Race, Politics, and Irish America

Race, Politics, and Irish America

A Gothic History

MARY M. BURKE

Great Clarendon Street, Oxford, OX2 6DP,
United Kingdom

Oxford University Press is a department of the University of Oxford. It furthers the University's objective of excellence in research, scholarship, and education by publishing worldwide. Oxford is a registered trade mark of Oxford University Press in the UK and in certain other countries

Published in the United States of America by Oxford University Press
198 Madison Avenue, New York, NY 10016, United States of America

British Library Cataloguing in Publication Data
Data available

Library of Congress Control Number: 2022943621

ISBN 978–0–19–285973–0

DOI: 10.1093/oso/9780192859730.001.0001

Printed and bound by
CPI Group (UK) Ltd, Croydon, CR0 4YY

For Maurice and Mella, who tolerated the many, many hours I spent in front of a computer during the long and lonely pandemic when I might have been with them.

Acknowledgements

My first book with Oxford University Press encompassed the descendants of nineteenth-century Irish Traveller emigrants to America, which obliged me to begin considering how certain Irish immigrants were both racialized and excluded by the common understanding of the term 'Irish America'. That became the seed of this examination of race and a variety of Irishnesses in the Americas. I am grateful to Oxford University Press for publishing my work once more and for the wonderful guidance of Jacqueline Norton (who has supported both books), Eleanor Collins, Jack McNichol, and Aimee Wright. I am also more grateful than I can convey to my readers for their invaluable attention to my manuscript during a pandemic. At the height of a global crisis, they generously gave their time and their bandwidth to my work. My earlier book was published during Barack Obama's presidency, a Black American whose Irish roots illuminate some of the complexities examined. Although this cultural history was begun during Obama's presidency, it continually evolved in response to the many recent wild pivots in American culture and politics. As such, I am grateful to the many people and institutions who supported me in that journey, not least my colleagues in the English Department and the University of Connecticut, whose generous funding and research sabbatical policy allowed me to work on this project and to present from it during its evolution. Likewise, my time as a Faculty Fellow at the University of Connecticut Humanities Institute was an opportunity for which I am deeply grateful. I also wish to express appreciation to the Aaron Warner Fund at the University Seminars at Columbia University for substantial help with images costs; material in this work was presented at Columbia's Irish Studies Seminar. My thanks also to UConn's Scholarship Facilitation Fund for assistance with publication costs and to Matt Mroz, Dan Schwartz, and graphic artist Michaela Abate for assistance with that application and the cover art. This project was initially seeded by a Boston College-Ireland Visiting Research Fellowship, a component of which was a one-day symposium on the Scots-Irish co-organized with Mike Cronin. Early iterations of the Henry James chapter were presented at the Research Seminar at NUIG and the Irish Seminar at UCD, while a recent invitation to speak at a Clinton Institute symposium at Dartmouth College consolidated the project, as did an invited talk on Grace Kelly at a regional American Conference for Irish Studies at Kutztown University. Indeed, the national and regional ACIS conferences have granted much airtime to what became my chapters. Diverse other organizations, events, conferences, or institutions whose speaking invitations or acceptance of my papers contributed incrementally to this volume include the American Studies Association, the American Literature Association, Boston College, Concordia University, the Costume Society, the Fitzgerald Society, Fordham University's Irish Women Writers Symposium, Glucksman Ireland House at NYU, the Henry James Society, the Hitchcock Area panel at SWPACA, MLA, NeMLA, NEPCA, NEASA, Sacred Heart University, and the Scotch-Irish Society. In addition, Jeff Cadman, Rich Gilligan, Sarah Hedlund, Eileen McGuckian, Francis P. O'Neill, and Annie Ryan graciously shared their work and expertise. I am likewise grateful to the colleagues who generously provided encouragement, feedback, and support, most especially Mary McGlynn, Diane Negra, Peter D. O'Neill, Lucy McDiarmid, Joseph Lennon, and Seamus O'Malley, as well as the following: Nicholas Allen, Lauren Arrington, Abby Bender, Kenneth Best, Claire Bracken, Jim Caroll, Lorna Carson, Sarah Churchill, David Clare, Mike Cronin, Christopher Dowd, Martin Doyle, Wayne Franklin, Marguerite Gannon, Crawford Gribben, Patrick Griffin, Tara Harney-Mahajan, Susan Harris, Melanie Hepburn, Michael Howarth, Margaret Kelleher, Mary C. Kelly, Liam Kennedy, Patrick Lonergan, Linde Lunney, Rachael and Brendan Lynch, Michael Malouf, Kelly Matthews, Nicole McClure, Maria McGarrity, Bill McGimpsey, Eileen Moore Quinn, Maureen Murphy, Rose Novak, Brian Ó Broin, Brian Ó Conhubhair, Ruan O'Donnell, Thomas O'Grady, Kevin O'Neill, James Ryan, Matt Shelton, Bob Smart, Kelly Sullivan, Kathleen Tonry, Sarah Townsend, Keri Walsh, and Cathal Woods. I am also grateful to the incredible UConn graduate students with whom I have recently worked or who took my Gothic and Irish-American fiction seminars, particularly Cassidy Allen, Leah Begg, Sarah Bertekap, Mollie Kervick, Imani Tucker, and Christina Wilson. I relied upon UConn's Babbidge library for this project, though pandemic conditions necessitated the use of HaithiTrust digital editions and Concord's Fowler Public Library during the final push, and to all I am thankful. I am also grateful to have received access to the following archives and collections: the Scotch-Irish Foundation Library and Archives Collection at the Historical Society of Pennsylvania; the Mitchel and Purroy Family Papers at the Rare Book and Manuscript Library, Columbia University; the Nigble Papers, Race Relations Collections, Williams Library at University of Mississippi; the Yerby Papers at the Howard Gotlieb Archival Research Center, Boston University. The Gotlieb kindly granted permission to quote from an unpublished Yerby letter. The discussion of 'The Real Thing' draws from my article, 'The Real Thing? The Irish immigrant ethnic hierarchy, S.S. McClure, and Henry James', *Henry James Review* 42.3 (2021): 248–51, while that of James's 'The Modern Warning' partly draws from 'The Marriage Plot and the Plot Against the Union', *Irish Studies Review* 23.2 (2015): 184–93. My work on the Kelly family evolved from 'Grace Kelly, Philadelphia, and the Politics of Irish Lace', *AJIS* 19 (2019): 31-46.

Note: This book considers various Irish, Irish-American, African-American, and American histories, identities, and cultural productions and aims for multiple readerships. To that end, endnotes or descriptors may sometimes detail events or figures that seem too well known for such treatment, but that may be the case for only one portion of the intended readership.

Contents

List of Illustrations xi

Introduction: The Past Is a Foreign Country 1
Immigrant Baggage: Irish America's Diverse Identities 2
Racialized Irishness: Redleg, Scots-Irish, and 'Black Irish' 3
Gothic: Jackson, Kennedy, and the Costs of Whiteness 5
Unassimilated: Queer, Multiracial, and Female Irish America 5
Chapter Synopses 7

1. Towards Scots-Irish Gothic 11
The Undead President 12
Irish History in American Gothic: *Edgar Huntly* (1799) 18
Poe, James, and Scots-Irish Gothic 24
Doppelgangers: Irish Patronyms and the Inescapable Past 30
Coda: The Convex Mirror 32

2. Closeted Irish: Henry James 34
Contagious Irish: James's *Daisy Miller* and Tóibín's Henry James 37
Illegible Irish: Norman Ancestry in James's Family and Fiction 41
Stand-in Irish: James's 'Off-White' Italians 46
Ulster Irish: The Marriage Plot and the Plot against the Union 50
Coda: Ancestor-Haunted: John Mitchel and John Purroy Mitchel 57

3. How the Irish Became Red: O'Neill and Fitzgerald 63
Redlegs: O'Neill's Black-Irish Caribbean 66
Irish Famine Gothic: *Long Day's Journey into Night* 74
Ulster Plantation Gothic: *Desire Under the Elms* 79
The Curious Case of Great-Grandfather Fitzgerald 83
'Half Black Irish': Tan Lines and Sunburns in Fitzgerald 89
Coda: Stage Irish: Fitzgerald in Hollywood 101

4. Complicit Irishness: Plantation Novels by Yerby, Mitchell, and Faulkner 103
Overlaps and Divergences: Yerby, Mitchell, and Faulkner 106
Neo-Gothic: The Pseudo-Aristocrat's Plantation House 110
Forget Haiti? *Absalom, Absalom!*'s Redleg Planter 113
Forget Culloden: Tracing the Compson Curse 120
Remember Ireland? *Gone with the Wind*'s Hypocritical Irish Planter 123
'Remember Haiti?' *The Foxes of Harrow*'s Ambivalent Irish Planter 127
Coda: Caste and Casting: Maureen O'Hara 132

5. White Wedding: Grace Kelly, Spectacle, and Irish Assimilation 135
The Kellys: 'Off-white' in a Scots-Irish City 137
America's 'Queerest Writer': George Kelly in the Ethnic Closet 144
WASP Performance: Grace Kelly, White Gloves, and Alfred Hitchcock 150
Haunted by History: Princess Grace of Monaco's Wedding Gown 156
Coda: Remembering Ann Lowe (1898–1981) 162

Epilogue: Kennedy Gothic 163
Bouvier Gothic: *Grey Gardens* 164
John F. Kennedy Gothic: Conspiracy 168
Ted Kennedy Gothic: The Family Curse 170
Jackie Kennedy Gothic: Blood and Red Roses 172
Coda: Irishness, the US Presidency, and Black Lives Matter 175

Endnotes 179
Selected Bibliography 230
Index 246

List of Illustrations

I.1. Nineteenth-century comic valentine of female Irish 'beauty' with the exaggerated philtrum (groove between nose and lip) seen in the simian Irishman of contemporaneous caricature. Collection of John A. McAllister. Courtesy of Library Company of Philadelphia. 6

I.2. Princess Grace of Monaco (formerly Grace Kelly) and John F. Kennedy in the White House, 24 May 1961. Photo by James Atherton. Courtesy of ALAMY. 9

I.3. Vintage tapestry of Robert Kennedy, Martin Luther King, Jr., and John F. Kennedy carried at a 15 January 2018 California gathering honouring Dr King. Courtesy of Wikimedia Commons. 10

1.1. The cover of an 1874 dime novel depicts Scots-Irish frontier folk hero Kit Carson violently fending off Native Americans. Courtesy of Wikimedia Commons. 15

1.2. Equestrian statue of Andrew Jackson (1853), President's Park, Washington, DC. It was graffitied on Indigenous Peoples' Day/Columbus Day, 11 October 2021. Courtesy of Wikimedia Commons. 17

1.3. 'William Wilson' illustration by Fritz Eichenberg for *Tales of Edgar Allan Poe* (1944). © 2022 Estate of Fritz Eichenberg / Licensed by VAGA at Artists Rights Society (ARS), NY. 27

1.4. Henry James, Jr. at age eleven, with his father, Henry James, Sr. 1854 daguerreotype by Mathew Brady. Courtesy of Wikimedia Commons. 31

2.1. Cybill Sheperd as the title character in the 1974 film adaptation of James's *Daisy Miller*. Courtesy of ALAMY. 39

2.2. Irish-American political operative Patrick O'Riley and his wife before a French sojourn, as illustrated in the Mark Twain co-authored *The Gilded Age* (1873). Courtesy of Northern Illinois University Libraries. 45

2.3. Patrick O'Riley and his wife after the French sojourn that transforms him into the Hon. Patrique Oreillé, as illustrated in the Mark Twain co-authored *The Gilded Age* (1873). Courtesy of Northern Illinois University Libraries. 46

2.4. 'John Mitchel, The First Martyr of Ireland in Her Revolution of 1848'. Lithograph by N. Currier, New York, 1848. Courtesy of Wikimedia Commons. 59

2.5. Monument to John Mitchel's grandson and former New York Mayor, John Purroy Mitchel, in Central Park, New York. Dedicated in 1928. Courtesy of Wikimedia Commons. 60

2.6. 1839 print by Edward W. Clay lampooning interracial romance. Contemporaneous Irish abolitionist Daniel O'Connell is the middle portrait on the wall. Courtesy of the Library Company of Philadelphia. 61

3.1. Ulster-American actor John McCullough as Othello in 1878. Theatre poster image courtesy of the Library of Congress. 65

3.2. 1937 production of O'Neill's *The Moon of the Caribbees* at the Lafayette Theatre, Harlem, New York. Courtesy of the Federal Theatre Project Collection, Library of Congress. 71

3.3. Ulster-American Mary Blair and Paul Robeson as interracial couple Ella and Jim in the 1924 New York production of Eugene O'Neill's *All God's Chillun Got Wings*. This hand-kissing scene led to threats from the Ku Klux Klan. Courtesy of Wikimedia Commons. 73

3.4. Cast of the Corn Exchange *Desire Under the Elms* production directed by Annie Ryan at the 2013 Dublin Theatre Festival: Fionn Walton (Eben Cabot); Janet Moran (Abbie Putnam); Lalor Roddy (Ephraim Cabot); Luke Griffin (Simeon); Peter Coonan (Peter). Photograph by Rich Gilligan. Courtesy of Annie Ryan and Rich Gilligan. 82

3.5. F. Scott, Zelda, and Scottie Fitzgerald at the beach, 1927. Courtesy of ALAMY. 90

3.6. Cartoon set in Philadelphia's environs depicting a Black man dressed in the style of the Irishman of lampoon, c. 1830. Attributed to Edward W. Clay. Courtesy of Library Company of Philadelphia. 92

3.7. Josephine Baker with long-term friend, Princess Grace of Monaco, *c.*1970. Courtesy of ALAMY. 98

4.1. Vivien Leigh (as Scarlett O'Hara) and Thomas Mitchell (as Gerald O'Hara) in the 1939 film adaptation of Margaret Mitchell's *Gone with the Wind*. Courtesy of ALAMY. 108

4.2. Rowan Oak, built by slave-holding Scots-Irish planter Robert Sheegog. Purchased and renovated by William Faulkner during the years that he worked on *Absalom, Absalom!* Courtesy of Wikimedia Commons. 119

4.3. Frank Yerby became the first African American to have a book purchased by a major Hollywood studio when 20th Century Fox optioned *The Foxes of Harrow*. Released in 1947, the adaptation starred Rex Harrison and Maureen O'Hara. Image of promotional poster courtesy of ALAMY. 132

5.1. Prince Rainier III of Monaco and Grace Kelly during their 1956 wedding ceremony. Courtesy of ALAMY. 136

5.2. Grace Kelly on 25 July 1949 (opening night) at the Bucks County Playhouse, Pennsylvania, in her stage debut as Florence McCrickett in *The Torch-Bearers* (1922), her uncle George Kelly's play. Photo by Richard W. Cauffman and courtesy of Jeff Cadman. 146

5.3. Lorraine O'Grady (in a dress hand-stitched from 180 pairs of white gloves), 'Mlle Bourgeoise Noire Beats Herself with the Whip-That-Made-Plantations-Move' from *Untitled (Mlle Bourgeoise Noire)*, 1980–83/2009. Silver gelatin fibre, part 10 of 14, 10.13×7.5 inches, *Edition 20 + 2AP*. Courtesy of Alexander Gray Associates, New York ©2022 Lorraine O'Grady/Artists Rights Society (ARS), New York. 152

5.4. Overdressed African-American steam laundry owners are importuned by a bedraggled Irishman with a dirty coat. *c.* 1831 lithograph in lampoon series *Life in New York.* Courtesy of Library Company of Philadelphia. 158

E.1. John Wayne (as Sean Thornton) and Maureen O'Hara (as Mary Kate Danaher) in John Ford's *The Quiet Man*, 1952. Courtesy of ALAMY. 165

E.2. Edith 'Little Edie' Bouvier Beale on the poster for the 1975 documentary, *Grey Gardens.* Courtesy of ALAMY. 167

E.3. Official portrait of First Lady Jacqueline Bouvier Kennedy by Aaron Shikler (1970) depicts her wearing a pleated Ulster linen gown by her personal friend, Irish designer Sybil Connolly. Courtesy of the White House Collection/White House Historical Association. 173

E.4. President and Mrs. Kennedy arrive in Dallas on 22 November 1963. Courtesy of ALAMY. 174

E.5. President Barack Obama celebrates St Patrick's Day in Washington in 2012 with his distant Irish cousins, Henry Healy and Ollie Hayes. Courtesy of ALAMY. 178

Introduction

The Past Is a Foreign Country

In the first decade of this century, the *Gone with the Wind* estate asked Pat Conroy (1945–2016) to write the sequel to the 1936 blockbuster of Margaret Mitchell, a fellow Southern Irish-American. However, it laid down the conditions that, in what will be argued to be the very Irish-American spirit of the original, there could be no homosexuality and no 'miscegenation' (interracial union). As Geraldine Higgins describes, after months of ultimately unsuccessful negotiation, the exasperated Conroy came up with the following opening involving the man that Irish-American plantation belle Scarlett O'Hara marries (Rhett) and another for whom she perennially pines (Ashley): 'After they made love, Rhett turned to Ashley Wilkes and said, "Ashley, have I ever told you that my grandmother was black?"'[1] A number of threads in Conroy's irreverent anecdote will be unpicked over the course of this cultural history of race and American representations of Irishness: divergent interpretations of the past between the Irish of different generation or political outlook, fraught Irish-American negotiations of race, gender, and sexuality, and the most basic fact that many well-known American creative works yield richer readings when their Irish contexts are given due weight.

Mitchell's historical novel is not Gothic literature, but, as my subtitle intimates, cultural expressions in that mode repeatedly emerge in this volume because history is undead in Irish-American narrative. That unfinished Irish past replays within American contexts of race, slavery, settler-colonialism, and ethnic hierarchies. As a result, this book expands the usual narrow post-Famine Catholic connotation of 'Irish America' to encompass a variety of 'Irishnesses' that evolved within racial categories in the Americas. Moments of African-Irish and Native-Irish solidarity consistently appear in this cultural history (not least because Black and Native Americans sometimes identified as Irish too), but so too do the repeated strivings to leave 'flawed' whiteness behind of Irish cohorts, from the indentured and transported Irish of all stripes in the Americas, to the Ulster Presbyterian immigrant in colonial America, and on to the Catholic post-Famine Irish. It is important to note that this racial barrier, as Peter D. O'Neill stresses, was 'not legal, but social and cultural'.[2] The range of Irish-American identities across both time and racial groupings necessitates the sundry cultural productions considered: fiction, drama, film, television, guerrilla art, fashion and beauty culture, journalism, caricature, historiography, viral pseudohistory, exhibition, song sheet, illustration, statuary, and gravestone inscription. Such endeavours explore, query,

Race, Politics, and Irish America. Mary M. Burke, Oxford University Press.
 DOI: 10.1093/oso/9780192859730.003.0001

or defend Irish aspirations to whiteness in locations from the seventeenth-century slave plantation Caribbean, to America's frontiers and antebellum plantations, and into the inter-war and postwar periods of its eastern seaboard.

The Irish pursuit of a whiteness perceived to be the secure social and cultural possession of 'Anglo-Saxon' America is critiqued and condoned by both canonical and somewhat lesser-known writers of Irish descent or connection such as Edgar Allan Poe, Henry James, Sarah Orne Jewett, Ellin Berlin, Ellen Glasgow, Margaret Mitchell, F. Scott Fitzgerald, John O'Hara, Eudora Welty, William Faulkner, Frank Yerby, and Eugene O'Neill. Also considered in this regard are past and present public figures of Irish connection known on both sides of the Atlantic, from Andrew Jackson, Frederick Douglass, and Oscar Wilde, to Grace Kelly, John Wayne, Maureen O'Hara, the Kennedy dynasty, Mariah Carey, and Rihanna. In addition, lesser-known or formerly popular Irish-American writers, critics, public figures, and actors are included, from journalist John Louis O'Sullivan (of 'Manifest Destiny' fame), and Broadway stalwarts, to the once widely read Ulster-born dime novelist, Mayne Reid, the 'Giant of the Westerns.' Finally, the transatlantic and archipelagic American scope of the enquiry required linguistic and geographic diversity. As such, all of the following are encompassed: A James Orr poem in Ulster-Scots dialect that refers to the Black-Irish encounter in America; a 1949 Máirtín Ó Cadhain Irish-language novel featuring mixed-race returned emigrants in Connemara; Afro-Caribbean Édouard Glissant's francophone scholarship; Jamaican-American Lorraine O'Grady's guerrilla performance art; an Irish Gothic-influenced 'Black revenge' story by Afro-Caribbean writer Eric Walrond.

Immigrant Baggage: Irish America's Diverse Identities

There were, as Kerby Miller delineates, cultural, ethno-religious, and linguistic divisions between the two broadly differing waves of Irish immigration before and after the Famine of 1845–52. The pre-Famine immigrant Irish tended to be relatively comfortable or skilled Anglicans, non-conformists, and Catholics from Ireland's more Anglicized and urbanized eastern seaboard, particularly the Presbyterian-dominated northern province of Ulster. By contrast, post-Famine immigrants were often unskilled Catholics from predominantly agricultural and Irish-speaking or somewhat bilingual western seaboard regions.[3] Nevertheless, and not least because cultural representations often overemphasized difference, this study also acknowledges the tremendous overlap and diversity of ethno-racial identity and ethno-religious allegiance within and between the pre- and post-Famine cohorts. As such, catch-all or vague terms such as 'Irish' and 'Celtic' are generally used carefully since they can efface distinctions—important to many of those considered—between micro identities with differing racio-ethnic, political, and denominational associations that are or were meaningful in Ireland and among its diaspora. These include Scots/Scotch-Irish (Ulster-Scots Presbyterian),[4] Norman (which can be British or Irish, Catholic or Protestant), mixed-race Irish, Jacobite peer (titles recognized only by Ireland's Catholic allies), and Gaelo-American (which can be Highland Scottish or native Irish). The last is my own coinage: Just as 'Irish' subsumes the many and sometimes antagonistic Irish identities charted, 'Scottish' does not always encompass the political significance and Irish links of Scottish Gaelic/Highland ancestry, which are central to my readings of both Fitzgerald and Faulkner.

Indeed, if scholars of a category called 'Irish-American literature' have customarily excluded canonical writers of Ulster Presbyterian origin such as Edgar Allan Poe, Henry James, Ellen Glasgow, and John Steinbeck, then an American writer of colour of Scots-Irish maternal ancestry such as Frank Yerby remains invisible within the Irish-American canon on *multiple* levels. Granular attention to Irish—or Gaelo-American—writers' racial, ethnic, class, political, and denominational roots yields evidence that belies their categorization in the American canon, thereby expanding standard interpretations of their works: Mitchell was of Franco-Irish gentry descent; Faulkner identified with ancestors he believed to be Gaelic-speaking survivors of Scotland's Battle of Culloden; the Henry James family intermarried with that of eighteenth-century Irish Protestant radical Robert Emmet; F. Scott Fitzgerald overlooked colonial-era Irish ancestry in overidentifying with his one colonial-period English family line; African American Yerby's self-ascriptions and literary themes suggest a critically unexplored identification with his mother's Scots-Irish heritage.

Similarly, US Americanist scholars often ignore Irish history in relation to canonical authors of Irish connection, even if the authors themselves do not. Therefore, the baggage of sectarianism, colonialism, and trauma brought with Irish deportees and immigrants from the disordered motherland over centuries is considered in cultural productions by or about their descendants. Such works often simultaneously conjure up the unfinished history of *both* Ireland and America. Besides the Famine of 1845, Irish histories that mark the canonical American literature considered include the transportations and ethno-sectarian division created by the consolidation of British power in seventeenth-century Ireland, the religious persecution of both Catholics and Presbyterians into the eighteenth century, crop crises that impacted Ulster prior to 1845, and the 1798 uprising against colonial rule by radicalized Catholics and Presbyterians that sent political refugees to America. Traditionally less-documented push factors in terms of Irish flight also hover, such as the conservative and patriarchal tenor of Irish culture, which made America an attractive alternative for women, the young, and the queer, as well as for the politically seditious. Nevertheless, the horrors they fled often followed the Irish to America.

Racialized Irishness: Redleg, Scots-Irish, and 'Black Irish'

One of the biggest histories hiding in plain sight in the narrative of Irish America is that of race, and it encompasses a variety of periods and locations: Irish relations with Native Americans and enslaved people; the internecine jostling of the 'Saxon' Scots-Irish and 'Celtic' post-Famine Irish for position in America's immigrant hierarchy; the overlooked contributions of Irish-American writers of colour; the Kennedy brothers' negotiations of Civil Rights just as their own ethnic cohort attained unconditional whiteness. In an archipelagic America in which race was always central, the Irish themselves were racialized and subsequently 'whitened' multiple times, beginning in the seventeenth-century slave-plantation Americas. This analysis pivots on racialized coinages applied to those of white Irish stock in the Americas that have, traditionally, had no corollary in Ireland: 'Redleg' (the transported Irish and Scottish), 'Scots/Scotch-Irish', and 'black Irish.' These labels speak to America's contexts of slavery and racial categorization and to the racism and the hierarchy of whitenesses that emerged from those primal sins. Thus, O'Neill's placement of working-class white Irish characters in Caribbean settings in certain early plays will be seen to evoke 'Redleg' history. In turn, this unfolds a theory that Irish and Scottish paleness (and thus, tendency to sunburn) became a racial liability in that context until strict differentiation between white transportee and enslaved African was codified. Ultimately, the early racialization of the *too* pale yields this study's groundbreaking reading of the meanings of Fitzgerald's fetish for tanning.

If the transported Irish were racially transformed by conditions in the Americas, so too were the Presbyterian Ulster Irish. The Scots-Irish are particularly plucked out in this study because they have often been subsumed or effaced by wider Irish, British, and Irish-American Protestant identities and cultural categories. (For this reason, Ascendancy/mainstream Protestant Anglo-Irishness, which has been much discussed by historians and literary critics, is considered only sporadically and mostly in relation to Oscar Wilde, Robert Emmet, and Elizabeth Bowen.) Predominantly Presbyterians of Lowland Scottish descent who had settled land confiscated from the native Irish in seventeenth-century Ulster, the Ulster Scots subsequently departed for colonial America in large numbers. By 1790, one half of the 400,000 US residents who were commonly labeled 'Irish' were of this descent.[5] The Protestant Ulster Irish attained only conditional 'whiteness' in Franklin's colony and on certain frontiers due to their role as a buffer population between Native Americans and Europeans. However, the more 'white Anglo-Saxon' coinage 'Scots/Scotch-Irish' gradually gained currency among this cohort as they assimilated, and the influx of poor and predominantly Catholic Irish immigrants during and after the 1845–52 famine strengthened the gulf between 'old' 'whitened' Irishness and a 'new' Irishness that *aspired to* unconditional whiteness. For Noel Ignatiev and David R. Roediger, the unskilled 'new' Irish in post-Civil War America failed to make common cause with African Americans because they competed with them for jobs or wished to differentiate themselves from fellow-workers who were people of colour.[6] This was a 'dangerous' equivalence, as suggested by a remark in *Gone with the Wind* that in post-slavery Georgia's brave new capitalist world, 'Irish [wage] slaves' were replacing 'darky slaves.'[7] As such, the convoluted histories of the slippery term 'black Irish'/'Black Irish', used in reference *both* to the marginalized nineteenth-century white Irish in America and Black Caribbeans of Irish connection, thread this study.

Gothic: Jackson, Kennedy, and the Costs of Whiteness

In their dealings with Native and African Americans, successive waves of Irish immigrants often—but not always—replicated the very colonial-settler mindset that had caused their flight from Ireland. The Irish were both colluders and victims within the racial order of both the colonial motherland and America. As such, this study theorizes 'Scots-Irish Gothic', a literary subgenre that is neither fully Anglo-Irish Gothic nor fully American Gothic. In Scots-Irish Gothic texts by Poe, James, Faulkner, and O'Neill, the traumas of the Irish motherland are both knowingly and unintentionally visited upon marginalized Americans, including, sometimes, other Irish cohorts. In particular, the troubling spectre of Andrew Jackson, son of Ulster settler-colonists, major slave-holder, and scourge of Native Americans, repeatedly haunts Irish-American narrative. Joe Cleary implies that Irish-American critics' overreliance on ethnic representation of the social realist kind has provided a very partial picture of Irish-American culture.[8] Therefore, as well as tracing Scots-Irish Gothic and moments in which past Irish trauma erupts into ostensibly realist narratives by the likes of Welty, Fitzgerald, and Yerby, the epilogue also names the contradictory cultural afterlives of the Kennedy dynasty as 'Gothic.' The Gothic mode expresses the complicity that achieving and maintaining power (whiteness) entails: after the postwar ascent to royalty and the presidential office of Grace Kelly and John F. Kennedy respectively, the finally attained dream slides into the genre that best expresses nightmare.

Unassimilated: Queer, Multiracial, and Female Irish America

This study's consideration of Irish-American performers, public women, and queer and multiracial authors expands the standard Irish assimilation narrative. Although Jackson and Kennedy used the presidency to bolster Scots-Irish and post-Famine Irish aspirations respectively, a traditional overemphasis on the roles played by public men in accounts of Irish 'whitening' is corrected for. So, also, is literary critics' traditional focus on the straight white male Irish-American author. Surveys of Irish-American history have sometimes divvied up attention between the Scots-Irish and post-Famine Irish, though surveys of Irish-American fiction generally elide the former. Nevertheless, both historiography and literary criticism have traditionally agreed that only straight white male Irish-American lives and authors deserve attention.

'Besides the clothes and makeup, politics is the most exciting thing about America', quipped a cousin of Jacqueline Bouvier Kennedy in 1972.[9] The business and practice of beauty has customarily been associated with women and queer people. Thus, due to what Tressie McMillan Cottom calls a 'masculinist strain of intellectualism' that considers such interests 'inferior',[10] it has been overlooked in considerations of the Irish quest for whiteness. As such, Critical Fashion and Beauty lenses are used to probe the negotiation of 'good taste' in queer authors Henry James and George Kelly (Grace Kelly's playwright uncle), as well as the evolving relationship between beauty norms, celebrity, social 'whiteness', and Irish status. For instance, the simian features of nineteenth-century caricature that have customarily been analysed only in relation to Irishmen are also present in caricatures of that period mocking Irish women's appearance (Figure I.1).

Christopher Dowd's examination of early American celebrity culture and Irish America would suggest that it is no coincidence that *Tender Is the Night*,

BEAUTY OF IRELAND.
Och, you're a beauty, mavourneen, my darlin'!
That swate Irish brogue, too, as thick as my ar-r-m;
Faith, when I see yez, I cannot help calling,
"St. Patrick presarve me, and kape me from har-r-m!"

Figure I.1 Nineteenth-century comic valentine of female Irish 'beauty' with the exaggerated philtrum (groove between nose and lip) seen in the simian Irishman of contemporaneous caricature. Collection of John A. McAllister. Courtesy of Library Company of Philadelphia.

Fitzgerald's most anxious examination of whiteness and beauty, opens with a film star based on Pittsburgh-Irish actress Lois Moran (his erstwhile lover).[11] Moreover, in what he called his 'finest hour', André Leon Talley (1948–2022; a rare Black presence in American fashion's upper echelons born in the Jim Crow South),[12] cast British-Jamaican supermodel Naomi Campbell as Scarlett O'Hara in a 1996 *Vanity Fair* spread.[13] Given such emphases, it is extraordinarily complex that the trend for suntanning in order to signal elite whiteness was popularized by Fitzgerald, yet he also denigrated himself as 'half black Irish'. That the racial implications of this contradiction have received no attention suggests that Irish and Irish-American Studies has ignored Critical Fashion and Beauty Studies to its detriment. There is much to consider in the fact that the only impactful full-length recent work engaging critically with such issues in the Irish context is by Emma Dabiri, an Irishwoman of colour.[14]

Chapter Synopses

Chapter 1 suggests that the commonplace that Irish Gothic literature pertains to the Anglo-Irish Ascendancy class does not account for Ireland's *other* settler-colonial cohort, the Ulster Scots. In addition, the category 'American Gothic' does not encompass texts by or about the latter community's descendants in America, the Scots-Irish. In response, the first chapter theorizes that works by Charles Brockden Brown, Edgar Allan Poe, Henry James, and William Faulkner that express the unease of the Ulster settler in America are *neither* fully Anglo-Irish nor American Gothic, but a subgenre that will be termed 'Scots-Irish Gothic'. In depicting the violence of the Old World being ceaselessly reprised in the New, these works question the legitimacy of Ulster Protestant presence in colonial Ireland and on the colonial American frontier, locations in which the Ulster Scots were oppressor and oppressed, white and off-white. The Scots-Irish Andrew Jackson, scourge of Native Americans, emerges as an undead presence who repeatedly returns to haunt both Irish-American fiction and American political culture down to the Trump administration. The chapter's closing discussion of Gothic's *doppelganger* (uncanny double) motif argues that deeply rooted Irish patronymic traditions render the male line 'ancestor haunted'. This emphasis is returned to throughout since surnames in Irish-American culture are often understood to dictate ethno-racial and political allegiance, even when acquired through marriage.

Chapter 2 argues that Henry James's Irishness, like his sexuality, was closeted, as the opening reading of Colm Tóibín's fictionalized James suggests. James's own fiction is fuelled by anxiety linked to the vexed issue of his paternal Scots-Irish ancestry, as well as to his mother's distinct and uninvestigated Irish ethnic roots. In James's lifetime, Emerson influentially represented the 'Saxon race' as the origin from which 'superior' American whites descended, a taxonomy that enfolded the Scots-Irish most but *not all* of the time. The chapter probes the submerged concern in James's 'Irish marriage plot' story, 'The Modern Warning', and in his novella *Daisy Miller*, that non-Gaelic, non-Catholic Irishness, originally the most common Irish ancestry in America, might be mistaken for what it is not: poor, Catholic, Gaelic, and post-1845 Famine. James's racio-ethnic anxieties are further examined through his depiction of both working-class and elite Italians, who stand in for differing relations to whiteness of diverse Irish identities in nineteenth-century America, from Hiberno-Norman and Jacobite peer, to Scots-Irish and Gael. The coda pivots to the impact of pro-slavery Irish nationalist John Mitchel and his namesake mayor grandson on the New York of James's lifetime.

Chapter 3 considers near-contemporaries Eugene O'Neill and F. Scott Fitzgerald. The latter over-identified with the one non-Irish branch of his family that exemplified 'Saxon' whiteness, an emphasis unquestioned by critics, who have left Fitzgerald's eighteenth-century Irish-American roots unexamined. This struggle is at the source of his oeuvre's anxiety regarding class and racial status, as the consideration of the term 'half black Irish' (a Fitzgerald self-ascription) suggests. By contrast, O'Neill's drama critiques the Irish presence in the Americas over centuries as one long failure to create solidarity with their fellow oppressed, especially peoples of colour. As a result, unfinished Irish histories (the Ulster Plantation and the 1845 Famine) return to haunt the American action of O'Neill's drama. In dermatologic classification (the Fitzpatrick Scale), those of white Irish ancestry have skin tones so light as to be 'flawed' due to being *too* white. Thus, a tendency to burn easily was a racial liability on fashionable 1920s Riviera beaches in which an even tan conversely signalled 'whiteness' (as depicted by Fitzgerald). It had also been a liability in the seventeenth century on Caribbean islands that witnessed indentured white labour and in which the easily sunburned Irish were racialized as 'red' (as evoked by O'Neill).

Chapter 4 considers three plantation novels that depict—in different registers—Southern planters of Scottish Gaelic and pre-Famine Irish origin: Margaret Mitchell's Gerald O'Hara in *Gone with the Wind*, William Faulkner's Thomas Sutpen in *Absalom, Absalom!* (both 1936), and Stephen Fox in *Foxes of Harrow* (1946), a bestselling novel by Frank Yerby, an African-American author of Scots-Irish maternal ancestry. (The film adaptation of the last, starring Maureen O'Hara, is also considered.) The chapter's discussion of the entwined roots of the slave-holding Southern plantation, the Caribbean Great House, and the Irish Big House encompasses an Elizabeth Bowen-inspired Eudora Welty story. The three planter novels centre on initially penniless and 'off-white' protagonists of broadly Irish association who transform themselves into the exploitative and unconditionally white landowner class to whom they themselves had once been subject. These three novelists were all of Southern birth in a period in which that region was still racially segregated, and all three claimed to be of Scottish Gaelic or Irish descent. Nevertheless, their origins do not conform to the dominant image of the Irish-connected writer as white, Catholic, and northeastern post-Famine by origin.

Chapter 5 suggests that the WASP persona movie studio executives created for film star Grace Kelly (later known as Princess Grace of Monaco) was meant to diminish the usual associations of her background. Her Famine-Catholic Philadelphia roots are explored through the neglected drama of her Pulitzer Prize-winning uncle, George Kelly. The symbiosis between 'whiteness' and the images of women used to sell products created by the beauty, fashion, and film industries is well documented. Such links, overlooked in male-centred accounts of the 'whitening' of Irish America, are are used to analyse Kelly's impact. In addition, in *Dial M for Murder,* Kelly performs a woman who duplicitously *performs* the role of a proper English wife, for which she was coached by director Alfred Hitchcock. They shared a surprisingly similar background: both were, by origin, Catholic Irish outsiders to elite WASP culture who learned to 'pass'. Kelly's wedding to Prince Rainier of Monaco in 1956 was one of the largest international media events of that decade, and constituted, to Catholic Philadelphia, the rejoinder of a 'hometown girl' to the 1953 spectacular of Elizabeth II's coronation. Grace's globally broadcast ascent to fairy-tale whiteness paved the way for 'America's royals', the Kennedy dynasty, as well as broader Irish America's assimilation. However, centuries of Gothic literature holds that where there is a fair princess in a castle, there is soon to be horror (Figure I.2).

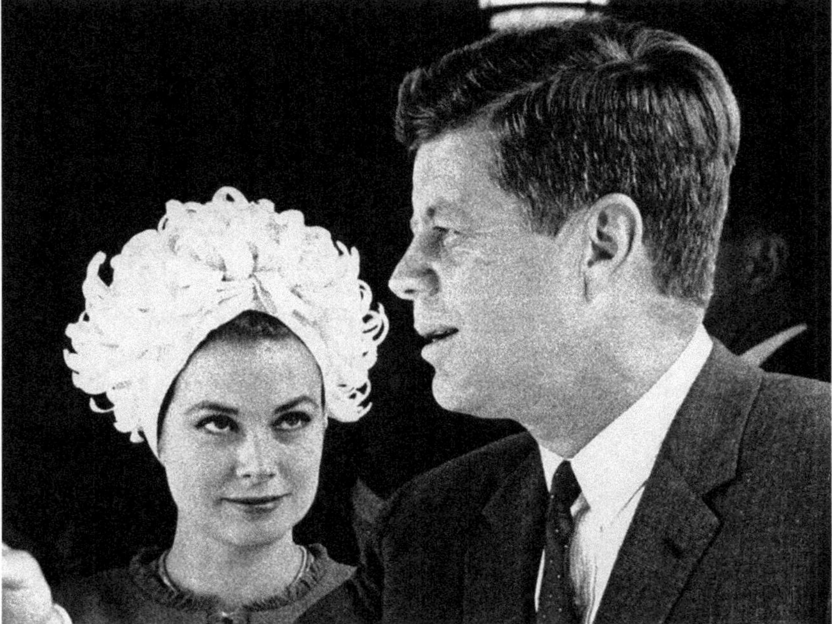

Figure I.2 Princess Grace of Monaco (formerly Grace Kelly) and John F. Kennedy in the White House, 24 May 1961. Photo by James Atherton. Courtesy of ALAMY.

The Epilogue turns to the Gothic cultural afterlives of the new and uncontestably white Catholic-Irish power elite in the 1960s and beyond. Gothic incorporates new aristocracies as they arise, and this iteration, which includes the Jacqueline Bouvier-associated documentary *Grey Gardens* (1975), is termed 'Kennedy Gothic'. Cultural and journalistic portrayals of the Kennedys encompass two distinct interpretations that generally break down along party lines. However, in both iterations the dynasty is enmeshed with the terror and violence with which Gothic has always been concerned. Liberals and Democrats held that Kennedy family members were *themselves* the innocent victims of sinister conspiracies, while for conservatives and Irish-American voters abandoning hereditary Democratic Party allegiance, the dynasty personified the moral decay at the heart of aristocratic power, an abiding theme of Gothic. This latter narrative was also entangled with Irish America's often-negative response to the Kennedy brothers' Civil Rights agenda. In the age of Black Lives Matter, the Gothicizing of Biden as a Kennedy-era 'revenant' does not bode well for the pact that the earlier administration attempted to forge between progressive politics and Irish America (Figure I.3).

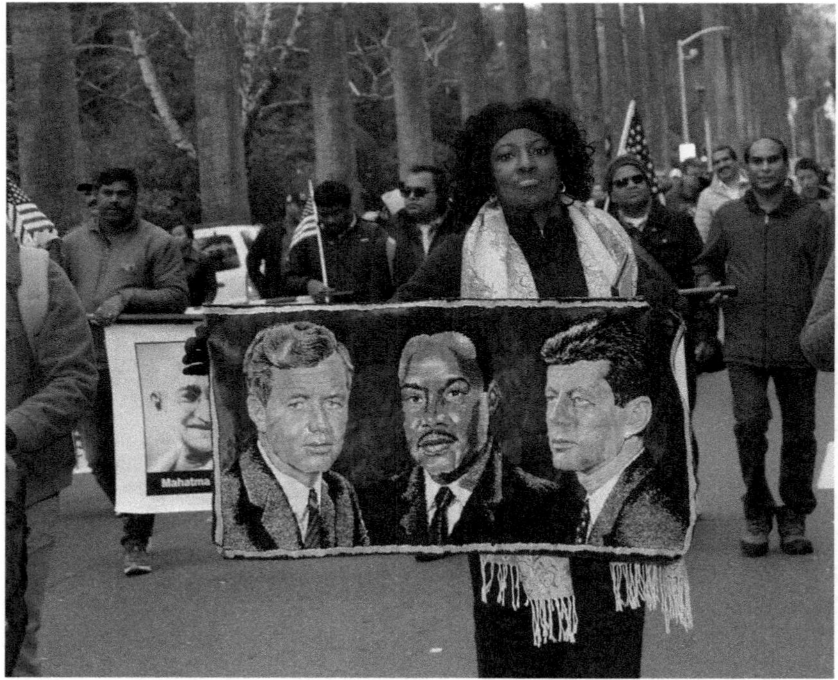

Figure I.3 Vintage tapestry of Robert Kennedy, Martin Luther King, Jr., and John F. Kennedy carried at a 15 January 2018 California gathering honouring Dr King. Courtesy of Wikimedia Commons.

1
Towards Scots-Irish Gothic

In the introduction to his bestselling and controversial memoir, *Hillbilly Elegy* (2016), author and aspiring politician J. D. Vance claims, 'I may be white, but I do not identify with the WASPS of the Northeast. Instead, I identify with the millions of working-class white Americans of Scots-Irish descent who have no college degree.'[1] In mid-2016 interviews, and based on his understanding of this white, and predominantly nonconformist Protestant grouping of deep Irish—and further back again, deep Scottish—ancestry, Vance correctly predicted Trump's ascent to the Office of President at a time when this seemed unlikely. Vance calls the Scots-Irish 'one of the most distinctive subgroups in America', but his ethnicizing of a great number of disaffected working-class whites as 'Scots-Irish' is, in fact, rare today, in contrast to the commonplace use of the label into the first half of the twentieth century. In addition, the implication that this cohort of predominantly Ulster Presbyterian origin would dominate Trump's voter base,[2] a widespread claim that later proved to be somewhat inaccurate,[3] partakes of old and contradictory positionings of the Scots-Irish as both Ur-white Americans and scapegoated 'buffer' population on the racial margins. A racially charged contemporary white Protestant nativism and inconsistent concepts of both unethnicized founding Americanness and aggrieved marginalized 'whiteness' certainly did gain visibility with the 2016 election cycle. Regardless of the degree to which the Scots-Irish formed that pro-Trump voter base, however, his emergence as a candidate returned those so labelled to mainstream American conversation for the first time in over half a century.

Prior to Trump, contemporary attempts to name Scots-Irishness remained rare in mainstream media outlets and any that did emerge tended to stress that it was an unethnicized ethnicity. As recently as 2012, a popular science magazine suggested that Scots-Irish identity had 'decoupled itself from any "Old Country" consciousness. A broad swath of the Eastern American Uplands is dominated by people who give their *ethnicity* as American. After 250 years [those of Scots-Irish ancestry] have only the vaguest recollections of the nature of their British antecedents.'[4] The concept of 'American ethnicity' refers to the following: maps of Scots-Irish settlement patterns mirror the 2000 Census map of the concentration (7.2 per cent) of citizens who identified their ethnicity as 'American' on returns.[5] This suggests an older construct of the Scots-Irish as foundational Americans that was cemented by the arrival of the Famine-generation and predominantly Catholic Irish in the 1840s

Race, Politics, and Irish America. Mary M. Burke, Oxford University Press.
 DOI: 10.1093/oso/9780192859730.003.0002

and after. The seemingly odd phrase 'American ethnic' is also pushed towards in historian and activist Roxanne Dunbar-Ortiz's critical take on her Scots-Irish paternal heritage in a 2006 memoir. (She is Native American on her mother's side.) The Scots-Irish are described as 'foot soldiers of empire', first in the service of the British in Ireland and then of the progressively westward white settlement of America. However, Dunbar-Ortiz suggests, this is not the self-image of those who share her paternal ancestry nor the 'popular imag[e]': 'We [Scots-Irish] consider ourselves to be the true native-born Americans, the personification of what America is supposed to be, and we know that means being Scots-Irish original settler, those who fought for and won the continent.' Such beliefs, Dunbar-Ortiz continues, 'transform[ed] the white frontier settler into an "indigenous people", believing that they are the true natives of the continent'.[6] Given Dunbar-Ortiz's maternal ancestry, her unspoken conclusion is that in imagining their 'native' Americanness, this early Irish cohort effaced Native Americanness. That the pre-Famine Irish erased Indigenous Americans in more visceral ways too will become a focus as this chapter unfolds.

The Undead President

The president-to-be was initially considered a controversial and 'outsider' candidate by the Washington Republican elite, despite his national celebrity and substantial property and business success. Newspapers impugned his private life and accusations of sexual improprieties were made into which his reclusive wife was dragged. Despite this opposition and open hostility, however, the momentum of popular opinion carried the nominee to a staggering win, and his victory was widely perceived as a shift towards populism in American political consciousness and the rise to power of a previously discounted voting bloc with a deep distrust of Washington. His inauguration was represented in the press as a mob occupation. On taking office, the president proceeded to sweep out previous administrative appointees and an enormous number of lesser federal office holders, some of whom had held their posts for decades. Even more astounding to the political establishment were the replacements the president made: he installed associates into high offices for which they had no relevant experience and members of his personal staff were awarded with official positions. Though revered by supporters as an advocate for the common people, his policies were contentious. He challenged the authority of the Supreme Court, and among the more impactful policies of the early days of his administration was his routing of minorities of colour, with the resultant deaths making headlines. His subsequent refusal to support a mass movement calling for the equality of Black Americans was also divisive. A thriving economy in the early years of the presidency ended in an economic crisis in the period surrounding his leaving of office.

The president described in the paragraph above is not Donald Trump, but Democrat Andrew Jackson, US President from 1829–1837 and the son of Ulster immigrants. Jackson's ascent to the highest office in the land signalled the social and racial arrival of the Scots-Irish from the 'off-white' wilderness of some of their earliest moments on the American continent. In Jackson's own case, whiteness was enacted by his extirpation of Native Americans and his ownership of human chattel. As an Army general, Jackson spent years leading ruthless campaigns against the Creeks in Georgia and Alabama and the Seminoles in Florida, campaigns that led to the transfer of vast swathes of land from Indian nations to white settlers. As president, he signed the Indian Removal Act in 1830, which ultimately forced Native Americans to vacate lands they had lived on for generations and, in some cases, journey on foot to their new allocations in the west in brutal conditions under which many thousands died. By the time of his death in 1845, Jackson's Nashville Hermitage plantation was being sustained by the unfree labour of 150 humans.[7] Ta-Nehisi Coates suggests that Trump was America's 'first white president',[8] but Jackson was the first president whose election *secured* his cohort's whiteness. Trump's aping—as well as accidental echoing—of Jackson has made visible and caused to be named the immigrant cohort from which Jackson emerged and which receded in the imaginary of the northeast in the era of the first president of Famine Catholic Irish origin, John F. Kennedy. The connection between Jackson and Trump was intimated on the very night of the latter's election, when prominent pro-Trump attorney and former New York mayor, Rudy Giuliani, named the ascent the 'greatest victory for the people of America since Andrew Jackson' on live network television.[9] (Strikingly, a clue that the 'people' alluded to were white emerged when the new administration postponed a long-planned replacement of Jackson on the US $20 bill with Underground Railroad heroine Harriet Tubman.[10])

Jackson's code and popular image was one of 'toughness, maleness, and whiteness',[11] and he became a template for the masculinist image that inserted the Scots-Irish into America's history of founding and rendered their whiteness unassailable. In the decades after Jackson, in particular, a period that saw fierce jostling for position in the American hierarchy of whitenesses, many US presidents stressed their Scots-Irish ('white') origins.[12] (President Clinton's later claims to that ancestry were made in the differing context of his role in negotiating peace in Northern Ireland.[13]) Thus, the election of a Catholic Irish president is an outlandish fantasy in an 1889 Sarah Orne Jewett depiction of an Irish aspirant to that office,[14] while in Fitzgerald's *This Side of Paradise* (1920), the disproportionately 'Nordic' colouring of past US presidents is audited.[15] *The Winning of the West* (1889), a work by president-to-be Theodore Roosevelt, praises the Scots-Irish as 'fitted to be Americans from the very start'.[16] This tallies with the 'cultural preadaptation' theme of turn-of-the-century literature extolling Ulster-America, which suggested that the purported cultural traits of Scots-Irish areas ('a warrior ethic, belligerence towards an indigenous population and metropolitan government, and a nonconformist religion') became the core traits of rural, white Protestant America itself.[17] In effect, and as Dunbar-Ortiz implies, the Scots-Irish were imagined to have been 'American' (in the nativist sense) *before* ever having left Ireland. The Ulster Irish had often occupied unauthorized tracts unpurchased from Native Americans, and early twentieth-century boosters cemented the Scots-Irish as founding Americans by glorifying what Patrick Griffin describes as their violent 'buffer' role against Native Americans on the colonial frontier.[18]

Furthermore, decades of folkloric, stage play, press, and dime-novel exaggerations of frontier 'escapades' of the likes of Davy Crockett (1786–1836), Kit Carson (1809–1868) (Figure 1.1), and 'Wild Bill' Hickok (1837–1876) made these Scots-Irishman the epitome of the frontier 'Injun-fighter' masculine ideal, allowing their ethnicity to stand in for white frontier Americanness itself.[19] One of the most prolific such myth-makers was the County Down-born Mayne Reid (1818–1883), dubbed the 'Giant of the Westerns' because of his dozens of adventure books of derring-do in the American West. Reid left Ulster to avoid following in the footsteps of his minister father, a senior figure in Irish Presbyterianism, and novels such as *The Scalp Hunters* (1851), in which the Creole hero hunts Indians who have kidnapped his daughter, were unchallenging enough regarding stereotypes of the West to be wildly popular throughout Europe, North America, and even Russia, particularly with boys; Reid villains tended to be 'morally inferior Indians, wicked Catholic priests, and dastardly Mormons'.[20] By the close of the nineteenth century, and in the context of the massive success of Frederick Jackson Turner's 1893 thesis that the frontier—and apparent Scots-Irish dominance therein—epitomized white America's egalitarian, democratic ideal,[21] the Crockett of cultural representation became a major figure in this masculinist American myth. The *real* Crockett was a more nuanced man, however: Elected to the US Congress in 1827, he vehemently opposed the Indian Removal Act of his fellow Scots-Irishman, Jackson. Nevertheless, this particular valour was ignored by turn-of-the-century Scots-Irish boosters who used the reputation of real-life Scots-Irish frontiersmen to affirm the cohort's whiteness.[22] Incidentally, the effacement of the category of 'Scots-Irish*woman*' in print culture by this incessant linking of Scots-Irishness to renegade white *machismo* spurred certain women writers of that background such as Ellen Glasgow (to be discussed) and the now-forgotten Jane H[udson] Corwin. The latter included a spirited dialogue in an 1858 collection in which a male bully harangues an 'Irish' female for daring to give voice to her thoughts in print.[23]

For Anatol Lieven, Trump is part of a Jacksonian American nationalism that privileges the white population of the republic.[24] However, the following examines not so much the traditional mainstream American representation of Jackson as the epitome of 'manly' white values, but the more ambivalent representation that emerged in the fiction of those who shared his ancestral ties to Ireland. Indeed, the interpretation of Jackson generated by the Gothic lexicon of such writers

Figure 1.1 The cover of an 1874 dime novel depicts Scots-Irish frontier folk hero Kit Carson violently fending off Native Americans. Courtesy of Wikimedia Commons.

suggests that Trump is but the latest iteration of Jackson's many returns. In what seems to be a submerged commentary on Jackson's ruthless Indian removal policy, the (un)dead president hovers over an 1876 Henry James story concerned with seizure and displacement. 'The Ghostly Rental' concerns an old man, Captain Diamond, whose curse upon his daughter had seemingly caused her death. Her ghost enacts vengeance by ousting her father from his large old home, offering to be his tenant, and having him go every quarter to his former home to collect rent. At the conclusion, the narrator discovers the very much alive daughter to be an 'audacious actress',[25] made up to look ghostly. In the final scene, the recently deceased father then begins to haunt his living daughter. Diamond is transformed into a ghost only at the very close of the action, but the narrator's odd earlier description of the then-living Captain suggests a deeper level of haunting in the narrative:

> His head reminded me, vaguely, of the portraits of Andrew Jackson. He had a crop of grizzled hair, as stiff as a brush, a lean, pale, smooth-shaven face, and an eye of intense brilliancy, surmounted with thick brows, which had remained perfectly black. His face, as well as his cloak, seemed to belong to an old soldier [...].[26]

The original ghost is false, and the real presence haunting this story of dispossession and fraudulent occupancy is Andrew Jackson. Not unsurprisingly, 'The Ghostly Rental' has often been described as one of James's most Poe-influenced stories, and this chapter suggests that the anxiety regarding Ulster Protestant ancestry that the authors share is central to that resemblance.

As a figure who represented the longed-for *attained* whiteness, Jackson haunts the pre-Kennedy Irish-American Catholic imagination of Fitzgerald somewhat differently: in the opening chapter of his posthumous and unfinished *The Love of the Last Tycoon* (1993),[27] Jackson is a monumental white supremacist presence/absence that annihilates. Jackson's history as slave-holder and scourge of Native Americans pulls together the novel's references to racial history and to the 'off-whiteness' of Mannie Schwartze, a failed Jewish film producer. At the novel's 1930s opening and in the company of Cecelia Brady, Schwartze attempts to visit Jackson's Nashville Hermitage plantation. Nashville itself was the site of a decisive Confederate loss during the Civil War, and ghosts unassimilated by the plantation 'heritage' industry emerge as the would-be visitors are driven to the estate in the pre-dawn hours: A Black cow-herder encountered *en route* to Jackson's plantation 'grew gradually real out of the darkness'.[28] Cecelia thinks that 'ghetto' Schwartze does not 'fit' 'at that raw shrine': 'Mannie Schwartze and Andrew Jackson – it was hard to say them in the same sentence.' Jackson's 'big white box' is not a heritage to which Schwartze, whose name translates from the German as 'black', has access. He commits suicide soon after the visit, enacting a kind of blood sacrifice for Jackson's 'shrine' to white supremacy.[29] Although a triumphalist Jackson was embraced in what Amy Clukey calls neo-Confederate iconography in recent Northern Irish loyalism (allegiance to the British crown),[30] Fitzgerald and James do not celebrate Jackson .[31] Similarly, speaking to a journalist in 1946, Eugene O'Neill seems to target Jackson in a diatribe against so-called 'great national heroes' whose 'portraits should be taken out and burned' due to their 'treachery [against] the Indians'.[32]

Thus, Jackson's troubling legacy (Figure 1.2) leaves traces in the works by James and Fitzgerald just considered, and his treatment of Americans of colour

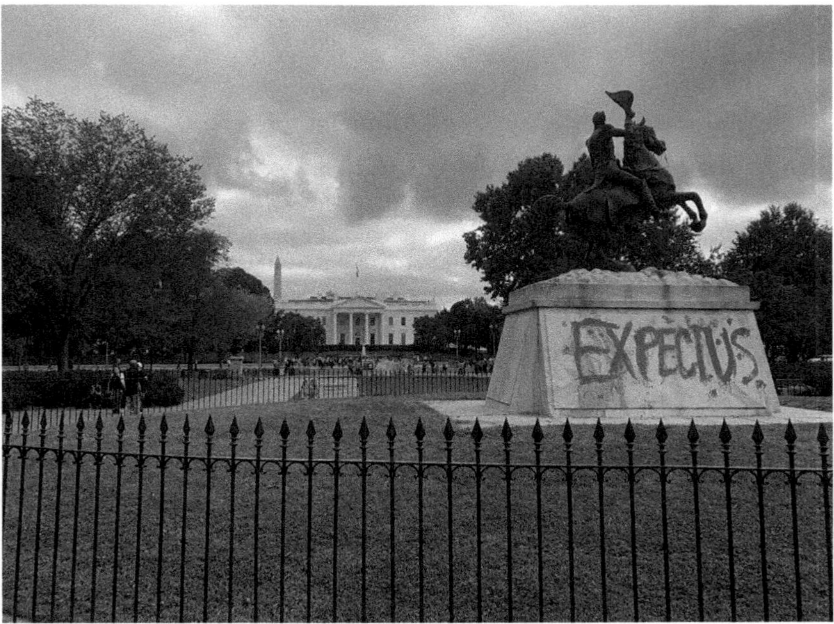

Figure 1.2 Equestrian statue of Andrew Jackson (1853), President's Park, Washington, DC. It was graffitied on Indigenous Peoples' Day/Columbus Day, 11 October 2021. Courtesy of Wikimedia Commons.

is, moreover, a history that uncomfortably echoes the role that ancestors of the Scots-Irish played in seventeenth-century Ulster. The unfinished business of the Irish past erupts again and again in America, 'a land primed for fatality and already cursed', in Faulkner's words.[33] As such, this chapter further examines the rendering of broader Irish and American histories of guilt and trauma in Gothic fiction by writers of Ulster settler-colonial origin. These narratives by Poe and James will be theorized as belonging to a subgenre related to but separate from both Anglo-Irish and American Gothic and which will be termed 'Scots-Irish Gothic'. However, it is first necessary to outline not just the trajectory of Scots-Irish identity in colonial America, but to go farther back again, to its origin in disordered colonial Ulster. Historian David H. Fischer goes back further still in beginning in the unstable Scottish borderlands: those who became the Ulster Scots originated in the historically violence-prone zone between Scotland and England, moving from there to early modern Ireland and from thence to colonial America's frontier in what Fischer describes as a recurrent cycle of violence and insecurity.[34] Griffin similarly suggests that this cohort straddled 'civilized' and 'savage' in both the Ulster and—later on—the colonial American frontier. Historiography's Gothicizing of this trajectory arguably takes its cue from literary representations of the Ulster Irish, which date to American literature's very beginnings. This troubled history makes an immigrant of Ulster roots a menacing presence in Charles Brockden Brown's *Edgar Huntly*, America's earliest Gothic novel, which is arguably Scots-Irish Gothic in the anxiety it expresses regarding colonial-period Irish immigration. This intial hostility towards the Ulster Irish in America will be laid out before the chapter considers Brown's 1799 novel.

Irish History in American Gothic: *Edgar Huntly* (1799)

The contention over 'whiteness' of the two distinct waves of Irish immigration before and after the Famine of 1845 must begin with the Plantation of the northern Irish province of Ulster. The New World's racial and ethnic contexts amplified and transformed the traumatic first encounter between Gaelic Ireland and those that America named the Scots/Scotch-Irish and Ireland eventually named the Ulster Scots. Medieval Gaeldom spanned Ireland and Scotland's Highlands and Western Isles, linking these regions culturally and linguistically, which created a trans-Irish Sea solidarity that persisted for centuries and even in the New World.[35] The colonization of Ireland's northern province, the so-called 'Plantation of Ulster', was intended to Anglicize, 'civilize', and make Protestant what had been the rural, Catholic, Irish-speaking, and culturally Gaelic stronghold of the powerful O'Neill family.[36] The 'Planters' were a linguistically, culturally, and denominationally diverse cohort, but many were Lowland Scottish in origin, Presbyterian, and speakers of Scots, which has been considered both an old variety of English and a distinct Germanic language.[37] The Plantation began in 1609 and led to ethnic and sectarian conflict, since most of the appropriated land was forfeited from members of a native Gaelic class that had collapsed following the Nine Year's War (1593-1603), a rebellion led by Hugh O'Neill against the Tudor reconquest. The last term refers to England's attempt to reassert control over Ireland centuries after the initial Anglo-Norman invasion of Ireland in 1169, spurred in part by the belief that this first so-called 'English' cohort had 'gone native'. In the Scottish context, a similar decimation of cultural and political power is set in motion for Gaelic Highland culture with the end of the Jacobite insurgency on the field of Culloden in 1746, a rupture that emerges in the imagining of the pan-Gaelic past and Gaelo-American present in work by Fitzgerald and Faulkner considered in this study.

In the wake of the consolidation of British power in seventeenth-century Ireland, Miller notes that although only one-fourth to one-third of Ireland's population were Protestants, they constituted about 75 per cent of all transatlantic departures between 1700 and 1776. Moreover, about 70 per cent of these Irish Protestant emigrants were Presbyterian.[38] As a result of various natural and man-made crises in Ulster throughout the eighteenth century, from rack-renting, crop failures, and persecution by the Established (Anglican) Church, Presbyterians fled in waves. They tended at first to emigrate in family groups led by ministers, perceiving themselves to be a 'communal exodus compelled by religious and political oppression.'[39] Ulster Presbyterians had been sent in by the British authorities originally, but to their chagrin, from the close of the seventeenth century and into the early decades of the following century, they became subject to some of the systemic religious and economic oppression enforced by the British authorities in Ireland under which the colonized native Catholic Irish greatly suffered.[40] James Anthony Froude linked this formative experience in Ulster to the subsequent eagerness of many Scots-Irishmen to take up arms against the British Crown during the American Revolution: 'The resentment which they carried with them continued to burn in their new homes; and, in the War of Independence, England had no fiercer enemies than the grandsons and great-grandsons of the Presbyterians who had held Ulster against Tyrconnell [O'Neill-controlled Ulster].'[41]

By 1790, one half of the 400,000 US residents who were often labelled 'Irish' descended from Ulster stock, and the majority of those were Presbyterians of Scottish descent.[42] The marked degree to which this cohort still gave evidence of many Scottish cultural, linguistic, and religious attributes in colonial America led to the use of the term 'Scotch-Irish' in areas settled by the Ulster Irish, though this did not take decisive hold in mainstream America or as a widespread self-designation until after the middle of the nineteenth century. What Charles Fanning has called 'the first Irish-American novel',[43] an 1817 publication under the pseudonym 'An Hibernian' and entitled *The Irish Emigrant, An Historical Tale Founded on Fact*, was written by Adam Douglass (1790–1847), the son of a politically radical Scottish-born settler of Ulster.[44] This radical tradition and Douglass's ease with a label denoting Irishness was effaced with the 'Britishing' (or, more accurately, the 'Scottishing') of Ulster Presbyterian identity in both Ireland and America in the mid-nineteenth century. Likewise, in frontier folk hero Crockett's 1834 memoir, he refers repeatedly to family members as being 'Irish', though their skill-set ('she was also a good weaver, as most of the Irish are, whether men or women') point to their more specific Ulster Irish culture,[45] since weaving and linen production were rural Presbyterian Ulster economic mainstays before the province industrialized. Peter Gilmore suggests that their relatively recent Scottish origins made Ulster Presbyterians 'distinguishable' from native Irish and Irish Anglican immigrants in the colonies, but their time in Ireland meant that were also culturally 'distinct from Scots.'[46] Thus, labouring-class Ulster-Scots poet Samuel Thomson (1766–1816) revealingly writes of being 'Irish' on the outside and 'Scotch within.'[47]

The influx of poor Irish immigrants after the 1845 Famine strengthened the growing distance between 'old' (predominantly Ulster Presbyterian) and 'new' (predominantly western seaboard Gaelic and Catholic) Irish Americans. The differentiating and more 'Saxon' coinage 'Scotch-Irish' also gained currency in response to 'New World' issues such as anti-immigrant feeling in the early republic, the Second Great Awakening, the creation of a post-Civil War unified Southern white Protestant identity in opposition to the active citizenship of the formerly enslaved, and the high status of Scottishness in elite America. The last was tied to that community's wealth in the colonial period but also to a wider *cachet* after a tartan-clad Queen Victoria made depopulated Scotland an outdoor playground for the British elite in the 1850s.[48] However, the differentiating coinage of 'Scotch-Irish' ultimately emerges from the sectarian tensions of the Irish motherland,[49] which leaves traces in America's first bestseller, *The Wide, Wide World* (1850), Susan Warner's novel of strong Presbyterian tenor. In nineteenth-century Ireland, both self-consciously evangelical Protestant and Catholic sentimental literature commonly depicted characters' willing conversion to 'the other side',[50] which illuminates an episode in Warner in which a poor Irish Catholic undergoes deathbed conversion through the offices of a rural New York Presbyterian minister.[51] Nevertheless, as Eileen Sullivan details, post-Famine Irish-American writers generally portrayed their community as bound by shared ethnicity more than by shared theology.[52]

Ignatiev outlines the gradual transformation of post-Famine Catholic Irish-Americans from 'off-whiteness' to mainstream whiteness within an American racial symbolic in which the powerful are invariably 'white'.[53] However, it is less often noted that the Scots-Irish underwent a similar process during the previous century and were subject to stereotypes that gradually transferred to the post-Famine cohort, as in Henry David Thoreau's mocking account of Ralph Waldo Emerson's feckless Scots-Irish servant.[54] Writing in 1757, Edmund Burke suggested that 'the Irish' were giving up their land in Pennsylvania and moving on to Virginia, Maryland, and North Carolina because they were 'not succeeding so well' as their 'more frugal and industrious' German fellow-immigrants.[55] New York state landowner Hector St. John de Crèvecoeur conveys a similar sentiment in 1783:

> The Irish do not prosper so well; they love to drink and to quarrel; they are litigious and soon take to the gun, which is the ruin of everything; they seem beside to labour under a greater degree of ignorance in husbandry than the others, perhaps it is that their industry had less scope, and was less exercised at home.[56]

As described by Griffin, the lifestyles of the colonial Irish became the very definition of rural white indigence: 'Poor and mobile, they scratched a precarious existence out of the woods beyond the reach of the law and polite society.'[57] Griffin suggests that the political marginalization of Presbyterians by the Established Church in Ireland, and their initial deployment in Ulster as a bulwark between the Crown and the native Gaels was replicated in the New World: as occupants of unauthorized tracts unpurchased from Native Americans, the Irish initially functioned as a buffer between European and native, legitimacy and illegitimacy, white and non-white. Popular depictions in the Pennsylvania press painted them as squatting, drunken, boisterous, dishonest, lazy, and comic. Most significantly, in light of the rhetoric of flawed whiteness implied by the poisonous 'white trash' construct, the Irish settlers were referred to as 'idle trash' in a 1734 letter to Thomas Penn, hereditary proprietor of the Province of Pennsylvania.[58] This makes them the implicit cultural ancestors of the unethnicized 'po' white folks' who later become subject to the dehumanizing 'trash' label.

The first wave of emigration from Ireland occurred from 1718 onward, and was made up of those who could raise the cost of their passage. However, the second wave, beginning in 1740, consisted of penniless indentured servants. James Leyburn's estimate suggests that 'not less than half, nor more than two-thirds of all white immigrants to the colonies were indentured servants or redemptioners or convicts', and that beginning in 1728, 'by far the greatest number of servants and redemptioners' came from Ireland.[59] Many Ulster immigrants of the second wave subsequently made their way along the eastern slope of the Appalachians to the back parts of Virginia, where the charge of being the 'Refuse of Mankind' was levelled against them.[60] Areas settled by the eighteenth-century Irish are today popularly perceived to be the epicentre of what is deprecatingly called 'cracker' culture. The phenomenon of white indentured servants is generally held to have led to the coining of the contemptuous term 'white trash' by enslaved African-Americans in about the early nineteenth century. However, as posited above, the word 'trash' had *earlier* attached itself *specifically* to the Irish, and their subsequent behaviour cemented this perception of 'defective' whiteness. To wit, Griffin suggests that Benjamin Franklin implied an initial 'flawed white' capacity for brutality when he called the Scots-Irish Paxton Boys, perpetrators of an indiscriminate massacre of Indians in Lancaster, Pennsylvania in 1763 'CHRISTIAN WHITE SAVAGES' whose brutality made them more barbarian than any Indian or 'poor unenlightened *African Negroe*' [...].[61] This conjoining of supposedly 'antithetical' categories suggests the threat posed to the entwined concepts of 'whiteness' and 'Christian civility' by the Paxtons' behaviour.

The reputation for violence of the frontier Scots-Irish provoked anxiety in America, as did the later involvement of radicalized Irish of all stripes in the French Revolution-inspired 1798 uprising against British rule in Ireland itself. The latter was part of the impetus for the *Alien and Sedition Acts* passed by the US Congress in the same year. The insurgency of the years surrounding 1798 in Ireland was a tradition to which the Henry James family was directly linked through multiple marriage ties to that of noted Irish Protestant radical Robert Emmet. However, late eighteenth-century radical Ulster Protestant proto-nationalism was later forgotten in both Protestant America and Presbyterian Ireland. In the Irish case, it was, as Guy Beiner suggests, at best ambivalently remembered in Ulster with the 'Britishing' of Protestant identity after the Union of Great Britain and Ireland in 1800 (after which the whole island was to be governed directly from Westminster for the next 120 years). In addition, the 'New Light' (liberal) Presbyterianism that had prompted participation in the 1798 Uprising fell away in the decades after.[62] Belfast's textile-centred industrial revolution inserted it into a wider British economic trajectory and was a further factor in why loyalty to the Crown became central to northern Protestant identity. However, although the Ulster Scots would go on to throw their lot in with Britain in the nineteenth century, this was *far from apparent* in the 1790s, as suggested by the anxiety regarding an immigrant of that background in one of the first and most sensationalist American Gothic novels, Charles Brockden Brown's *Edgar Huntly* (1799).

Edgar Huntly tells of sleepwalking, murder, and frontier violence in the rural Pennsylvania of the 1780s. The title character relates the consequences of his chance encounter with a local servant named Clithero Edny, a mysterious immigrant whose violent history in Dublin follows him to the New World. There Clithero had, he believes, killed both his wealthy Anglo-Irish benefactress, Mrs Lorimer, and her brother. (She actually survives.) Huntly tracks the fleeing Clithero, and both plunge into the wilds of the colonial territories of the Delaware basin. Due to his mistaken belief that they had murdered his family, Edgar Huntly encounters and kills a number of Delaware Indians, the region's displaced original inhabitants, and both he and the Irish Clithero live like animals in their respective flights. However, these actions never seem to displace Huntly's belief in his own civility and his repeatedly stated distaste for violence, nor his equally unconvincing insistence on Clithero's lack of culpability for his (Clithero's) violent actions in Ireland, despite evidence to the contrary.

Jared Gardner situates *Edgar Huntly* in the immediate context of the Alien and Sedition Acts (which the novel's author supported), suggesting that it creates American identity by exorcising from the land the 'alien' aboriginal Indian and the equally 'alien' Irish immigrant.[63] The Alien and Sedition Acts of 1798 were a response to the perception in the 1790s that French and Irish 'alien forces' were at work within the heart of the nation. During a congressional debate on naturalization, it was made clear that 'hordes of wild Irishmen', with their incendiary political ideas, were not welcome in the land of the free.[64] The Irish with French republican political beliefs came to epitomize the alien for the Federalists because many 'of those active in the 1798 Irish Rebellion were believed to be in exile in the US, and the professed affinities between the United Irishmen [the instigators of the rebellion] in [America] and the pro-French revolutionaries in Ireland sparked widespread hostility towards this immigrant population'.[65]

Gardner notwithstanding, attention to the Irish political subtexts of *Edgar Huntly* tends to be the stuff of footnote, when acknowledged at all. Moreover, as with many analyses of American literary texts with Irish characters, Gardner's otherwise groundbreaking reading of *Edgar Huntly* does not consider the *specifics* of Clithero's background. In fact, details suggest that the servant is of Ulster settler-colonial origin: Clithero is from Armagh; is implied not to stand out in any way as denominationally anomalous in his Protestant enclave in Pennsylvania; is the son of a tenant farmer 'of the better sort' and the possessor of a British surname. Moreover, on fleeing Ireland, he takes the predominant Ulster-Scots immigrant route of the era of travelling from Belfast to Philadelphia. Thus, Clithero is almost certainly to be understood as being of Ulster 'Planter' (seventeenth-century settler-colonial) stock. This would explain the ease and kindness with which he is accepted into the fold of the elite and implicitly Ascendancy (Anglo-Irish Anglican) Lorimer family of Dublin. Despite their difference in class, both Clithero Edny and the Lorimers originate from the post-Williamite War Protestant and so-called 'New English' order that stepped into the vacuum created by the definitive banishment of the Catholic and Jacobite Gaelo-Norman order at the Battles of the Boyne and Aughrim in 1690 and 1691 respectively.

In addition, the character named Sarsefield, in a coincidence that reeks of the kind of supposed transatlantic conspiracy that galvanized the Alien and Sedition Acts, was both Clithero's mentor in Ireland and later emerges as Edgar's instructor in rural Pennsylvania. Ireland is dangerously close in this novel: a number of Irish characters—Mrs Lorimer and her daughter, as well as Sarsefield—come and go from its shores seemingly easily and quickly. More damningly still, this latter Irish immigrant's name strongly recalls Patrick Sarsfield (1655–1693), a landowner and a celebrated Catholic Irish Jacobite commander of Old English (Norman) descent in the doomed 1690s campaign.[66] From the Counter Reformation period onward, those of Norman/Old English ancestry in Ireland who remained Catholic generally began to see themselves as Irish, while, as noted, many radicals of Ulster Presbyterian origin had participated in the 1798 Rebellion against the British Crown. Thus, in the long context of Irish history, Sarsefield and Clithero represent the 'Old' and 'New' English colonies in Ireland, respectively, two cohorts who had, it seemed by the 1790s, *both* 'gone native' in terms of political allegiance to the Irish radical cause. Unconvincing rationalizations are repeatedly offered by Huntly as to why Clithero entered Mrs Lorimer's chambers with a dagger in his hand soon after killing her brother, but when Clithero's actions in Ireland are described in bare-bone terms, the imputation is treachery to his own, given the settler-colonial origins he shares with the siblings.

Brown continually circles on issues of the precarity of settler 'civilization' in a novel in which both Edgar and Clithero easily descend into a 'savagery' overtly associated in the novel with Indians and wild animals. As such, his Irish immigrant characters' Old and New English backgrounds may be read as a warning to the Anglo settler-colonials of America of the danger of identifying with the causes of savage aboriginals, be they the Gaels of Ireland or the Natives of America. As Gardner nicely puts it in summing up how Edgar alone ultimately throws his lot in with Anglo-American civilization after his spell of savage living *precisely because* he massacres native inhabitants: 'Aliens [such as Clithero] become Indians' but 'Americans [such as Huntly] become Indian-killers'.[67] Huntly's violence is in the service of his white settler community, while Clithero's actions in Dublin suggest he has turned on members of the Anglo garrison there and may do the same in his new home. Indeed, Philip Barnard and Stephen Shapiro draw attention to the Irish violence on American soil with which Brown, a Pennsylvania Quaker, would have been immediately familiar, which is the 'Christian White Savage[ry]' of the Paxton Boys' actions in 1763. The Paxtons 'challenged Quaker authority on the Pennsylvania frontier' and led that community to 'blame backcountry Irish settlers for conflicts that [went] back to the original Quaker colonization and landgrabs', a manoeuvre echoed in Edgar's continual shifts of responsibility for violence.[68]

Thus, for the careful reader of the 1790s, the ethno-religious *specifics* of Clithero Edny's Irish background prefigure which side of the divide between wild and civilized he is destined to come down upon. His closing appearances in the novel, living destitute in the hut of defiant Delaware hold-out 'Queen Mab' and then dying by his own hand in the throes of lunacy, confirm what knowledge of Old and New English disloyalty to Anglo civilization in Ireland would have predicted to a white Anglo-American reader, which is this: Clithero was a settler-colonial who had 'gone native' before ever setting foot in Pennsylvania. *Edgar Huntly* is undoubtedly a novel of incongruities, inconclusiveness, and inconsistencies, but Clithero cannot be unequivocally read as an 'Irish savage',[69] nor is he an Irish Catholic immigrant:[70] more terrifying yet to a white American reader of the 1790s, he appears to be a British Protestant settler-colonial who had first degenerated into savagery *in Ireland* and brings that disorder with him to the sister colony in America.

Poe, James, and Scots-Irish Gothic

Although *Edgar Huntly* is generally categorized as American Gothic literature, this chapter will imply that it might also be claimed for a subgenre to be named 'Scots-Irish Gothic.' Broadly defined, Gothic is fiction with a grotesque, sinister, or claustrophobic atmosphere in which the vanquished, the past, or the dead return. This basic definition fits both American and Anglo-Irish Gothic literature, aside from the former's often overt anxiety concerning race. The latter, whose best-known text may be Bram Stoker's *Dracula* (1897), likewise possesses features specific to its country of origin: Jarlath Killeen reads Anglo-Irish Gothic's emphasis on the return of the dispossessed Other as an expression of the 'siege-mentality' preoccupation with impending extermination of authors from or connected to Ireland's Anglican ruling elite.[71] However, dominant understandings of Irish and American Gothic do not account for *the other settler-colonizer cohort in Ireland*, the Ulster Scots, nor for the cultural productions of or about their settler-colonizer descendants in America by Brown, Poe, and Faulkner, in whose work the violence of the Old World is ceaselessly reprised in the New. If 'the past is a foreign country',[72] then for American writers of Gothic, that country is often Ireland.

Indeed, Robert Smart has recently theorized that colonial-era settlers from Ireland brought the Gothic trope to American writing.[73] Altogether, works expressive of the unease of the Ulster settler-colonial cohort in America are *neither* Anglo-Irish Gothic nor American Gothic, but a subgenre to be termed Scots-Irish Gothic.[74]

The tropes of invisibility and silence have invariably attached themselves to narratives that seek to recover Scots-Irishness as an identifiable but submerged historical presence or an Irish or diasporic literary or linguistic tradition. Griffin's masterful study of the Scots-Irish in America is entitled *The People with No Name*, and for all the attention they have received from literary critics,[75] the Scots-Irish might equally be termed 'The People with No Literature', as Glasgow's 1925 novel, *Barren Ground*, implies.[76] Likewise, Ivan Herbison's 1996 pamphlet on Ulster's 'Rhyming Weaver' Poets (a self-taught and politically radical eighteenth-century Presbyterian textile worker cohort) was the evocatively titled '*The Rest is Silence*', and linguist Lorna Carson has noted that most contemporary speakers of Scots dialect as it has evolved in Ulster have no name for the language variety.[77] Altogether, just as the Ulster-Scots voice is hardly accounted for in the Irish canon, the Scots-Irish voice is a kind of *doppelganger* of the Irish-American literary canon, a troubling double that perennially haunts but is only occasionally discerned.

Scots-Irish Gothic potentially enfolds both depictions of the Scots-Irish such as *Edgar Huntly* and works by authors of that ancestry, among which may be counted one conventionally considered to be the founding father of American Gothic, Edgar Allan Poe (1809–1849). Both an heir to Irish Gothic and a progenitor of its American iteration, Poe is central to a bastard offspring that might be—but never has been—named Scots-Irish Gothic. Poe's paternal grandfather was born in Dring, County Cavan in the province of Ulster in *c.* 1742 to a comfortable Presbyterian tenant farming family,[78] and eventually settled in Baltimore, Maryland. After Edgar's father abandoned the family and his English mother died, he was fostered by a Virginia family of Scottish connection. Farther back still, the Poes were descended from a 'Planter' (settler-colonial) family in Ulster.[79] Edgar's convoluted family origins are emblematic of the questions of legitimacy of the Ulster Irish presence in colonial Ireland and the colonial American frontier, where they were both oppressor and oppressed. *Neither and both* Irish and British, Ulster Irishness is caught in no-man's-land of identity and allegiance somewhere between Ulster, Scotland, England, and, ultimately, between loyalist and patriot America in the period of the Revolutionary War. Thus, in both the British Isles and American contexts, there is no Other upon whom violence may be visited who is not the Self, to some degree. This could serve as a one-line summary of Poe's *oeuvre*.

For Killeen, Gothic emphasizes 'hesitancy over certainty' and 'refuses to dissolve binaries such as living/dead, inside/outside, friend/enemy, desire/disgust'.[80]

In Poe's best-known stories, 'The Black Cat', 'The Pit and the Pendulum', 'The Cask of Amontillado', 'Ligeia', 'The Fall of the House of Usher', and 'Morella', the lines between the diseased living and the red-cheeked dead, and between mansion and prison, grave and cell, are porous. However, the slave-holding Southern culture of Poe's upbringing is only the latest settler-colonial culture in which his protagonists must suffer, cursed to do, receive, and witness violence. Reading Poe's work alongside Gothic texts from Ireland illuminates its echo of earlier settler-colonial complicity, as suggested by a comparison of 'The Legend of Stumpie's Brae' (*c.*1839) with the American author's ballad-like 'The Tell-Tale Heart' (1843). The latter Poe story concerns the motiveless murder and dismemberment of an old man whose concealed corpse haunts the murderer with a thumping sound. 'The Legend of Stumpie's Brae' is a murder ballad in *faux* Ulster-Scots dialect attributed to Derry-based Anglican hymnist Cecil Frances Alexander (of 'Once in Royal David's City' fame). The ballad was inspired by an eighteenth-century Donegal legend about a poor Planter farming couple who kill and dismember a travelling peddler.[81] After his burial, the clomp of the victim's stumps is heard by the couple, so they flee to the American colonies, but 'the very first sound' they hear on the deck of their emigrant ship is 'the tappin' o' them bare knees'. The chilling fourth-last verse develops the horror in 'wild America', where Stumpie 'haunted them to their dying day/And he follows their children yet'.[82] The ballad's use of Ulster-Scots celebrates the dialect of the 'Rhyming Weaver' Poets. However, thematically, Planter culpability in Ireland and, in turn, colonial America, is evoked by the suggestion that unfinished history and violence is carried from Ulster to the New World and to the pen of Poe.

The Poe story that best expresses the horror of inescapable and inherited violence is 'William Wilson', his 1839 autobiographical *doppelganger* tale (Figure 1.3). It concerns the eponymous young man who meets another boy at his school who is also called William Wilson. The students also share a similar appearance and have even been born on the same date—19 January—which was Poe's own birthday. The protagonist's early educational career in a school in England follows that of Poe himself, and the author even gives the story's fictional headmaster the exact name of the man who led the school he attended from 1817 to 1820.[83] Most eerily of all, however, is that no one but the narrator appears to notice the other William. In the years after school, William is haunted by his double, who thwarts his plans at every turn. The name that both young men carry points to a shared ethnic or national background, a connection in what the story terms some 'infinitely remote' past that cannot be severed.[84] Moreover, 'William Wilson' also indicts the maddening inescapabilty of patrilineal inheritance. The son of William is 'Will's son', the origin of the British surname 'Wilson', of course. One is damned from the outset by the stamp of the forefather, who precludes individuality and free will as much as any Puritan God. As with the pair of Williams who are also sons of Williams ('Wilson') in Poe's story, no past, individuality, or closure is permissible.

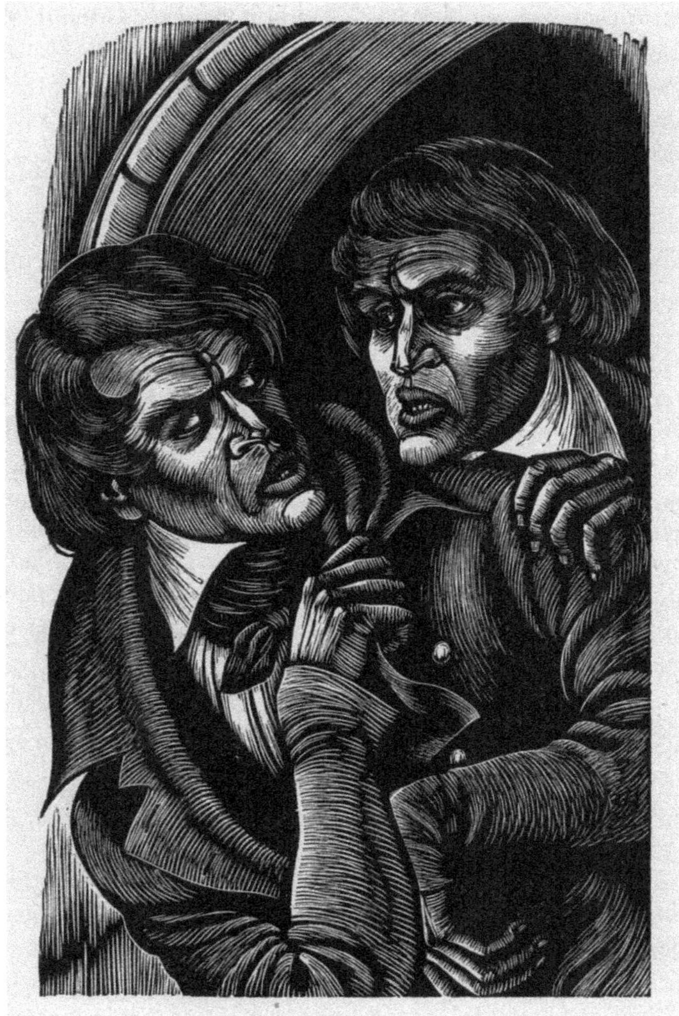

Figure 1.3 'William Wilson' illustration by Fritz Eichenberg for *Tales of Edgar Allan Poe* (1944). © 2022 Estate of Fritz Eichenberg / Licensed by VAGA at Artists Rights Society (ARS), NY.

(*'Maybe we are both Father,'* thinks Quentin in Faulkner's *Absalom, Absalom!*, *'Maybe nothing ever happens once and is finished.'*[85]) The father's lineage, heritage, and name are inescapable curses, and obligatory allegiances and prejudices handed down from the ancestors allow for no freedom of action or thought. Thus, the body is a tomb from which the dead speak in Poe's 'The Facts in the Case of M. Valdemar' (1845), in which a mesmerized dying man reports first that he is dying and then that he is dead. In Irish and British association, 'William' is the

Ur-conqueror name, carried by William, Duke of Normandy, who led the Conquest of England in 1066 that ultimately profoundly altered the British Isles. (The Norman invasion of Ireland out of Wales occurred a century later.) It is also a first name associated with Protestant hegemony in Ulster to this day due to William III of England's 1690 victory in Ireland over a Jacobite army.[86] It is no random choice of verb then, when at the close of 'William Wilson' the *doppelganger* whispers to his assassin and double that he/they had been '"conquered"'.[87] 'William' is also—whether Poe knew it or not—the first name of the man a nineteenth-century Irish historian surmised to be the first in the Poe family's line in Ireland, William Powell, an original undertaker of the Plantation of Ulster.[88]

Walt Whitman was attuned to the implications of Poe's fragmented national and familial origins. Speaking at the reburial celebration for Poe in Baltimore, Maryland in 1875 (a very Gothic event in itself), Whitman recalls a 'lurid dream' of a figure who turns out to be Poe in which he perceives him as an immigrant or refugee on the water, already battle-worn by the nightmare of inherited history and trauma before he has ever reached shore:

> In a dream I once had, I saw a vessel on the sea, at midnight, in a storm. It was no great fullrigg'd ship, nor majestic steamer, steering firmly through the gale but seem'd one of those superb little schooner yachts...now flying uncontroll'd with torn sails and broken spars through the wild sleet and winds and waves of the night. On deck was a slender, slight, beautiful figure, a dim man, apparently enjoying all the terror, the murk, and the dislocation of which he was the centre and the victim.[89]

In contrast to Whitman, and possibly resistant to Poe precisely because they shared so much in terms of anxiety of ancestry, James wrote in an 1876 review that 'to take [Poe] seriously is to lack seriousness one's self'.[90] And yet, one of James's most Gothic tales, 'Owen Wingrave' (1892), follows Poe's lead in depicting a cursed patrilineal line whose violence is brought down upon its latest member, the title character who is both 'the centre and the victim' of the inheritance. '"Ah, we're tainted—all!"' notes Owen of his ancestors.[91] The scion of a British military family, Owen is 'the first [in the male line] for three hundred years' to abandon military training.[92] Generations of Wingraves have been felled in colonial conflicts,[93] and their mansion is a kind of British Empire in miniature for Miss Julian of the 'long Eastern eyes', a 'vanquished and captive' Wingrave dependent who 'could fight with her back to the wall'.[94] James more explicitly conjures up Britain's annexed 'Celtic' margins by endowing Owen with an old Welsh name and his military coach (who seems surprisingly ambivalent about soldiering) with the Gaelic Irish surname of 'Coyle'. Hell-bent on conserving their centuries-long pattern of 'winning' graves, Owen's living—and it will ultimately seem—his dead family members collude in persecuting him regarding his abandonment of military training in the manner of an invading army. ('"They've cut off his supplies—they're trying to starve him out."'[95]) Strikingly, although living male *and* female members of the Wingrave household participate in the harassment of Owen, only *dead* Wingrave forefathers do so: '"I've started up all the old ghosts"', Owen tells Coyle. '"The very portraits glower at me on the walls. There's one of my great-great-grandfather [...] that fairly stirs on the canvas—just heaves a little—when I come near it."'[96] This man, Colonel Wingrave, is believed to haunt the family's gloomy mansion: He had killed his own son in a fit of violence and had then committed suicide in a room that is now sealed off. Owen's living grandfather, Sir Philip, 'a merciless old warrior',[97] has begun to be violently angry with his grandson. Unsettlingly, he is uncannily similar in appearance as well as in temperament to Colonel Wingrave.[98] Having spent the night in the sealed-off room, the defiant Owen is found 'dead on the spot on which his ancestor [Colonel Wingrave] had been found. He looked like a young soldier on a battle-field.'[99] Even in his attempted rebellion Owen Wingrave cannot escape his forefathers' demands. They kill him but he dies—as family members both living and dead had insisted he would—a soldier.

At the time of James's death, he left behind an unfinished novel—published in 1917 as *The Sense of the Past*—that likewise recalls Poe's 'William Wilson'. It is also a striking departure from James's usual mode of realism in encompassing the theme of time travel. The narrative of the collapse of distance between generations of the same family, *The Sense of the Past* concerns a young New York man, Ralph Pendrel, who is bequeathed an eighteenth-century London house by a distant relative. In his new residence, Ralph discovers a portrait of his ancestor, also named Ralph Pendrel. Prowling the house in the darkness by the light of a hand-held candle later in the action, the American 'saw what was indeed beyond sense': the figure in the painting has come to life and his 'face – miracle of miracles, yes – confounded him as his own'.[100] Pendrel is ultimately thrust back into the past, where he takes on his *doppelganger*'s identity. As in Poe's narrative, the mirroring *doppelganger* enfolds a threat of murder/suicide: 'what he had taken for a reflection of his light was only another candle. [...] He raised his [eyes] still higher to be sure, and the young man in the doorway made a movement that answered; but so, while almost as with brandished weapons they faced each other [...]'.[101] The repeated trope of the threatening *doppelganger* of Ulster-American non-realist fiction suggests that writers such as Poe and James process a central complex of the heritage they shared, the psychic heaviness of which is suggested by the tortured tone of James's notebook record of his drafting of *The Sense of the Past*.[102] It is fitting that *The Sense of the Past* remained unfinished and perhaps even unfinishable, an incompleteness that complements the unfinished history of the Ulster Irish, as does its theme of the threatening forebear who rises from the dead. Since the weight of history carried by the patronym is a thread that runs through the James and Poe works just considered and recurs throughout this study, this chapter now pivots to a theory of the male line as 'ancestor haunted'.

Doppelgangers: Irish Patronyms and the Inescapable Past

Queer African-American poet and scholar bell hooks (1952–2021; born as Gloria Jean Watkins) adopted her maternal great-grandmother's name (though without capitalization). This was a triply significant manoeuvre since, traditionally, the possibility of possessing a surname and /or passing on one's surname to offspring was unavailable to enslaved people, married women in most Western cultures, and those for whom sexuality precluded legal marriage to those they loved. Though Frank Yerby's *Foxes of Harrow* portrays how the plantation's unofficial Black matrilineal line eventually converges with the white Irish planter's patrilineal line, women, like the enslaved, generally had little choice but to take the name given to them by the man who had legally sanctioned control over their lives and bodies. As Irish-American feminist Jane O'Reilly explains regarding her decision to revert to her Irish maiden name after a divorce, 'We [women] are the people who lose our names when we marry, the also-rans of recorded history, the unidentified half of "mankind". We travel incognita in our own culture.'[103] Thus, gender intersects with the perception of Irishness or the assumption of its absence through the tradition of a woman's name change upon marriage, which could often mean the bride's loss of ethno-religious identity along with her birth surname. Kate Chopin (née O'Flaherty; 1850–1904) is, with the exception of Bryan Giemza's attentions,[104] lost to the Irish-American canon because of the French surname she acquired through marriage. Indeed, Chopin's story 'Athénaïse' (1896) protests against the tradition of the effacement of a woman's identity as well as her birth surname upon marriage.[105] The daughter of a Galway-born businessman, Chopin's Irish ancestry is more immediate than many male writers of distant Irish ancestry readily designated 'Irish American' because they possess a recognizably Irish surname through the male line.

Such considerations aside, however, 'William Wilson' suggests that the father's name is a curse for the male inheritor. Ireland has one of the oldest traditions of patrilineal hereditary nomenclature in the world,[106] and even some of its Norman 'invader' surnames go back a thousand years. Shared names are at the root of intergenerational haunting in James's *The Sense of the Past* and 'Owen Wingrave', and the Irish male body is itself an ancestor-haunted text, inscribed with the inescapable imprint of *doppelganger* forebears who demand allegiance to the ethno-religious heritage and politics with which the family name is associated. Strikingly, the ancestor-as-self motif in *The Sense of the Past* also features in what is conventionally considered to be the very first Gothic novel in Anglo-Irish tradition, Charles Maturin's *Melmoth the Wanderer* (1820). John Melmoth, a Trinity College Dublin student of settler-colonizer family, finds a portrait of an ancestor with his own name who turns out to be immortal because of a pact with the devil. Indeed, this first John Melmoth had come to Ireland as a soldier in Cromwell's brutal campaign to punish rebellious Ireland, Gothicized into twentieth-century

Figure 1.4 Henry James, Jr. at age eleven, with his father, Henry James, Sr. 1854 daguerreotype by Mathew Brady. Courtesy of Wikimedia Commons.

folk memory as a 'curse'. (Cromwell's ravaging throughout the 1650s resulted in the wholesale redistribution of land, the death of perhaps 20 per cent of the population, and the transportation of thousands of men.)[107] In Dubliner J.S. Le Fanu's 1872 novella *Carmilla*, the seductive female vampire is blood kin to her female victim, but it is a rare exception to the usual patrilineal and heteronormative contexts of the ancestor/Self *doppelganger* theme (Figure 1.4).[108]

British control over a native Gaelic populace and the settlement of Ireland by many with British surnames made that culture exquisitely attuned to the associations of patronyms. To that end, the Irish and British surnames with which characters with links to Ireland are endowed in American cultural productions carry significant weight, since an Irish protagonist's surname, ethnicity, denomination, and behaviour often neatly matches the commonplace stereotype of that particular community. Even in ostensibly realistic texts concerned with Irishness, surnames often operate within a Gothic imperative to evoke traumatic return in the manner of Poe's 'William Wilson'. The greater difficulty of 'locating' those with Hiberno-Norman names in this manner will be seen in the ever-subtle James, since Hiberno-Norman ancestry lies ambiguously on what was often a rigid post-Elizabethan Irish binary of British Protestant and Gaelic Catholic. In reality, assimilation, marriage, religious conversion,[109] post-Emancipation naming patterns among African Americans,[110] and the Anglicization or 'standardization' of Gaelic surnames in colonial Ireland or at Ellis Island all make Irish surnames in America unreliable as evidence of exact origin and allegiance. Thus, it is a given that Irish ethnicities are subjective, perceptual, and ascribed categories. As Richard Alba's work suggests, Irishness—most particularly so in the multi-ethnic American context—is a social phenomenon as much as a biological one.[111] After a few generations in America, successive intermarriages with other racio-ethnic and religious cohorts and assimilation often culminates in the choice or effacement of a particular Irishness.[112] However, *for this very reason*, the Irish or British surnames given to Irish protagonists in certain texts examined convey the writer's aspiration to fix what could often be a heterogeneous origin: An accent that matches a surname 'outs' a character seeking to hide her lineage in James's 'The Chaperon', in which a Mrs Donovan who insists that she was 'of the English Donovans' is implied to be lying when she speaks in the author's rendering of a 'brogue'.[113]

Nevertheless, the Ulster Irish Presbyterian immigrants who become the Scots-Irish often had Lowland Scottish surnames, while the majority of post-Famine immigrants had names of Gaelic or Hiberno-Norman origin, so in the American context Irish names tended to be understood as evidence of political and religious identity. (Anna Burns depicts this as remaining true of Northern Ireland in 2018's *Milkman*.[114]) As such, characters' surnames will be critical to readings of certain texts in this study, since they carry the baggage of Irish history down the male line. Of course, even when all family lines led back to Ireland, those who adamantly identified as Scots-Irish sometimes effaced native Irish ancestry, and *vice versa*, as in the case of Margaret Mitchell, who did not identify strongly as Irish Catholic, though claimed by that community. Thus, of equal interest in this study as a whole is the choice to *not* be Irish/Scots-Irish: in the case of writers James, George Kelly, and Fitzgerald, the available association was downplayed or even repudiated, and their characters likewise generally possess an Irishness that must be excavated. Moreover, and for reasons of racism, the identification of Black writer Frank Yerby with his maternal Scots-Irish ancestry cannot be encompassed by conservative definitions of Irishness that insist upon dermal whiteness; it is a sad fact that even after centuries of Irish presence in multi-racial America, *every* face in the 2004 coffee table book *The Irish Face in America* is white.[115]

Coda: The Convex Mirror

M. H. Abrams's classic study suggested that mirrors have long been regarded as symbols of art conceived as a faithful mimetic representation of external reality; writing of *Dubliners*, James Joyce described his stories about the Irish capital city as a 'nicely polished looking-glass'.[116] When it comes to reading Irishnesses in American literature, however, more useful than Joyce's flat mirror is the convex mirror of the sort used on the side of cars. This gives a wider field of view and requires that one bears in mind what might be creeping up from behind during forward motion. Thus, that which is at one's back is simultaneously present at all times and is ignored at the driver's peril. When the literature of Irish America is considered as a convex mirror whose distortion nevertheless allows for a stereoscopic vision of history, then both realistic and non-realistic texts emerge as reflections of unfinished Irish and Irish-American pasts that continue to inform. The convex mirror signifies how historical trauma warps the texture of the present and causes inexact but still informative reflections: at the close of Poe's 'William Wilson', the enraged protagonist murders his identically dressed double, after which a large mirror suddenly appears from nowhere and in which he sees 'mine own image, but with features all pale and dabbled in blood'.[117] Although Gothic was a genre supremely suited to representing the disordered conditions of both colonial Ireland and colonial America, even ostensibly realist narratives that invoke Irishnesses in America are disrupted by non-realistic elements, as may be seen in 'The Modern Warning', James's explicit intervention in Irish identity and politics, to which the following chapter turns.

2
Closeted Irish
Henry James

William James Sr, the grandfather of celebrated American realist author Henry James, was born in 1771 on a 25-acre flax farm in County Cavan in the northern Irish province of Ulster. After he immigrated to America in 1789, William left his relatively modest Presbyterian farming origins behind, making his fortune in dry goods and land speculation in Albany, NY, and at length became one of the wealthiest men in America.[1] Upstate New York had been settled by the Ulster Irish beginning with the great immigration wave of 1718, and they were of sufficient number in Albany by 1760 to organize a Presbyterian church.[2] Moreover, Alfred Habegger notes that William Sr became a major player in 'a rich Scotch-Irish [...] brotherhood' of businessmen operating in New York State in the early 1800s.[3] Culturally very Ulster Presbyterian, William of Albany, as he is also known, sent his son Henry Sr (1811–1882), the author's theologian father, for divinity training at Princeton, the educational and religious capital of Presbyterian America.[4] Grandson Henry James Jr was born in 1843 into what was by then a patrician and somewhat bohemian (though no longer fabulously wealthy) New York city family. There appears to have been enough residual feeling for Ireland into the second generation that Henry Sr visited the Cavan homestead in 1837 (though the Black manservant who accompanied him, Billy Taylor, was remembered more vividly in the lore of the Irish Jameses than their American cousin).[5] An extreme though not wholly uncritical Anglophile, Henry Jr, by contrast, chose to become naturalized as a British citizen in 1915 after many years of residence in England. Among members of the northeastern *elite* of James's lifetime, it was assumed that the America that mattered socially, racially, and culturally was one of purely British descent,[6] and by this period the Ulster Protestant Irish in America had become more and more identified with British America. A 1913 autobiographical piece by the Scots-Irish syndicator of some of James's work, S.S. McClure (written with Willa Cather, who was of part-Ulster origin), is typical of post-Famine Scots-Irish self-fashioning in stressing Protestantism, Scottish roots, and racial separateness from Catholics to the degree that Ulster becomes a small waystation between the important beginning and end points of Scotland and America. His father's people, McClure begins, 'were from Galloway, Scotland. The family had come across the North Channel about two hundred years ago and settled in Ulster.' He continues that among 'both

Race, Politics, and Irish America. Mary M. Burke, Oxford University Press.
 DOI: 10.1093/oso/9780192859730.003.0003

Protestants and Catholics the feeling against intermarriage was so strong' that it 'had kept both races pure'.[7] James's convoluted description of his Ulster Presbyterian maternal grandfather as being 'from' an Irish home'—rather than simple stating that he was Irish—gives a similar impression of Ulster as waystation.[8]

The Irish influx after the 1845 Famine strengthened the chasm between 'old' (predominantly Ulster Presbyterian) and 'new' (predominantly Catholic) Irish-Americans. The opening description of William Sr in a 2013 Albany newspaper article as 'a dirt-poor Irish farm boy who sailed to the new world with a few coins in his pocket' would likely have made his refined grandson wince.[9] However, the phrase does the service of suggesting how William's modest but far from 'dirt poor' origins would potentially have been recast by the visibility of genuinely dirt-poor Irish farm boys and girls in America after 1845. Christopher Newman, the title businessman character of James's novel, *The American* (1877), has worked for a living since the age of ten and made a large fortune. With the exception, perhaps, of the 1908 *doppelganger* ghost story 'The Jolly Corner',[10] *The American* is the closest portrait in James's fiction of his own grandfather, William of Albany, another 'new man' whose own modest background spurred the creation of a massive fortune. Having become rich by his thirties, Newman travels to the continent to find a wife who can elevate him socially, one who is, as he explains to the expatriate American Tristrams, '"beautiful in mind and in manners, as well as in person"'.[11] When Mrs Tristram asks if Newman would object to a foreign bride, her somewhat obtuse husband, Tom, interjects, '"No Irish need apply"'.[12] It is striking that this shorthand for anti-Irish immigrant prejudice appears in a novel whose central character seems inspired by the James family's own self-made Irish immigrant progenitor.

Nevertheless, the centrality of James's ancestry to understanding both his work and his uneasy relationship with Irishness has been ignored, set aside as unassimilable,[13] or even misunderstood by James scholars: The Author Note in the prefatory pages of the distinguished collection, *The Portable Henry James,* describes James as being 'of Scottish and Irish ancestry',[14] a description that over-simplifies Scots-Irishness. Moreover, the term 'Scots-Irish' seems sometimes to have been misconstrued in relation to the James family even by acquaintances: to wit, an essay on Henry James by William Dean Howells begins with a description of James's 'race' as 'Irish on his father's side and Scotch on his mother's'.[15] (His mother's actual Irish origins are considered presently.) Attention to antagonistic relations between Irish identities in Ireland and America answers George Monteiro's question as to why, when James 'came from Irish stock', no one 'ever seems to have identified James with his Hibernian countrymen'.[16] John Kaag, a scholar of James's brother, the philosopher William James (1842–1910), suggests that the uneasy relationship with Irishness of an elite family of Ulster Presbyterian origin may be explained by the fact that 'second- and third-generation immigrants, [Henry and William] tried to brush off the dust of poverty.'[17] For Kaag, wealth alone created distance from Irishness among William of Albany's bookish grandsons, but this does not account for the role played by inter-Irish sectarian tension in both the motherland and within slave-holding America's complex racio-ethnic hierarchy. The cultural historiography of whiteness and Irishness tends to consider the nineteenth-century Famine cohort alone, but their drive for status was often most vehemently opposed by the earlier immigrants out of Ireland's north who had first claimed unconditional whiteness.

Born in 1843, a mere two years before the Famine began, James grew up seeing the transformation that took root in his native New York city due to the subsequent influx of Irish refugees, and did not much care for it. The brand of Catholicism of the continental aristocratic culture that so many of James's Americans abroad find aesthetically pleasing is far removed from that to which desperate Irish immigrants so visibly clung. The Washington Square-area location of James's birth is also the setting of his major 1880 novel of that title, but of greater interest here is that the peripatetic James family had moved to West Fourteenth Street in Manhattan when Henry was a young boy. That street had, by the close of the century, evolved in the 'geographical imagination of New Yorkers' as the 'boundary' between 'the orderly and modern' gridded streets above and the chaos of the 'warren-like' immigrant slums of 'Old New York' below.[18] In his autobiography, *A Small Boy and Others,* James describes that childhood world as a territory of 'pigs', 'poultry', and 'Irish [public] houses', and in *Washington Square*, genteel Mrs Penniman decides against a meeting in Manhattan's southern tip as it 'was rather cold and windy, besides one's being exposed to intrusion from the Irish emigrants who at this point alight [...]'.[19] Thus, the violent boundaries between 'civilized' and 'savage' that the Ulster Irish had precariously straddled in colonial and frontier America became an urban frontier in New York, and what had been James's childhood home eventually sat on that border.A further menace to Irish-American Protestant status that had been directly relevant to the first generation of the James family in America is processed in Henry's writing. This is connected to the reference made in Congress for the need to keep out 'wild' Irish political refugees in the lead-in to the 1798 Rebellion (which has alredy been discussed in relation to *Edgar Huntly*). Despite the fact that the Protestant cohorts of Ireland had originated as settler-colonists, the radicalized among them played a pivotal role in the United Irishmen-led uprising against British rule in Ireland, a coalition of mostly eastern seaboard Ulster Presbyterians, Anglicans, and Catholics. However, the political energy that had facilitated rebellion was defanged by the Union of Great Britain and Ireland in 1800, and the insurgency's failure saw numerous Irish Protestant participants flee to America. The James family was entwined with this radical generation through both friendship and marriage with the immediate family of transnationally known executed United Irishmen leader Robert Emmet.[20] (His doomed romance with the daughter of a Frederick Douglass-associated Irish abolitionist inspired Washington Irving.[21]) Henry's sense of bemused distance from Emmet martyrology is palpable in an aside on a cousin named after his rebel uncle: 'the latter name, being naturally, among *them* all, of a pious, indeed of a glorious, tradition' (stress added).[22] The vulgar Gerald O'Hara in *Gone with the Wind* bellows a Thomas Moore lament for Robert Emmet when drunk,[23] suggesting the kind of populist Irish nationalism that James will be seen to skewer in 'The Modern Warning'. Beiner's work on Ulster (dis)remembering intimates that James's downplaying of kin links to the 1798 Uprising was a manoeuvre conducted by many of Ulster Presbyterian tradition after loyalty to the British Crown grew central to the identity.[24] Indeed, similar mental gymnastics were required of late nineteenth-century Scots-Irish boosters when accounting for colonial-era ancestral disloyalty to the Crown during the American Revolution.

Contagious Irish: James's *Daisy Miller* and Tóibín's Henry James

James's critics and biographers have tended to dispense quickly with his family's ties to Ireland (if they are addressed at all). However, the consideration given to this heritage by Irish novelist Colm Tóibín, which he calls 'a key' that unlocks the vast store of James's imagination,[25] is a distinguished exception. In Tóibín's *The Master*, a 2004 biofiction of James during the years 1895–1899, the fictionalized James refuses to engage with his Irish heritage. Tóibín creates a liberal Anglican Oscar Wilde as James's shadow self, not simply because Wilde is open about his sexuality in a way that James is not, but because he flaunts his Irishness. *The Master* begins with James attending a Wilde play on the night his own play, *Guy Domville*, opens to a bad reception, which is historically accurate. Tóibín's James is 'jealous' that Wilde's audience 'laugh at lines which he thought crude', and seems relived that the 'loud and large and Irish' Wilde is absent.[26] Nonetheless, *The Master* stresses the similarity of Wilde and James: both had privileged and Irish backgrounds, both were outsiders who lived in and wrote about London, and both were gay. In Tóibín's telling, there are profound differences between the two queer Protestant Irish authors, however: James disdains America's lack of aristocrats, Roman coins, and ruined abbeys, and this uncritical Anglophilia is implicitly contrasted to Wilde, in whose comedies about the British aristocracy 'imitation [serves as] the sincerest form of mockery'.[27] *The Master* draws upon Wilde's own *The Picture of Dorian Gray* to frame the literary peers as *doppelgangers*: the reticent James is the closeted portrait, Wilde the exuberant public aspect. After the theatre scene, *The Master* then moves to elite Dublin, where James hobnobs with members of the British garrison, having fled to Ireland after the humiliation of the *Guy Domville* failure and the contrasting success of Wilde's play. Tóibín's novel ends with a scene in which the American author discusses the vulgarity of commercial London theatre with these same characters. Thus, Tóibín bookends the portrait of James in Irish contexts and contrasts him with his flamboyantly Irish rival throughout.

Tóibín is now out of the closet, but such would not have been possible in the Ireland of his youth, nor even during his tenure as an editor in 1980s Ireland. The *New York Times* review of *The Master* opens by drawing attention to Tóibín's slow journey in this regard, implying that his account of James's suppression of his sexuality is disguised autobiography.[28] Indeed, critics have generally read the central concern of *The Master* as being James's closeted sexuality, but Tóibín's novel is just as much about James's *closeted Irishness*, since it deftly weaves issues of suppressed ethnic and sexual identity together. Consider the gossip swirling around Wilde's 1895 trial for gross indecency among James's circle in *The Master*:

> James remembered something vague being told to him about Wilde's parents, his mother's madness or her revolutionary spirit, or both, and his father's philandering or perhaps, indeed, his revolutionary spirit. Ireland, he supposed, was too small for someone like Wilde yet he always carried a threat of Ireland with him.[29]

Moreover, James's friend Sturges is perplexed that Wilde's mother 'believes he has delivered a great blow against the Empire'.[30] Altogether, Wilde's unconcealed sexuality and loud Irishness are double threats to James's reticence about his secret Irish and queer selves. In the following passage set during a dinner at Dublin Castle (the seat of British power), Tóibín invokes the language of the closet, *not* in reference to James's sexuality, but with regard to his humble Irish roots:

> 'Mr. James, are you going to visit any of your Irish kinsmen while you are here?'
> 'No, Mr. Webster, I have no plans of any sort.' He spoke coldly and firmly......
> 'What was the name of that place, Lady Wolseley? [asks Webster]
> Bailieborough, that's right, Bailieborough in County Cavan. It is where you will find the seat of the James family.'
> Henry noticed Lady Wolseley blushing and keeping her eyes from him...
> Henry felt as though he had been struck with something and...with all his secret energy he concentrated on what had just been said...it was the sneer on Lady Wolseley's face when Webster had mentioned Bailieborough that Henry remembered ...He also knew that Webster and Lady Wolseley had discussed him and his family's origins in County Cavan. He did not know where they had got their information.[31]

Tóibín's portrayal of James's closeted ethnicity will be a jumping-off point to explore how Irishness—and corollary European immigrant 'off-whitenesses'—are a submerged and troubling theme in the latter's short fiction. In a 1970 review of

Principato,[32] Irish-American academic Julian Moynihan caustically suggests that James should have been a pillar of ethnic American fiction, but instead posed as the chronicler of elite Anglo-American Protestant life:

> The cause of the American ethnic novel took quite a pasting when Henry James Sr., an Albany-based hyphenated American from County Cavan, married to a woman named Walsh, took his two boys to Europe and the younger one, the heavily built one named Junior who had the peculiar groin injury and never married, mislaid his ethnicity and founded...the modern American WASP novel.[33]

Moynihan's intersectional shaming of James connects closeted Irishness, closeted sexuality, and closeted disability. Tóibín, like Moynihan before him, suggests that James was uneasy with Irishness. However, the Master's work will be read as expressing the *more specific* anxiety that the hard-earned racial and social status of Protestant Americans of pre-Famine Irish origin is endangered by the post-Famine influx. In the otherwise binary racial world of *Gone with the Wind*, contagion enters the Irish planter's family not by way of enslaved people, but through contact with 'white trash' Irishwoman Emmie Slattery.[34] Thus, danger inheres not so much in the racial Other as in the proximity of elite whiteness to 'off-whiteness', a logic that also fuels James's novella, *Daisy Miller: A Study* (1879) (Figure 2.1).

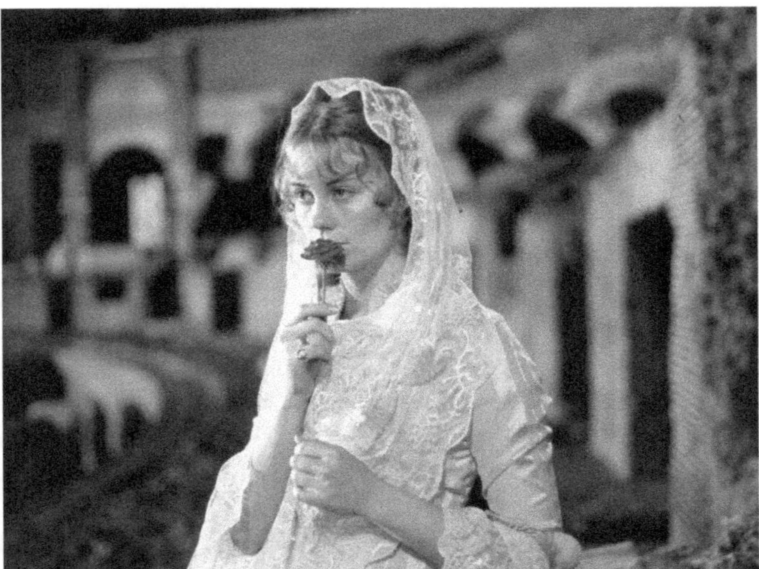

Figure 2.1 Cybill Sheperd as the title character in the 1974 film adaptation of James's *Daisy Miller*. Courtesy of ALAMY.

Daisy Miller centres on a pair of vacationing Americans, Frederick Winterbourne and the eponymous young woman, who initially meet in Switzerland. Both are members of the leisured classes of the northeast, though Daisy's free-spirited behaviour ultimately endangers her social position, and thus, her 'whiteness'. Daisy is flirtatious, so Winterbourne pursues her, despite the disapproval of his stiff aunt, Mrs Costello, who finds the relaxed Millers wanting. Daisy is on easy terms with Eugenio, the family's Italian courier (guide), prompting Mrs Costello to scathingly remark that Daisy is unable to distinguish a polished employee from a 'real' gentleman. This is one of many instances in James in which fine clothes and acquired tastes are central to an anxiety regarding the danger of the not-quite-white or the *nouveau riche* being mistaken for the 'real thing'. (The moment in which James's *The Turn of the Screw* comes out of the closet as Gothic begins with the horror of an uppity—and for John Carlos Rowe, an Irish—servant who is *wearing* his master's clothes.[35]) To be too exactingly presented is to inspire suspicion that one is 'passing': Daisy emerges as being both racially and socially suspect in an exchange between Mrs Costello and her nephew *precisely because* her clothing is impeccable:

> 'She has that charming look they all have,' [Mrs. Costello] resumed. 'I can't think where they pick it up; and she dresses in perfection—no, you don't know how well she dresses. I can't think where they get their taste.'
> 'But, my dear aunt, she's not, after all, a Comanche savage.'
> 'She is a young lady,' said Mrs. Costello, 'who has an intimacy with mamma's courier.'[36]

Interestingly, in light of the story's anxieties regarding new wealth, Daisy's suspect provinciality is implied to be the result of her upbringing in the upstate New York location of Schenectady, a mere twenty miles from Albany, the origin of the James family's own fortune.

In Rome, where Daisy and Frederick meet again, she is regularly seen in the company of local gentleman Giovanelli, which causes her to be shunned by the American colony. One night, Winterbourne takes a walk through the Colosseum and sees Giovanelli with Daisy. Winterbourne admonishes the Italian for taking the lady where she runs the risk of contracting malaria ('Roman fever'), which Daisy appears to do as she dies a few days later. This has generally been interpreted as a coded reference to Daisy being sexually active, but since miscegenation is simultaneously racial and sexual 'pollution', it also refers to the contagion of Giovanelli's off-whiteness, which seems to have led to a heavier 'viral load' for Daisy than her association with Eugenio. Fear of racial pollution is also pertinent in the case of Winterbourne's supposedly 'blue blood' aunt, Mrs Costello, since her surname undermines commonplace readings of *Daisy Miller* as a clash of Anglo-American decency, artlessness, and innate gentility with a continental culture that is the opposite of all those things. In fact, the surname 'Costello' suggests instead a submerged concern with a third heritage, that of Americans of Hiberno-Norman descent.

'Costello' originated with the first Norman family in Ireland to 'go native' by assuming a 'Mac' prefix.[37] In Ireland, the dynasty's *conquistador* aura survived into James's lifetime: the 'nob[ility]' and 'white hands' of a Costello heroine are discussed in a J.M. Synge play.[38] However, that this surname could be puzzlingly non-WASP in *the American context* is implied by a 1932 dramatization of *Daisy Miller* in which Mrs Costello becomes Mrs Suydam, an 'old' Dutch New York surname.[39] Moreover, as if to underline the proper place of an Irish name in such a setting, Mrs Suydam is provided with an Irish maid in the adaptation![40] Since the connotations of the surname 'Costello' are ambiguous, an outline of the fluctuating understanding of 'Normanness' within much broader 'Saxon' and 'Celtic' Irish, British, and American taxonomies is necessary before returning to James's character of that name.

Illegible Irish: Norman Ancestry in James's Family and Fiction

Contemporary ideological requirements in an America flooded by an influx of poor Irish Catholic immigrants understood to be Gaelic shape *English Traits* (1856), Ralph Waldo Emerson's volume on white America's Saxon heritage, which will be described presently. In order to understand the invasions of both Britain and Ireland that Emerson uses to lend heft to his hierarchy of European 'whitenesses', a potted history as well as some discussion of the coded presence of such ideas in James's work (outside of *Daisy Miller*) and in his wider circle is first necessary. It should be understood that although the effects of the invasions to be delineated may have been more social, linguistic, and cultural than genetic, the notion of distinctly different invader and native 'blood' was useful to the Irish and their diasporas. To begin: The Angles, Saxons, Jutes, and Frisians, 'Germanic' (or 'Teutonic') peoples of northern European origin began settling England in the fifth century in the vacuum left by the Roman withdrawal. Their collective 'Anglo-Saxon' culture came to dominate that of the indigenous Celtic Britons. Vikings of Danish and Norwegian origin—yet more invaders of northern European origin and speakers of Germanic offshoot Old Norse—began raiding and settling in England in the eighth and ninth century. The Normans ('Norsemen'), descendants of Scandinavian Viking settlers of what came to be known as Normandy in northern France, invaded England in the eleventh century, effectively wiping out the existent English elite.[41] The Normans spoke a Romance language that was a forerunner of French, so the Norman invasion was a linguistic one too: it injected

10,000 new Latinate words into English as spoken in England (though much less so the Scots spoken in Lowland Scotland, which remained more Germanic in sound and vocabulary as the Normans never formally invaded Scotland). Nevertheless, fraught relations between England and France over subsequent centuries and the seventeenth- and eighteenth-century rise of a political paradigm that imagined the roots of England's parliamentarian system in Saxon culture meant that the ruling class of Great Britain did not stress its Norman-French roots.[42]

A century after their arrival in geographic Great Britain, the Normans who had settled England and Wales then invaded Ireland starting in 1169, marking the origin moment of what is retroactively called the 'English' presence in Ireland. Initially, Norman and native Irish relations were wholly antagonistic. A document protesting their presence in Ireland was sent to Pope John XXII in or about 1317 by the powerful Gaelic Ulster leader, Domhnall Ó Néill, who was an ally of Scottish king, Robert the Bruce. Ó Néill presents the Gaelic Scots of the Highlands and the native Irish as sharing 'blood...language and habits'. In addition, the resonant term 'middle nation' is used by Ó Néill of the Hiberno-Normans: 'the English inhabiting our land, who call themselves of the middle nation, are...different in character from the English of England'.[43] However, a degree of cultural assimilation is apparent in the poetry of members of the Cambro-Norman FitzGerald dynasty. Maurice FitzThomas FitzGerald, 1st Earl of Desmond (*c.* 1295–1356), wrote poetry in Norman French,[44] but Gerald FitzGerald, the 3rd Earl of Desmond (1335–98), composed in Irish.[45] The more decisive English incursion came with the Tudor reconquest of Ireland, Henry VIII's restoration of the central authority that gradually receded after the initial Norman conquest. To an Elizabethan such as Edmund Spenser of the so-called 'New English' settlement (the largely Protestant wave who came to Ireland after the Tudor reconquest), the 'Old English' Hiberno-Normans had 'degenerated' due to their adaptation of native Gaelic culture and their retention of Catholicism after the Crown's official split with Rome in the 1530s. Spenser's *A View on the Present State of Ireland* (written 1595–96; published 1633) elucidates this Elizabethan view, and seems particularly affronted by the 'contagion' of Gaelic culture.[46]

In the wake of the Reformation, European powers stressed religious difference to evolve or maintain rivalries, and predominantly Catholic Ireland became a pawn in the collisions of its powerful neighbours, particularly Catholic France and Protestant England. As a result, in post-Elizabethan Ireland, Hiberno-Norman identity dissolved in two broad directions under these pressures: elite families of 'Old English' origin who adapted Protestantism aligned with the 'New English' and generally Anglican establishment (as did subsequent Protestant settlers such as the French Huguenots, the German Palatines, and, after the 1798 Uprising, the Scots who had settled Ulster). By contrast, and in the interests of an oppositional pan-Catholic Irish identity, the many of Norman ancestry in

Ireland who remained Catholic began to see themselves as unequivocally Irish, especially as the Counter Reformation required Catholic Hiberno-Normans to graft themselves onto the Gaelic record. Writing in the Irish language that the Normans had long-ago adopted, Geoffrey Keating, a seventeenth-century priest of 'Old English' descent, coined the term *Éireannach* ('Irish' or 'person from Ireland/*Éire*'). This was distinct from the preceding Irish-language term *Gael*, which was used in *both* Ireland and Scotland and, thus, did not necessarily imply Catholicism in the manner of the Counter-Reformation-era term *Éireannach*. That coinage aimed to create a joint Gaelo-Norman identity that excluded the seventeenth-century 'New English', the predominantly Protestant cohort that enfolded the Lowland Scots 'Planters' of Ulster.[47] Later, the widespread adaptation of 'Celtic' during the Irish Cultural Revival allowed non-Catholics of Norman and 'New English' ancestry such as Wilde and W.B. Yeats to become 'Irish'. However, Douglas Hyde—a prominent Church of Ireland (Anglican) nationalist of Norman ancestry and a future president of an independent Ireland (1938–45)—excluded what he called the 'Saxon' Ulster Scots from this warm and fuzzy catch-all.[48] Thus, the Saxonist discourse used in Emerson's America to exclude the Gaelic Irish from full 'whiteness' migrates into Victorian-era Irish nationalist writing, though in the service of writing the Ulster Scots *out* of a pan-Irish ('Celtic') history!

The strong emphasis on the origin of family names in Irish (and diasporic Irish) culture meant that an awareness of the roots of Norman surnames sporadically survived into the nineteenth century in America, and continues in present-day Ireland to a very minor extent.[49] Nonetheless, Norman identity generally gets subsumed by previous and subsequent waves of settlers and invaders in both the British and Irish contexts. In the post-Reformation Irish context, the dominance of the increasingly fixed binary of Catholic/Gaelic and English/Protestant rendered 'Normanness' a quasi-illegible identity going forward. This ambiguity seemingly makes Hiberno-Norman identity irresistible to the over-subtle James when he engages with the fine distinctions of ethnicity, class, and denomination of those of British Isles descent.

Given the illustriousness of so many male Jameses and Irish-American historiography's traditional focus on prominent individual males, James's maternal line is generally unexamined. Indeed, in a photomontage of William James's parents in a 1920 edition of his letters, the caption reads 'Henry James, Sr., and his Wife'.[50] Arguably, the identities of married women of Irish descent had the potential to be particularly effaced, given the culture's certainty regarding the ethno-religious allegiances conveyed by surnames. In fact, the name of Henry James Sr's spouse (and Henry James Jr's mother) was not 'his Wife' but Mary Walsh. She was the daughter of Hugh Walsh, who emigrated from Ulster to colonial America in the 1760s. Born in New York in 1810, Mary was raised as a devout Presbyterian.

She adored young Henry, and his touching description of the effect of her passing in 1882 suggests her centrality to his sense of identity: 'She was our life, she was the house, she was the keystone of the arch. She held us all together, and without her we are scattered reeds.'[51] Of interest to this study is that Mary's maiden name is one that evolved in Ireland as a result of the Norman invasion. 'Walsh' (i.e. a Welsh person) is the fourth most common surname in Ireland, 'given independently to many unconnected families in different parts of the country' in the wake of the Norman invasion of Ireland launched out of Wales.[52] Thus, James's maternal surname as good as translates as 'Norman' in the Irish context, so he was almost certainly conscious both of his maternal ancestry and of how 'wild Irish' such a name may have seemed to some in his circles who were unaware of Ireland's fine ethnic distinctions. The difficulty of situating those of Norman descent in the post-Williamite Catholic nationalist/Ulster Unionist binary emerges in *Gone with the Wind*: Sectarian Irish Catholic planter Gerald O'Hara can readily slot his Ulster Protestant neighbours in Georgia into his taxonomy of Irishnesses. (He files them under 'damned'.) However, when Rhett Butler, who carries a prominent Hiberno-Norman surname, refuses to join in with a lament for executed Irish radical Robert Emmet, O'Hara accuses him of being an 'Orangeman' (an Ulster Protestant in favour of maintaining Ireland's Union with Great Britain).[53]

Indeed, descendants of exiled members of the Gaelic and Hiberno-Norman Catholic gentry are a distinct and often overlooked cohort in the make-up of Irish America. Journalist John Louis O'Sullivan (1813–95) coined the phrase 'manifest destiny' in an 1845 article on the boundary dispute with Great Britain in the Oregon Country that promoted the annexation of Texas and the Oregon Country to the United States.[54] O'Sullivan descended on his father's side from a prominent Kerry family whose estate had been confiscated by the English Crown after the Irish Rebellion of 1641, in which many Ulster Protestant settlers perished.[55] Though merely an Irish immigrant newspaper editor in America, under the Jacobite peerage system O'Sullivan was entitled to style himself as the fifth Baronet O'Sullivan, a title conferred on his Irish Jacobite grandfather in 1753 for leadership at the Battle of Culloden in 1745.[56] The nineteenth-century view that white settlers were ordained to expand across the American continent, 'manifest destiny' enfolded a belief in white American cultural and racial superiority. Thus, what Robert J. Miller sees as O'Sullivan's surprising imperialism,[57] which would have been anathema to anti-colonial Irish nationalists, makes sense if his family's royalist loyalties to the Stuarts are considered. In short, O'Sullivan was more *emigré* than immigrant, but such distinctions are often fudged in accounts of Irish America. James's work betrays finely tuned antennae for such obscure distinctions, perhaps because of an awareness that his mother's heritage was sometimes illegible in America.

Similarly, the Mark Twain co-authored satire, *The Gilded Age* (1873), published in the same decade as *Daisy Miller*, suggests mockery of Irish pretentions to Norman connection or at the least jabs at the Jacobite peerage system under which Irish Stuart supporters were granted titles that were recognized only by France, Spain, and the Papacy.[58] In the novel, Patrick O'Riley, a corrupt operative in Tammany Hall, the New York seat of post-Famine Irish-American power, flees to France in order to escape investigation, and on his return to the United States has transformed into the Hon. Patrique Oreillé. The illustrations of O'Riley/Oreillé (Figures 2.2 and 2.3) portray his initial Irish-American incarnation as possessing a long philtrum in the mould of Victorian Anglo-American caricatures of the bedraggled Irish and the African-American as equally ape-like.[59] When he and his lady return to the United States wearing unconvincing French finery, evidence that the Gallicized couple remain low on the evolutionary scale is still evident in their facial features.[60]

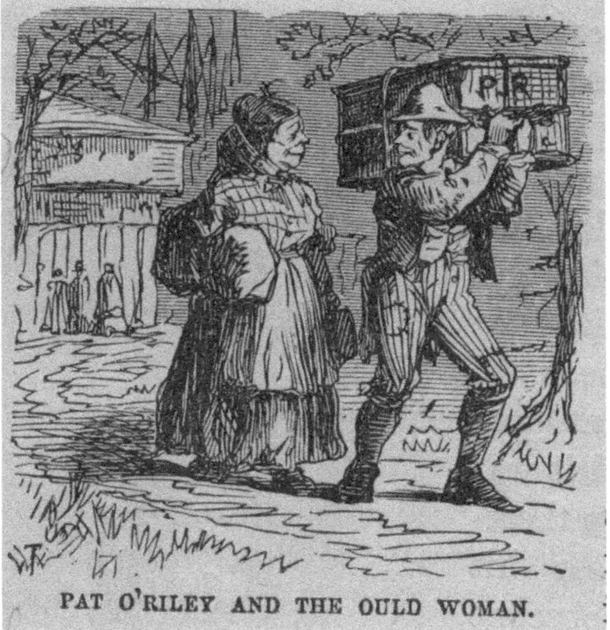

Figure 2.2 Irish-American political operative Patrick O'Riley and his wife before a French sojourn, as illustrated in the Mark Twain co-authored *The Gilded Age* (1873). Courtesy of Northern Illinois University Libraries.

Figure 2.3 Patrick O'Riley and his wife after the French sojourn that transforms him into the Hon. Patrique Oreillé, as illustrated in the Mark Twain co-authored *The Gilded Age* (1873). Courtesy of Northern Illinois University Libraries.

Stand-in Irish: James's 'Off-White' Italians

Hiberno-Norman or Jacobite peer Irish backgrounds were rendered illegible in mainstream America by the predominant image of the Irish immigrant after the 1840s. Nevertheless, a desire to confirm the 'Englishness' of Hiberno-Normans is of interest to certain nineteenth-century elite Americans due to the pervasive Saxonist discourse in which 'Northmen' were sometimes held to be a 'cousin race' of Saxons. Critics primed to think of whiteness as monumental and undifferentiated interpret the insistence on Daisy's 'white muslin' clothing as indicative of anxiety regarding blackness, as in Bryan Washington's reading of the story.[61] However, if one attends to James's conjuring up of non-Gaelic Irishness with the name 'Costello' and *Daisy Miller*'s concern that 'dusky' Italians are 'not-quite-white', then the novella seems to be equally concerned with what Matthew Frye Jacobson has described as the hierarchy of whitenesses created in response to the influx of masses of poor Irish, Italian, and European Jewish immigrants.[62] Between around 1880 and 1924, more than four million mostly southern Italians immigrated to the United States. They began to be increasingly depicted as 'racially suspect', and faced exclusion from or segregation within certain schools, churches, movie theatres, social group, and labour unions.[63] This anxiety concerning Italian whiteness is probed as early as James's 'The Last of the Valerii' (1874) and later in 'The Real Thing' (1893). These stories will be considered briefly before this chapter returns to *Daisy Miller*'s anxieties regarding the potential for confusion between 'white' ('old' Protestant) and 'off-white' ('new' Catholic Gaelic) Irishness.

'The Last of the Valerii' concerns the union of the American narrator's goddaughter, Martha, to a handsome and wealthy Roman Count. The unnamed narrator opens by informing the reader that he 'had had occasion to declare more than once that if my goddaughter married a foreigner I should refuse to give her away'.[64] Thus, the narrator is plainly in possession of the commonplace prejudices of his White, Anglo-Saxon Protestant *milieu*, even if the particular continental Catholic to whom Martha becomes engaged is the kind of Italian unlikely to end up in the immigrant slums of New York. The opening description's stress on Conte Valerio as one whose 'dusky' and 'deep glowing brown' looks contrast with Martha's 'yellow locks' suggests the narrator's unease regarding the betrothed's not-quite-whiteness. Nevertheless, this threat begins to be moderated when the narrator discerns that the '"good and strong and brave"' count possesses none of the effete and dissembling refinement that the American obviously associates with the Italian aristocracy.[65]

Anxieties concerning race connect to uneasiness regarding Catholicism, for the narrator begins to warm to Conte Valerio after it becomes apparent that the nobleman possesses no real religious enthusiasm.[66] From about this point onward, the Count is increasingly associated with the domain of ancient Rome: 'The young man's hair grew superbly; it was such hair as the old Romans must have had when they walked bareheaded and bronzed about the world.'[67] Moreover, the Italian aristocrat seems to be returned to a decidedly pre-Christian Rome when the story begins to culminate with the excavation of an ancient statue of the Goddess Juno in the grounds of his family's villa, a beautiful effigy 'with an almost human look' that Valerio afterward starts worshipping in secret.[68] By returning the Count to the scene of his very distant ancestors, he is inserted into a world before Catholicism and prior to the fixed taxonomy of skin tone that emerges with Atlantic world slavery; the 'bronzed' skin of the ancient Romans indicates rugged power. This is the 'Ancient Rome' of Anglo-American fantasy, a font of elite, white European culture in opposition to the degraded spectacle of contemporary Rome, with its showy Catholicism. In a remarkably rapid journey backward through 'the Count's interminable ancestry', he is stripped of the troubling accretions of recent history, making him an acceptable spouse for Anglo-American Protestant Martha: 'Back to the profligate revival of arts and vices – back to the bloody medley of medieval wars – back through the long, fitfully glaring dusk of the early ages to its ponderous origin in the solid Roman state, back through all the darkness of history it stretched itself [...].'[69] In choosing the paganism of his ancestors over Catholicism, the Count becomes a crusading Cromwellian Puritan of the sort that ravaged seventeenth-century Irish churches. The narrator encounters the aristocrat at the Pantheon, described as still holding 'a vague reverberation of pagan worship' and as being a 'Roman monument' whose 'Christian altars have but half converted' it into a church, and this partial Catholicization angers the Count: '"This...place...is worth fifty St Peter's...I should like to pull down their pictures, overturn their candlesticks, and poison their holy water!"'[70] This refutation appears to lighten the skin tone of the aristocrat. Having been referred to as 'dusky' twice by Martha's uncle, after this encounter the Count is described as follows when spied worshipping the unearthed statue: 'The moonlight blanched his face, which seemed already pale with weariness.'[71]

'The Real Thing', published nineteen years after 'The Last of the Valerii', returns to the anxiety of *Daisy Miller* that that the not-quite-white or lower class can pass as genteel. The narrator, an unnamed British artist, hires the down-at-heel but refined Mr and Mrs Monarch as models when he is commissioned to create illustrations of aristocrats. The Monarchs are the '*real* thing' in the narrator's initial estimation,[72] since they had moved in upper-class circles during their prosperous days. However, the artist finds that they do not look like the 'real thing' once they pose for him, unlike 'sallow' Oronte, an Italian street vendor-cum-artist's model. The Monarchs consider Oronte a 'foreign vagabond', but he passes for an 'Englishman' when the artist puts him 'into some old clothes of my own'.[73] At the beginning of the action, the artist assesses the couple's potential, but since both he and they are genteel, he is embarrassed to find himself 'appraising [them] physically, as if they were animals on hire or useful blacks [...]'.[74] Thus, once the Monarchs are forced to earn an hourly wage, the spectre of race erupts.

James's Italian stories speak to an unease that America would conflate the ethno-religious and class differences of which Irish Americans themselves were painfully aware. *Daisy Miller*, too, is concerned with where non-Gaelic Irish identity (Scots-Irish or Hiberno-Norman) fits within the hierarchy of whiteness in an America unsettled by bedraggled Catholic Irish and Italian immigrants. In *Daisy Miller*, the dubious whiteness of Daisy's Italian suitor is placed alongside the WASP-like Mrs Costello because of an anxiety that the proximity of the new Catholic Gaelic Irishness to the established Protestant Irishness will threaten the whiteness of the latter, returning it, in the *specific* case of the Scots-Irish, to its racially ambiguous status in colonial America. Consider James's remark in an 1882 letter that the town of Washington 'is too n*****ish, & that has rubbed off on some of the whites'.[75] Thus, whiteness may be lost by proximity to the Black *or* the not-quite-white.

Is it farfetched to imagine that Henry James might have had knowledge of the Irish particulars of the Costello dynasty? Perhaps not, given that the name was discussed in an early number of the *Atlantic Monthly*, co-founded in 1857 in Boston by a member of the James family's circle. (Indeed, that publication generously championed the difficult fiction of an unknown called Henry James Jr when it published his first short story in 1865.) An article on Edmund Spenser's years in Ireland published in an 1858 issue speculates on the Edmund Spenser family's marriage connections to a prominent Norman-Irish gentry family named Nagle, and refers twice to the fact that 'Costello' was the Connacht branch of the Nagle line.[76] Thus, it is possible that the then fourteen-year-old Henry James read this intriguing instance of a discussion of the lineage of the Costelloes. Published just as the post-Famine influx had flattened out Irishness in America, this article would have contributed to young Henry's sense of the complexity of Ireland's ethno-religious identities. At the very least, the *Atlantic Monthly* article suggests that an interest in upper-crust and non-Gaelic Irishness was part of the broader northeastern Saxonist obsession with issues of 'breeding'. Edmund Thomas Bewley's history of the Poe family in Ireland castigates poet Sarah Helen Whitman for creating a spurious aristocratic Norman lineage for Poe's ancestors in an 1860 book,[77] further suggesting the *cachet* of things Hiberno-Norman in elite northeastern circles. In the very period of Whitman's volume, the theorist of Saxonism most interested in Norman identity in the British Isles was Ralph Waldo Emerson, the towering intellectual of his age and a friend of Henry James's father. It is to him that this chapter now turns.

In *English Traits* (1856), a history of the British 'race', Emerson followed the lead of his mentor, Thomas Carlyle, in considering Normans to be merely Norsemen (Vikings) who had learned to speak French. For Carlyle, according to Nell Irvin Painter, this change of language 'had not altered their blood, their basic nature, or their manly might'.[78] In Emerson's estimation, the 'Norman noble was the Norwegian pirate baptized', a member of a cousin race of the Saxons whose admirably 'brutish strength' made England—and by extension, those of Saxon heritage in the New World—great.[79] Within three months of publication, 24,000 copies of Emerson's *English Traits* were in circulation in the United States and Britain: His views on a Viking/Saxon/Northman (Norman) racial continuum dominated white America's fantasy of its origins and destiny for generations. It is important to note when considering how the Scots-Irish fitted into Emerson's taxonomy that Carlyle, of Lowland Scottish origin, considered himself to be a Saxon. Thus, the Scots-Irish, despite their Irish motherland, strove to emphasize their Lowland Scottish roots in the *milieu* of Saxonist America. This was not least because *English Traits* linked physical characteristics associated with Saxon ancestry to moral, cultural, and political superiority:

> On the English face are combined decision and nerve with the fair complexion, blue eyes and open and florid aspect. Hence the love of truth, hence the sensibility, the fine perception and poetic construction. The fair Saxon man, with open front and honest meaning, domestic, affectionate, is not the wood out of which cannibal or inquisitor, or assassin is made, but he is moulded for law, lawful trade, civility, marriage, the nurture of children, for colleges, churches, charities, and colonies.[80]

The echo of these lines in James's 'The Romance of Certain Old Clothes' suggests that he had read *English Traits*.[81] At any rate, to Emerson the openness of the white Saxon Protestant face contrasts with the implied treachery of what is coded as the non-Christian ('cannibal'), the Catholic ('inquisitor'), and the Oriental ('assassin') visage, effortless references that carry the weight of centuries of Protestant Northern European stereotypes of domestic and colonial Others. Moreover, the crucial difference between failing Ireland and thriving England is Saxon blood: 'In Ireland are the same climate and soil as in England, but less food, no right relation to the land, political dependence, small tenantry, and an inferior or misplaced race.'[82]

Although Emerson's authoritative pronouncements theoretically bolstered the racial credentials of the settler-colonial Irish, room for ambiguity remained, however, even in the case of the wealthy and highly educated Scots-Irish/Hiberno-Norman James family. The description of the Jameses as 'Irish' and 'under[bred]' by their Boston Brahmin friend Oliver Wendell Holmes Jr is particularly hair-raising since, in his subsequent role as a Supreme Court Justice, Holmes advocated the use of forced sterilization in order to a maintain racial fitness.[83] Furthermore, an 1860s account of the Jameses by Emerson's son, Edward, associated that family with the lowly 'Gaelic' rung of Emerson Sr's racial hierarchy in using vocabulary ('wit' and 'blunder') that had long circulated regarding supposed 'native' Irish garrulousness: 'In their speech, singularly mature and picturesque, as well as vehement, the Gaelic (Irish) element in their descent always showed. Even if they blundered, they saved themselves by wit.'[84] Altogether, Edward Emerson's statement suggests that Irishes 'new' and 'old', Planter and 'wild', Gaelic and non-Gaelic could indeed be confused in the post-Famine period, just as James's own narratives fear.

Ulster Irish: The Marriage Plot and the Plot against the Union

The tone of James's echo of an Emersonian vocabulary of English blood superiority in 'The Romance of Certain Old Clothes' is uncertain. Likewise, it may be that Mrs Costello's anxieties regarding the threatened whiteness of America's earliest Irish cohort is treated with ironic distance in *Daisy Miller*. However, any such detachment is abandoned in James's 1888 story 'The Modern Warning' in the context of a heated-up Home Rule debate a decade later. James does not draw explicit attention to Norman ancestry in the case of Mrs Costello, but does so in the case of the shared Norman heritage of his warring British and Irish characters in 'The Modern Warning'. This he does so as to indicate all that they unknowingly have in common, genetically, linguistically, culturally, and—most importantly in this Home Rule-era story—politically.

Home Rule was a constitutional movement towards a national All-Ireland parliament partly under Westminster, and thus for quasi political independence. The First Home Rule Bill was defeated in the House of Commons in 1886, two years before James published 'The Modern Warning' and second and third attempts were vetoed and suspended in 1893 and 1914 respectively. Throughout this whole period and until the Government of Ireland Act of 1920 that laid the groundwork for Partition, the so-called 'Irish Question' bitterly divided Victorian and Edwardian Britain and Ireland. Indeed, it is a lens that can entirely reframe even well-analysed events of the period. For instance, discussions of Edward Carson's role as defence attorney in the 1895 Wilde trial rarely consider the significane of the fact that he later became the most visible anti-Home Rule Unionist leader. As such, the significant political chasm between the pro-Home Rule Wilde and Carson, the Dublin-born son of a Scottish Presbyterian,[85] doubtlessly coloured their courtroom encounters.[86] Clothing history is another little-considered aspect of the Home Rule story that demonstrates how the question saturated every aspect of Irish life: the handmade lace used on Diana Spencer's 1981 wedding gown had belonged to Queen Mary, a present from the Unionist women of Belfast to demonstrate loyalty during the royal couple's state visit to Ireland in 1911 when the Home Rule debate was reaching fever pitch.[87] In general, Catholics and nationalist Anglicans lobbied for limited self-government while Ulster Presbyterians fought to maintain the Union with Great Britain of 1800. This cemented the image of Ulster Protestants as a distinct political constituency in Ireland *and* in America, where it was also widely debated. For instance, in a 1917 one-act by Eugene O'Neill (whose middle name of 'Gladstone' honoured a pro-Home Rule British Prime Minister), an Irish sailor in a London dive bar shouts 'To hell wid Ulster!' a propos of nothing, suggesting that the playwright could assume audience knowledge of 'the Irish Question'.[88] Indeed, Home Rule-era Scots-Irish boosters explicitly linked the Ulster Presbyterian fight to remain in the Union with the positive stereotype of the unbowed, independent Scots-Irish frontiersman: towards the close of his term as US Ambassador to the Court of St James, the eminent Scots-Irish politician and author of *The Scot in America and the Ulster Scot* (1912), Whitelaw Reid, delivered a well-received anti-Home Rule lecture tied to his historiography in Belfast in March 1912.[89] On 28 September of that year, almost half a million people signed the Ulster Covenant in Belfast, an oath whereby Unionists pledged to fight the threat of Home Rule. Carson was the first person to sign, and the event was the greatest marshalling of Unionist public demonstration ever witnessed on the island of Ireland.[90]

By the period of the Home Rule crisis, the differentiation between 'old' and 'new' Irish America allowed certain of those of pre-Famine northern Irish Protestant origin to identify with the predominant position of their Presbyterian brethren in Ulster.[91] Joseph Conrad implies that James's *Irish Presbyterian* background is central to understanding his work;[92] this is a more specific category than Tóibín's portrayal of James's 'Irishness'. Indeed, a very identifiably Ulster Protestant engagement with Home Rule emerges in the relatively obscure 'The Modern Warning', whose critical neglect may be traced to the fact that James's American critics overlook the Home Rule context. Ultimately, James's engagement with politics connected to his paternal ancestry conjures up this study's repeated consideration of the Irish-American male body as an ancestor-haunted text, inscribed with the inescapable imprint of *doppelganger* forebears and their allegiances.

James's most celebrated fiction examines the encounters of forthright Americans with urbane Europe. Although patently of this mode, 'The Modern Warning' further addresses the question as to how people of pre-Famine Irish origin in the British *milieu* of elite urban northeast America grappled with the contemporaneous politics of Ireland. Although such political views divide the story's protagonists, Ireland's central role in the plotline is disregarded: 'The Modern Warning' is consistently discussed as the story of an American woman torn between her brother and her English husband over their attitudes to their respective countries. For instance, the following paragraph-length synopsis contains no reference to the significance of Irish ancestry to the protagonists:

> Young American Macarthy Grice, visiting his mother and sister [Agatha Grice] who are in Europe...finds them...on the Italian lakes. They are very friendly with the conservative Englishman, Sir Rufus Chasemore. Macarthy determines that the Grices will leave [...] the next day [...]. The impending sudden departure forces Sir Rufus to propose to Agatha Grice [...] but she tells him it is impossible because of his and her brother's mutual national suspicion. Five years later, the couple have been married one year [...] and they are making their first trip to America [from England] [...]. On [Rufus's] return he makes it clear he is going to write a book about America. Lady Chasemore tells her brother that she will feel very uncomfortable if the book is very severe on the country. A further year on, Lady Chasemore finds a bundle of proof-sheets [...]. When Sir Rufus returns next day he finds his wife distraught at the content [...] and eventually volunteers to give up its publication. However after a few weeks during which Agatha believes his attitude towards her has changed, she re-opens the subject, asking him to proceed with his book. He finds her neurotic about this and the day her brother arrives from America for a holiday [...] she takes a lethal dose of poison.[93]

However, the exact source of the Grices' hostility to England is that they are partly of Gaelic Irish origin, a descent memorialized by the given name of Macarthy, which, as Denis Flannery notes, 'functions as an endless reminder of Ireland' for James's readers.[94] The MacCarthys were an influential Munster Gaelic family, certain branches of whom openly resisted the Crown,[95] and this history inspires the politics of James's protagonist of that name. What is more, the family trees of all three British and Anglo-American protagonists encompass names of Gaelic and Norman origin: Macarthy's family name, 'Grice', is an Anglo-Norman surname,[96] and the Fitzgibbons, Rufus Chasemore's antecedents, were a Norman-Irish family.[97] These facts emerge in an early discussion between Agatha and Rufus in which she initially spurns her English suitor because of her brother's Irish nationalism:

> we are of Irish descent, on my mother's side. Her mother was a Macarthy. We have kept up the name and we have kept up the feeling.
> I see—so that even if the Yankee were to let me off the Paddy would come down! [...] But [...] I am quite as Irish as you can ever be. I had an Irish grandmother—a beauty of beauties, a certain Lady Laura Fitzgibbon [...].
> Oh, well, she wasn't of our kind! the girl exclaimed, laughing. [...]
> Good God! do you mean to say that an hostility of race, a legendary feud, is to prevent you and me from meeting again?[98]

'Norman' is implied but never named in the exchange, and Agatha's cryptic remark ('our kind') creates an Anglo/Gaelic binary.[99] This entirely overlooks the Norman ancestry that Grice and Chasemore share, which bubbles beneath the story's surface as a subtle conduit of trans-Irish Sea connection. It is unclear as to whether James's withholding of the key term 'Norman' assumes ignorance or an urbane understanding of the niceties of Anglo-Irish intermixing in his readership. If the latter is the case, then the story ironizes the Grise siblings' enthusiasm for an Irish connection whose complexity they do not understand. This would make 'The Modern Warning' a very early iteration of what became, in the postwar period, the literary and cinematic theme of the danger to the diasporic or returned emigrant Irishman of his shallow understanding of the motherland.[100]

'The Modern Warning' is Irish in form as well as content since James invokes the traditional Irish literary trope of the marriage of a visiting Englishman and a native woman as allegory for political union, deployed (in various registers) from Lady Morgan's *Wild Irish Girl* (1806) and G.B. Shaw's *John Bull's Other Island* (1904) to Brian Friel's *Translations* (1980). Indeed, the trope followed the Irish across the Atlantic: in the crucial year for Home Rule of 1912, *Peg o' My Heart*, a Broadway iteration of the Irish marriage plot, was wildly successful.[101] 'The Modern Warning' deploys the marriage plot as metaphor for the political Union between Ireland and Great Britain in 1800 in order to contend with a moment in which that alliance is—for Ulster Unionists—in danger. Incontestable evidence that James was familiar with the Irish 'marriage-as-Union' literary trope emerges in his favourable review of Dion Boucicault's *The Shaughran* for its première run at Wallack's Theatre in New York in 1874–75.[102] A significant subplot of this Irish play centres on the romance and eventual marriage between a nationalist maiden of Hiberno-Norman surname and a British officer who carries an Anglo-Norman patronym. As soon as the Act of 1800 began to be discussed, Claire Connolly notes, 'one of the main metaphors' used was that of 'the union as marriage'.[103] In addition, and long after the Act of Union itself, the marriage-as-political-alliance trope continued to be called upon by Irish writers to either endorse or query the Anglo-Irish relationship. The marriage metaphor gave Irish writers licence to endow the relation of potential wives to would-be husbands with colonial implications because 'efforts to legitimate English rule in Ireland so often involve disputed rights to land and property'.[104] Indeed, the marriage-as-political-Union lens reframes certain Irish cultural productions as being *only seemingly* about marriage: consider, for instance, how Wilde's Irish nationalism potentially opens up the satire of wedlock of *The Importance of Being Earnest* (1895).

Nation, marriage, family, and political loyalties are continually associated in 'The Modern Warning' in a manner that makes the Anglo-American union of Agatha and Rufus a stand-in for cross-Atlantic relations. Consider the description of Macarthy's strong feelings for his sibling and his initial anxiety regarding her beau:

> But [Macarthy's] mother and sister *were* his home [...] He was so fond of his sister that he had a secret hope that she would never marry at all. [...] On the day she should marry an Englishman she would not throw him over—she would betray him. That is she would betray her country, and it came to the same thing. Macarthy's patriotism was of so intense a hue that to his own sense the national life and his own life flowed in an indistinguishable current.[105]

Rufus and Agatha's alliance represents the potential of Anglo-American relations, but the happy union is threatened by a combination of Macarthy's politics and Agnes's parroting of her brother's Irish and American nationalist beliefs. In rejoinder to Agatha's anger that her husband's manuscript condemns American democracy's corruption, Rufus argues that this is irrelevant since she has become English through marriage: 'My dear girl, what is a woman's country? It's her house and her garden, her children and her social world.'[106] Rufus considers this threat to their union as being akin to a sudden rift between unified nations: 'He had forgotten that America was hers – that she had any allegiance but the allegiance of her marriage. [...] He had assimilated her, as it were, completely, and he had assumed that she had also assimilated him and his country with him [...].'[107] In response, Agatha conflates her Irish and American roots, reminding her astonished husband that she could claim 'Irish blood'.[108] Altogether, the Grices' seemingly foolish Irish nationalism constitutes the warning of the title, which is the danger to the Anglo-American relationship of Irish-American support for the dissolution of the Union of 1800.

According to Fred Kaplan, during the 1880s James 'declined to identify with Irish aspirations, even with any broader principle of equity and liberalism', and had only two concerns: that 'Anglo-American relations not be damaged by the differences of national interest that the issue provoked and that Britain itself not be weakened in its efforts to deal with Ireland'.[109] Ireland would, James wrote in an 1886 letter,

> injure England less with [Home Rule] than without it [...]. She seems to me [...] a country revelling in odious forms of irresponsibility & license. And, surely, how can one speak of the Irish as a 'great people'? [...] they seem to me an inferior & 3rd rate race, whose virtues are of the cheapest & shallowest order, while their vices are peculiarly cowardly & ferocious. They have been abominably treated in the past—but their wrongs appear, to me, in our time, to have occupied the conscience of England only too much to the exclusion of other things.[110]

Sara Blair's work suggests that James's image of an 'inferior' Irish 'race' clearly derives from the 'negroid' Irishman figure in late nineteenth-century political cartoons skewering the Irish/Irish-American clamour for Home Rule.[111] What is fascinating in James's statement is not his low opinion of the Irish, for such maps accurately onto establishment American opinion of the period, but that he is able to speak of the country in the aloof manner of one who is obviously certain that ancestral ties to Ireland count for nothing by the 1880s. The 'abominabl[e] treat[ment] in the past' of the Irish is a phrase that might enfold the sense of mistreatment at British hands that drove earlier Ulster Presbyterians like his Emmet kinsman across the Atlantic. However, there is no hint of this possibility in the author's phrasing.

'The Modern Warning' presents Macarthy's patriotism (both Irish and American) as ridiculous and as part of the impetus for Agatha's rather melodramatic suicide. 'The Modern Warning' does not conform to James's general tendency to subtlety and interiority, as exemplified by the novel, *The Portrait of a Lady* (1881), and the story was not well received by critics. This uncharacteristic lack of authorial command and what Flannery calls its 'thin realism' indicates that the theme came from a place of personal anxiety for James.[112] The story continually stresses that the Americans and the Englishman have much in common in terms of shared language and cultural heritage, which was also a belief of the author. James casually refers to the 'English and American' contemporaries with whom he was schooled in 1857 during a family sojourn in Paris as 'young men and women of the Anglo-Saxon family',[113] and in a letter to William James written in the year of publication of 'The Modern Warning' he notes: 'I can't look at the English and American worlds, or feel about them, any more, save as a big Anglo Saxon [*sic*] total, destined to such an amount of melting together that an insistence on their differences becomes more & more idle and pedantic.'[114] James's belief partakes of the demands for the '"reunion" of Britain and the United States, the two great "Anglo-Saxon" powers ordained to reorder the world' that peaked in the 1890s, and that sometimes (as in his case too, of course) aligned with anti-Home Rule beliefs.[115] Viewed through the lens of 'The Modern Warning', the subtext of James's pro-unification language is that any claim to Irish separateness must be subsumed by the Anglo-American relationship. Strikingly, 'The Modern Warning' was initially published in *Harper's New Monthly Magazine* as 'The Two Countries' (in June 1888), a title that implies a pointed dismissal of the third country invoked by the Grices' allegiance to the country of their maternal ancestors. The plotline raises up the spectre of Ireland, but that ghost is exorcised by the original title's firm statement that the conjoined fates of England and America alone is what is at stake. Ireland cannot have a separate existence beyond its Union with Great Britain, just as Agatha has to perish once she can no longer take on her husband's loyalties.

It is no coincidence that in the same 1888 letter to William, Henry dismisses the wearisome subject of Irish Home Rule, as personified by Charles Stewart Parnell, president of the Irish National Land League. Given that the latter was the product of a marriage between an Irish landowner and an American mother of impeccable Scots-Irish Philadelphian descent,[116] 'The Modern Warning' might be read further as a Unionist warning against the monsters created by political 'miscegenation'. Monteiro argues that 'The Modern Warning' was initially inspired by *The Great Republic,* a now-forgotten study of American democracy by a disapproving Englishman called Lepel H. Griffin that James read in 1884.[117] Monteiro examines the contents of Griffin's book broadly and does not refer to the role that Irishness plays in the story it inspired; *The Great Republic*'s chapter on 'The Foreign Element' supposedly ruining American democracy opens with condemnations of 'the Irish question', the 'demagog[ic]' Parnell, and the ruinous Irish nationalism of Irish immigrants in New York.[118] The first two sentiments are echoed in James's own letters, and the latter belief doubtlessly struck a chord with the native New Yorker. For Griffin, the ill-informed and illiterate post-Famine New York Irish were dangerously undemocratic because they voted according to their priests' orders. (This belief reemerges with force later during John F. Kennedy's electioneering.) The implicit racial undertones of the opinion that the nationalist Irish were a threat to American democracy explicitly emerges in Griffin's follow-on discussion of the 'problem' of the African-American voter: 'the negro is as fit for the franchise as the monkey he closely resembles'.[119]

Hugh Stevens's work suggests that in James's fiction, that which is unspoken by the character is often meant to reveal much more than anything stated aloud.[120] It is interesting, therefore, to note that the clamour Macarthy makes about his Gaelic given name distracts from his silence regarding his Anglo-Norman surname. Grice's obliviousness to his paternal ancestry suggests disregard for where his political loyalties should lie, which, apparently, should *not* be on the side of his 'rebellious' maternal ancestors. The Normans had conquered both Ireland and England, but in the former country they were sometimes ambiguously positioned in the polarized spectrum of Gaelic Catholic and Anglo Protestant. Therefore, the Norman ancestry as well as the Anglo-American culture that the male protagonists in 'The Modern Warning' share imply that Macarthy's stress on their lack of commonality is both anachronistic in terms of the contemporary climate *and* factually incorrect. 'Grice' means 'grey' in Norman French, but the ideologically rigid protagonist of that name thinks only in black and white. In James's *The American,* a description of the background of Lord Deepmere, a wealthy English aristocrat, suggests the manner in which strict boundaries between 'Irish' and 'English' collapse in the case of the cosmopolitan elite. Lord Deepmere praises his Dublin social life so enthusiastically at a dinner in Paris that Newman quietly enquires afterwards if he is Irish and is told that though his title is English, the grandee is the grandson of an owner of '"great Irish estates"'.[121] Altogether, in its political concerns and theme, its awareness of the ambiguity of Hiberno-Norman ethno-religious allegiance, and its use of the marriage-as-Union trope, 'The Modern Warning' suggests that although James may have been a secular American, his Ulster Presbyterian and Hiberno-Norman origins cannot be ignored.

Coda: Ancestor-Haunted: John Mitchel and John Purroy Mitchel

James remained an American citizen until World War I when, angry at his native land's delay in entering the fray, he finally took out British citizenship. He died in February 1916, a little over two months before the Easter Rising in Dublin, which was effectively the beginning of the end of British rule for most of Ireland. These conflicts involving James's distant and adopted motherlands impacted the Irish political scene of his American hometown, particularly in the case of John Purroy Mitchel (1879–1918), a World War I-era New York mayor of famous Ulster Presbyterian ancestry. The binary of Irish-Americanness as either Protestant/Scots-Irish/Unionist or Catholic/nationalist into that period and that so marked James led to the forgetting of this once-prominent politician because he did not fully fit either category. This was not least because of the mayor's *doppelganger* grandfather, John Mitchel (1815–75), whose troubling legacy opens up the Irish engagements with race in the Americas examined in the following two chapters.

At his death James left behind the unfinished *doppelganger* novel, *The Sense of the Past.* It was published during the final year of the New York mayoralty of Mitchel, in whose own life the threatening *doppelganger* trope of Ulster-American non-realist fiction plays out. Mitchel (in office 1914 to 1917), was the second youngest ever mayor of New York. His 'New Light' (liberal) Ulster Presbyterian ancestor and namesake had been a militant leader of the nationalist Young Irelanders and a descendant of a United Irishman. The tail-end of the kind of radical Ulster Presbyterian politics that had led to the 1798 Uprising in Ireland,

Mitchel *grandpère's Jail Journal* (1854) and *The Last Conquest of Ireland (Perhaps)* (1861) remain central to Irish nationalism. The latter volume cemented the view of the 1845 Famine as deliberate genocide by the British authorities.[122] This belief moulded the politics of post-Famine Catholic Irish America and, in the period of his grandson's mayoralty, shaped its antagonistic attitude to American participation on what was perceived to be the 'British' side of the Great War. Successive Irish food crises spurred early waves of Ulster Presbyterian emigration from 1728 onwards,[123] a history effaced by the mayor's lifetime due to his grandfather's melding of the Famine with nationalist Catholic grievance.[124] *Jail Journal* is a caustic critique of British colonial policy that details Mitchel *grandpère*'s devastating first-hand witness of the Famine. It further details his penal transportation to Bermuda in 1848 for advocating militant resistance in the lead-in to the Young Irelander Rebellion of that year, his escape from that fourteen-year sentence in 1853 after his transfer to Van Diemen's Land, and his eventual arrival in New York in 1854. There he was, and remained, a hero to Irish nationalists, inspiring the violent Irish Republican tradition of Irish America up to his grandson's generation (Figure 2.4).[125]

In Betty Smith's semi-autobiographical *A Tree Grows in Brooklyn*, pre-pubescent Irish Catholic Francie Nolan and her father enjoy watching the cavalcade of an unnamed New York mayor-to-be in her Brooklyn neighbourhood,[126] almost certainly based on William Jay Gaynor (1849–1913), a Tammany-backed Irish Catholic Democrat who held office from 1910 to 1913. Gaynor preceded John Purroy Mitchel,[127] and the manner in which the Nolans celebrate Gaynor as 'one of their own' contrasts to how Mayor Mitchel was increasingly distrusted by Catholic Irish America during his tenure. The Columbia-educated Mitchel was raised Catholic but, as John F. McClymer details, his Republicanism and pro-war and Reform politics—which saw him take on a case against Tammany Hall as a young lawyer in 1907—put him at odds with the New York Irish Democratic political machine and facilitated accusations in Irish-American media that his loyalty was with Britain.[128] Mitchel's reformist bent made him popular with the broader electorate, however,[129] so when, aged thirty-eight, he died in uniform during Air Service training on 6 July 1918, he was given one of the largest public funerals ever seen by his city. Mitchel lay in state at New York City Hall, followed by a massive procession up Fifth Avenue for a funeral service with full military honours at St Patrick's Cathedral, symbol *par excellence* of the aspirations of post-Famine Irish New York.[130] An enormously impactful event for New Yorkers, a city in which F. Scott Fitzgerald had resided, the shocking crash seems to have inspired a poignant cameo in Fitzgerald's *The Beautiful and Damned.* Gloria's former Ivy League flame, Tudor Baird, reconnects with her during the Great War when relocated by the Aviation Corps. Gloria kisses him 'sentimentally one night' and afterward is glad, 'for

Figure 2.4 'John Mitchel, The First Martyr of Ireland in Her Revolution of 1848'. Lithograph by N. Currier, New York, 1848. Courtesy of Wikimedia Commons.

next day when his plane fell fifteen hundred feet at Mineola [airfield, New York] a piece of a gasolene engine smashed through his heart' (Figure 2.5).[131]

Nine days after Mitchel's death, the former mayor and his grandfather were referred to in the widely reported trial in the Federal District Court in New York of John A. O'Leary. The latter was leader in America of Sinn Féin, the Irish republican political organization then pushing back against America joining a 'British' war. Meanwhile, O'Leary's brother, Jeremiah, was President of the American Truth Society, which was under surveillance for its pro-German stance. John O'Leary had been charged with having aided in Jeremiah's flight from the jurisdiction of the court. During cross examination, reference was made to a 1917 letter written by

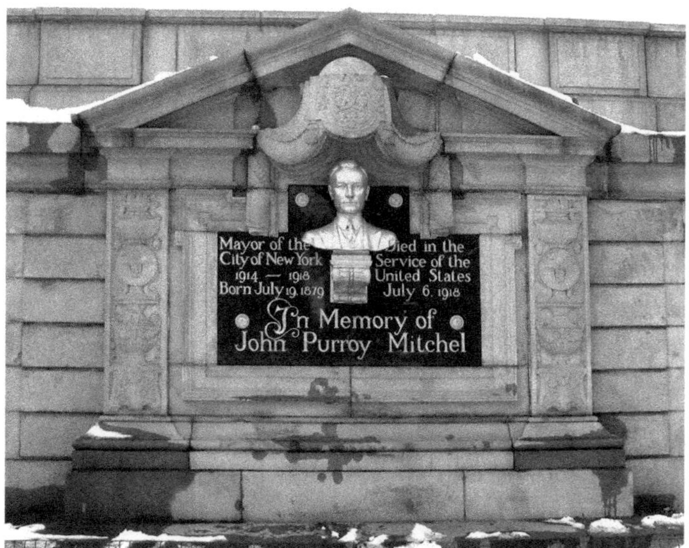

Figure 2.5 Monument to John Mitchel's grandson and former New York Mayor, John Purroy Mitchel, in Central Park, New York. Dedicated in 1928. Courtesy of Wikimedia Commons.

Jeremiah in which he castigated British military forces and the 'degenerate Irishman', Mitchel.[132] John O'Leary then produced a copy of *Jail Journal* and in what the *New York Times* called an 'outburst', the chief witness declared:

> when I said that John Purroy Mitchel was a degenerate Irishman I meant that he did not agree with the sentiments of his grandfather, who did not fear jail in support of his convictions. He was put into jail unlawfully, as I have been. [...] you have no right to keep me in jail [...] because I want to see old Ireland free.[133]

The use of the racialized term 'degenerate' to denounce the late former mayor's pro-British stance opens up a submerged politics of Mitchel *grandpère*'s *Jail Journal*, that of white supremacism. The term implied that John Purroy Mitchel had failed not just to replicate his grandfather's politics, but his championing of Irish aspirations to whiteness also.

Jail Journal, Mitchel *grandpère*'s 'ultimately supremacist story of victimization', conjoins anti-imperialism with the incipient anti-abolitionism he would express in his American journalism. It did so by, as Peter D. O'Neill demonstrates, co-opting the conventions of the slave narrative's 'tropes of kidnap, of Middle Passage dehumanization and commodification, of escape, and of liberation'.[134] In Ireland, Mitchel's militancy had caused him to break with his former nationalist ally, the

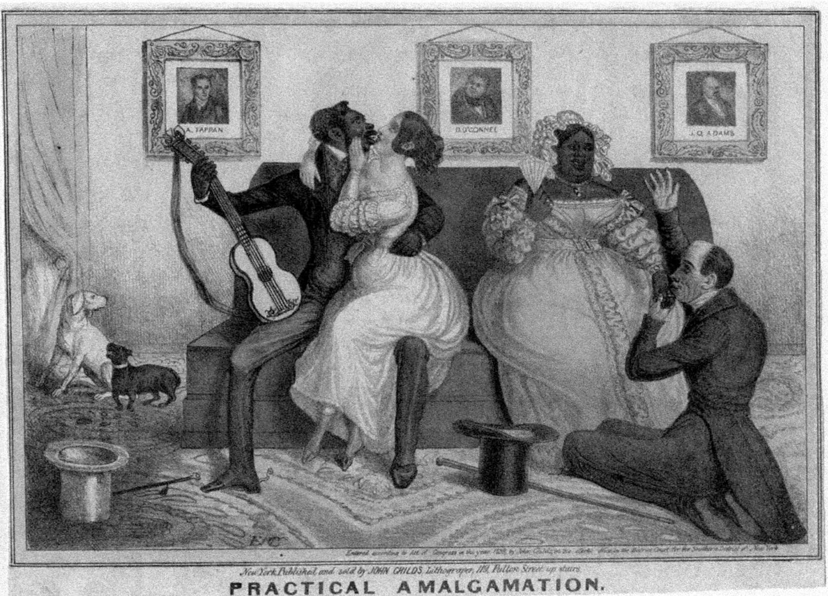

Figure 2.6 1839 print by Edward W. Clay lampooning interracial romance. Contemporaneous Irish abolitionist Daniel O'Connell is the middle portrait on the wall. Courtesy of the Library Company of Philadelphia.

pacifist Daniel O'Connell, who spear-headed the 1829 removal of anti-Catholic restrictions (Catholic Emancipation) and pushed for repeal of the Union of Ireland with Great Britain of 1800. O'Connell had worked to align the causes of Irish nationalism and abolitionism to the degree that William Lloyd Garrison's Preface to Frederick Douglass's memoir proclaimed O'Connell 'the distinguished advocate of universal emancipation'.[135] However, the Irish abolitionist was labelled a 'blackguard' in an 1843 caricature by the Philadelphia-born Edward W. Clay for this very stance.[136] In addition, O'Connell is a background detail in an 1839 print by the same caricaturist lampooning interracial romance (Figure 2.6). In America, Mitchel directly opposed O'Connell's abolitionism.[137] As Anthony G. Russell details, in articles for his *Southern Citizen* newspaper in the late 1850s, Mitchel's original sympathy for the plight of the degraded Irish rural poor transmutes: he compares Britain's relationship with Ireland to that of the industrial, abolitionist North's desire to impose its will upon the agrarian South.[138] (Startlingly, Wilde and Yeats expressed similar sentiments,[139] while 'Giant of the Westerns', Mayne Reid, became a loud Irish-born abolitionist voice.[140]) In the *Southern Citizen*, Mitchel would go on to suggest the reasonableness of Southern slavery when the enslaved were well treated, his public repetition of which angered fugitive Harriet Jacobs.[141]

In the following *Jail Journal* passage on what Mitchel witnessed when docked for supplies in Brazil during his 1848 transportation, that view is incipient in the commonplace of the Irish peasant as his landlord's 'slave':

> I surveyed [the enslaved Africans] long and earnestly, for before this day I never saw a slave in his slavery – I mean a merchantable slave, a slave of real-money value [...] The poor slaves I have been accustomed to see are [...] of no value. [...] These slaves in Brazil are fat and merry, obviously not overworked nor under-fed. [...] Is it better, then, to be the slave of a merciful master and a just man, or to be serf to an Irish land-appropriator.[142]

For Anthony R. Hale, Mitchel invokes the notion of the 'Irish slave' not to question the racial basis of slavery but to emphasize the outrageousness of the degradation of those *who would be white.*[143] Irish units served in both the Confederate and Union armies during the Civil War, an ideological flexibility that Dennis Clark traces to conditions in the motherland,[144] and Mitchel's three sons were among the *c.* 40,000 Irish who fought for the Confederacy, though the Union Irish were not necessarily abolitionist either.[145] The only survivor among the Mitchel boys, James, went on to father John Purroy Mitchel.[146]

Shared names are at the root of intergenerational haunting in James's *The Sense of the Past*, and John Purroy Mitchel is likewise inscribed with the inescapable imprint of a *doppelganger* forebear with whom he was as odds and whose outsize reputation among Irish nationalists bedevilled the mayor's public life. Mitchel becomes a dissonant presence in WWI-era Irish New York due to the period's increasingly fixed idea of 'Irishness' as post-Famine, Catholic, ethnically Gaelic, and Irish nationalist. This has contributed to his current neglect by historians and his general absence from the Irish-American pantheon,[147] though his namesake ancestor remains a central—if contested—figure in current Irish historiography. Chapter 4 considers twentieth-century novels in which modestly born Irish plantation owners transform themselves into the class (race) that has oppressed them. As with Mitchel *grandpère*, these protagonists' response to their oppression is to become the oppressor. Mitchel *grandpère* did not make common cause with African Americans, but that did occur in certain Irish-American writing. As such, the chapter that follows opens with some early Eugene O'Neill drama that takes its cue from shared Irish-African experience in the seventeenth-century Americas.

3

How the Irish Became Red

O'Neill and Fitzgerald

Writers Eugene O'Neill (1888–1953) and F. Scott Fitzgerald (1896–1940) were near contemporaries in terms of lifespan and period of productivity and shared similar backgrounds: both were raised in comfortable Irish-American homes and both were mindful of their immigrant roots. Fitzgerald's fiction, which will be considered in the second half of this chapter, generally hews closely to his own time, place, and social class. During Fitzgerald's 1920s heyday, the post-Famine Irish were vulnerable to Ku Klux Klan race rhetoric and that decade's anti-immigration legislation: the Klan opposed both 'off-white' Catholic immigration and Al Smith, the first Irish Catholic nominee of a major party when he ran as Democratic candidate for US President in 1928. In the period after the Famine refugee influx, Irishness became synonymous with being Gaelic, while the earlier Irish cohort had assimilated to white Americanness: the novels that inspired the touchstone Klan film, *The Birth of a Nation* (1915), portrayed 'the true American nation as Scotch-Irish in descent and inspiration'.[1] Partly as a result of such contexts, Fitzgerald over-identified with the one non-Irish branch of his family that exemplified uncontestable whiteness. Moreover, his struggles with his 'off-white' Irish ancestry inform the obsession with the class and racial status of immigrant whiteness vis-à-vis WASP and Black America in his fiction. Fitzgerald's striking self-ascription as 'black Irish' (or 'half black Irish', to be exact) is a phrase used in America in reference to the dermally white Irish, though it is unknown in Ireland in that iteration. Thus, like the coining of 'Scots-Irish' to describe those of Ulster Presbyterian origin, 'black Irish' is a term that emerges in response to America's ethno-racial politics, as will be explored. The centenary of the Irish Free State in 2022 will be followed in short order by that of the best-known novel by a member of Ireland's enormous diaspora, Fitzgerald's *The Great Gatsby* (1925). In order to bring these centenaries into dialogue, the presence and effacement of Irishness in Fitzgerald's oeuvre and sense of his paternal ancestry will be foregrounded.

By contrast with Fitzgerald, the O'Neill works considered bring a wide lens to bear upon his ethnic cohort, and critique the Irish presence in the Americas over centuries as one long failure to create solidarity with their fellow oppressed, especially peoples of colour. Those of the white Irish ancestry that O'Neill and Fitzgerald shared often have very light skin tones, with the most common type

Race, Politics, and Irish America. Mary M. Burke, Oxford University Press.
 DOI: 10.1093/oso/9780192859730.003.0004

among this population being the palest on the widely accepted (though not uncontroversial) numerical classification schema for human skin colour developed by Irish-American dermatologist Thomas Fitzpatrick.[2] What beauty magazines call 'Celtic skin' burns easily in the sun or more visibly reddens with inflammatory conditions (such as the 'curse of the Celts', rosacea).[3] Thus, Irish dermal whiteness is 'flawed' due to being *too* white. This tendency was a racial liability in two locations evoked in the work of Fitzgerald and O'Neill, respectively: on fashionable 1920s Riviera beaches in which an even tan conversely signalled 'whiteness' as well as on seventeenth-century Caribbean islands in which the indentured and transported Irish were racialized as 'red' due to their propensity to burn. Thus, a point of convergence in the work of Fitzgerald and O'Neill is 'defective' Irish whiteness, both dermal and social.

American playwright and Nobel laureate Eugene O'Neill (1888–1953) was born in New York to Irish Famine refugee and stage actor James O'Neill and Mary Ella Quinlan, who was of more 'lace curtain' (aspirational) Irish descent. In his childhood, O'Neill's father was often on tour with a theatrical company, but the family reunited in the summers at a modest beach home in New London, Connecticut that would form the setting for Eugene's masterpiece, *Long Day's Journey into Night* (1941–42, first published posthumously in 1956). O'Neill critics generally concur that the histrionic melodramas in which his father specialized were both an education and a template against which to rebel for the emerging playwright. Like Fitzgerald a decade later, O'Neill aspired to the Ivy League but found himself a bad fit therein: he lasted only a year (1906–07) at Princeton. Also like Fitzgerald, he struggled intermittently with depression and alcoholism throughout his life. In 1910, as a twenty-one-year-old shirking an ill-advised first marriage, O'Neill booked passage on a boat out of Boston bound for Buenos Aires. Once he arrived in Argentina, he lived hand-to-mouth for months and then as a near-vagrant, after which he took ship to Portuguese East Africa.[4] O'Neill's description of this formidable experience, which must have seemed akin to that of his father's hard early years in Famine Ireland, suggests a racializing experience in which his previous identification as white ('a gentleman') disintegrated: 'I landed in Buenos Aires a gentleman, so called, and wound up a bum on the docks.'[5] O'Neill returned to the US as a crewman on a British merchant ship, whose anchoring in Trinidad inspired the setting for his early play, *The Moon of the Caribbees*.[6]

O'Neill's drama career was launched by the Provincetown Players collective, which produced many of his early works in their theatres in Provincetown, Massachusetts and Greenwich Village, New York. His expressionist and realist plays were among the first to include speeches in American English vernacular and to depict social outsiders. Eugene's insistence that only a Black actor could take on the role of the title African-American character in his play, *The Emperor Jones* (1920), gave the first opportunity to a Black performer to play a major role on the Broadway stage.[7] This was audacious 'in a theatrical universe in which

Figure 3.1 Ulster-American actor John McCullough as Othello in 1878. Theatre poster image courtesy of the Library of Congress.

Othello was regularly played by white actors in blackface', James O'Neill and his Ulster-American *doppelganger*, John McCullough (Figure 3.1), included.[8]

This analysis begins by considering O'Neill's early explorations of shared Black-Irish histories in his drama before pivoting to *Long Day's Journey into Night*. A play so personal that O'Neill did not want it produced or published during his lifetime, this late career *magnum opus* is regarded as the autobiography of O'Neill's family of origin since its plot points and characters follow the contours of their life trajectories and personalities. However, the playwright's reading of cutting-edge historiography on early modern Ireland at about the time that he was working on *Long Day's Journey into Night* allowed him to bring the wide lens of the early plays considered presently to bear upon familial history, thereby transforming one family's pain into an audit of centuries of traumatic history, both Irish and American. This opening-out is further generated by reading *Long Day's Journey into Night* alongside O'Neill's *Desire Under the Elms* (1924); when paired, the plays critique the settler-colonial mindset adapted by Scots-Irish and Famine Irish immigrants in America, an interpretation pursued in Annie Ryan's landmark 2013 Dublin production of *Desire Under the Elms.* O'Neill's letters and biographies give ample evidence that he was, as implied in a conversation with his son, avidly aware of both Irish history and current affairs: 'The one thing that explains more than anything about me is the fact that I'm Irish. And strangely enough, it is something that all the writers who have attempted to explain me and my work have overlooked.'[9] O'Neill's understanding of the deep historical contexts of the tumult of early 1920s Ireland means that *Desire Under the Elms* is also marked by Irish Partition in 1921, which emerges as merely the latest historical rupture that the plays audits. However, in order to examine O'Neill's portrayals of Irish encounters with the Atlantic world's ethno-racial hierarchy, we must begin with his earliest work.

Redlegs: O'Neill's Black-Irish Caribbean

Two of O'Neill's earliest plays, *Thirst* (1913) and *Moon of the Caribbees* (1918), conjure up the period and location of the first contact between Irish and African in the Americas, which was the seventeenth-century Caribbean. In a 2018 group interview on O'Neill and Irish theatre that included Christopher Morash, Christopher Murray, and Anthony Roche, David Clare evoked the theory of cultural survivals from African roots that is a given in African American Studies to suggest that there should be 'an understanding of cultural survivals within Irish American experiences'.[10] (Clare has recently developed this idea in discussing the influence of O'Neill on Jamaican playwright Dennis Scott's 1974 'race memory' plantation play, *An Echo in the Bone.*[11]) A major caveat before examining the shared Black and Irish historical hinterland of O'Neill's early work is that in the seventeenth-century Caribbean, the Irish were both planter and debased deportee, and the low status of the latter should not efface the imperialist role played by some elite Irish in that sphere.[12] Nor will this chapter endorse the inaccurate but popular pseudohistory—readily available online—that the Irish were 'white slaves'.[13] Librarian and independent historian Liam Hogan notes that this narrative has become 'a favoured derailment tactic' for those wishing to shut down conversations about race, reparation, and slavery.[14] Without minimizing the suffering and premature deaths of many Irish transportees (or even voluntary emigrants) to the Caribbean, it is vital to acknowledge that 'Irish slavery' rhetoric creates a false equivalence between an indentured servitude that was, in its worst iterations, what Peter Kolchin calls 'temporary slavery', and the much more systemic and sustained debasement of people of African origin and their descendants in the Americas as chattels *in perpetuity.* Indenture contracts for voluntary servants in Barbados between 1635 and 1680 ran an average of 6.75 years, while the forcibly transported 'served ten years and longer'.[15] Abbott Emerson Smith makes the conclusive statement that although the English authorities plainly treated the transported as human detritus on numerous levels, 'there was never any such thing as perpetual slavery for any white man in any English colony'.[16] The internet-age argument that the Irish were enslaved is an egregious descendant of Mitchel's emphasis on the Irish as victims but never as perpetrators. (It also effaces the fact, delineated by Michael Malouf, that twentieth-century Black Caribbean politicians and writers such as Marcus Garvey and Derek Walcott identified with Irish nationalism.[17])

In 2015, a photograph surfaced of Betty Fenty, the great-aunt of Rihanna (Robyn Rihanna Fenty; b. 1988-), the Black Barbadian pop singer. Betty appeared to be of white European ancestry,[18] but the *Irish America* magazine article concerned labelled her a 'Redleg'. It also discussed the fact that she and many contemporary 'Redlegs' on the Caribbean island of Barbados, a former and very early British colony, identify as Irish. (Although Redlegs have Scottish associations too, as will emerge sporadically in the following, the term tends to be most associated with the Irish.) As described in the *New York Times* in 1973, Redlegs are strikingly—even excessively—pale, yet are not considered to be white:

> Today the 'Redlegs'—usually identified by complexions which seem almost bleached of all color, straw-like hair and pale blue eyes—are pariahs, a subculture unto themselves, aloof from the environment and era. Though their roots in the Caribbean now go back 300 years, they have never assimilated.[19]

In the seventeenth and eighteenth centuries, huge cash crop plantations in the Caribbean islands under French and English control were worked by enslaved Africans, but a heterogeneous white underclass also worked on the English-controlled islands: 'Some came as slaves: losers in Protestant–Catholic conflicts, debtors and other convicts or kidnapping victims, Others came as indentured servants, some willingly, some not'.[20] Though Richard Dunn gives evidence that some Irish had voluntarily gone as indentured servants to the Caribbean,[21] the 'losers in Protestant–Catholic conflicts' is what will be detailed here.

In response to a threatening alliance between the Irish Catholic elite and English Royalists, English Republican and Puritan Oliver Cromwell invaded Ireland on behalf of the English Parliament in 1649. Cromwell introduced Penal Laws that punished the majority Catholic population and confiscated large amounts of Catholic-owned land, which was granted to colonists with a British Protestant identity. The ferocity of these actions went on to create support for the Jacobite cause among elite Gaelo-Normans, and a further consequence was the subsequent transportation of many thousands of Irish to Caribbean islands. Peter Linebaugh and Marcus Redike estimate that some 34,000 men were 'shipped out of Ireland and sold abroad in the aftermath of the 1649 conquest. By 1660 there were at least twelve thousand Irish workers in the West Indies, and nine years later, eight thousand in Barbados alone.'[22] The Gothic horror of this scenario is suggested by the fact that references to Cromwell open and close Maturin's *Melmoth the Wanderer.*

Dunn details the appalling mortality rates for both Blacks and whites that made seventeenth-century Barbados the wealthiest—but in human terms, the costliest—colony in English America. The Southern United States was only the northernmost outpost of a plantation system for the large-scale cultivation of staple crops that encompassed many Caribbean colonies too. The initial demand for labour 'was largely color-blind', and the basis of the seventeenth-century work force in the southern two-thirds of the English mainland colonies was indentured labourers, mostly servants, whom Kolchin, as noted, defines as 'temporary slave[s]'.[23] Although earlier indentured servants were English, in eighteenth-century America, servant ranks were swelled by Irish emigrants and by English convicts transported in lieu of prison terms or death. However, after the 1680s, mainland colonies underwent a massive shift from indentured to slave labour, in the initial period of which there was often 'little clear demarcation between blacks and lower-class whites.'[24] Kolchin notes that, in the absence of the 'racial contrast' that went on to become central to the 'we-they' dichotomy between master and 'those who might legitimately be enslaved', other attributes, 'such as religion and nationality' could serve.[25] Thus, in the specific case of Irish indentured servants, not just Catholicism but the kind of extreme paleness that caused skin to redden rather than tan emerges as a marker of difference. (A relationship between the 'reddening' of the pale and indentured and the mid-eighteenth-century 'reddening' of Indigenous North Americans detailed by Nancy Shoemaker is possible but requires exploration.[26]) Barbadian historian Hilary Beckles suggests that most indentured servants on Barbados, regardless of British Isles ethnic origins, experienced punitive treatment, but that the Irish had a particularly low status.[27] Donald Akenson suggests that on Hiberno-Norman controlled Montserrat, by contrast, the indentured Irish enjoyed better conditions.[28]

The ideological degradation of 'all manual labor' rapidly pervaded Caribbean plantation society after the large-scale importation of Africans in the late seventeenth century.[29] However, long after the very pale-skinned were no longer subject to temporary chattel status, their pallor—and that of any equally pale descendants—still served as a reminder of their former degradation as clearly as any brand. Anthropologist Sheila S. Walker proposes that 'honky', a slur for 'poor white', may derive from a term in the West African Wolof language meaning 'red ears'.[30] This suggests that to some of African origin, the propensity of the pale to burn at their bodily extremities may have meant, in effect, *defective* whiteness. If darker-skinned African-Americans have carried the stigma of forced labour long after abolition because skin tone is understood to be evidence of ancestry, then in the hot Caribbean climate this became equally true of the hereditarily extremely pale. For Beckles, the deeply impoverished contemporary Barbadian

'Redleg' descendants of indentured whites are 'living empirical evidence that in slave society, a white skin did not necessarily symbolize wealth, power, and status'.[31] In short, in the Caribbean context, when 'white' did not connote such attributes it became 'red'.

In order to frame O'Neill's interest in the historical ties between oppressed cohorts, it is important to glimpse moments of Black-Irish alliance in the Americas. In Barbados in 1675, 1686, and 1692, Irish 'redshanks' and 'African slaves' conspired together to resist or kill their masters,[32] while in 1661 in Bermuda, 'a threatened insurrection of Irish and Negroes' was suppressed.[33] The co-operation in rebellion between enslaved and indentured people was discouraged in Barbados by the codification in law of a division between white servant and Black enslaved person in 1661, which placed the former 'above' the latter within the plantation system. A similar code was later adopted in South Carolina.[34] As a consequence, in terms of real numbers, indentured servitude was effectively replaced by slavery. Nevertheless, those of 'red' Irish descent persisted on Barbados, alienated from planter wealth and power even as they clung to compensatory whiteness.[35] By the nineteenth century, no trace of the seventeenth-century alliance between Black and marginalized white on Barbados remained: visitors repeatedly record that the degraded 'Redlegs'—notwithstanding creolization and despite existing in a manner that suggested they were the lowest stratum—considered themselves superior to their neighbours of African descent.[36] Thus, as Harvey O'Brien argues in an article on *Redlegs* and *Barbado'ed*, two 2009 documentaries on descendants of such seventeenth-century Irish and Scottish deportees, these 'abject doppelganger[s]' of the contemporary Irish and Scottish 'complicate' any easy vision of historical pan-Gaelic victimization and lie outside the 'restorative trajectory' of the contemporary 'oppressed-Irish-made-good' narrative beloved of the Irish diaspora in North America.[37]

In his time at sea, O'Neill followed routes that had been charted by the mercantile and slave-trading interests that had shaped the Atlantic world. This interlude became the experiential bedrock of his earliest artistic negotiations of that past. O'Neill's diatribe to a journalist regarding the oppression that the US government had sanctioned 'since the beginning of our history – and before that too' suggests the depth of his historical vision.[38] Thus, by placing the working-class white Irish back in the scene of ancestral indenture and transportation in *Thirst* and *The Moon of the Caribbees*, the racial ambiguity and troubled race relations this created plays out. *Thirst* (written in 1913), a critically neglected expressionist one-act included in the first published collection of O'Neill's drama in 1914, portrays a raft as a microcosm of the toxic dynamics produced in the cauldron of the seventeenth-century Atlantic world. Three shipwreck survivors, the Dancer, the Gentleman, and the West Indian Mulatto Sailor, are adrift on an unnamed 'tropic sea'.[39] The West Indian's descriptor of 'mulatto' (mixed race) and his listlessness (he 'croons a monotonous negro song to himself as his round eyes follow the shark fins in their everlasting circles') suggests the broken spirit of an enslaved person. The merciless sun is slowly transforming the white Gentleman, sitting in the tatters of evening dress, into a 'half black' 'Redleg': his bald spot is 'burnt crimson by the sun' and his moustache dye has run, 'making a black line down the side of his lean face, blistering with sunburn'.[40] The sole female, also white, is being racially transformed into red/black in the tropical heat too, and the description of her body is suggestive of famine: dressed in dance costume, a 'diamond necklace can be seen glittering coldly on the protruding collar bones of her emaciated shoulders. Continuous weeping has made a blurred smudge of her rouge and the black make-up of her eyes.' She had been beautiful 'before hunger and thirst had transformed her into a mocking spectre of a dancer'.[41]

The Belfast-built *Titanic*, whose 1912 sinking seems to be overtly invoked (though not necessarily mourned) in the description of what characters have endured,[42] is only the most recent maritime history that haunts the action. O'Neill explicitly explores the collective memory of the Middle Passage in *The Emperor Jones*, when the African-American title character hallucinates that ancestral trauma, but this and other harrowing forced sea journeys haunt *Thirst*, whose title hints at the sea's boundless desire for blood. When the Gentleman muses that the sea's red colour may be 'the blood of all those who were drowned th[e] night [of our shipwreck] rising to the surface',[43] it evokes the countless bodies thrown overboard into the world's waters,[44] from the Middle Passage to the popular memory of the dangerously overcrowded so-called 'coffin' ships that transported Irish Famine refugees. As with Rivers Solomon's mythopoetic *The Deep* (2020), in which water-breathing descendants of pregnant Africans tossed overboard during the Middle Passage persist underwater,[45] *Thirst* ultimately brings to the surface history assumed to be safely drowned. The interactions of *Thirst*'s shipwreck survivors broadly replay the downward trajectory of Black-abject white relations in the Caribbean, from initial collaboration ('He is only a poor negro sailor – our companion in misfortune. God knows we are all in the same pitiful plight'), to division and violence, as the action descends into madness, intimations of prostitution and cannibalism, and murder.[46] The ghosts of seventeenth-century transported sex workers and human chattel seem to emerge from the sea: hallucinating that the sailor has somehow hidden water, the Dancer offers her diamond necklace and then her body in exchange for it, shrieking that he is a 'dirty slave' when rebuffed.[47] At the close, all three are dead in the water and only the diamond necklace remains on the raft, the ultimate emblem of what W.E.B. Du Bois theorized as the Atlantic world's extractive mindset;[48] in Fitzgerald's 1922 story, 'The Diamond as Big as the Ritz' (to be discussed), contemporary lineal descendants of George Washington run a secret diamond mine on unfree labour.

O'Neill's 1917 exploration of deep African-Irish history, *The Moon of the Caribbees* (staged in 1918 by the Provincetown Players), is one of a quartet of one-act plays about seamen written during the Great War that drew from O'Neill's

Figure 3.2 1937 production of O'Neill's *The Moon of the Caribbees* at the Lafayette Theatre, Harlem, New York. Courtesy of the Federal Theatre Project Collection, Library of Congress.

own maritime experience (Figure 3.2). The play's break with Aristotelian theatrical conventions—it relies on poetic mood for dramatic effect—was inspired by O'Neill's attendance of productions of a number of landmark Irish Revival dramas in New York in 1911.[49] *The Moon of the Caribbees* explores the rowdy interactions between British and Irish seaman on the *Glencairn* and a group of local West Indian women who come aboard to sell alcohol and sex. *Moon* opens on the main deck as, from the distance, a 'melancholy Negro chant, faint and far-off, drifts, crooning, over the water'.[50] As the men smoke together and await the women's arrival, the emphasis is on race from the outset, with Irishman Driscoll using an Irish dialect variant on the 'n'-word ('naygur') in the very first line of dialogue.[51] Soon after referring to one of the West Indian women as a 'monkey', a cockney seaman calls 'Liverpool Irishman' Paddy an '"airy ape', a racialization that angers the latter.[52] The racist belief that African Americans resembled apes was pseudoscience into O'Neill's lifetime,[53] and the 'simian' Irish were also subject to this belief to some degree as well as to the slur 'white n*****'.[54] Quickest to use a racial slur—and one native to Hiberno-English dialect at that—the Irish are also the first to be racialized, enacting the toxic Atlantic World dynamic whereby the 'defective' whites who might have made common cause with Black people were often the least likely to ultimately do so. As if to reiterate his whiteness in the wake of any doubt created by the insult to his fellow Irishman, Driscoll soon praises some of the West Indian women to the British Davis as 'near as white as you an' me'.[55] The

Irish sailors are entangled in a racial nexus created centuries before their birth and thousands of miles from Ireland, one that they unwittingly enter both in being cast as racially inferior and in utilizing Irish variants of globally circuated slurs.

This deep history also gives resonance to O'Neill's expressionistic *All God's Chillun Got Wings* (1924), a timbre amplified by his casting decisions in the original production. It was the third O'Neill play to feature a Black protagonist and the first drama to feature an interracial couple on the Broadway stage.[56] *All God's Chillun Got Wings* portrays the working-class and white Ella, who marries an ambitious African-American man named Jim. On the surface it is very much a story of its era in its highly controversial depiction of 'miscegenation', what novelist Frank Yerby—born in 1916 to a Black father and a mother of Scots-Irish ancestry—called 'one of the two or three ugliest and most insulting words in the English language'.[57] Interracial marriage was still illegal in the majority of American states in 1924, and when word got out before *All God's Chillun Got Wings* opened in the Manhattan Provincetown Playhouse that Ella would kiss Jim's hand, a national uproar and a threat to O'Neill's family from the Ku Klux Klan ensued (Figure 3.3).[58] Ella was being played by Mary Blair (1897–1947), the Swedenborgian (Neo-Christian) daughter of a Belfast family,[59] while performer Paul Robeson was playing Jim, a role that launched his career.[60] The Klan newsletter seemed to unconsciously perceive this contact between the Irish immigrant actress and the Black performer as an echo of joint Black-Irish rebellion of the sort that periodically roiled seventeenth-century Barbados: '[O'Neill] is a Catholic and hence doubtless trying to stir up the Negroes to arm, march on Washington, and burn down the Nordic White House'.[61] Even moderate white America called the play a provocation, with a *New York Times* journalist advising O'Neill in an interview that when 'the community's social code [...] didn't like the notion of a black man and a white woman married on the stage the dramatist should not present such a play'.[62] In order to assuage counter suspicions within the Black community in the lead-in to the opening, O'Neill enlisted the support of both Langston Hughes and Du Bois, not least because the play's depiction of the plight of ambitious African Americans drew from the conclusions of Du Bois's own *The Souls of Black Folk* (1903).[63]

Set in a mixed-race neighbourhood, *All God's Chillun Got Wings* opens with Jim and Ella as child playmates. The latter is not explicitly named as Irish, but her surname (Downey) and her speech patterns infer as much.[64] Since the play is often discussed simply as a depiction of Black-white tensions, it is important to stress that Ella is *Irish* American, since that is altogether not the same thing in 1924 as being an unethicized 'white' woman; this was the very year in which the federal Johnson–Reed Act effectively banned 'off-white' immigration. As a child, Ella appears to possess no negative racial stereotypes, but the older Ella who marries the ambitious Jim as a route out of a downward spiral has developed that outlook. The drama tracks Jim's self-doubt and inability to complete his law studies due

Figure 3.3 Ulster-American Mary Blair and Paul Robeson as interracial couple Ella and Jim in the 1924 New York production of Eugene O'Neill's *All God's Chillun Got Wings*. This hand-kissing scene led to threats from the Ku Klux Klan. Courtesy of Wikimedia Commons.

to the racist hostility of his wife. With illness, Ella declines into delusional white supremacist views, a reprise of the earliest collaboration and subsequent alignment with their white 'betters' of the Irish on Barbados, as suggested by the references to Ella's pale and 'red' complexion. In a kind of reversal of blackface, the extreme paleness of the young Ella is mocked with the nickname 'Painty Face'. She hates her indentured Irish 'red "n" white' colouring, telling her young playmate, Jim, 'I wish I was black like you.' He meanwhile, wants to have white skin.[65] Jim's self-debasing marriage proposal, when he promises to become Ella's 'black slave',[66] marks the point at which they settle into the firm racial nexus that emerges after slavery displaces indentured servitude in the Americas.

Richard Brucher suggests that the depiction of a white woman who destroys her Black husband in *All God's Chillun Got Wings* constitutes a Jim Crow-era writing back to *Othello*,[67] while Shannon Steen reads the fact that the play's interracial couple come close to sharing the names of the playwright's own parents (James and Mary Ella) as evidence that O'Neill identified on some level as 'mulatto'.[68] Indeed, James O'Neill, the 'off-white' immigrant who had married a younger, genteel woman, associated his own union with that of Othello and Desdemona.[69] It is to this family of origin that the chapter now turns in tracing the entwined familial and national traumas of O'Neill's *Desire Under the Elms* and *Long Day's Journey into Night.*

Irish Famine Gothic: *Long Day's Journey into Night*

From 1935 onward, O'Neill worked on an ambitious cycle of plays that would trace the history of America through one family over several generations, to be entitled *A Tale of Possessors Self-Dispossessed.* The chronologically earliest play in the cycle concerns the first ancestor in colonial America, and imagines a different kind of settlement history. Harford has escaped a hard-scrabble farm in Ireland (or Wales in one outline) by joining the British side in the French and Indian War (1754–1763), which ultimately gave Great Britain enormous territorial gains in North America. Captured by Indians, he comes to appreciate their attitude to the land, which they use just enough for support, but do not wish to own. After he is released, Harford settles a while on a frontier farm with a needy widow, but restless on the land, he ultimately strikes out for the wilderness to travel and develop his mind.[70] On the frontier farm, Harford was a 'possessor' who 'self-dispossessed' in order to finally escape imperial values. He also leaves his newborn son in the care of the widow's family, abandoning the allied nexus of patrilineality also. O'Neill never completed this play (nor the cycle), but its theme illustrates the connections he made between Irish and American history, which I suggest is reflected in the scope of two plays on Irish-American patriarchs and their fateful forgetting of that from which they had fled.

O'Neill's realist family drama *Long Day's Journey into Night* (hereafter *LDJIN*), written in 1941–42, is conventionally considered to be an abandonment of the wide-lens view of many earlier plays. However, a consideration of its Famine hinterland and thematic connection to *Desire Under the Elms* (1924) suggests that it meditates on the forgetting of generations of Irish immigrants in America in adapting a settler-colonial mindset. *LDJIN* is set in a claustrophobic, fog-bound summer home in New London, Connecticut in 1912, and centres on Irish Americans Mary and James Tyrone and their adult sons Edmund and Jamie. All seem incapable of keeping negative memories of the past to themselves. Tyrone patriarch James, like the playwright's own father, is an Irish-born and overbearing former stage actor, and *LDJIN* is generally read as autobiographical. However, it is more ambitious than a portrayal of the trauma of an individual family, but instead engages with the trauma of a whole ethnic cohort by auditing its silences. As many historians have noted of the Irish in general, the Tyrones remember too much, but it might equally be argued that the Tyrones forget too much. Altogether, the domineering father, the oppressive atmosphere, and the hovering presence of traumatic pasts, both immediate and historical, suggest a play in a Gothic realist mode. Matriarch Mary Tyrone's lines in this tenor, 'The past is the present, isn't it? It's the future, too', are the play's most chilling.[71]

Despite frequent outbursts, the Tyrones skirt around the issues that fuel their unhappiness. Most significantly, in terms of what cannot be named for most of the action is that Edmund, who has persistent coughing fits, is suffering from tuberculosis. However, TB is cover for a further undiscussed contagion that haunts the family patriarch, that of the mass deaths from transmittable diseases that hit Ireland during the Famine of 1845–1852, which killed many already weakened by starvation and fever. James Tyrone's birth year in Ireland can be calculated to have been 1847 (according to his age in the action), which is close to the year of birth of the playwright's famine-survivor father, which Arthur and Barbara Gelb have traced through Irish records to 1845.[72] The evidence regarding the deep impoverishment of James O'Neill's roots in Kilkenny that the Gelbs uncovered so profoundly altered their earlier assessment of his son's oeuvre that it motivated the highly unusual step they took of rewriting their 1962 biography of the playwright, *O'Neill*, as *O'Neill: Life with Monte Cristo* (2000). [73] The fictional James Tyrone's birth year of 1847 was two years into the famine, but like his namesake, James O'Neill, James Tyrone never explicitly mentions the trauma because the era's memories of starvation and death by contagious disease evoked shame and guilt in that cohort. The Famine may have been a powerful trope within post-Mitchel nationalism, but for many actual survivors, it was unnamable. According to Mary C. Kelly, the multi-generation Irish progress from tenement to mainstream, and from stigmatized, off-white refugee to white establishment necessitated amnesia regarding the Famine.[74]

James O'Neill was born in Ireland at the outset of the Famine, and immigrated to Buffalo, New York with his large family in 1851 at the age of five, when the catastrophe was still not fully over. His tenant farmer father's relatively advanced age at the time—he was about sixty years old—suggests desperation. The Gelbs bear out Kelly's thesis in suggesting that though the trauma experienced by James as a child refugee 'scarred him unforgettably',[75] he was utterly silent on the subject:

> James, however, never publicly acknowledged the famine's devastation, preferring to present a romanticized account of his beginnings: 'It was Kilkenny—smiling Kilkenny...where I was born one opal-tinted day in October, 1847', he wrote for a theater magazine three years before his death in 1920. [...] Of far

> greater significance than James's two-year slurring of his [real] birthdate [of October 15, 1845], was his failure to note that on the 'opal-tinted day' he commemorated, potato fields throughout the south of Ireland had blackened from a wind-born fungus that devastated the countryside with fever and famine. On James's actual birthdate, [...] the disease had already begun to kill the potato crop in Kilkenny.[76]

James Tyrone's similar maintenance of his ethnic cohort's *omertà* in *LDJIN* exemplifies what Kelly identifies as the manner in which the Famine functioned as a traumatic silence at the core of aspirational Catholic Irish America.

Although unmentioned by O'Neill's James Tyrone, the Famine *is* obliquely present in his vocabulary, however. Tyrone is land-hungry and mocks Shaughnessy, a tenant on a Connecticut farm he has purchased. Despite being able to afford the purchase of land, however, on at least five occasions in the action, the overly frugal James expresses fear of ending his days in the poorhouse. As the action peaks, he finally gains insight into the link between this terror and the struggles of his Famine-survivor mother:

> TYRONE: Her one fear was she'd get old and sick and have to die in the poorhouse. [...] It was in those days I learned to be a miser.[77]

Fear of the 'poorhouse' reveals Tyrone's unprocessed survivor trauma, and is based on a trait O'Neill noticed in his own father.[78] The 'poorhouse' or 'workhouse' was a colonial British institution for the destitute whose harsh rules and inhumane regime—particularly the policy of separating families and couples on entry—made it a hellish last resort during the Famine.[79] The workhouse also facilitated contagion by crowding the weak and diseased together indoors. Stuck in their small, fog-bound house with the tubercular Jamie, the Tyrones replicate the very workhouse conditions that James appears to fear, as suggested in the play's 2003 Plymouth Theatre New York production in which Santo Loquasto's set rendered the cottage as a 'monumental wooden tomb'.[80] The late Eavan Boland's poem 'Quarantine' (2001) suggests that the word 'workhouse' still carries the baggage of famine, contagion, and colonization in Irish culture. A love poem with a Famine backdrop, Boland depicts a couple who *choose* to set out walking from the workhouse in which the wife has caught 'famine fever' (epidemic typhus). This is really a choice to die *together* of starvation and exposure rather than remain separated within the workhouse walls. Boland's poetry typically draws on myth and folklore to imagine the unrecorded histories of women and the poor, and when the terrifying reputation of the workhouse in Famine lore is understood,[81] the motivation for the couple's stark decision becomes patent.

Tyrone's boast to his son that, 'I educated myself. I got rid of an Irish brogue you could cut with a knife',[82] intimates that a further dislocation of memory may be language shift; Eugene's Famine-refugee grandmother, Mary, 'spoke Gaelic and could not write English.'[83] Linguistic transition was hastened by the Famine, which wiped out many Irish speakers and the culture associated with the native tongue: An Aodh Mac Domhnaill poem of 1846 described the Famine as '[An] c[...]ogadh lucht Béarla a sháraigh orainn le dlí' (the war of the English-speakers who have conquered us with law).[84] The directness of the reference in an Irish-language poem written *as the Famine was occurring* contrasts with its later overt forgetting among the Anglophone Irish and Irish Americans. This suggests that it became an inarticulable memory in part because, as Kevin Whelan puts it, '[t]he language—Irish—in which the experience of the Famine was actually lived by the bulk of its victims was itself one of its casualties.'[85] The decisive seventeenth-century defeat of the Gaelo-Norman elite was the end of Irish as a language of high culture. Thereafter, Irish gradually became stigmatized as the language of Ireland's poor western margins until the turn-of-the-century Irish Cultural Revival, during which the rhetoric of its resurrection evaded the biggest reason for its decline: The Famine.

After the failure of the potato crop upon which many of the island's nine million inhabitants depended, food continued to be exported from a disordered colonial Ireland in which the poor were subject to the exploitation of the landlord class. Combined with the inadequate response of the British administration, landlords' mismanagement led to the deaths of over a million people and set in motion a culture of emigration that made Eugene O'Neill an American rather than an Irish playwright. O'Neill skewers his character's lack of insight into the history that had created his family dynamics by depicting Tyrone as land-hungry and as behaving pettily towards his own patently 'Irish peasant' tenant, Shaughnessy. In short, on his Connecticut smallholding Tyrone replicates the toxic conditions that caused his family to flee Ireland in playing the 'squireen.'[86] Thus, Tyrone suppresses not just his own suffering, but that of others too.

The historical hinterland of *LDJIN* goes back farther than the Famine, however. The name of the central family (Tyrone) is evidence of O'Neill's sense of the role played historically by carriers of his name in Ulster, originally the stronghold of the powerful Gaelic O'Neills, Earls of Tyrone. The fictional Tyrone family's inability to escape from or even adequately agree upon their past is easily read as an allegory of Ulster's history of internecine conflict. Although Eugene had devoured popular Irish histories in his youth,[87] in the period in which he wrote *LDJIN* he read a sophisticated history of Hugh (Aodh) O'Neill, an Earl of Tyrone whose failed seventeenth-century rebellion against the Crown was the Gaelic elite's last gasp. This illuminated how his immediate family fit within a longer and deeper tapestry of loss, connecting the dots between the upheaval of the early modern Atlantic World evoked in his early sea plays and the nineteenth-century famine that his father had endured. That book, *The Great O'Neill* (1942), was written by cosmopolitan Irish man of letters Seán O'Faoláin (1900–1991), an impactful public intellectual of the Irish twentieth century. O'Faoláin's ground-breaking treatment of Hugh O'Neill as a culturally hybrid and politically complex product of his period and multiple contexts challenged the older and essentialist school of nationalist hagiography that had presented Hugh O'Neill as a proud 'defender' of the Catholic faith or a kind of proto-nationalist would-be King of Ireland. (No less an author than John Mitchel *grandpère* had produced one of the better-known such histories.[88])

Indeed, James O'Neill had himself commissioned a blank-verse romance from William Greer Harrison called *The Prince of Ulster, or O'Neill* about Shane O'Neill (*c.* 1528–1567), a chieftain of the dynasty who had also clashed with the English authorities. James performed the melodrama for the five-year-old Eugene,[89] and went on to stage it in San Francisco in March of 1894. The play's swashbuckling 'lusty Irish chieftain', who peremptorily demands Irish independence from Queen Elizabeth, was cheered on by James O'Neill's Irish immigrant audience.[90] In addition, Eugene signed with the name 'Tyrone' when—in an association of Shane's rebellion with his own stance against white supremacy—he sent a Klansman an expletive by return mail when threatened over the interracial marriage theme of *All God's Chillun Got Wings*.[91] Nevertheless, *The Prince of Ulster* was exactly the kind of romantic nationalist history that made Eugene recognize the clarity of O'Faoláin's scholarship, as suggested in a 1943 letter to Irish-American novelist James T. Farrell:

> I learned from it a lot of Irish past I had mislearned before. You know what most Irish histories are like—benign Catholic benediction-and-blather tracts, or blind jingo glorifications of peerless fighting heroes, in the old bardic fashion. Hugh O'Neill, as O'Faoláin portrays him in the light of historical fact, is no pure and pious archangel of Erin, but a fascinatingly complicated character, strong proud and noble, ignoble shameless and base, loyal and treacherous, a cunning politician, a courageous soldier, an inspiring leader— -but at times so weakly neurotic he could burst openly into tears [...].[92]

Critics agree that *LDJIN* was completed some time in 1942, while O'Faoláin's book was published on 25 September of that year.[93] While it is not conclusive that O'Neill had read O'Faoláin's history *before* completing the play, its atmosphere of a family caught up in forces much bigger than they can understand suggests as much. The play's historical sweep is amplified when it is paired with *Desire Under the Elms*, an earlier but thematically connected O'Neill drama. It, too, centres on a patriarch with roots in disordered seventeenth-century Ulster who also replicates settler-colonialism on New England soil. *Desire Under the Elms* and its recent landmark production in Dublin will close the analysis of O'Neill.

Ulster Plantation Gothic: *Desire Under the Elms*

Protestant-dominated Ulster's growing differentiation from the rest of the island as the nineteenth century progressed culminated in 1921 with the Partition of Ireland. This monumental event for both Ireland and Irish America haunts O'Neill's 1924 play, *Desire Under the Elms,* which centres on land-hungry New England farmer Ephraim Cabot. Indeed, so Irish and Partition-era is this drama that T.C. Murray's *Autumn Fire*—a play of Irish setting but nearly identical plotline—was staged at the Abbey Theater on 8 September 1924, only a few weeks before the première of Neill's play at the Provincetown Players' Greenwich Village venue on 11 November 1924. However, *Desire Under the Elms* audits Partition as only the latest Irish upheaval by meditating on the interconnected 'Planting' (in the verb's Irish historical sense) of both Irish and American soil.

The seventeenth-century Plantation of the former O'Neill stronghold of Ulster by predominantly Scottish settlers, which entailed the seizure of Catholic-held lands, was justified as the righteous cultivation by God's chosen people of land left sinfully idle by the Gaelic Irish. This reasoning was repeated in the New World by British settler-colonials, as elucidated by Nicholas Canny's influential thesis that Ireland was a practising ground for English policy in the Americas.[94] Although the colonization of Ireland is submerged content in *Desire Under the Elms*, the allied Jacksonian annexation of Native American territory becomes manifest with patriarch Ephraim's boast that he'd 'killed Injuns in the West afore ye was born – an' [scalped] 'em too.'[95]

O'Neill's engagement with Scots-Irishness in *Desire Under the Elms* has been overlooked or, at best, misunderstood as engaging with the land politics of the post-Famine Irish. Wei H. Kao's reading of the 'desire for land' of the Cabots as evidence that they are what is now commonly understood by the term 'Irish immigrants' ignores the fact that Cabot is seventy-five years old at the time of the play's setting in 1850, during the very famine that profoundly shifted Irish emigration patterns.[96] As noted, Tyrone in *LDJIN*—whose pettiness in his role as Connecticut 'squireen' suggests wilful forgetting—has been born in 1847, a mere three years earlier than the setting of *Desire Under the Elms* and two years into the Famine. Placed end-to-end, the lifespans of Cabot and Tyrone meet at the handover point between two distinct waves of Irish immigration and the national trauma that punctuated those scatterings. If Cabot is Irish, then his birth year and the Bible fluency and land hunger that he shares with Samuel Hamilton, John Steinbeck's explicitly Ulster-Scots immigrant character in *East of Eden* (1952), suggests an Ulster Presbyterian origin. As such, the disputed ownership of the farm that constitutes the centre of the Cabots' world takes on symbolic value in light of what would have been the recent Partition of Ireland at the time of the play's premiere.

In *Desire Under the Elms*, Ephraim Cabot, a tyrannical patriarch in the Old Testament mould, returns to his rural New England farm in 1850 with a new young wife, Abbie. Ephraim is already the father of two older sons by a first wife, and a younger son, Eben, by his second spouse. Fearing disinheritance, Eben hates his new stepmother, but this soon gives way to lust. The ensuing affair unleashes tragic consequences when Abbie kills the child her step-son has secretly fathered. O'Neill's play partakes of Scots-Irish Gothic, and the tradition's recurring role of endangered *doppelganger* falls to the newborn, the 'dead spit "n" image' of Eben.[97] The baby's identity within the patrilineal line is so overdetermined by his being both the legal son and biological grandson of Ephraim that he does not even have a name in the action.

Cabot's farm has been his whole life and its continued possession and viability justifies all coldness and cruelty. Eben hates Ephraim because he believes that the obdurate patriarch dispossessed his mother (Ephraim's second wife) of the farm and then 'slav[ed] her to her grave',[98] though these are claims that Ephraim dismisses:

> CABOT: Ye lie! 'Twas yer Maw's folks aimed t'steal my farm from me.
> EBEN: Other folks don't say so.[99]

As with the island of Ireland, there are only conflicting claims of possession that emerge from contending versions of history and incompatible belief systems.

Ephraim's mindset and speech is saturated by the language of the Bible: when Abbie queries as to whether she will inherit the farm, he attempts to distract her with compliments that are a series of garbled lines from the Song of Songs.[100] Cabot's description to Abbie of how he obtained the farm does not recognize Eben's claim through his mother's line, and utilizes the Old Testament terminology of God's favour, prudence, and righteousness in justifying seizure:

> CABOT: I was jest twenty an' the strongest an' hardest ye ever seen—ten times as strong an' fifty times as hard as Eben. Waal—this place was nothin' but fields o' stones. Folks laughed when I tuk it. They couldn't know what I knowed. When ye kin make corn sprout out o' stones, God's livin' in yew![101]

In Cabot's settler-colonial mindset, the land is an uninhabited *tabula rasa*, there for the taking for one of God's chosen people. As the play's references to marauding Indians suggests, it is a space from which the original inhabitants (and subsequent female possessors) have been extirpated. Cabot's two older sons readily abandon the flinty patriarch for the boat to the gold fields of California as soon as he returns with his bride. This, in turn, constitutes their participation in the overrun of land that had been occupied by mostly Spanish-speaking people and Native Americans rather than the *tabula rasa* that they imagine California to be.[102] The weight of this ongoing history of seizure and dispossession and the language of Godliness that cloaks its naked rapacity are as woven into the dialogue of the play as in an ostensibly casual encounter between a young Ulster Catholic farm child and his elderly Presbyterian neighbour in 'The Other Side', a Seamus Heaney poem published in 1972, one of the most violent years in Northern Ireland's violent history. In comparing his own fertile acres to his neighbours' poorer soil, Heaney's old farmer judges with the moral certainty of an Old Testament prophet or, indeed, an O'Neill patriarch.[103]

An insightful production of *Desire Under the Elms* in this regard was the Corn Exchange staging at Smock Alley Theatre during the 2013 Dublin Theatre Festival under the direction of Annie Ryan. Although Ryan did not explicitly move the setting from New England to the North of Ireland, when we spoke in July 2021 the director told me that her production had been located in what she called 'a dream space' that was simultaneously Ulster and America.[104] Ephraim Cabot was played by Belfast native, Lalor Roddy, and for one Irish reviewer, Ryan's choice to have 'her cast locate their accents in the North' cracked open O'Neill's script: 'That the rhythm and flow of their speech feels naturally aligned with the playwright's rhythms is a revelation, another layer peeled back, another discovery made.'[105] Further evidence that Ulster haunts this play is that O'Neill himself cast the Scots-Irish actor Walter Huston (1884–1950; the Canadian-born father of filmmaker John Huston) as Ephraim in the original production, describing Huston in 1948 as one of the few actors who had ever realized his characters.[106] The sense of some third space that is both Ulster and America was reinforced by Northern Irish academic Michael Hinds's lyrical programme note for Ryan's production. *Desire Under the Elms,* Hinds wrote, could have been set 'anywhere in a hillbilly archipelago that runs peak-to-peak up the Appalachians and across the Atlantic to [Northern Ireland's] Sperrins, where young men still cry *yee-hah* as they gun their motors on Saturdays'.[107]

Born and trained in America, Ryan moved to Ireland in 1990, and the richness of vision that she brings to directing the first-generation immigrant Irish-American dramatist is rooted in her feeling that she is 'neither and both' Irish and American by now. This hybridity allowed her to perceive a buried concern with the Ulster Irish/Scots-Irish in *Desire Under the Elms* where an unhyphenated Irish or American director would only see unethnicized white Protestant Americanness. Ryan emphasizes that her *modus operandi* in directing American plays for Corn Exchange has been to 'culture swap': that is, to unlock Irish themes in dramas of rural America by playwrights such as Tennessee Williams and the Cuban-American María Irene Fornés. In combination with the Ulster emphasis that Ryan, the actors, and Hinds's programme note brought to the Corn Exchange

Figure 3.4 Cast of the Corn Exchange *Desire Under the Elms* production directed by Annie Ryan at the 2013 Dublin Theatre Festival: Fionn Walton (Eben Cabot); Janet Moran (Abbie Putnam); Lalor Roddy (Ephraim Cabot); Luke Griffin (Simeon); Peter Coonan (Peter). Photograph by Rich Gilligan. Courtesy of Annie Ryan and Rich Gilligan.

production, Rich Gilligan's uncanny promotional photograph of the cast emerging like ghosts out of the fog of the Dublin Mountains in their American farm garb is a further interpretation of *Desire Under the Elms* as a prime slice of Scots-Irish Gothic (Figure 3.4).

The *doppelganger* imperative explored by Poe, James, and O'Neill is also seen in the playwright's own patrilineal line: it is likely that James O'Neill named his son in honour of Owen Roe O'Neill/Eoghan Ruadh Ó Néill (*c.* 1585–1649), since 'Eugene' was a name by which the English authorities in Ireland knew that O'Neill dynasty leader.[108] Both *LDJIN* and *Desire Under the Elms* suggest that his weighty surname gave Eugene O'Neill imaginative access to Irish history. Another Irish dynasty, the Hiberno-Norman Fitzgeralds, served as both all-powerful representatives of colonial interests and prominent rebels against that order.[109] However, the acclaimed Irish-American author of that surname had a different relationship with his storied patronymic: F. Scott left his paternal ancestry beyond his grandfather's generation unexplored in print, and abandoned curiosity about Ireland and the Fitzgerald dynasty once youth had passed.[110] Nevertheless, the precarity of Irish racial status in America haunts Fitzgerald's fiction, and the following exploration opens with the complex connection between forgotten ancestors and that anxiety in his work.

The Curious Case of Great-Grandfather Fitzgerald

The marriages of the Fitzgerald patrilineal line in America
Edward Fitzgerald *c.* 1770–*c.* 1836; m. Maria (King?), 1774–1858 in 1796(?)
Michael (or Michel) T. Fitzgerald, 1805–1855; m. Cecilia Ashton Scott in 1850
Edward Fitzgerald 1853–1931; m. Mary McQuillan in 1890
F. Scott Fitzgerald, 1896–1940; m. Zelda Sayre in 1920

F. Scott Fitzgerald was born into what was ultimately a monied family in St. Paul, Minnesota, and was raised primarily in New York state. His mother was Mary McQuillan, the daughter of an 1840s Irish Catholic immigrant who had made a fortune in the wholesale grocery business. His genteel but professionally unsuccessful father, Edward Fitzgerald, was a Catholic from Maryland. F. Scott tended to stress family connections to the Maryland elite through his paternal grandfather's marriage into the Anglo-American establishment Scott family. Although the novelist always discussed the Irish ancestry that embarrassed him as being on his mother's side alone, this chapter unfolds the discovery that the direct Fitzgerald line in America was Irish and went right back into the late eighteenth century. This fact was unincorporated into the author's boasts regarding his deep roots in America. Fitzgerald attended Princeton University beginning in 1913 but, to his abiding disappointment, he failed to achieve either academically or on the football field, and effectively dropped out to join the Army in 1917. Moreover, biographers stress that his failure to see action during the Great War was a further source of personal discontent. In the years immediately after the publication of the first of four finished novels, *This Side of Paradise* (1920), which centres on World War I-era Princeton student, Amory Blaine, Fitzgerald enjoyed enormous fame as the voice of his era, and he and his socialite wife, Zelda Sayre, frequented Europe. However, by the 1930s they were both in free-fall, he from alcoholism and she from mental illness. In addition, the financial difficulties caused by the declining popularity of his work forced F. Scott to turn to full-time Hollywood screenwriting later in that decade. By the time he died of a heart attack at the age of forty-four in 1940, Fitzgerald was considered a 'has-been' whose finest hour had been his first novel. Poignantly, *The Great Gatsby* only began to be considered the Great American Novel after the author's passing.

By Fitzgerald's lifetime, 'Irish' ancestry is generally understood only under a post-Famine rubric, and biographers consistently discuss the author's complex regarding his Irish heritage as being rooted in his McQuillan maternal ancestry. This takes at face value F. Scott's repeated implication, by way of a stress on his father's 'old' Maryland links, that the pro-Confederate Edward Fitzgerald possessed a deeply contrasting heritage to that of his wife. (Critics have routinely parroted the author's own problematic implication of a connection between Edward's 'gentlemanly' ways and his politics, thereby naturalizing the association of slave-holding with so-called 'aristocratic' bearing.) Before turning to the McQuillan side and then to the connections between race and Irishness in Fitzgerald's fiction, this chapter reads two early stories, 'The Camel's Back' and the better-known 'The Curious Case of Benjamin Button' to assess the family heritages that the author emphasized and ignored. Critics and biographers invariably lavish great attention on the fact that Francis Scott Fitzgerald was namesake and second cousin three times removed of American national anthem author Francis Scott Key (1779–1843). The 1850 marriage of the author's paternal grandfather, Michael Fitzgerald (1805–1855), to Cecilia Ashton Scott (1832–1924), the daughter of Eliza Scott (*née* Key),[111] inaugurated the much-discussed Fitzgerald connection to the Key family and, through them, to the Maryland colonial elite. Though the Scotts were Catholic, Cecilia was the granddaughter of Philip Key (1750–1820), a prominent Maryland Episcopalian of English descent. In a forward to the tony 1939 title, *Colonial and Historic Homes of Maryland*, Fitzgerald describes himself as a native of Maryland 'through ancestry', discussing the family 'legends' of his Maryland-born father, 'memories' that go back before 1755 and that involve the Keys and their ilk.[112] He signs it 'Francis Scott *Key* Fitzgerald' (emphasis added) in order to underline his links to this *milieu*. This is the name on the gravestone that memorializes his burial in Montgomery County, Maryland in the year after he wrote the forward.

The son of Michael and Cecilia, the novelist's father, Edward Fitzgerald (1853–1931), was born on the farm near Gaithersburg, Montgomery County in 1853 that his parents had acquired a short while before his birth.[113] In the *Colonial and Historic Homes of Maryland* forward, as elsewhere, F. Scott is silent regarding the memories or pre-1853 location of any direct Fitzgerald ancestors prior to his father's generation. This has led, in quick surveys of Fitzgerald's background, to an interesting reversal of the gender dynamic that named Mary Walsh only as '[Henry James Sr's] Wife': Paternal Grandfather Michael is relegated to the role of sperm donor, the generally unnamed conduit through which the novelist may be connected to established Maryland families. Fitzgerald chronologies—even one co-created by 'Scottie', his daughter with Zelda[114]—generally use his father's birth year of 1853 as year zero of the author's patrilineal beginnings. This follows the dead end that F. Scott created by repeated sleights of hand, which stress his connections back into eighteenth-century Maryland through the Keys but say nothing of his direct paternal lineage. Indeed, F. Scott claimed much closer kinship to his second cousin three times removed than he actually possessed, referring to the national anthem author as a 'great, great uncle'.[115] The desirable Key connection illuminates a character of that surname in the early Fitzgerald story 'May Day', who, despite his unenviable present-day circumstances, carries 'a name hinting that in his veins, however thinly diluted by generations of degeneration, ran blood of some potentiality'.[116] Exactly where 'degeneration' comes from in such cases emerges in Fitzgerald's early stories.

'The Camel's Back' (1920) processes anxieties created by the marriage at the heart of Fitzgerald's complex regarding his paternal background, that of grandfather Michael Fitzgerald to Cecilia Scott in 1850. Beneath the story's surface farce lies unease regarding the social legitimacy of an alliance that flouts ethno-racial boundaries and WASP *mores*. 'The Camel's Back' concerns the impeccably white Perry, possessor of 'nice teeth' and 'a Harvard diploma'.[117] His intended, Betty, throws Perry over after he secretly obtains a marriage licence in an attempt to force her hand. Drunk and despairing due to this rejection, Perry appropriates a camel costume and pays an impoverished taxi driver to be the rump to his front. In this disguise Perry arrives *incognito* to a raucous high society costume party. Betty, it turns out, is in attendance in brownface 'barbaric paint' as an Egyptian snake charmer. She flirts with the front end of the camel, not realizing who is within the costume. Both snake charmer and camel are awarded 'Best Costume', and in the event's carnivalesque spirit, a mock wedding of the winners ensues. A Black waiter named Jumbo is enjoined to play minister, but after the vows, Perry admits to his possession of a real marriage license, at which point Jumbo reveals that because he is also a Baptist minister, the ceremony is binding. A story regarding a costumed groom who encompasses both working class and perfect WASP (taxi driver and Harvard man) illuminates Fitzgerald's anxieties concerning the marriage between Michael and Cecilia, upon which he ventured his sense of himself as one with a stake in Maryland's old stock. Despite the Black minister's accepted ability to perform a valid wedding ceremony, the story closes with a reconciliation in which Betty says that if Perry 'can wake up a [white] minister at this hour and have it done over again', she'll (re)marry him. Thus, the story is uneasy regarding the social legitimacy of anything that lay beyond white Protestantism—be that Catholicism or African-American non-conformism.

'The Curious Case of Benjamin Button' (1922), a narrative of a boy who ages backwards, reveals a similar anxiety regarding the male ancestor, and likewise corrects for the perceived shames of the Fitzgerald record, both ancestral and personal. The title character of Fitzgerald's story is the baby-cum-grandfather of the wealthy Buttons, whose money, like that of the McQuillans, originates in a wholesale business. Benjamin is born as an uncouth old man of seventy years in 1860 in antebellum Maryland (a strikingly similar *milieu* to that of the author's father) and proceeds to age backward until he loses consciousness and the narrative fades out in the haze of babyhood. Ironically, given what will be argued to be the story's excision of Irishness, 'The Curious Case of Benjamin Button' appears to draw upon the changeling baby tradition of rural Irish Catholic lore, in which malevolent fairies replace a human baby with a wizened, cantankerous elder of their own kind. Since the story was published in 1922, Benjamin's year zero would, it seems, be 1930, then eight years into the future, suggesting that the 'appalling apparition' has yet to be exorcised.[118] Ordered by the hospital staff to take the giant newborn home on the day of his birth, Benjamin's shocked father imagines how walking about with his uncanny baby would destabilize the certainties pertaining to class and race of his wealthy white family: 'People would stop to speak to him, and what was he going to say? He would have to introduce this—this septuagenarian [...] and they would plod on, past the bustling stores, the slave market—for a dark instant Mr. Button wished passionately that his son was black [...]'.[119] The implication is that Mr. Button is tempted to sell his wizened newborn into bondage, an appalling moment that casually conjures up the slave-holding reality of earlier Maryland. Benjamin makes good on such disruption as he ages backward, however, effectively reliving and then erasing the blots of Fitzgerald's own youth: accused of being an imposter due to his aged appearance when still only twenty in real years, he is kicked out of Yale. This proves to be the 'biggest mistake that Yale College had ever made' when, passing as young later, Benjamin is accepted to Harvard, where he single-handedly eviscerates the Yale football team in a game. By degrees, Benjamin learns how to conceal—in a very telling phrase—the 'grotesque story of his origin',[120] marrying well and becoming a professional success. However, as time flies on and Benjamin begins to resemble his own young male direct descendants, he becomes, once again, with a circular inevitability, 'a source of torment' to his kinfolk.[121] At one point, a ludic iteration of the *doppelganger* motif occurs when, sixty years after his birth, the by now seemingly ten-year-old Benjamin becomes the playmate of his own grandson.

'Almost nothing is known about' Michael Fitzgerald, according to the four-line entry on him in Mary Jo Tate's 2007 reference book on his famous grandson.[122] However, traces of Michael are discoverable. What is more, they intimate that F. Scott's paternal antecedents were deeply rooted in American soil. Michael Fitzgerald (along with Cecilia) appears in the 1850 US Census for Baltimore, Maryland as 'Michel'.[123] (Poignantly, a 'Grace Fitzgerald', born in 1815 in Maryland and also a Fitzgerald household member at the time of the census, is entirely absent from accounts of the novelist's antecedents.) Although F. Scott described his paternal grandfather as a 'wholesale hardware m[erchant]' in his *First Families of America* entry,[124] in the 1850 Census Michael's occupation is listed as 'farmer'. Most revealingly, in terms of the overlooked depth of F. Scott's paternal ancestry in America, the census confirms Michael's birthplace as Maryland. In Scottie's 1981 essay on her father's 'colonial ancestors', the Fitzgerald branch gets *not a single line*, but Michael's 1805 birth in Maryland means that the author's paternal grandfather almost certainly had parents who were resident in America during or soon after the colonial period. This is intimated in the one locatable published reference to F. Scott's paternal great-grandparents: Janet Thompson Manuel's chapter on local genealogy in a 1978 Montgomery County history describes Michael as the 'son of Edward and Maria (King) Fitzgerald of Baltimore'.[125] A 'spouses' cross-reference of both names on *FamilySearch.org* within a time range that would be reasonable in terms of their son's birth date throws up an 'Edward Fitzgerald' born in *c.*1770 in Ireland and who dies 'before 1836' in Baltimore, MD. His wife, Maria King, is given as being born in Ireland in 1774 and as dying in 1858. A subsequent consultation with Francis P. O'Neill, a reference librarian at the Maryland Center for History and Culture with a specialty in Maryland genealogy, corroborated these dates for Maria (though not her maiden surname). O'Neill's unpublished research, drawn from marriage and death notices and Baltimore directories, appears to indicate that Maria and Edward married on 27 October 1796 in St Paul's Episcopal Church in Baltimore and that 'Edward Fitzgerald of Ireland and Baltimore', styled 'Esquire' in his daughter's marriage announcement, is listed intermittently through the late 1830s as a 'collector' (landlord's agent).[126] (Assuming this is the correct couple and given the Catholicism of his descendants, it is possible that Edward was Catholic but married in his wife's church.)

My search for the Fitzgerald patrilineal line turned up details of the presence of other families of that name in Montgomery County in the colonial period. Although they may not be related to the author's direct line, they are of interest in imagining the county's Irish history, particularly in relation to the issue of slave-holding. The 1790 United States Census counts seven men named Fitzgerald (or its variants) who were Montgomery County residents, some of whom held one enslaved person.[127] After 1715, the still heavily forested country that would become Montgomery County in 1776 saw the first European settlers arrive from other parts of Maryland.[128] Although local histories suggest that Montgomery County was predominantly settled by the Scottish and English and was 'British' in 'character',[129] a smattering of surnames of Irish Gaelic and Hiberno-Norman origin in the 1790 Census returns suggest an Irish presence too.[130] Most of the British settlers were small farmers, though many such owned human chattel,[131] a broader cultural *milieu* that contextualizes Edward Fitzgerald's Confederate sympathies. Given the patronymic's origins, it is striking that Fitzgerald deploys a ludic surplus of 'Normanness' in 'The Diamond as Big as the Ritz' for the first name of slave-owning diamond mine operator, Fitz-Norman.[132] Even if no slave-holding Montgomery County Fitzgeralds were direct ancestors of the author (though they may have been connections of some sort), his father, born there just over a half century after this census, was raised in a community in which, within living memory, even modest farming families held enslaved people.[133] Divergent Irish and African experience in Montgomery County over centuries intersect in St Mary's Cemetery, which contains 'the remains of prominent Rockville citizens, Catholics from the nearby County Almshouse, slaves who were owned by local Catholic families, and F. Scott Fitzgerald.'[134]

The preceding discussion of F. Scott's paternal great-grandparents and their possible kin in 1790s Montgomery County has had to be somewhat speculative and tentative since the research was conducted under pandemic limitations and will, one hopes, be refined in the future. Nevertheless, this initial research does the service of pointing up the dearth of such investigation into Fitzgerald's deeper patrilineal roots in what is by now a century of published commentary on his life and work. The holdings and archives of the present reflect the prejudices of the past, and Maryland archives and histories and Fitzgerald biographies give overwhelming attention to the Key connection and related genealogy alone. At the least, Fitzgerald's very partial discussion of his paternal ancestors—and the manner in which scholars have accepted this at face value—suggests the effacement of Irish identities that do not fit the post-Famine paradigm. The roots in America of the author's great-grandparents, Edward and Maria, seem go back to at least the late eighteenth century, and F. Scott once slapped Zelda when she 'cuttingly referred to his father as an Irish policeman',[135] a stereotyped post-Famine Irish male immigrant occupation. There is a marked silence regarding the patrilineal line in Fitzgerald's fiction,[136] and a late essay intimates a sense of loss at all that he had put aside in this regard.[137] In WASP-centric American historiography, the Irish cannot be—to borrow Scottie's term—'colonial', even when they lived in colonial America, as many Maryland families named Fitzgerald certainly did. In the period after the 1845 Famine, all Irish Americans are lazily understood to have fled hunger, as becomes apparent on considering the discussion of Fitzgerald's maternal ancestry.

F. Scott wrote friend and critic Edmund Wilson that 'I'm not Irish on Father's side—that's where Francis Scott Key comes in [...]'.[138] He may have denied that he was Irish on his father's side, but could hardly do so in the case of his mother. Mary McQuillan was born in 1860 to an Irish immigrant of modest origins who became wealthy as a wholesale grocer in St Paul. Both Edward Fitzgerald and Mary McQuillan Fitzgerald were raised as Catholics, and sent their son to good private Catholic schools throughout his youth. Nevertheless, the new money and lack of cultural capital of the McQuillan background made reading James Joyce's *Ulysses* uncomfortable for F. Scott: 'there is something about middle-class Ireland that depresses me inordinately—I mean gives me a sort of hollow, cheerless pain. Half of my ancestors came from just such an Irish strata or perhaps a lower one. The book makes me feel appallingly naked.'[139] Suppressed folk Catholicism haunts the urbane and half-Irish Amory Blaine in *This Side of Paradise*: In the midst of a dissolute evening, Amory sees a strange man whose moccasins appear to conceal what are implied to be hooves and stutters, '"I think I've—I've seen the devil [...]"'.[140] This is the devil of folklore, a hooved man spotted at 'sinful' card games or country dance halls in rural Catholic Ireland right into the 1950s.[141] Fitzgerald attended a tony Jesuit-run school in New Jersey between 1911 and 1913, and his story, 'Benediction' (1920), struggles with the suspicion that Irish-American Catholicism was down-market, not just in comparison to the Protestantism that predominated at Princeton even into his youth,[142] but even in comparison to continental Catholicism.[143]

As with much to do with Fitzgerald's Irish background, confusion reigns with regard to the McQuillans' exact *milieu*. The author's McQuillan maternal grandfather, Philip (1834–77), had, as a child, emigrated with his family from Fermanagh in the province of Ulster in 1842,[144] so Fitzgerald's description of them to an interviewer in 1927 to as 'straight 1850 potato-famine Irish' is carelessly incorrect.[145] The McQuillans are 'Famine-era' since they emigrated in the *decade* of the famine's onset, but they left Ireland *before* that catastrophe began in 1845 so they cannot be understood to be refugees in the manner of James O'Neill. Moreover, the family's origins and their subsequent settlement in Illinois suggests the pre-Famine Ulster Irish-dominated immigration pattern. The McQuillans' departure prior to the Famine is an important distinction as it—and the multiple Illinois land purchases the family appear to have made soon after arrival[146]—suggests that their background, though possibly modest, was not as reduced as that of many who would flee Ireland as the food crisis wore on. Philip's wife, Louisa Allen (1841–1913), whom he married in *c.* 1860, was an Irish immigrant carpenter's daughter,[147] a skilled trade that likewise suggests a background that was *not* penurious. The acceptance of the baggage-laden label 'potato-Famine Irish' by Fitzgerald critics in reference to the McQuillans is typical of the pattern whereby critics of Irish-American writers, though scrupulous in rendering the facts of American history accurately, sometimes take less care with those of Irish history.

'Half Black Irish': Tan Lines and Sunburns in Fitzgerald

Fitzgerald's fantasies and anxieties regarding ancestral lines both hidden and overemphasized saturate the novels to be considered, *The Beautiful and Damned*, *The Great Gatsby*, and *Tender Is the Night*. Walter Benn Michaels implies that the stress on 'good' (white) 'breeding' and 'good' (white) family in inter-war American literature and society slid class difference into racial difference.[148] Thus, insults to the class status of white characters in Fitzgerald can be racially charged: in the 1922 'Winter Dreams', a well-paid teen caddie of 'off-white' immigrant descent quits his country club job after a member calls him 'boy', a belittling form of address for African-American males of all ages.[149] Although Fitzgerald embraced contemporaneous Irish cultural nationalism and its 'ethnic pride' boosting briefly in his youth, an early description of being 'Teutonic' on the outside but 'Celt' within—the author was fair-haired—suggests racial passing.[150] Fitzgerald's work probes the symbolic racialization caused by modest origins or social decline, as well as the differing social and racial meanings of brown skin, which depend on whether it is an *inherent* or *temporary* attribute. Racialization due to social decline structures the narrative arc of the 1922 novel, *The Beautiful and Damned*, while Fitzgerald's self-ascription as 'half black Irish' in a 1933 letter is read against the complicated maneuvre in *Tender Is the Night* (1934) of associating tanned skin with elite whiteness. Strikingly, the paradigm-shifting fashion for tanning was consolidated on the 1920s French Riviera by the author's social circle (Figure 3.5). Moreover, Fitzgerald's self-outing as a 'Gael' in the same 1933 letter opens up the disruptive

Figure 3.5 F. Scott, Zelda, and Scottie Fitzgerald at the beach, 1927. Courtesy of ALAMY.

presence of Gaelic identity in its broadest Scottish-Irish iteration in *The Great Gatsby*, undermining standard readings of narrator Nick Carraway and his cousin, Daisy, as unassailably WASP. These three novels are considered chronologically to illuminate how racial anxiety becomes progressively more explicit in Fitzgerald's work. A culminating self-hating alignment with post-Famine Irish stereotypes grew with the author's sense of personal and professional failure as he aged, as expressed in the 'Pat Hobby' story series upon which he worked up to his death, the consideration of which caps this chapter.

In a letter to fellow Irish-American author, John O'Hara, written while he worked on *Tender Is the Night,* Fitzgerald discusses his 'intense social self-consciousness' regarding his background:

> I am half black Irish and half old American stock with the usual exaggerated ancestral pretensions. The black Irish half of the family had the money and looked down upon the Maryland side of the family who had, and really had, that certain series of reticences and obligations that go under the poor old shattered word 'breeding'...I suppose this is just a confession of being a Gael...[151]

Since Fitzgerald was central to the 1920s about-face in the relationship between skin colour and beauty norms in white America, his self-ascription as 'half black Irish' to denote feelings of inferiority regarding his maternal ancestry requires analysis. The phrase 'black Irish' had currency among the Irish in the inter-war period when signalling their cohort's ambiguous placement within America's complex of race, ethnicity, and class: Fitzgerald used it in response to O'Hara's introduction of himself as 'the son of a black Irish doctor'.[152]

Although the term 'black Irish' is absent, it hovers over a *c.*1830 lampoon set near Philadelphia that includes a traveller or job-seeker of seemingly African-American features and stereotyped Irish clothing and speech (Figure 3.6). The exact origins of the term 'black Irish' (as applied to white Irish Americans) appear to be undocumented, but it almost certainly consolidated to racialize the post-Famine Irish in America since it implies an unstated, preexistent 'white Irishness'. Moreover, what may be one of the earliest mentions in print has a racial context and involves no less a person than James O'Neill. The actor made a splash when he alternated the role of Othello with the famed Edwin Booth in Chicago in 1874.[153] O'Neill's appearance in that decade—'black hair, black eyes, [and a] rather dark complexion'—becomes conjoined to this celebrated turn in an 1875 argument that Othello was not a 'negro' but merely dark-complexioned: 'black Irish' was given as an example of the latter.[154] Closer to midcentury, the term seems to begin shedding its overt racial overtones. Speaking in 1946 to Croswell Bowen, O'Neill's former New London neighbour describes the playwright as a 'Black Irishman', which he explains was one who had 'lost his [Catholic] Faith'.[155] However, this seems to be his modification of 'black Protestant', a commonplace sectarian insult (meaning 'immoderate' or 'bigoted') among Irish Catholics into that period.[156] A 1948 *New Yorker* profile of O'Neill shows the beginnings of the current American emphasis on colouring alone and the falling away of the any sectarian baggage in citing the Irish Protestant Yeats as an exemplar of the 'black Irish' type: one 'set apart from other Irishmen, according to the Irish, by their black hair, dark eyes, and mystic natures'.[157] (To reiterate: the white Irish in Ireland do *not* use this self-ascription.) Bowen himself takes the phrase to mean a 'brooding,

Figure 3.6 Cartoon set in Philadelphia's environs depicting a Black man dressed in the style of the Irishman of lampoon, c. 1830. Attributed to Edward W. Clay. Courtesy of Library Company of Philadelphia.

solitary [...] drinking man', listing Fitzgerald and O'Hara as 'Black Irishmen', with O'Neill as 'the blackest one of all'.[158] Strikingly, neither Bowen nor his New London informant refer to the playwright's *appearance*, though Yvonne Shafer claims that O'Neill was able to play the 'mulatto' in the original 1913 production of *Thirst* 'without make-up because of his black hair and tan',[159] a moment in which O'Neill is 'black Irish' in two registers.

The seeming deracializing of the term 'black Irish' in reference to the white Irish in the aforementioned post-war contexts may be connected to its emergence to describe Afro-Caribbeans of Irish ancestry, as given in *Whence the 'Black Irish' of Jamaica?*, a 1932 title by an Irish Jesuit missionary priest. However, Fr. Williams's attempt to link current-day Jamaicans of Irish surname with Cromwellian-era deportees met with resistance in Ireland: one reviewer insisted that the surnames were merely evidence of 'the prevailing habit of giving to emancipated slaves the family name of their masters'.[160] A Black Caribbean islander might indeed have acquired an Irish surname by this route: a rapacious 'neo-feudal' Irish planter class of predominantly Catholic Old English/Hiberno-Norman origin held sway on the Caribbean island of Montserrat in the seventeenth century, and Marcus Garvey's surname came by way of a Caribbean-Irish slave-holding family.[161] However, the Irish reviewer's refusal to countenance the *possibility* of mixed-race Irishness speaks to the suppression of historical Afro-Irish Caribbean links forged in the racial cauldron that created the Redlegs. In a contemporary America in which the Irish are still too often perceived to be simply 'white'—a truism promoted by the coffee table book *The Irish Face in America* but complicated by the work of Diane Negra, Sinéad Moynihan, and Jennifer Nugent Duffy[162]—'black Irish' denotes a person of white Irish heritage with 'dark hair and blue eyes'.[163] To this is sometimes appended a long-debunked theory of descent from Spanish Armada survivors in Ireland.[164] Performer and entrepreneur Mariah Carey, of white Irish and Afro-Venezuelan heritage, is a rare prominent contemporary American to utilize the self-ascription 'Black Irish' to refer to dual racial heritage, though she does so in the interest of promoting her cream liqueur of that brand name![165] Moreover, Carey's use of the term as a seemingly straightforward descriptor effaces its ambiguous history. As such, the impugned whiteness implied in Fitzgerald's use of the phrase as self-ascription undergirds the following consideration of his work.

Fitzgerald's 1922 novel, *The Beautiful and Damned*, tracks the deterioration of 1910s golden couple Anthony and Gloria Patch into disinheritance, pariah status, alcoholism, marital breakdown, and eventually, racial demotion. (The inheritance is ultimately regained, but the Patches have been blighted by their ordeal by then.) At the outset, the couple is spectacularly white: Gloria is a 'Nordic Ganymede' and Anthony is the presumptive heir to a tycoon.[166] However, an incident during Anthony's World War I service that marks a turning point in his fortunes is presaged in his musing that 'all strongly accentuated classes' divide men into 'their own kind—and those without': To 'the Catholic there were Catholics and non-Catholics, to the negro there were blacks and whites, [...] and to the sick man there were the sick and the well.'[167] At this moment, the privileged Anthony is on the winning side of these binaries, which makes him oblivious to other realities: well read in the Euro-centric history he had learned at Harvard, slavery is a phenomenon he associates only with Ancient Rome, and he is so willfully ignorant of links that may have been created by English and French control of Caribbean slavery that he arrogantly declares the 'British accent' of a 'Martinique negro' to be 'incongruous'.[168] However, Anthony is forced to the losing side of the binaries after making a foolish choice: returning to camp after curfew one night, he gives the false Gaelic Irish surname 'Foley'. His lie discovered, he is subsequently reduced in rank and has his movements confined for a month. Further degradation follows: 'With this blow a spell of utter depression overtook him, and within a week he was again caught down-town, wandering around in a drunken daze, with a pint of boot-leg whiskey in his hip pocket.'[169] In earlier scenes of carousing with old Harvard cronies—one of whom gave up on charity work in Catholic immigrant slums due to the impossibility of 'making sow-ear purses out of sows' ears'—the Patches had drunk brand-name whisky (Canadian Club), and imagined their hard partying to be in the style of 'the British aristocracy of a hundred years ago'.[170] However, by publicly consuming *whiskey* (the 'e' denotes that the illicit spirit has been distilled in the Irish style), Patch has truly transformed into the shanty Irish 'Foley'. By the lowest point of the Patches' degradation, a former female friend berates them for their down-at-heel, heavy-drinking lifestyle like a '"lady slum-worker"';[171] the fallen Patches have become the object of the paternalism usually directed at poor Catholic immigrants. Drinking in dive bars with inane drunks towards the close of the action, Anthony hears harangues about socialism and 'the Irish problem', though the actual 'Irish problem' Anthony soon encounters is the 'Mick' bank manager who forces him to close his overdrawn account,[172] just one more humiliation in his socio-racial descent.

In Fitzgerald's *The Great Gatsby* (1925), WASP Tom Buchanan, whose wife, Daisy, is coveted by the self-made title character, impugns Gatsby's 'breeding' (whiteness).[173] Gatsby's racial identity has been the subject of speculation: Michaels reads him as Jewish, while Carlyle Van Thompson suggests that Gatsby is a light-skinned Black man passing as white.[174] Although George Bornstein's work stresses the connections between being Black, Jewish, or Irish in Fitzgerald's America,[175] Gatsby's ambiguity is ultimately rooted in Fitzgerald's anxiety regarding his own ancestry, which marks the novel in ways that remain unexcavated. Fitzgerald's self-ascription as 'Gael' in his 1933 letter opens up not *Irish* but *Gaelic* identity in its broadest Scottish and Irish iteration in *The Great Gatsby*. It does so in relation to Nick Carraway, muddying readings of the novel's narrator—and his cousin Daisy—as deeply rooted American WASPs. In one of the novel's most ambiguous moments, Buchanan praises *The Rise of the Coloured Empire*, a fictional pseudo-scientific book on the threat to the 'white race' that draws upon Emerson's model of 'white' to mean peoples of deep Scandinavian ancestry. Addressing Nick, who sits with Daisy and her friend, Jordan, Tom explains: '"This idea is that we're Nordics. I am, and you are, and you are, and—" After an infinitesimal hesitation he included Daisy with a slight nod [...]'.[176] In order to probe Buchanan's seeming apprehension regarding his wife's placement in the ethno-racial hierarchy, we must go back to her cousin Nick's opening description of the specifics of his—and, we assume, her—Scottish ancestry.

Medieval Gaeldom spanned Ireland and Scotland's Highlands and Western Isles, linking these regions culturally and linguistically, but Gaelic Scotland was decimated by the Jacobite defeat at the Battle of Culloden in 1746, after which Lowland Scottish culture dominated. A further catastrophe that spanned the tattered remnants of what had been medieval Gaeldom was the potato blight that struck the Highlands in 1846 at about the same time as Ireland, the subsequent response to which was both coerced and voluntary emigration, which T.M. Devine frames as the second wave of the Highland Clearances (the first having been post-Culloden uprootings).[177] The harshest of these displacements came in the 1840s and 1850s, at precisely the time Nick notes that a Carraway forebear leaves Scotland (1851). This man, his family 'tradition' held, was 'descended from the Dukes of Buccleuch'. This is a real and extant title in the Peerage of Scotland, but 'tradition' is suspiciously vague. Much more convincing due to its concrete details is the Carraway lore concerning the founder of the line in America, his 'grandfather's brother, who came here in fifty-one, sent a substitute to the Civil War, and started the wholesale hardware business that my father carries on today.'[178] Thus, one of the traumatic pasts into which characters in *The Great Gatsby* are 'borne back ceaselessly' is that of Famine-era Scotland.[179] As well as piercing the assumption that cousins Nick and Daisy are the epitome of WASP privilege, this origin also muddies readings in which the character of Gatsby alone is interpreted as a working-through of Fitzgerald's own anxiety regarding his background. Moreover, placing the Carraway ancestry alongside that of Fitzgerald himself exposes the chasm between fantasy ('great, great uncle' Francis Scott Key / 'the Dukes of Buccleuch') and the mundane reality of immigration out of the Union's blighted Gaelic margins and family money acquired through trade. Altogether, Carraway, of Famine-era Scottish immigrant extraction, more plausibly stands in for Fitzgerald than what turns out to be, in the end, a title character of immigrant Lutheran German origin.[180]

Among *The Great Gatsby*'s main characters, only Tom Buchanan is unassailably WASP, and in the identity's most unsheathed iteration of white supremacist at that. His surname suggests that he, too, is Scottish-American, but the lack of detail regarding Buchanan's origins obliges us instead to consider his name's contemporaneous associations. For the American reader of the 1920s, the surname would have evoked James Buchanan (1791–1868), the last President during the long era of slavery. After Jackson, Buchanan may be the most immediately Scots-Irish of the many of that heritage who took up residence in what a 1924 Klan newsletter called the 'Nordic White House':[181] Buchanan was the son of a Donegal Presbyterian father who emigrated to Pennsylvania in 1783 and a mother whose Presbyterian antecedents had left Ulster for the same state in 1756.[182] Buchanan's legacy in relation to African Americans intimates why Fitzgerald borrowed his surname for Daisy's white supremacist husband, since historians judge Buchanan to have been so partial to supporting the white South and slavery as to have been treasonous. The President backed the upcoming Supreme Court decision in the Dred Scott case in 1857, which denied the petition of the enslaved man of that name for freedom. Furthermore, he joined in the attempt to admit Kansas to the Union as a slave state, antagonizing both Republicans and northern Democrats. Weeks after Lincoln took over from Buchanan as president, Southern states began seceding from the Union, and the Civil War ensued.[183] Altogether, as with his evocations of Jackson (in *The Love of the Last Tycoon*) and Washington (in 'The Diamond as Big as the Ritz'), race erupts when Fitzgerald conjures up this American president too.

If ethno-racial concerns rumble beneath *The Great Gatsby*, then repeated attention to the skin tones of both Black and white characters in Fitzgerald's *Tender Is the Night* makes racial anxiety even more explicit. Set in the French Riviera, Paris, and Rome, the novel opens in the mid-1920s with vacationer Rosemary Hoyt, a teen film star based on Grace Kelly's *doppelganger*, Lois Moran (1909–1990). (The Pittsburgh-Irish Moran, with whom Fitzgerald conducted an affair in 1927 during an initial Hollywood foray, shared Kelly's heritage and cultivation.[184]) Hoyt arrives in summer when the Riviera is deserted as the fashion for vacationing in order to suntan is being created *at that very moment* by the elite circle she meets, led by the charming and permanently tanned white American couple, Dick and Nicole Diver. Soon after, the action goes backwards to 1917, when Dick is an emerging psychiatrist in Zurich and Nicole is a wealthy young patient with whom he becomes entangled. A shadier picture of the golden couple's relationship develops, and the action then jumps to the late 1920s, when the Divers' mid-decade veneer of glamour has been lost: Nicole is behaving erratically and Dick is descending into alcoholism, professional failure, and public outbursts of 'contempt for some person, race, class, [or] way of life'.[185] Suzanne del Gizzo notes that Dick's use of racio-ethnic slurs increase as he declines,[186] so before delving into the action that leads to Dick's own racial demotion, the new social meaning of brown skin in the 1920s must be considered.

In her seminal history of American beauty culture, *Hope in a Jar* (1998), Kathy Peiss details that in the nineteenth century, skin whitener was the most popular cosmetic among Black and white American women, from society belles to Irish immigrants. Strikingly, however, Peiss notes that Madam C.J. Walker (1867–1919), an African-American entrepreneur and activist who made millions manufacturing and selling beauty products to Black women, refused to market such bleach.[187] The opening of *Gone with The Wind* literally sets *the tone* in recounting that Southern-Irish belle Scarlett O'Hara possesses 'magnolia-white skin—that skin so prized by Southern women and so carefully guarded with bonnets, veils and mittens against hot Georgia suns'.[188] Thus, the terrifying threat that looms on the horizon in the 1861 opening of Margaret Mitchell's novel is not the soon-to-arrrive Civil War, but the sun. (The earliest homemade beauty treatment Peiss details is a Civil War-era recipe for sun-exposed skin.[189]) In Scarlett's antebellum world, only 'white trash' with no stake in the black/white binary allow their skin to get brown: the enslaved Mammy warns Scarlett to wear a shawl over her bare shoulders when outdoors, lest she end up '"lookin' brown lak Ole Miz Slattery"', who is, significantly, 'poor white' Irish.[190] Well-born white men, too, took care in this regard: an 1817 English traveller in the South noted that plantation owners in Virginia were much paler than both poor whites *and* their class equivalents in England since they wore hats with extraordinarily wide brims when outdoors.[191]

In her 1858 advice book *The Arts of Beauty,* the cosmopolitan Anglo-Irish courtesan, Lola Montez (born Eliza Rosanna Gilbert), warns that going outdoors without bonnet or veil is 'ruinous' for a woman's skin.[192] Today, however, the tanned skin of a privileged white globe-trotter sometimes approximates to the skin tone of a mixed-race person, but the respective trajectories by which that complexion arises exposes the fissures of racial history: as African-American poet Caroline

Randall Williams devastatingly puts it, 'I have rape-colored skin'.[193] Historians of beauty can pinpoint the exact moment when monied, dermally white Americans first *chose* to tan their skin as evidence of leisure. Given the Irish-American drive for social whiteness, it is extraordinary that this trend was popularized in the Anglophone world by two Catholic Irish-American men and their wives in the mid-1920s French Riviera: F. Scott and Zelda Fitzgerald along with Gerald Murphy, a wealthy Irish American living in that location with his wife, Sara.[194] The latter woman's *penchant* for tanning in pearls is often cited as the inspiration for the erotic description in *Tender Is the Night* of Nicole sunning with her bathing suit 'pulled off her shoulders and her back, a ruddy, orange brown, set off by a string of creamy pearls [...]'.[195] So quickly did tans become fashionable that *Vogue* magazine was soon carrying advertisements for tanning lamps.[196] Thus, in the 1920s, as Susan L. Keller notes, and 'despite the long history of darkness being associated with racial and class inferiority', tanning was 'a new social practice' that Fitzgerald documented and popularized by associating it with the elite in *Tender Is the Night*.[197] This trend has consistently been read as emerging from the fact that as whites began to work in factories and offices more than on farms, tanned skin became less associated with outdoor labour.[198] Writing in 1843 of Irish immigrants working on a Massachusetts railway line extension, Thoreau stresses that this cohort is 'tanned'.[199] However, after the millions of factory jobs created in America from 1900 to 1920 were filled by eastern and southern European immigrants, the increasing paleness of 'off-white' immigrants precipitated the sudden *cachet* of tans among the privileged.[200]

In the early 1930s, bleach creams continued to be marketed to white American women through 'traditional appeals' to 'Anglo-Saxon superiority' and the kind of 'Old South' imagery that went global after the release of the film adaptation of *Gone with the Wind* later that decade.[201] Thus, at first glance, tanning (as 1920s-inaugurated social practice) undoes the conventional racial order. This seems especially true in its French iteration, which was inspired, not just by designer Coco Chanel, but by Paris's favourite 'caramel'-skinned expatriate, African-American performer Josephine Baker (Figure 3.7).[202] However, in *White* (1997), his influential book on the assumed unremarkability of images of pale-skinned people, Richard Dyer claims that a 'tanned white person is just that – a white person who has acquired a darker skin. There is no loss of prestige [...]'.[203] Nonetheless, the 'risk' of tanning is probed in Fitzgerald's *The Beautiful and Damned*. Prompted by a dazzling socialite's tan, Anthony's white friend, Maury, muses that he used to '"get a pretty good tan"', and Anthony's teasing response suggests an underlying anxiety regarding sun-darkened white skin: '"Heiress elopes with coast-guard because of his luscious pigmentation! Afterward found to be Tasmanian strain in his family!"'[204] Tasmania, now an island state of Australia, was originally populated by Aboriginal peoples, and as Van Diemen's Land it became a notorious nineteenth-century British penal colony; thus, it has both 'brown native'

Figure 3.7 Josephine Baker with long-term friend, Princess Grace of Monaco, *c.*1970. Courtesy of ALAMY.

and 'red' deportee associations. Altogether, given the history of sun-altered skin as liability for the indentured and deported of pale complexion in the seventeenth-century Americas, tanning was a tricky negotiation for a pale Irishman such as Fitzgerald, an anxiety that plays out in *Tender Is the Night.*

Although Fitzgerald wrote that *Tender Is the Night* is a 'woman's book',[205] the mainly male critics of his generation generally read it as an indictment of Nicole's parasitic reliance on Dick in order to regain her mental health. In addition, Fitzgerald's depiction of the thinly sketched 'Afro-European' Jules Peterson, whose corpse winds up dumped in Rosemary's hotel room bed, has been read as a mere logistical headache for the three-dimensional white characters. In fact, attention to the structure of the novel suggests that Fitzgerald parallels how institutional discrimination destroys *both* Jules and Nicole. As Sarah B. Fryer audits, the latter is utterly failed when she seeks help from the male-dominated field of psychiatry as a result of being raped as a child by her father:[206] He openly confesses to the crime to his daughter's psychiatrist in Switzerland, fearing no repercussions, and that analyst later casually posits Nicole's 'complicity' in discussing the rape with Dick.[207] In Jules's case, the *gendarmes* and Dick's drunkard friend, Abe, find it merely farcical that the 'Afro-European' is being hounded by other Black men in Paris for ratting on one of their number in aid of Abe. This good citizenship eventually leads to Peterson's murder. Structural (and moral) balancing occurs when it later emerges that Abe, who had nonchalantly walked away after Jules's homicide, has met with an ignoble death in a speakeasy brawl.[208] Having moved Peterson's corpse from Rosemary's bed in order to cover up its initial location so as to prevent scandal attaching to the film star, Dick deploys his white male authority and the medical training that bolsters it: when he calls the hotel manager to report a 'negro' in the hallway, he uses the title 'Doctor' for the first time in the action.[209] The utter disregard with which both Jules and Nicole have been treated coalesce when Dick unthinkingly forces his wife to relive her childhood rape in the parental bed when he has her clean Peterson's blood from Rosemary's bedsheets, at which point Nicole loses control.[210] Nicole's unconscious identification with the racism that the 'Afro-European' ('Black Irish'?) Jules endures explains her seemingly confused declaration that 'my baby is black'.[211] Although the white male characters' treatment of Jules reveals their racism, on a structural level that which threatens is the ambiguous tanned zone between Black and white rather than unambiguous Blackness. As the novel notes of the Franco-American Tommy Barban's complexion: 'His handsome face was so dark as to have lost the pleasantness of deep tan, without attaining the blue beauty of Negroes—it was just worn leather.'[212]

Fitzgerald stages Dick Diver's social decline as a sequence of racially charged clashes during which the clout of his whiteness ebbs away. The pivot in Diver's fortunes begins in Rome when his haggling with a taxi driver escalates and he ends up in a jail cell, from which he shouts that the police are '"dirty Wops!"'[213] Significantly, after this episode, Dick defines himself explicitly as white (a 'mature Aryan'), and feels a 'vast criminal irresponsibility' at his 'humiliation':[214] Dick's identity as uncontestably white has begun to unravel, and the remaining action audits his ensuing rampages of anger, drunkenness, and racism. After the seventeenth century in the Americas—and with only a few exceptions such as the Redlegs—to be dark-skinned was analogous with subservience. Dick has internalized this belief, and one of the earliest incidents in his decline denotes the moment in which this is challenged. Drinking heavily in a Roman nightclub, he peremptorily summons over a Black Bahamian orchestra leader that he considers to be 'conceited and unpleasant' and an antagonistic exchange ensues.[215] The key to this scene is the man's national origin: as Walter Johnson details, the Bahamas was the location of the most successful slave revolt in US history in terms of numbers freed.[216] By his mutinous refusal to be servile, the orchestra leader unconsciously evokes this national memory in Dick. After this episode, the thin veneer of civilization that always only barely covers the violence necessary to maintain the racial hierarchy erupts in Dick's slew of slurs.

The Divers subsequently visit the second husband of Abe's widow, the 'Asiatic' Conte di Minghetti, whose title is 'merely [...] papal' and whose complexion is 'not quite light enough to travel in a Pullman south of the Mason-Dixon'.[217] Dick uses the word 'spic' in the Conte's presence,[218] and berates a veiled woman in his entourage whom he takes to be a servant. She turns out to be the Conte's sister, and Dick and Nicole are obliged to hastily depart.[219] The very next scene, back in the Riviera, opens with an actual servant, but one who is far from submissive, since she is brandishing a knife at Dick, angered that he has berated her for drinking the household wine.[220] Altogether, Dick's ability to recognize or control his 'inferiors' is slipping as he sheds whiteness. Yet another structural and moral balancing occurs at this juncture, when Dick himself suffers the institutional discrimination and dismissal to which Jules had been subject years earlier: he threatens the mutinous servant with the police, and she snorts derisively that her brother is a *gendarme*. Dick calls the station anyway, and, as predicted, the police merely laugh at his complaint.[221]

Dick claims descent from 'Mad' Anthony Wayne (1745–96), a real-life American military officer and statesman of settler-colonial Irish stock, though Nicole's 'worldly' sister 'measured [Dick] with the warped rule of an Anglophile and found him wanting [...]'.[222] Dick's colouring may be the cause: His 'complexion was reddish and weather-burned', as 'was his short hair', the very hallmarks of defective indentured whiteness.[223] Indeed, for all of the theorizing of Fitzgerald's *tan*, a contemporary description of his appearance on the Riviera in 1926 suggests that a discussion of the fair-haired author's *sunburn* would have been more apt.[224] Thus, even with the kind of 'Teutonic' colouring of which Emerson would have approved, one could still remain 'black Irish'.[225]

As Keller documents, fashion arbiters of the 1920s from Chanel to *Vogue* magazine 'laid out an intricate series of rules' to distinguish 'the cosmopolitan tan from its quotidian lower-class counterpart'. A central tenet was that tan lines were to be avoided as they suggested outdoor labour, in response to which French designer Jean Patou introduced swimsuits cut for maximum skin exposure.[226] Tan lines take on a more complicated meaning as *Tender Is the Night* concludes, however. As the action culminates, Nicole has tired of Dick's obnoxiousness, and countenances a break with him by writing Barban a 'provocative letter', setting in train her eventual divorce.[227] After consummating the affair with Tommy, Nicole is revealed to have been only temporarily 'half black': 'He inspected the oblong white torso joined abruptly to the brown limbs and head, and said, laughing gravely: "You are all new like a baby."'[228] The erotic charge of the passage is not that Nicole is naked, but that she is revealed to have *become* white again: the '[cosmetic] powder had dampened on her to make a milky surface', and 'as Tommy kissed her she felt him losing himself in the whiteness of her cheeks and her white teeth [...]'.[229] While tethered to Dick, Nicole had been 'half black', both symbolically (through association with her racially compromised husband) and literally (due to her tan lines). However, in her nakedness it emerges that hers has only been a *temporary* darkness, and unencumbered by Dick, she is racially reborn.

Coda: Stage Irish: Fitzgerald in Hollywood

From 1937 until he died of a heart attack in December 1940 at the age of forty-four, Fitzgerald turned to full-time Hollywood screenwriting. The 'Pat Hobby' series, seventeen short stories published between January 1940 and May 1941,[230] convey the disappointment of this final act. The title character is a self-defeating and penniless Hollywood screenwriter who 'had never written much'.[231] Briefly successful during cinema's silent age, Hobby is now reduced to hack work. (His surname suggests amateurishness.) Hobby is an alcoholic, gambler, and reprobate, and most stories depict him as engaged in some ploy for money, which usually ends only in further embarrassment. Foolish, dishonest, grovelling, drunken, and incompetent, Pat is followed by repeated and pathetic ill-luck that is mostly of his own making. Physically, he is vaguely repulsive, in possession of 'red-rimmed eyes and a soft purr of whiskey on his breath'.[232] Much of his low character and air of failure is conveyed in the opening of '"Boil Some Water – Lots of It"':

> Pat Hobby sat in his office in the Writer's Building and looked at his morning's work, just come back from the script department. He was on a 'polish job', about the only kind he ever got nowadays. He was to repair a messy sequence in a hurry, but the word 'hurry' neither frightened nor inspired him, for Pat had been in Hollywood since he was thirty—now he has forty-nine. All the work he had done this morning (except a little changing around of lines so he could claim them as his own)—all he had actually invented was a single imperative sentence, spoken by a doctor.[233]

Alcoholism, increasing obscurity, and financial woes had assailed Fitzgerald since his own 1920s heyday, and obituary notices at the time of his death gave little impression that this writer 'might ever be read again'.[234] In short, Pat is a self-hating pen picture that conjures up the most atavistic stereotype of the 'off-white' Irish, conforming in many ways to the 'Stage Irishman' cliché, down to his very name:

> The stage Irishman habitually bears the generic name of Pat, Paddy or Teague. He has an atrocious Irish brogue, makes perpetual jokes, blunders and [absurd

> statements] in speaking, and never fails to utter, by way of Hibernian seasoning, some wild screech or oath of Gaelic origin at every third word: he has an unsurpassable gift of 'blarney' and cadges for tips and free drinks. His hair is of a fiery red; massive, and whiskey-loving. His face is one of simian bestiality, with an expression of diabolical archness written all over it.[235]

The original publisher of the Pat Hobby stories, *Esquire* magazine's Arnold Gingrich, notes that, while the series is not a novel, it constitutes 'a full-length portrait'. Fitzgerald, Gingrich claims, 'thought of it as a comedy'.[236] If so, its laughter is in the bitter Irish mould of Tom Murphy's play, *Bailegangaire* (1985), in which a long tale of merciless bad luck culminates with manic laughter. The Pat creation converges with Fitzgerald's own heavy drinking and sense of failure at his life's close. Poignantly, this is a portrait of the artist as the worst old stereotype of the heritage from which he had always attempted to distance himself. Alan Margolies details that Fitzgerald worked extremely hard in Hollywood on a variety of projects, but to little credit, and indeed, the Warner Bros./Turner Entertainment F. Scott Fitzgerald Screenplay Collection at the University of South Carolina contains 2,000 pages of the manuscripts, revised typescripts, and working screenplay drafts that Fitzgerald wrote for Metro-Goldwyn-Mayer from 1937 to 1938. Thus, there is a huge chasm between the work-shy Pat and Fitzgerald's own conscientiousness. Altogether, as a sudden, unanticipated halt to Fitzgerald's decades of grappling with his ethnic identity in print, the Pat Hobby stories evoke only discomfort.

David O. Selznick bought the movie rights for Mitchell's *Gone with the Wind* and in January of 1939 Fitzgerald participated in two frustrating weeks of writing on the script: he was required to adhere closely to Mitchell's style, to his deep irritation.[237] Fitzgerald read the novel in preparation for the adaptation, and wrote Scottie that he found it unoriginal if 'workmanlike'.[238] Fitzgerald was only one of a number of writers pulled in to help with the mammoth task of condensing Mitchell's 1,037-page novel into a manageable screenplay. It must have been yet a further galling affirmation of his decline that his near-contemporary, Sidney Howard (1891–1939), was the writer honoured with a posthumous Academy Award for adapted screenplay in February of 1940. More galling still must have been that Fitzgerald's lifelong struggle with the topic of race and Irishness never achieved the kind of success that Mitchell's dishonest representation of that history won. After all, Fitzgerald's 'The Diamond as Big as the Ritz' had earlier mocked the fudge that scaffolds Mitchell's romance, which is that enslaved people welcome bondage.[239] In the following chapter, Mitchell's tome is considered, not just as a bad faith representation of African-American history but, consequently, as a bad faith rendering of Irish history too.

4

Complicit Irishness: Plantation Novels by Yerby, Mitchell, and Faulkner

Writing in 1854, a year after his escape from bondage in Van Diemen's Land, John Mitchel aspired to 'a good plantation well stocked with healthy negroes in Alabama'.[1] Six years later, 110 men, women, and children from Benin and Nigeria were brought ashore in that very state under cover of night. This last illegal transport of human chattel from Africa to the United States was undertaken as a wager by first-generation Irish-American businessman, Timothy Meaher (or O'Meagher; 1812–92), who was of Kilkenny Jacobite Catholic gentry descent.[2] The self-evident myopia of nineteenth-century Irish-American nationalism in relation to slavery that those words and events suggest unfold in this chapter. It considers three novels that depict planters of broadly Irish connection in the antebellum and post-Civil War South: Margaret Mitchell's Gerald O'Hara in *Gone with the Wind*, William Faulkner's Thomas Sutpen in *Absalom, Absalom!* (both 1936), and Frank Yerby's Stephen Fox in *Foxes of Harrow* (1946). The works differ in register: Faulkner writes difficult Gothic modernism that simultaneously mourns and condemns the 'Old South', while the more accessible historical romances of Yerby and Mitchell portray slavery in diametrically opposed ways. Nevertheless, all three fictions centre on penniless and initially 'off-white' protagonists of pre-Famine Irish or pan-Gaelic association who transform themselves into the white exploitative landowner class to whom they themselves had once been subject. Moreover, all three authors were of Southern birth in a period in which that region remained racially segregated, and all claimed pre-Famine Irish or Scottish Gaelic descent. However, their family origins deviate from the dominant image of the American writer of Irish connection in various ways, as the opening survey of their backgrounds suggests. That will be followed by a discussion of the overlaps and divergences between the three plantation novels before the chapter considers each work individually.

Frank Yerby (1916–1991) had published thirty-two historical novels of diverse setting and period by the time of his death. By 1954 alone, he had produced eight historical novels that had sold eight million copies in hardback and was estimated to be America's highest-earning novelist.[3] However, Yerby was long associated with antebellum Southern settings due to the success of his break-out bestseller of 1946, *The Foxes of Harrow*. Covering a forty-year period (1825–1865) from the height to the nadir of white Southern fortunes, this historical romance chronicles Stephen

Race, Politics, and Irish America. Mary M. Burke, Oxford University Press.
 DOI: 10.1093/oso/9780192859730.003.0005

Fox, a poor Dublin immigrant who rises to the uppermost stratum of Louisiana society by acquiring a slave plantation. *The Foxes of Harrow* was adapted to the big screen a year later (in a production starring the Irish actor, Maureen O'Hara), making Yerby the first African-American author to achieve this distinction.

Yerby was born in Jim Crow-era Augusta, Georgia, to Rufus Garvin Yerby (1886–1961) and Wilhelmina 'Willie' Yerby (née Smythe; 1888–1960). Rufus was blue-collar African American by descent, while Yerby's mother was of Scots-Irish ancestry. The family home was in the Terry, once an area of Irish settlement known as Verdery's Territory that became a thriving Black district after the Civil War. In 1937, Yerby graduated from Paine College with a BA in English. His brother, Alonzo, went on to become the first African-American head of Harvard School of Public Health's Department of Health Policy and Management and helped to write America's Medicare programme in 1965.[4] Alonzo was named for the family's maternal side,[5] which suggests that the Smythe-Yerby family saw itself as being what Frank referred to as a 'mini-United Nations',[6] despite the 'one-drop' mentality of Southern culture.[7] Unsurprisingly in the segregated South, the ambiguity of the Yerby family's racial identity caused trouble: in his youth, an Augusta policeman attacked Yerby for 'walking with a White girl'.[8] That woman was Yerby's sister.

Scholars Gene Andrew Jarrett, Stephanie Brown, Matthew Teutsch, and Veronica T. Watson have spearheaded a recent resurgence of interest in Yerby after decades of neglect. Nevertheless, his identification as part-Irish remains unexamined but for a Korey Garibaldi article. This, despite the fact that Yerby told his uncredited *Contemporary Authors* interviewer in the 1980s that he had 'far more Irish blood than Negro'.[9] Yerby's negotiation of what he patently perceived to be his dual heritages is apparent in 'Myra and the Leprechaun' (date uncertain), which is told from the title female character's point of view. Although set in America, the short story draws on the Irish lore of the alluring fairy who entices a human away from the quotidian world. Yerby racializes the supernatural figure by endowing him with 'heavy curling black masses' of hair and 'brown' skin.[10] This chapter's reading of *The Foxes of Harrow* (hereafter *Foxes*) and its 1947 screen adaptation give weight to the Irish heritage that Yerby himself always claimed, suggesting that protagonist Stephen Fox's 'guttersnipe' Irishness challenges the certainties of the South's black-white binary as much as the novel's mixed-race and racially ambiguous French characters.

'The ones I feel sorry for', says a bigoted white woman in a story by Georgia-born Irish-American author Flannery O'Connor, 'are the ones that are half white'.[11] The either/or imperative that has structured American ideas of difference from Christian/savage and Native/European to Black/white, obscures the degree to which, as LeiLani Nishime notes, America 'ha[s] always already been mixed race'.[12] Nonetheless, Yerby's hybridity alongside the whiteness of many of his protagonists were understood by certain Black contemporaries as a refusal to confront race, as Jarrett explicates.[13] Brown, however, voices the growing contemporary reassessment of *Foxes* as profoundly engaged with race and interraciality,[14] as this chapter further explores. However, it also reads the character of Stephen Fox as a negotiation of Yerby's *mother's* heritage, especially as the author posits a link between slavery and those his maternal ancestry would have primed him to understand as Scots-Irish: *Foxes* repeatedly makes sympathetic references to the 'poor whites up in the hills' whose *paid* labour is not needed in the Southern slave economy.

Margaret Mitchell (1900–1949), was born into a prominent Atlanta, Georgia family. Her only published novel in her lifetime, *Gone with the Wind* (1936; hereafter *GWTW*), appeared in an era of unremittent lynch terror in the South. As such, the bestseller and its massively successful 1939 film adaptation were and remain controversial for opening with a vision of an antebellum world of grace. Set mostly during the American Civil War and the subsequent Reconstruction period,[15] *GWTW* follows Scarlett O'Hara, born on the Georgia cotton plantation of Tara to Irishman Gerald. Mitchell was Scottish Methodist on her father's side and Catholic Irish on that of her mother. She left Catholicism behind in young adulthood, identifying more with her father's Methodism.[16] However, she was wholeheartedly embraced as 'one of our own' by conservative Catholic Irish America,[17] with an 'ethnic pride' study proclaiming *GWTW* the Irish-American *Odyssey*.[18] Nevertheless, Mitchell's Irish ancestry is more complex in terms of class status and denomination than has been popularly understood. To wit: the rise of Gerald O'Hara appears to draw from Mitchell's maternal great-grandfather, Phillip Fitzgerald (1798–1880), whose name is hidden in plain sight in *GWTW* as the given name 'Gerald'. Phillip was an immigrant who was born in Fethard, a walled Norman settlement in County Tipperary. In 1836 he acquired a house in Clayton County, Georgia when that land was—to quote Gerald O'Hara's funeral eulogy in *GWTW*—'part wild and the Injuns had just been run out of it'.[19] In the 1810s, Andrew Jackson had consolidated his image as a military aggressor when he led brutal campaigns against the Creeks in Georgia and Alabama and the Seminoles in Florida, which resulted in the mass transfer of land from Indian nations to white settlers. (*GWTW*'s partial account of what it calls the Creek 'uprising' only describes Indians 'scalping' Europeans.[20]) Historic structure expert Tommy H. Jones was commissioned to create a study of the site, construction, and evolution of the ancestral Fitzgerald house and lands, which the Atlanta-raised Mitchell often visited. He concludes that by the mid-1840s, the author's great-grandfather owned over 1,000 acres in the area and by the eve of the Civil War, Phillip Fitzgerald was one of Clayton County's richest planters, owning at least thirty-four enslaved people.[21] Moreover, his 'good wife', Eleanor McGhann Fitzgerald, as a Mitchell biographer unironically records, 'saw to it that every one of them was instructed and baptized in the Catholic faith'.[22]

Jones draws on a handwritten 1917 Mitchell family history and similar papers to sketch the family's own origin narrative, which runs as follows: Phillip was born in the mid-eighteenth-century house in Fethard probably built by his grandfather, John Fitzgerald (1719–1798), who had died on the 'rebel' side during the 1798 Uprising. Several of Philip's siblings immigrated to America in the 1820s and 1830s, including James (1791–1835), who purportedly attended Trinity College in Dublin before leaving Ireland for America.[23] The details of the Fitzgeralds' origins provided by Mitchell's biographer, Darden Asbury Pyron, broadly dovetail with that of Jones, but that the former makes no mention of a death during the 1798 rebellion. However, Pyron takes the further detail from a family record that the Hiberno-Norman Fitzgeralds fled to France as a result of the uprising, where Phillip was raised. At any rate, in either telling the Fitzgeralds were a gentry family who easily fell in with the planter order on arriving in Georgia. Ironically, although Mitchell was in possession of the kind of elite Fitzgerald origins for which the young F. Scott Fitzgerald might have longed, she imagined her maternal ancestors as having been akin to the semi-literate and uncultured Gerald O'Hara.[24] Nonetheless, the mapping of her family's gentry roots in Ireland onto those of Georgia seems evident in her phrase that the 'Southern Irish became more Southern than the Southerners';[25] this is an obvious repurposing of the cliché that the 'Old English' Fitzgeralds and their ilk became 'more Irish than the Irish themselves'.[26]

William Faulkner (1897–1962) was known for his novels and stories set in the fictional Yoknapatawpha County, which was based on Lafayette County, Mississippi, where he spent most of his life. He is considered to be one of the finest exponents of modernism and Southern Gothic in the American tradition, though this chapter's reading of *Absalom, Absalom!* concludes that it may belong equally to the Scots-Irish Gothic subgenre. Joseph Blotner traces the origins of the author's paternal side to John and Elizabeth Falkner,[27] who emigrated out of England in 1665 and whose descendants identified the couple's origins as Ulster Irish, Huguenot, and Scottish,[28] though Joel Williamson was 'struck by the almost total neglect' of Faulkner's maternal line, the Butlers, who may have been Hiberno-Norman.[29] Most interestingly, the writer's family seem to have shared something of Yerby's dual British Isles-African heritage: Williamson's attention to the Butler side broke new ground in uncovering the fact that Faulkner's maternal grandfather had a 'shadow family' with an enslaved woman called Emeline Lacy Falkner, an open secret within the 'official' family that illuminates the interracial Sutpen family tree in *Absalom, Absalom!*[30] Nevertheless, and despite all the options Faulkner possessed in terms of choosing his heritage, his purported Gaelic-speaking Scottish Highland ancestors became central to his imagining of Sutpen, though Scots-Irishness emerges strongly in the author's imaginative landscape too.

Overlaps and Divergences: Yerby, Mitchell, and Faulkner

The sometimes converging Irish and American literary, generic, and cinematic contexts of *GWTW*, *Absalom, Absalom!* and *Foxes* will be examined presently, and that survey encompasses Kate Chopin, Ellen Glasgow, Elizabeth Bowen, Maureen O'Hara, Eudora Welty, and John Banville. Firstly, however, the degree to which the three novels both overlap and diverge is surveyed. The most discussed such intersection is that Faulkner published *Absalom, Absalom*! in the same year as *GWTW*, stripping away Mitchell's Southern mythology to reveal the consequences down through the generations of the original sin of forced labour in the Americas. Faulkner's 'poor white' Sutpen, who secures status by becoming a plantation master, will be read as a critique of the very earliest attempt by those of British and Irish origin in the Americas to become white. Mitchell, by contrast, unapologetically *claims* whiteness for the Catholic Irish by installing the O'Haras as the equals of a neighbouring Scots-Irish-owned plantation.

Yerby and Mitchell were both born and raised in Georgia during segregation by mothers of Irish descent. However, their socially assigned racial identities created divergent approaches to representing the antebellum and Reconstruction South in their respective historical romance novels. *GWTW*, in a which a plotline justifies the Klan as needed protection from the sexual predation of white women by freed male slaves,[31] was being written right about the time that a young Yerby was harassed for walking with a sister perceived to be white. Indeed, these were also the very years in which America was galvanized by the Alabama Scottsboro Boys' trials, which involved Black teenagers falsely accused of rape by two white women.[32] Yerby writes accessible romance fiction in the Mitchell mode, but is able to simultaneously debunk what Du Bois had indicted as the 'southern white fairytale' of graceful plantation life. (Du Bois was writing in 1935, a year before that fantasy started to go global with the *GWTW* novel and film adaptation juggernaut.[33]) In a *Foxes* scene that anticipates a similar event in Toni Morrison's *Beloved* (1987), the unfree Sauvage attempts to take her baby with her when she jumps to her death, exposing the stark reality of the desperation created by enslavement.[34] By contrast, Mitchell propounds the myth of the cherished and 'happy darky' by having Scarlett claim that 'house slave' Peter is '"family"',[35] though this claim is certainly not meant to suggest *interracial* ties of the sort depicted by Yerby and Faulkner![36] *GWTW* is able to evade slavery's harsher realities by individuating only 'house slave' characters, who would not have suffered the physical hardship that field hands picking cotton endured.[37] This partial representation, combined with the lack of meaningful reference to slavery as a cause of the Civil War, is a crater in the narrative flow for readers with even a cursory knowledge of American history, not least because *GWTW* gives evidence of solid historical research in other ways.[38]

Brown notes that Yerby's readers in 1946 'would have been struck by the points of convergence' between his characters in *Foxes* and those of *GWTW*.[39] As a young man in Ireland, Mitchell's Gerald murders a landlord's agent for whistling a Protestant folksong that celebrates the victory of William of Orange ('King Billy') in the Battle of the Boyne, and subsequently flees to America.[40] Arriving in the South in 1822, O'Hara wins both his first enslaved man and a neglected plantation in northwestern Georgia in games of poker, and further 'whitens' by marrying into the local French elite. The plot points of both novels converge as follows: Yerby's

Figure 4.1 Vivien Leigh (as Scarlett O'Hara) and Thomas Mitchell (as Gerald O'Hara) in the 1939 film adaptation of Margaret Mitchell's *Gone with the Wind.* Courtesy of ALAMY.

Fox, too, is a hardscrabble Irishman who emigrates in the 1820s in dubious circumstances; he, too, wins a plantation through gambling; he also 'marries up' into a local French family.[41] However, in an insightful departure from the easy interpretation of Yerby as merely derivative, Mark C. Jerng calls *Foxes* 'a prequel to *GWTW* that centers on the Gerald O'Hara figure'.[42] As such, he receives more attention in this chapter than his daughter, Scarlett (Figure 4.1).[43]

Mitchell's planter sees no connection between the sectarian oppression in Ireland that he had fled and the South's slave system. The origins of Yerby's Fox, by contrast, are an implicit source of his ambivalent view of that way of life. Yerby puts words in his planter's mouth of the sort likely never before uttered by 'the master' in a Southern plantation romance: '"slavery is a very convenient and pleasant system—for us...I have my leisure, which I haven't earned, and my wealth, which I didn't work for"'.[44] Most importantly, Yerby deviates hugely from Mitchell in depicting rebellious, articulate, and prominent African-American characters, particularly those on the enslaved Caleen's matrilineal line. Similarly, Yerby is alert to the manner in which, as both Du Bois and Roediger theorize, the ability to share spaces with their 'betters' was sold to poor Southern whites as adequate compensation for exploitative class relationships, thereby preventing common cause with enslaved people or their descendants.[45] On the eve of the Civil War, Stephen queries the certainties of his classist and racist son, Etienne: 'What of your landless white? Your mountaineer—your swampfolk? Must they go on eating the clay of the earth to keep from starving?'[46] In Mitchell, by contrast, the low status of the unsympathetic 'poor white' Irish Slatterys is presented as evidence of their innate inferiority.

Strikingly, however, and with the exception of Jarrett, Yerby is not given credit for drawing from *Absalom, Absalom!*.[47] This reluctance probably stems from his early dismissal as a writer of 'potboilers' in a canon-making study of the African-American novel.[48] Although Yerby's romance differs hugely from Faulkner's modernist Gothic novel in terms of accessibility and genre, there are interesting plot overlaps beyond the obvious central one of a self-made antebellum planter of Irish association: both involve a morganatic marriage in New Orleans between an elite male and a 'mulatta';[49] both feature a son named Etienne; the planter in both turns to his sister-in-law after the death of his first wife. Indeed, the opening scene of *Foxes,* in which a young Stephen Fox is dumped on a Mississippi sandbar in 1825 by a riverboat captain for cheating at cards, suggests both that Yerby took this cue from a line in *Absalom, Absalom!* and that he read Sutpen as an Irishman on the make: Faulkner's protagonist materializes in Mississippi in 1833 and narrator Rosa implies that he risked 'being put ashore on a sandbar' for gambling on Mississippi steamboats in order to obtain seed money for his plantation.[50]

Stylistically, too, Yerby draws from Faulknerian Southern Gothic in what is, effectively, the short second-person prologue describing the plantation house at Harrow before *Foxes* opens in the third-person in 1825 with Stephen's story. The prologue's unidentified voice lyrically describes Harrow's degraded appearance in the 1945 present tense,[51] and with the benefit of hindsight regarding the novel's arc, the passage speaks in a forked tongue:

> It is better to see Harrow at night. The moonlight is kinder. The North Wing has no roof and through the eyeless sockets of the windows the stars shine. Yet at night when the moon is at the full, Harrow is still magnificent. By day you can see that the white paint has peeled off and that all the doors are gone, and through them and the windows you can see the mud and the dust over everything. But at night the moon brings back the white again and the shadows hide the weeds between the flagstones...You walk very fast over the flagstones and resist the impulse to whirl suddenly in your tracks and look back at Harrow. The lights are not on. The crystal chandeliers are not ablaze. There are no dancers in the great hall.[52]

The preamble is a strikingly Gothic note within Yerby's otherwise picaresque plantation romance, reminiscent of the celebrated opening of Daphne du Maurier's 1938 Gothic romance, *Rebecca*. Altogether, the prologue demonstrates the heights of prose that a writer accused of churning out 'potboilers' could reach. Mitchell and Faulkner both lead the reader to the threats to or degradation of their central plantation homes late in the action,[53] by which point a reader may feel nostalgia for the loss. By contrast, Yerby's Gothic opening presents the destruction of Harrow as a fait accompli. The African-American author foregrounds the inevitability of the slave plantation's demise, as later theorized by Martinican poet and scholar,

Édouard Glissant.[54] In short, Yerby reminds his readers upfront, before giving them leave to wallow in Southern nostalgia for a while, that the antebellum order is dead. Should Yerby's Gothic opening have been an epilogue rather than the preamble, an elegiac note might have emerged. However, this danger is prevented by placing the passage at the outset, before readers have become attached to either setting or characters. The preamble is also, by dint of its implicit present-day date and second-person address, as direct an authorial assessment of antebellum Southern history as can occur in a 1940s work of fiction by a quasi-racially closeted author for a predominantly white mainstream readership.[55] While the tone regarding the South's lost glory is sometimes ambivalent in Faulkner, and most of Mitchell's characters unambiguously mourn the loss of white dominance after the Civil War, Yerby's Gothic opening is a dance upon the grave of the planation system: The prologue's last words are, 'And you don't look back.'[56]

Neo-Gothic: The Pseudo-Aristocrat's Plantation House

There is a further significant plot convergence in the three novels: all the planters-to-be as good as camp out on newly acquired land while their unfree labour builds the plantation house. In doing so, these transplanted Irishmen uncritically replicate the very architectural structures first developed in the colony of Ireland. Canny's work explicates how the plantation system associated with the antebellum South was, in fact, originally created by the seventeenth-century 'New English' economic and cultural domination in Ireland. In Amy Clukey's formulation, the difference in Irish and American terminology for similar phenomena 'obscures' their 'commonalities': Irish 'landed estates and big houses' equate to 'plantations; landlords replace planters; and the Anglo-Irish Ascendancy supplants the North American plantocracy'.[57] 'Big House' is an Irish usage for the manor houses of the Anglo-Protestant elite and is also the name of the Irish literary genre in which such dwellings are central. Thus, the Southern plantation novel and Ireland's 'Big House' novel emerge as the same genre separated by water. In addition, the slave-plantation Caribbean's 'Great House' (and that context's potential to 'contaminate' whiteness) hovers over this comparison too, as suggested by Afro-Caribbean Eric Walrond's 1926 *Dracula*-inspired story of Black revenge:[58] In 'The Vampire Bat', a white Caribbean heir journeying by night to Waterford, his family estate,[59] is rendered a 'white and bloodless' husk by a vampire in the shape of a Black foundling.[60]

In self-consciously postcolonial iterations such as John Banville's *Birchwood* (1973), the Big House novel takes a postmodern Gothic turn in order to grapple with its problematic roots in the romanticization of colonial culture. This is paralleled by American fiction's movement from nineteenth-century celebrations of plantation life to its critique by Faulkner.[61] Consider the structural and thematic overlaps between *Absalom, Absalom!* and Banville's *Birchwood*: beyond the shared mood of decadence and decay and the dense language, both centre on the mansion of the usurping settler-colonial family who depose the natives; both invoke the melodrama of brother–sister incest; both ruined homes are ultimately inhabited by the reduced remnants of the usurpers; both imply travelling backwards in time to a moment of rupture (the Famine in Banville and the American Civil War in Faulkner). The latter congruence denotes that the Irish experience of an undead past in which historical trauma has always just occurred 'last Thursday week' plays out in both novels and both contexts.[62]

Unsurprisingly, then, the Southern writer is sensitive to the ghosts of the mirror settler-colonial culture. To wit: Faulkner's Mississippi contemporary, Eudora Welty, who seldom used non-Southern settings, summons up unfinished American and Irish history in a rare story boasting Irish characters called 'The Bride of the Innisfallen' (1951). Significant to this discussion is that the story was inspired by Welty's 1950 visit to the ancestral mansion of novelist Elizabeth Bowen in southwest Ireland. Welty's recall of the trip, Dawn Trouard notes, conflates the landscapes and terminologies of Ireland and the American South: the fuchsia hedges of Bowen's Court reminds Welty of Savannah, while the Irish novelist's hospitality is ambiguously ascribed to her status as '*Southerner*' (the emphasis is Welty's).[63] Bowen's Gothicizing of the Big House in her 1929 novel, *The Last September*, emerged from self-awareness regarding her family's origin.[64] The descendants of a Welsh ancestor granted confiscated land in Ireland because he had fought with Cromwell, the Bowens, Elizabeth wrote, 'drew their power from a situation that shows an inherent wrong', replicating in Ireland the very 'colonial' conditions that had made the Welsh motherland untenable. Her ancestral manse in County Cork was, Bowen concludes, 'built of anxious history'.[65]

Welty's ostensibly present-tense 'The Bride of the Innisfallen' is attuned to that anxiety. It opens with a troubled American woman fleeing the English capital in the crowded compartment of a boat train coursing out of London towards a Welsh port. All other initial passengers in her compartment are Irish since the vessel to which the train travels is bound for Cork. Incongruous opening references to an Irish passenger in a hat 'like an Indian bonnet' (battle headdress), and another wearing a 'hat like old Cromwell's' evoke the colonial strife of both Ireland and America.[66] When the Irish travellers sing 'The Wild Colonial Boy', a ballad celebrating an Irish convict transportee, it is a further omen that traumatic communal memory has been generated by the gathering of so many unmoored Irish people in a confined and kinetic space. An Irish boy brings out a harmonica to accompany the singing 'as he would a pistol', echoing the culmination of the ballad's action, when the Irish outlaw draws his gun and is shot by the police.[67] A Welshman joins the easy-going party for a while, and his insistent questions about religion and habits suggests that he holds colonial views regarding Irish Catholic backwardness.[68] The Welshman is both disparaging about Irish culture and sinister,[69] demanding to see the identity papers of fellow passengers, who readily obey.[70] To the consciousness of one female Irish passenger looking out the window in the corridor outside the compartment, 'Wales was formidable, barrier-like [...] dense and heraldic',[71] evocative of the might and armorial bearings of the Norman incursion. Thus, the history that produces both the Welshman's peremptoriness and Irish acquiescence is that of the first wave of colonization of Ireland out of Britain which, like the journey that will cap the action, was from Wales to the Irish southern coast. (And, of course, Bowen's own marauding Welsh ancestor haunts the story too.)

This woman's statement on returning to the compartment conjures up the convex mirror of Poe's 'William Wilson': '"Ah, in the windows black as they are, we do look almost like ghosts riding by".'[72] Hurtling through the night, the train is increasingly adrift from reality and linear time, as implied by a returning emigrant's talk of a ghost-addled Norman castle he will visit in Ireland: 'She comes first because she's mad, and he slow—got the dagger stuck in him...and while you look [they] go leaping in the bright air, moonlight as may be, and sailing off together cozy...to start it again.'[73] Returning from the dinner car, another Irishwoman tells of the alterations in time, space, and selfhood of a fellow passenger: '"A man left us but returned to the car to say that while we were eating they shifted the carriages about and he had gone up the train, down the train, and could not find himself at all...He said his carriage was gone, yes."'[74] Welty proselytized the Chekhovian use of strangeness in fiction,[75] and here defamiliarization works to indicate how historical rupture warps and impoverishes the present. In this Irish Big House-inspired story, the homicidal dead are more real than the living.

With the passage of time and the fading of bloodstains, in both Ireland and America the settler-colonizer was generally naturalized as a deeply rooted aristocrat. Conservative iterations of the Big House novel defuse the rupture of the Anglo-Irish mansion by emphasizing its long history,[76] but the twentieth-century Southern plantation house novels surveyed here both deliberately and inadvertently expose that edifice as *arriviste*. In Faulkner and Yerby, the notion of 'aristocrat' in the Southern context is queried, ultimately exposing the shallowness of the plantation's roots. Indeed, beyond old colonial towns like Charleston, as writer and Scots language activist Billy Kay's Southern travelogue drily points out,

> the 'Old South' lasted a mere 40 years—from the planting of cotton in the wilderness of Mississippi and Alabama to the outbreak of the Civil War in 1861. There was scarcely enough time to tear down the old family shack, set up the neo-classical porticos, and claim the ancestry of a gentleman cavalier before riding off to defend the way of life from the Yankee hordes.[77]

As Welty's story implies, the distance of centuries endows the initially *parvenu* estates of the Old World with the patina of aristocracy. The planters in the three novels considered rush that process, but aristocratic time is measured not in months or years, but centuries. In the slave-holding context, however, aristocratic time is speeded up due to the racial gulf between whites and the enslaved: 'Having no ancestors, I am become one', declares the young Stephen Fox grandly.[78] Listening to Rosa Coldfield's account of Sutpen's clearance of his land with the forced labour of twenty enslaved males in Faulkner's novel, Quentin Compson envisages a creation out of the void. Although he thereby effaces that toil as well as the land's original Native American inhabitants, Quentin inadvertently exposes the swiftness of the creation of an edifice intended to signal deep-rooted presence:

> Then in the long unamaze Quentin seemed to watch them overrun suddenly the hundred square miles of tranquil and astonished earth and drag house and formal gardens violently out of the soundless Nothing and clap them down like cards upon a table beneath the up-palm immobile and pontific, creating the Sutpen's Hundred, the *Be Sutpen's Hundred* like the oldentime *Be Light*.[79]

Like Supten, Fox hastily imports the ready-made splendour of chandeliers, tiles, and carpets to soften the rawness of the shiny new mansion built on recently cleared land. Indeed, Yerby and Faulkner depict their protagonists building and furnishing plantation houses with such speed as to recall nothing so much as the ready-to-assemble neoclassical suburban mansions sold with complete building instructions by Sears, Roebuck and Company in pre-World War II America.[80] Glissant describes the Caribbean planter class as a 'pseudoaristocracy' lacking both roots and organically evolved traditions.[81] Likewise, to call the thin plantation culture depicted in the novels surveyed 'aristocratic' is either a wilful misunderstanding of that word—or mockery. In the case of Mitchell's novel, it is the former, and in those of Faulkner and Yerby, it is the latter. Indeed, in the Southern racial symbolic, all whites above the 'trash' cut-off are gentry by default: Faulkner's Rosa, a storekeeper's daughter, considers herself to be a 'gentlewoman'.[82] All that is seemingly needed to become a Southern 'aristocrat' overnight in the Faulkner and Yerby novels is to own enough men to be able to build a plantation quickly. Rather than celebrating the aristocratic fallacy, as detractors assumed, Yerby was 'an entertaining debunker' of such 'myths',[83] as was Faulkner. All in all, when read together, the three Irish planter novels suggest—in admittedly different registers—that to fell the wilderness and build a mansion quickly is America's ultimate fable of instant whiteness, be that in the antebellum South or the twentieth-century suburb.

Forget Haiti? *Absalom, Absalom!*'s Redleg Planter

Absalom, Absalom! flows back and forth between the early nineteenth and early twentieth century and a number of narrators, but the coldly ambitious Sutpen is the centre around which the story eddies. A chronologically linear (and necessarily flattening) rearrangement of the novel's plot is provided in the following, but its crisscrossing structure, in which originary historical violence incessantly returns, suggests an undead past. In particular, Rosa's vitriolic repetitions suggest a continual reliving of unprocessed trauma. In her opening narration, Sutpen appears 'out of nowhere and without warning upon the land with a band of strange n*****s and built a plantation' in Yoknapatawpha County, Mississippi.[84] By degrees, the dispersed pieces of Sutpen's backstory, as told and retold in fragments by a number of narrators, cohere (somewhat) into a chronology (of sorts): Sutpen was born poor white in the Appalachians in 1807; he vows to rise socially and racially when snubbed by an effete enslaved butler in plantation Virginia as a bedraggled migrant child; he takes ship to Haiti as a teenager where he marries into the French gentry after suppressing a slave rebellion in that Caribbean country; his wife turns out to have African 'blood', so he abandons her and their son to go create an uncontestably white dynasty; he arrives in Mississippi in 1833, obtains a 'hundred miles of land which he took from a tribe of ignorant Indians, nobody knows how';[85] he builds a plantation and marries Ellen Coldfield in 1838, a woman of respectable family and sometime narrator Rosa's older sister.

Other characters move into view: by possible design, Sutpen's now-adult Haitian son, Charles Bon, who, like his mother, presents as white, becomes the college roommate of Sutpen's heir, Henry, at the University of Mississippi in 1859. The older and worldlier New Orleans-raised Bon wins both the unsuspecting Henry's affections and, dangerously, also those of Sutpen's daughter, Judith. She is, of course, Bon's half-sister, and they become engaged. Sutpen later reveals Bon's African ancestry and his blood connection to the family, and a combination of this first fact alongside unease regarding Bon's earlier morganatic marriage to a 'mulatta' eventually leads Henry to murder Bon. This occurs in 1865 at the Civil War's close after the young men have been in the Confederate Army together.[86] Henry flees after the killing, leaving the broken-hearted Judith behind with her half-sister, Clytie, Sutpen's adult daughter by an enslaved woman. By 1869, and now a widower without male heir or human chattel whose plantation is being diminished by the redistribution policy of Reconstruction, Sutpen proposes to Rosa. However, he then enrages the latter by asking her to produce a boy child before they can marry. Subsequently, he sires a child upon squatter Wash Jones's 'poor white' teenage granddaughter, Milly, but both women thwart Sutpen's plans for ensuring the patrilineal line: Rosa's dignity has been affronted and she breaks with Sutpen, while the teenager births a girl, to Sutpen's disgust. An incensed Wash Jones kills mother and newborn and then slays Sutpen. The following year sees the emergence of Charles Etienne, the child of Bon's morganatic marriage in New Orleans, and he and his family eke out a marginal existence on the plantation's remnants. Sutpen's shell of a property is eventually burned to the ground in about 1910. Thus, Sutpen's rejection of his own Black Haitian dynasty entwines with the failure of his grand design for plantation and white dynasty. In the discussion that follows, it is demonstrated that his family line begins as well as ends as creolized, a further circular movement in the novel.

As an illiterate child migrant, Sutpen does not know his date of birth, seems unfamiliar with his real surname, and is unconscious of race until his poor mountain-dwelling family migrates to coastal Tidewater Virginia.[87] Although the ten-year-old Sutpen may not understand race, it understands him: when he knocks on the door of a Virginia plantation house, the sophisticated Black butler takes one look at 'his patched made-over jeans clothes and no shoes' and orders him 'never to come to that front door again but to go around to the back'.[88] Prior to the rebuff, '[Sutpen] was no more conscious of his appearance...or of the possibility that anyone else would be than he was of his skin'. Afterwards, however, young Sutpen 'learned the difference not only between white men and black ones', but 'between white men and white men'.[89] Young Sutpen, who 'knew neither where he had come from nor where he was nor why', possesses the ignorance regarding exact ancestry of the abject,[90] but seems to be dispossessed British-Irish by origin and culture. The ethnically incoherent product of the ethno-religious divisions and connections that crisscross Britain, Ireland, and their diasporas, he is the detritus of Empire destined to become the 'trash' of America. Sutpen is born poor white in the Scots-Irish enclave of what becomes West Virginia, his grandmother speaks only Scottish Gaelic, and 'the first Sutpen'—presumably a transported English or Welsh convict—comes to Jamestown, Virginia on a 'ship from the Old Bailey',[91] a pre-'Mayflower' origin that undermines the northeastern myth of the 'pure' descent of America's earliest whites.[92] Sutpen's paternal and maternal roots, which may be English, Welsh, Scottish Gaelic, Scots-Irish, Irish, or some combination of all of these, go back to the earliest moments of the dispossessed white presence on American soil. Altogether, the indentured servitude of the first in his male line in seventeenth-century Virginia—as well as Sutpen's own red hair and tendency to sunburn[93]—suggests 'Redleg' ancestry.

In the century of arrival of this first in Sutpen's line, Virginia was the northernmost outpost of the slave plantation system of the Americas, and the cauldron in which North American race was made. The first Africans were landed in Virginia in 1619 and English courts began to send convicts thence as a way of alleviating England's large criminal population from 1615. Within the hierarchy of early Virginia, Sutpen's first ancestor was from the very bottom rung: Between 1700 and 1775, Emily Jones Salmon writes, of the approximately 52,000 convicts who sailed for the colonies, more than 20,000 went to Virginia, where their terms (generally seven to fourteen years) could be purchased 'for a lower price than [those of free] indentured white and enslaved African laborers'.[94] Convict and dispossessed British by earliest origin and Scots-Irish 'hill-billy' and Scottish Gaelic by culture and more recent ancestry, Sutpen's lowly British-Irish existence in the New World fixes him as 'white trash' as soon as he reenters the symbolic that created the racial identity of his first forebear in America when he knocks on the Tidewater mansion door.[95] Glissant concludes that the multiracial Southern US-Caribbean zone of Faulkner's imaginative range forecasts a creolized American future ('une nouvelle poétique' [a new poetics]).[96] However, Sutpen's multiplicity arguably also recuperates a creolized British-Irish past.

'The Plantation', Glissant notes, 'displays most clearly the opposed forces of the oral and the written at work'.[97] Before they migrate from their isolated mountain, Sutpen's nameless family of origin seem to have retreated from formal history, the racial symbolic, and print culture. Faulkner's complex style is highest modernism, but given the enslaved-African and abject British-Irish roots of Sutpen and the sprawling family lines he seeds, the novel's repetitions and meanderings also draw upon the oral or non-literate worlds of all who came before Sutpen and Bon's unnamed mother: the enslaved and forcibly transported from Africa and the convicted, defeated, or indentured shipped out of the British Isles. The childhood decision of the 'off-white' Sutpen to *become* white is a return to the pivotal moment in the seventeenth-century Americas when the sporadic solidarity of enslaved African and indentured Irish terminated with the legal division of white servant and Black slave. Faulkner's derangement of linear time in portraying Sutpen putting down a Haitian slave revolt in the 1820s (when Haiti had been independent since 1804) allows the past to replay. This non-linearity fuels the logic of Sutpen's journey backward after his humiliation at the plantation door to a prime site of shared African and Irish history, the West Indies.[98] Moreover, Faulkner furthers the impression of Sutpen's descent into the Dreamtime of whiteness by abruptly placing him in Haiti rather than depicting his journey thence.[99]

Nevertheless, as with *Edgar Huntly's* Clithero and the Paxton Boys' episode in Pennsylvania, a careful reading of *Absalom, Absalom!* suggests that the Scots-Irish-associated Sutpen carries sins that should also be ascribed to 'genteel' settler-colonial society as a whole. The Coldfields, modest business people and God-fearing Methodists, feel morally superior to Sutpen but, as Rosa admits, the promise of 'slaves underfoot' entice the family to allow daughter Ellen to marry into his planation.[100] The novel leaves an afterimage of Sutpen as monster, but when read with care, it emerges that descriptors of him drawn from dark fairy-tale, demonology, and Gothic ('Bluebeard', 'ogre' and 'djinn') are used by Rosa alone,[101] whose judgement has been clouded by his affront to her chastity. Rosa's narration is a perfect example of how a belief repeated often enough is eventually taken for truth. She uses 'demon' in reference to Sutpen approximately *sixty* times in her narration. Tellingly, Quentin's college roommate, who has listened to many reports of Rosa's story, also begins using the descriptor when referring to Sutpen. That this language *creates* Sutpen-as-demon in the minds of others is suggested by the fact that when Charles Etienne appears at the plantation, locals readily assume that he is Sutpen's child by his own mixed-race daughter, Clytie.

In contrast to conventional plantation romances, there is no gold veneer over the dung heap in *Absalom, Absalom!* The uncouth Sutpen is a 'demon' because he strips the planter role of its obfuscating facade of civility and sophistication, closing the distance between 'savage slave' and 'genteel master' that fine clothes and power wielded through mediators usually creates (see Figure 5.3). Sutpen does so by exposing domination in its most elemental form of one man's physical over-powering of another. Consider what Ellen discovers in a stable in which she knew that Sutpen used to have the enslaved males fight each other before spectators:

> Ellen seeing not the two black beasts she had expected to see but instead a white one and a black one, both naked to the waist and gouging at one another's eyes...the father of her children standing there naked and panting and bloody to the waist and the negro just fallen evidently, lying at his feet and bloody too...and the spectators falling back to permit her to see [her son] Henry plunge out from among the negroes who had been holding him, screaming and vomiting.[102]

The spectacle of Supten's brutality reveals that 'savagery' does not inhere in the African, as antebellum justifications of slavery would have it. Slaveholding, like the description of colonization of Martinican scholar and poet Aimé Césaire, 'works to *decivilize* the colonizer, to *brutalize*' and 'degrade him'.[103] (Moreover, Sutpen's bald proposition to Rosa that she should prove her ability to produce a male child before they marry unmasks the mercenary patrilineal imperative behind *every* heterosexual alliance within plantation culture.[104]) As we shall see in the following, Faulkner's interest in pointing out how the Scots-Irish carried the sins for more diffuse and systemic ills emerged in his activism too.

If the term 'Scots-Irish' recedes in the urban northeast after Kennedy, then its trajectory in the South is different. There it continued to be used as a self-designation but also as a stand-in for 'white' by many not necessarily of that ancestry. The South was settled by large numbers of English, Irish, Scots, German, and French. However, because the Scots-Irish dominated the earliest push into the southern backcountry,[105] claims to that origin could function as code for deep white pedigree. Kay details his experience in the Southern city of Charleston in the early 1970s, a period after violent desegregation when racism remained 'an open wound':

> 'Y'all have any n****r problem over there in Scotland?' asked the boys in the truck festooned with the St. Andrew's cross of the Confederate battle flag as they drove me across the South Carolina line. As a hitchhiker in the South, you quickly learned to avoid discussions with gun-toting racists, so I changed the subject and survived. The boys all had some 'Scotch-Irish' in them, though none knew that meant they were of Ulster Scots extraction. Their ethnic identity was distant and vague, and what they were not—black—was far more important to them than what they were.[106]

Moreover, as Kay adds, the blanket association of Scots-Irishness with white supremacy also discounted the honourable history of covenanting ministers in Ulster-Scots communities who led their congregations away from the 'slavery-tainted' South 'on a great folk migration west to Illinois and Indiana'.[107]

By 1962, Robert Kennedy, in his role of US Attorney General in his brother's administration, brought Faulkner's hometown of Oxford under the global spotlight when he sent in forces to implement a federal court order allowing the admittance of the first Black student to the University of Mississippi.[108] In the midcentury South's explosive atmosphere regarding racial integration, Faulkner attempted to steer a 'moderate' course, a position criticized by writer-activist James Baldwin.[109] Nonetheless, Faulkner was involved in an interesting push-back against racism in the lead-in to the UMiss crisis that does the double work of querying why the Scots-Irish alone are depicted as the carriers of white supremacist views. In 1956, Faulkner worked on a lampoon tabloid targeting racism with activist and editor P.D. East called *The Southern Reposure*, which revised, edited, and gained a much wider readership for *The Nigble Papers*, two editions of a mimeographed satirical newspaper produced near UMiss on February 17 and 18 May, 1956. The papers inverted racist discourse regarding Black 'threats' to race purity and white womanhood in describing the Scots-Irish. One parody trial report describes a 'Scotch-Irish boy' who is charged with insulting a Southern woman by calling her a 'wee bonnie lassie'. A prosecuting attorney is quoted on the dangers of 'the Scotch-Irish menace' and the threat to 'pure' blood of 'monegrelizing with the Scotch-Irish'.[110] In order to make clear that what is called 'Scotch-Irish' is a jumbled fantasy, the boy's details and parody letters to the editor about the trial conflate every known stereotype of Irish, Ulster Scots, Lowland Scottish, and Highland culture, speech, and naming patterns: he 'wear[s] the plaids of his clan', uses Scots dialect, his people drink 'Uisgebeatha' (Scotch), perform 'such dances as the jig or the highland fling', and the 'tragic results' of intermarriage with his kind would be 'red-haired, freckle-faced children with such names as Patrick or Andrew'.[111] (Thus, the racialized pale transportee 'Redleg' hovers in the parody too.) In this effort, Faulkner recognized, as he had done in having Rosa project the sins of white culture upon Sutpen alone, that the free-floating label of 'Scots-Irish' had become a convenient stand-in for a much more diffuse Southern white supremacy.

Moreover, Faulkner had already probed broader white culture's stereotype of Scots-Irish society in a 1941 story. Almost a merely sentimental story but for a macabre—and very Faulknerian—cameo by an amputated leg, 'The Tall Men' depicts the self-sufficient McCallums, sympathetic Depression-era farmers whose surname denotes Ulster or Scottish origin. Set during the years when America readied itself for possible entry into World War II, 'The Tall Men' opens with a government investigator sent to rural Mississippi to arrest two of the McCallums for neglecting to register for the draft. The investigator reels off a sequence of stereotypes regarding shiftless, dishonest poor whites in his head before he meets the McCallums, but his encounter with the dignified and straightforward men leaves him nonplussed.[112] Called 'MacCallum' in Faulkner's *Flags in the Dust* (1929) and *As I Lay Dying* (1930), the family is a constant in the Yoknapatawpha universe. The women of the clan are rarely mentioned in narratives featuring the hunter, farmer, horseman, and soldier MacCallums/McCallums. Their masculinist virtues of courage, independence, and loyalty across generations and wars—and the peculiar absence of womenfolk from the narratives—imply their derivation from earlier valorizations of the frontier Scots-Irishman. Thus, in refuting the easy association of the Scots-Irishman with backwardness, Faulkner arguably came dangerously close to embracing the old idealized image instead.

Faulkner may also have been able to imagine a hybrid British-Irish Sutpen of part Scots-Irish association because he purchased and renovated the small plantation home of a slave-holding planter of Ulster origin called Robert Sheegog in the very years that he worked on *Absalom, Absalom!* (Figure 4.2)[113] Indeed, in

Figure 4.2 Rowan Oak, built by slave-holding Scots-Irish planter Robert Sheegog. Purchased and renovated by William Faulkner during the years that he worked on *Absalom, Absalom!* Courtesy of Wikimedia Commons.

a suggestion of the mixed-race descendants of planters so central to its plotline, a variant of the surname ('Shegog') is given to a Black preacher in the novel. Despite his multiple Irish associations, however, and although critics routinely name him as being of Scottish and English descent, Supten's Scottish ancestry is his only *named* ethnicity in the novel. Moreover, since his birth in the action (1807) makes his grandmother who 'never did quite learn to speak English' a probable Highlander refugee of the Battle of Culloden (1746),[114] it is most accurate to name Sutpen's only known ethnicity as Scottish *Gaelic*. This is a cultural origin over which, in Quinlan's nice phrase, Irishness 'hover[s]': in the Culloden period, the ideo-cultural links between the Highlands and Ireland were understood enough in slave-holding Maryland for Irish Catholics to be barred from its militia.[115] Yet again, the neologism 'Gaelo-American' seems necessary to express this pan-Gaelic identity.

Forget Culloden: Tracing the Compson Curse

Culloden was the defeat of Britain's own Gaelic margin, and the vanquished Highland Other of British identity remains unfinished history that repeatedly returns in contemporary culture, from Alexander McQueen fashion collections (entitled 'Highland Rape' and 'Widows of Culloden') to the 2012 Bond film, *Skyfall*.[116] Culloden-era Highland ancestry is significant both to Faulkner's imagining of his own background and as a cultural hinterland of the fictional Yoknapatawpha County. Faulkner either had—or wished to have had—Culloden roots. Reminiscing about the extended Faulkner family history, as conveyed to him by the author, Faulkner's editor, Malcolm Cowley, gives the impression of 'the clan' as a kind of living museum of the Scottish Highland past:

> His section of Mississippi was Scotch, Highland and Lowland...Faulkner's [maternal] great-grandfather, [John Young] Murry, who lived to be a hundred, spoke Gaelic. When his old wife berated him, he used to go up to his room, dress in his kilt, buckle on his [sword] and come down and sulk in the chimney corner.[117]

Murry had supposedly inherited the sword from his own grandfather, who had carried it at Culloden. Although Faulkner's aunt scoffed at the old man's claim (and Murry actually died at the age of 86 in 1915, so the tale is somewhat tall), a Scottish-born friend nevertheless described Faulkner as one who 'saw himself as a highlander living in exile in Mississippi'.[118]

Faulkner's output was intertextual, so the illumination of Sutpen's Highland connections within *The Sound and the Fury* will close this discussion of the author. This 1929 Faulkner novel tracks the social decline of the Compson family of Yoknapatawpha County in the first three decades of the twentieth century. Narrator Quentin Compson III in *Absalom, Absalom*! is of this line. In 1946, the 200th anniversary of Culloden, Faulkner published the Compson Appendix, a history of the family that begins with that battle. Despite small discrepancies between it and *The Sound and the Fury*, the Appendix makes explicit the occult Gaelic hinterland of that novel's twentieth-century action, proffering an explanation for the eventual debasement of the Compsons. The Appendix intimates that Faulkner, like Poe and O'Neill, envisaged the sins of settler-colonial America as being entwined with primal sins and traumas that crossed the Atlantic with those of Irish and Scottish origin. The Appendix traces the family line in America back to Quentin MacLachlan Compson. Raised by his maternal MacLachlan family in the Highlands, he flees to Carolina from the battlefield at Culloden Moor with a sword, 'the tartan he wore', and 'little else'.[119] (The real MacLachlan clan, of Ulster O'Neill descent, was particularly decimated at Culloden, where its chief died.[120]) At eighty, 'having fought once against an English king and lost', Quentin 'would not make that mistake twice',[121] so in 1779, during the American Revolutionary War between the colonies and Great Britain, he flees with his infant grandson and the tartan.

In 1811, this very grandson, Jason Lycurgus Compson, obtains, through mercenary means, the square mile in Mississippi on which he builds a slave-run estate from Chickasaw Indian chief, Ikkemotubbe, thus unthinkingly dispossessing another, in turn. This acquisition was meant 'to avenge the dispossessed Compsons from Culloden',[122] but it is vengeance enacted upon blameless Native Americans.[123] Thus, Faulkner portrays the long and transatlantic arc of a family who are ultimately punished for their too-easy equation of Gaelic Scotland's 'Lost Cause' with that of the South.[124] Faulkner clearly envisaged the troubles of the twentieth-century Compsons as retribution for the unthinking sins of the fathers: Ikkemotubbe is introduced in the Appendix as a 'dispossessed American king' who 'granted' a parcel of land to the 'grandson of a Scottish refugee who had lost his own birthright by casting his lot with a king who himself had been dispossessed'.[125] The spectre of Andrew Jackson that haunted James, Fitzgerald, and O'Neill also emerges in Faulkner's Appendix. In its unstable chronology, Jackson, the son of Irish settler-colonists who ruthlessly expanded the American settler-colonial dominion, appears as the 'Great White Father with a sword' who 'patented sealed and countersigned the grant' of Jason's land in 1811.[126] Through references to swords, Jackson and Quentin are linked to the violence that has followed them out of their motherlands to reemerge on American soil.

The 'Lost Cause' of Culloden is reenacted in the family line with the first Jason's grandson, Jason Lycurgus Compson II, who becomes a Confederate general. In turn, his son, Jason III, fathers the family portrayed in *The Sound and the Fury*: a daughter, Caddy, and three sons, Quentin III, Benjy, and Jason IV. By the time of the novel's action, the remnants of the family land have been sold off to a golf club, and the family, too, has dwindled: the last generation consists solely of Caddy's illegitimate daughter since Jason is a bachelor, Quentin III commits suicide, and the so-called 'idiot', Benjy, has been castrated. Quentin III's decision to kill himself is generally attributed to his emotional enmeshment with his promiscuous sister's difficulties. However, by endowing this character with the exact name of the first in the patrilineal line in America (as later revealed by the Appendix), Faulkner implies that centuries of family sin come to rest upon the head of the *doppelganger*. 'Quentin Compson' is also the name of the suicide's niece, but it is unclear within the Gothic logic of Faulkner's oeuvre if the blighted heritage can finally be exorcised by the first *female doppelganger* in the line, whose gender and 'illegitimacy' disrupts the Compson patrilineal record.[127] Altogether, the Appendix renders *The Sound and the Fury* an iteration of yet another possible subgenre of Gothic, which could be termed Gaelo-American Gothic. This tenor is generated by the novel's unexamined culminating engagement with both James Joyce's vision of history and a Culloden-era legend of the real-life MacLachlans.

In the enigmatic final scene of *The Sound and the Fury*, the Compsons' Black servant, Luster, turns the family buggy to the left instead of the right at the monument in the town square. This upends a normal pattern and, thereby, provokes anguished cries from the routine-loving Benjy.[128] Two possible sources for this ending suggest the influence of a representation of the undead Irish past, on the one hand, and evidence that the 1946 Culloden backstory of the Compsons was already forming in Faulkner's mind while completing the 1929 novel, on the other. Faulkner owned all of Joyce's works,[129] and the close of *The Sound and the Fury* echoes a similar moment in 'The Dead' (1904). This culminating story of *Dubliners* centres on Anglicized Dubliner Gabriel Conroy, who is alienated from his native culture and history. An anecdote Gabriel tells about the day his Catholic grandfather drove out with 'the quality' to a military review reveals the forgetting that rising socially in colonial Dublin necessitated. Dressed in the manner of his 'betters', Gabriel's mill-owner grandfather also mimics the diction of the Anglicized elite as his mill nag enacts his owner's unthinking admiration for colonizer might by endlessly circling a triumphalist equestrian commemoration of William III of England ('King Billy'), whose 1690 victory at the Boyne over James II secured Protestant Ireland.[130] Benjy's beloved monument is a statue of a 'Confederate soldier [who] gazed with empty eyes beneath his marble hand into wind and weather',[131] a representation that, like King Billy, denotes the death stare of unfinished history. Decades before the Appendix, this echo of 'The Dead' points to *The Sound and the Fury*'s occult message that those who have not learned from history mindlessly repeat it. The intellectually challenged Benjy is the unwitting carrier of the trauma and sins of earlier male Compsons, shrieking in horror for reasons he cannot verbalize.

In addition, Faulkner may have layered the meanings of the counter-clockwise drive, since it re-enacts a Culloden legend associated with the MacLachlans, the maternal Highland antecedents of the Compsons, which runs as follows. After clan chief Lachlan MacLachlan had raised his men for that battle, he stopped to pray at a cross at the chapel of Killevin. On remounting, his restive horse turned around the monument 'thrice widdershins' (counter-clockwise), which MacLachlan took as an omen that he would die.[132] Assuming that Faulkner had already somewhat conceived the 1946 origin story of the Compsons by 1929, then the 'thrice widdershins' echo at the close of *The Sound and the Fury* may denote that the cycle of violence and dispossession that begins at Culloden with Quentin MacLachlan Compson has ended. However, Faulkner would go on to disinter that corpse in 1946.

Remember Ireland? *Gone with the Wind*'s Hypocritical Irish Planter

Margaret Mitchell's *Gone with the Wind* has sold over twenty-five million copies and has been translated into twenty-seven languages. Thus, the degree to which the 1936 novel and its supremely successful 1939 film adaptation created the popular idea of the Civil War and Reconstruction cannot be underestimated, particularly in the many countries in which little-to-no American history is taught. Pitted against *Absalom, Absalom!*, Mitchell's novel won the 1937 Pulitzer Prize, but was criticized from the very start as a work in which 'the Old South and its Lost Cause were glamorized, sanitized, and merchandised'.[133] Even contrarian African-American commentator George Schuyler fell into step with the consensus of the Black intelligentsia when he called *GWTW* 'Rebel propaganda',[134] a sentiment echoed by Pat Conroy, who called it 'the last great posthumous victory of the Confederacy'.[135]

Dowd writes of *GWTW* that 'more people are familiar with the de-ethnicized film adaption than the novel'. As a result, the 'centrality' of Irishness to the work is mostly overlooked.[136] Vanquished in Ireland, Gerald O'Hara vows in his early years in America that the 'fortunes of the O'Haras would rise again',[137] though unfree Black labour allows for the come-back. The real O'Haras were Gaelic landowners associated with Sligo and Antrim, and there are late sixteenth-century records of the confiscation of O'Hara estates in Sligo.[138] However, one branch of the real O'Haras maintained its land and status after this period through complex legal manoeuvrings and conversion to Protestantism. They became, in Thomas Bartlett's words, the very model of the 'survival and revival' of a very small minority of the native Gaelic elite after the 'New English' incursion.[139] Strikingly, there is record of a John Fitzgerald of Fethard converting to Protestantism in 1766,[140] so Mitchell's own maternal ancestors may have availed of this strategy in Ireland also, as James Fitzgerald's purported (though unverifiable) attendance at Protestant-ethos Trinity College Dublin further intimates.[141] That Mitchell may have researched O'Hara traditions is suggested by the fact that she makes Gerald O'Hara the lone short male in a large family of extremely tall men,[142] since, in a well-known sixteenth-century lampoon of reduced Gaelic chieftains, the recently dispossessed branches of the 'tribe of O'Hara' are described as 'men of some height'.[143]

Thus, the fictional Gerald replicates the historical seizure of the ancestral lands of some of the real O'Haras in taking on an estate in Clayton County on the frontier of northwest Georgia, land originally occupied by Muskogean-speaking Creek Indians.[144] Indeed, the original mansion on the property O'Hara acquires was burned to the ground, suggesting the kind of so-called 'native insurgencies' that were common in the colonies of both Ireland and America. Furthermore, Gerald resembles the real O'Hara branch that chose to 'survive and revive' by any means necessary in conforming to Anglo norms, just as Mitchell's own Fitzgerald ancestors may have conformed to Anglicanism in a period in which that allowed elite Irish Catholics to hold onto property. Firstly, Gerald marries into an entrenched slave-holding class: Scarlett's French maternal grandparents had fled Haiti in the successful slave insurrection of 1791, through which the Caribbean country won independence.[145] In addition, O'Hara assimilates into the predominant elite by espousing its ideology and social norms: 'poker and horse racing, red-hot politics and the code duello, States' Rights and damnation to all Yankees, slavery and King Cotton, contempt for white trash and exaggerated courtesy to women'.[146] Gerald thereby shakes off any instinctive empathy he might have felt for enslaved or Native peoples. This, despite the fact that O'Hara flees Ireland in the early 1820s, the years of the ascent of Daniel O'Connell, whose campaign on behalf of Catholic rights was enmeshed with his abolitionism. O'Hara is a perfect demonstration of Frederick Douglass's insight that the Irish who 'at home, readily sympathize with the oppressed everywhere, are instantly taught when they step upon our soil to hate and despise the Negro'.[147] Gerald does not make any connection between the colonial-settler cultures of Ireland and America in that he loathes the former and embraces the latter. Moreover, he unthinkingly holds onto the animus created by 'divide and conquer' British policy in Ireland: He instinctively hates the only other elite Irish family in the locale, the Scots-Irish McIntoshes, for their 'Orange' (Irish Unionist) politics, even as he otherwise conforms to white Anglophilic cultural norms. Finally, although Gerald flees to America because he killed a landlord's agent, a particularly reviled class in colonial Ireland, he feels no hostility towards Wilkerson, his plantation's slave overseer, an equivalent 'middleman' mediator between elite and subjugated.[148]

Gerald is heedless of his replication in Georgia of the settler-colonial order that had caused his exile. Characters in the novel also falsely conflate 'Old World' conflicts with the so-called 'oppression' of white planters in Georgia and, farther back, Haiti: 'Run out of France with the Huguenots, run out of England with the Cavaliers, run out of Scotland with Bonnie Prince Charlie, run out of Haiti by the n*****s and now licked by the Yankees. But we always turn up on top in a few years'.[149] Could Gerald but recognize it, his Irish rebel origins actually align him with the Haitian cause. A mere three months before *GWTW*'s publication (and two years after the US occupation of Haiti had concluded), Trinidadian historian C.L.R. James staged a play in London about Haitian revolutionary Toussaint L'Ouverture, with Paul Robeson as the title character.[150] In 1938 the same author's iconoclastic study, *The Black Jacobins*, further unravelled the belief that the Haitian revolt was a chaotic riot, framing it as an insurgency that, like Ireland's 1798 Uprising, was inspired by the French Revolution.[151] Thus, on the O'Hara plantation, everything that rightly belongs to Black people—their bodily autonomy, their labour, and even their history of resistance—is co-opted by the Irish master. John Mitchel's comparison of Britain's relationship with Ireland to that of the North's 'oppression' of the South illuminates Gerald's postwar cognitive dissonance, as described by Dowd: 'Gerald equates the South's loss with Ireland's and considers Southern rebels (including the Ku Klux Klan) to be the equivalent of Irish militant nationalist groups.'[152]

Despite the centrality of a planter family of dispossessed Catholic Irish stock, *GWTW* is concerned with plural *Irishnesses* in depicting a zero-sum inter-Irish struggle for whiteness. For instance, Gerald also shakes off any instinctive empathy he might have felt for the 'white trash' Slatterys, whose native Irish surname suggest that they share his embeggared Irish origins. While the novel overtly depicts a binary racial world in antebellum Georgia, strikingly, typhoid enters the O'Hara household due to contact with Emmie Slattery. Thus, the danger of 'pollution' inheres not so much in the Black Other as in the proximity of elite Irish to 'off-white' Irish.[153] *GWTW* audits every Irishness created by America's ethno-racial hierarchy and Ireland's own colonialism, sectarianism, and linguistic shift: 'wild' Irish-speaking Union Army recruits; the 'shiftless', over-fecund 'poor white' Slatterys; Scarlett's post-war 'hillbilly' caretaker, Archie, implicitly of hard-scrabble Scots-Irish stock; 'lace curtain Irish' businessman and Scarlett's second of three husbands, Frank Kennedy; Will Benteen, the small farmer of possible indentured convict descent; the planter McIntoshes, whose Ulster Presbyterian roots, 'Orange' politics, and abolitionism 'damned them forever' in Gerald's eyes; 'Shanty Irish on the make' labourer and Scarlett's mill overseer, Johnnie Gallegher; former 'Irish Bridget' (maid) and carpetbagger Mrs Flaherty; elite Rhett Butler, carrier (like Mitchell's own Fitzgerald kin) of the name of one of the most powerful Norman dynasties in Irish history.[154] The novel attempts to assert landed Catholic Irish whiteness and elite status and to slough off the Irish castes considered less desirable for reasons of 'off-white' status (the Slatterys) or politics and/or denomination (the McIntoshes and Mrs Flaherty).

By contrast with Mitchell, Scots-Irish Southern realist Ellen Glasgow's treatment of much of the same history in *The Battle-Ground* (1902) depicts issues of class prejudice in pre- and post-Civil War Virginia sympathetically. The Pulitzer Prize-winning Glasgow (1873–1945) is, like her fellow Scots-Irish-writer Yerby, sympathetic to the manner in which the plantation system disenfranchised poor whites. However, in a distortion that Mitchell replicates, enslaved African Americans are depicted by Glasgow as being mainly contented. Thus, Mitchell and Glasgow both raise up their own particular Irish ethnic cohort in their depictions of the Old South, whilst sentimentalizing enslaved people. Since even Wash Jones is stereotyped as shiftless poor white in *Absalom, Absalom!*, it is, as we shall see presently, left to Yerby, the supposed spinner of entertaining yarns, to provide a systemic vision of the South that is sympathetic to *both* poor white and enslaved Black.

Faulkner's Supten and Yerby's Fox ultimately pay for their punishment of the blameless, since their plans to maintain their legitimate white patrilineal line in plantation splendour for generations come undone. No such punishment is meted out by Mitchell, however, since Gerald's mill-owner daughter thrives in the postwar economy by replacing slave labour with that of poorly fed convicts (a reversal of the sequence in seventeenth-century Virginia). The latter population was, ironically, heavily poor Irish immigrant in the Georgia of the period.[155] Scarlett's ruse echoes the theme of an Irishwoman's 'empowerment' by way of exploitation in Glasgow's *Barren Ground*, a copy of which Mitchell was gifted on its publication in 1925.[156] Glasgow's near-present-tense narrative centres on Dorinda Oakley, of modest Virginia Scots-Irish Presbyterian background. Deeply betrayed by her plantation-stock lover, Dorinda buys land, cutting-edge machinery, and cattle. She works hard to become rich, marrying, as does Scarlett, for business reasons rather than for love. *Barren Ground* rejects the Southern nostalgia that the antebellum scenes of *GWTW* embrace, yet Dorinda relies wholly on the competence of her largely unindividuated Black workforce for material success. In both novels, the Irish/Scots-Irish woman gains independence and wealth and laudably disrupts the Southern code that assigned physical labour and its overseeing to Black and poor white bodies alone, but this autonomy is gained through exploitation.[157] Slavery may have been abolished, but convict 'white trash' Irish and Black bodies provide the sweat that allows Irish wealth to be accumulated in both *GWTW* and *Barren Ground*.

Despite the status of the fictional Irish planter family in *GWTW*, Mitchell's blockbuster is of a period when, as explicitly rendered by the racialized self-ascriptions of writers F. Scott Fitzgerald and John O'Hara, real-life Irish Catholics were still not uncontestably white. Indeed, Klan opposition to the Democratic Party's nomination of Al Smith for president in 1928 was still a recent memory by the time *GWTW* was published. Actual Irish slave-ownership in no less than Fitzgerald's ancestral Maryland county hides in plain sight in *Uncle Tom's Cabin* (1852),[158] the most influential abolitionist novel in nineteenth-century white America. Likewise, the former planter family paying the price for ancestral sins in Paul Green's Southern Gothic drama, *The House of Connelly* (1931), is implicitly Irish. Nevertheless, Pyron notes that there were, in reality, few Irish Catholic planters in the South's interior, with most Irish transplants to be found living modest lives in coastal Charleston and Savannah.[159] Thus, in inserting the nineteenth-century Catholic Irish into the South's antebellum elite, Mitchell's novel seeds the past with the fallacy of long-standing Irish whiteness. In effect, *GWTW* answered the needs of the embattled Irish of the 1930s. In truth, the nineteenth-century Irish immigrant who wanted to pass as Southern elite generally had to get creative: in 1857, poor Dublin immigrant Ellen Walsh falsely claimed to be the daughter of a Louisiana planter,[160] a subterfuge that saw her marry into the family of a pro-Confederacy New York mayor referenced in Yerby's 1985 novel, *McKenzie's Hundred*. As we shall see presently, at the close of his career Yerby, too, wished to rewrite the past of the Irish in the Americas. However, he wished to do so for quite different ideological reasons.

'Remember Haiti?' *The Foxes of Harrow*'s Ambivalent Irish Planter

Stephen Fox is introduced in *The Foxes of Harrow* as a dishonest gambler being ejected from a Mississippi riverboat onto a sandbar.[161] In his 'Dublin guttersnipe' youth in pre-Catholic Emancipation Ireland, the illegitimate Stephen 'slept in the streets, and lived by begging food'.[162] In New Orleans, he gambles his way to acquiring the land upon which he will build his Louisiana plantation, Harrow. The implied racial ambiguity of Stephen's heritage is made explicit in the description of his son Etienne's Texan bride, the daughter of a squatter who was '"part Navaho and part Irish – two very savage races"'.[163] Once Fox is in possession of his plantation, he upgrades his social status and whiteness by marrying Odile, a local elite French woman who is described as being white Creole. However, in the novel's racially fluid French Louisiana, mixed-race characters in the novel speak French and are part-French, most notably Desiree, a refined woman who becomes Stephen's 'shadow wife' through morganatic marriage after his union with Odile sours. Moreover, the intimation that French Creole ancestry is, ultimately, racially mixed, emerges in the description of Etienne, Stephens's son by Odile: 'He had reached far back among his swarthy Mediterranean ancestors for a complexion that was as dark as a mulatto's, and inky hair that curled in great masses.'[164] Kolchin suggests that there was indeed room for generative ambiguity with regard to the term 'Creole', as used in the antebellum Louisiana of the novel's setting.[165] 'Creole', a self-ascription of whites of colonial French or Spanish origin, was *also* a self-ascription of paler-skinned free people of colour with colonial French or Spanish ancestry that they used to differentiate themselves from the dark-skinned and enslaved.[166] In Louisiana, especially, free 'Creoles of color' comprised a third racial category under French and Spanish rule, becoming educated and cultured, taking the names of white fathers or lovers, and often receiving property from such 'protectors', as *Foxes*'s Desiree does.[167]

However, after the US negotiated the Louisiana Purchase in 1803, the increasing numbers of white Anglo-American settlers in New Orleans in the decades that followed imported a starker racial binary, as Yerby depicts. This narrowing of possibilities over the course of the nineteenth century is portrayed in the Creole-Irish Chopin's story, 'Désirée's Baby' (1893).[168] Désirée, a foundling of unknown parentage, marries Armand, the planter son of a Creole family who had been raised in France. When their partially clothed baby is suddenly perceived to be dark-skinned when seen in proximity to an 'octoroon' child,[169] Armand asserts that his wife must be mixed-race and spurns her. Désirée takes their baby and walks into a bayou, never to be seen again. Later, Armand discovers that his mother—and, thus he, also—is of African descent, which was why his parents had lived in France.[170] Chopin tracks the movement from the *possibility* in French American that a person of known African blood may be discreetly accepted as a spouse, to a white Anglo-American mindset in which death is the only possible outcome if the lover is revealed to be mixed-race.

Both Sutpen and Fox plot to secure their respective legitimate male lines in perpetuity, but Faulkner and Yerby mock such ambition by making some of the descendants of both 'illegitimate' and mixed-race young men and women. As the planters' respective lineages multiply, so too does the headcount of mixed-race characters. Faulkner explicitly parallels the dual African and Irish Sutpen lines. However, when read without the blinders of caste, gender, and the patrilineal, *Foxes* likewise turns out to be a novel of Caleen's surname-less matrilineal line as much as Stephens's 'official' patrilineal line. (Indeed, her name sounds like 'colleen', the common Irish-American synonym for 'Irishwoman'.[171]) Caleen, the shrewd *materfamilias* of Harrow's enslaved cohort, upon whose deep knowledge of weather patterns and medicine Stephen relies,[172] is everywhere in the novel's action. She even haunts the ruins of Harrow in the Gothic prologue: its implied camera lens glides from the mansion's formerly grand spaces to its kitchen at the prologue's penultimate paragraph, where the ovens 'wait' for Caleen 'to bake her master's bread', a strikingly individuating focus on Black spaces and unfree labour in a mass-market plantation novel.[173] Judged by the prologue alone, Caleen, its only named character, is the real centre of the narrative. She is, moreover, the nexus of all its sedition: She is the widow of an enslaved man who was hanged in New Orleans for rebelling against the French in 1795, the mother-in-law of the defiant Sauvage, who jumps into the plantation's levee right after childbirth rather than remain in slavery, and the grandmother of the erudite Inch, Sauvage's rescued newborn who grows up to become a leader during Reconstruction, and to whom she (Caleen) teaches reading and passwords for the Underground Railroad.[174] Caleen shrewdly makes herself indispensable to Stephen, but all the while she strategizes for her family and its future, as protective of bloodline as any white planter. From his birth, Caleen quietly pursues the goal of her grandson's eventual escape from slavery:

> 'Inch', I will call him, [Caleen] mused. 'Little Inch', after his grandfather...His body will they enslave, yes, but never his mind and his heart. I will teach him, me. And

> in him the blood of his grandfather and of [his dead mother, Sauvage]. A man, him. A warrior, yes! She smiled slowly to herself.[175]

In comparison to the threatening *doppelganger* of white lineage and white Gothic, this is a positive ancestral haunting that will strengthen Inch for what lies ahead.

Moreover, in a subtext that draws attention to the fallacy of differing skin colour as barrier to kinship, the intelligent and judicious Inch is, in a kind of authorial vengeance, the son Stephen might have wished for, since his actual son, Etienne, is sadistic and amoral. Inch accompanies Etienne to France for the latter's education, and strategizes to study there too, returning better educated than his master.[176] Indeed, Stephen has more in common with the resolute Inch than with Etienne: both educate themselves in youth in order to lay the groundwork for later escape from dire circumstances, and both become self-made men.[177] Indeed, at the moment of his escape from slavery, when he starts a new chapter by entering the Mississippi from a steamboat, Inch unknowingly reenacts the social rebirth of the young Stephen on a sandbar in Louisiana. The dynastic lines of Caleen and Stephen converge at the close with Cyrus, Stephen's red-headed son by mixed-race Creole Desiree. Young Cyrus becomes Inch's stepson when the latter marries the boy's mother, a repudiation of the unyielding insistence on racially 'pure' and 'legitimate' patrilineal bloodline that proves to be the undoing of Faulkner's Sutpen.

Towards the close of *Foxes*, the ageing Stephen mulls on his origins and on 'the faces of the dead', a juxtaposition that suggests regret that he had not resisted participating in the exploitation of others: 'In Ireland he had hungered. In Ireland he had begged, lied, schemed, and stolen…They were all there, black and white alike, and the mind made no distinction.'[178] Hunger is about to come to Harrow with the Civil War as Stephen has these thoughts so, as in Faulkner's oeuvre, a refusal to learn from history on one side of the Atlantic leads to its recurrence on the other. Moreover, Stephen begins to recall other ominous histories: '"Remember Haiti?"', he reminds his son when arguing that slavery is doomed.[179] Stephen's age in the action places his birth at about the time of the 1798 Uprising, the opening clash of which, the Battle of the Harrow, he seemingly unironically memorializes in naming his plantation.[180] Like Mitchell's Gerald O'Hara, Stephen flees disordered colonial Ireland for America in order to gain 'freedom for himself and his sons',[181] but achieves this by denying it to others, as he ultimately becomes aware. '"For a little while"', muses Stephen in his final line of dialogue in the novel, '"we lived like gods. I'm not sure that it was good for us".'[182]

It is difficult to credit that earlier critics who dismissed Yerby as apolitical could not hear the emerging rhetoric of the Black Civil Rights movement of the 1950s and 1960s in his language. Consider Stephen's stream-of-consciousness reverie on the eve of the Civil War. He not only foresees the destruction of Harrow and accepts this as needed retribution, but also perceives the spirit of executed abolitionist John Brown persisting:

> Black, black, black...three million blacks sweating in the sun...and John Brown out of his grave and marching the earth through the whirlwind and the fire. They hanged him in Virginia but he is not dead...no, not dead, not ever dead; you cannot kill an idea. And because of that idea Harrow must perish.[183]

After the war, and close to the novel's conclusion, Inch becomes Commissioner of Police of New Orleans during Reconstruction, and through his influence Stephen is released from a Union prison.[184] Yerby's depiction of Reconstruction as a process that gives authority to the capable Inch is a counter-narrative to its representation as a postwar reign of terror and incompetence by African Americans and their degenerate white allies in *GWTW* and *The Birth of a Nation.* With Reconstruction, the formerly enslaved characters of *Foxes*—freed both from bondage and from the margins of the typical Southern historical romance—increasingly become the focus of the action. Stephen is philosophical at the upending of the hierarchy, unlike his white supremacist son, Etienne. The latter protests to the new Police Commissioner that authority would inevitably revert to 'the race for whom God intended it'.[185] Inch, foreseeing the soon-to-occur backlash to Reconstruction of the Jim Crow era, despondently concurs that the change has been too rapid to succeed. However, when Etienne goes on to claim that the formerly enslaved will *never* be equal, there is quiet prophecy in Inch's rejoinder: '"Never is a long time."'[186]

In the notorious 1863 New York riots, protests by Irish immigrants against a Civil War draft transformed into sustained attacks on African Americans. One of the darkest intersections of Irish and African histories, it greatly troubled the dual-heritage Yerby. This is suggested by the granular details of the murder of a Black child by Irish rioters in his final published novel, the Confederate spy romance, *McKenzie's Hundred* (1985). The Civil War-era and Tammany Hall-backed Mayor of New York, Fernando Wood (1812–81), a vocal opponent of the Thirteenth Amendment (abolishing slavery), once suggested to the New York Council that the city should secede in order to maintain its cotton trade with the Confederacy.[187] In *McKenzie's Hundred,* a fictional pro-Confederate intriguer in Wood's circle plots to further New York secession by bribing working-class Irish people to begin a 'nice bloody riot' against African Americans. The intriguer and his associates surreptitiously direct the rioting Irish 'b'hoys' and 'colleens' at street level.[188] As with the Paxton Boys' massacre and the demonization of Faulkner's Supten, the behind-the-scenes manipulation in *McKenzie's Hundred* exposes the process whereby the Irish become the public face of a much more diffuse and systemic racism. After a lengthy panorama of attacks on property at various locations in the city, Yerby closes in on a particularly hellish scene involving a lone unevacuated child at Manhattan's Colored Orphan Asylum, who is butchered to a pulp by Irishwomen wielding crowbars and brickbats.[189] The gruesome scene shows that, nearly forty years after his first bestseller about a slave-holding Irish adventurer, Yerby still struggled with the more disquieting historical overlaps of his Irish and African heritages.

As Yerby aged, he became increasingly interested in Irish history in the Americas and in his own Irish ancestry. In the 1986 interview in which he declared that he had 'more Irish blood than Negro', Yerby was promoting what turned out to be his final novel, *McKenzie's Hundred.* He told the interviewer that he was planning a next book on the Saint Patrick's Battalion (Batallón de San Patricio), a US Army unit of predominantly Catholic Irish immigrants. A year before the abortive rebellion of Mitchel's Young Irelanders as famine in Ireland dragged on, the unit deserted for the Mexican side in the Mexican-American War (1846–48). This conflict was a follow-on from the 1845 US annexation of Texas—which Mexico considered its own territory—by the administration of Andrew Jackson's *protégée*,[190] the Scots-Irish James K. Polk (1845–49). The reasons given for the mass desertion have centred on the shared Catholic culture of Irish and Mexican,[191] though discussions of the ethics of Polk's intervention pay little attention to the probable role played by the fact that the war delayed America's official response to the Famine. (In one of the great ironies of Irish-Native history, the Choctaw Nation of Oklahoma, who had been routed out of northern Mississippi in 1831 by Jackson, sent money to the starving Irish.[192]) However, Yerby implies that the Irish deserted out of a sense of solidarity with a people of colour invaded by its powerful Anglo Protestant neighbour. 'It was', Yerby told his interviewer in 1986, 'one of the first desertions, I think the *only* desertion en masse of American citizens who turned against their own country.'[193] The battalion is not memorialized in America, unsurprisingly, and has only received detailed scholarly attention since about the 1990s.[194] Yerby quotes the declaration by the eighteenth US president, Ulysses S. Grant, that the Mexican-American conflict was '"the most unjust war in the history of our country"', but wryly concedes that the battalion would make a 'very unpopular subject for a novel'.[195] Thus, the San Patricio episode went against the bestselling author's well-honed instinct for the commercial, but may have been the kind of meaningful topic he had in mind when he wrote his agent that he would like to write 'some good books before I die'.[196] Yerby's interest in what was, in 1986, an obscure moment of Irish solidarity with a non-white cohort suggests his search for a counter to the bleak history of African-Irish relations that he explored in *McKenzie's Hundred.* With the San Patricio project, the dual-heritage Yerby makes peace of sorts with this blighted past in locating an event in the Americas in which the possibility of a different trajectory flared for a moment.

Coda: Caste and Casting: Maureen O'Hara

Figure 4.3 Frank Yerby became the first African American to have a book purchased by a major Hollywood studio when 20th Century Fox optioned *The Foxes of Harrow*. Released in 1947, the adaptation starred Rex Harrison and Maureen O'Hara. Image of promotional poster courtesy of ALAMY.

In 1946, Yerby became the first African American to have a book purchased for screen adaptation by a major Hollywood studio when 20th Century Fox optioned *The Foxes of Harrow* (Figure 4.3). Nevertheless, at the film's preview in Augusta,

Georgia, Yerby's family was segregated.[197] The 1947 Oscar-nominated adaptation, which starred the Irish-born Maureen O'Hara and the British actor Rex Harrison, defanged its source material in presenting the South's racial make-up as a black/white binary. This contrasts with the racial spectrum of French Louisiana in the novel, in which 'mixed' and ambiguously 'white' characters are central. The screenplay focused mainly, as Matthew Teutsch notes, on the marriage of Odile and Stephen, and made alterations that cut or downplayed the Black experience depicted in the novel: the action concludes before the Civil War, Inch is only shown as an obedient enslaved child, Desiree becomes a white character, and Frederick Douglass's cameo in the novel is cut altogether.[198] In addition, Fox's 'guttersnipe' origins are excised in the film, where he becomes the 'natural' son of the aristocratic Irish House of Harrow. For Phyllis Klotman, this social elevation eradicates the novel's mockery of the plantation system's *creation* of instant aristocrats.[199] Indeed, Fox is played with an upper-class British accent by Harrison, whose background led to tension with the Irish nationalist O'Hara.[200] Yerby, unsurprisingly, 'despised the film adaptation', as did many fans of his novel.[201] Baltimore's *Afro-American*, a leading Black newspaper, complained that from 'the cadaver emerges only the customary boy-gets-girl formula', and that the source novel's condemnation of 'the entire social system of the antebellum South' is 'completely killed'.[202]

However, the casting of natural redhead O'Hara as Odile will be seen to have inadvertently reintroduced some of the class and racial ambiguity that the screenplay attempted to excise. (Odile has dark hair in the source novel.) In the past century, as Diane Negra charts, female stars of Irish connection have both challenged and cemented Hollywood's representations of the unethnicized white woman and the 'off-white' ethnic woman.[203] The Abbey Theatre-trained O'Hara was born Maureen FitzSimons, and shared her prominent Anglo- and Hiberno-Norman surname with Thomas Fitzsimons, an Irish-born signer of the United States Constitution. The name apparently sounded too 'WASP' for an Irish redhead in mid-century America, since FitzSimons was reassembled as a 'lower-caste colleen' by being forced to change her name to 'O'Hara' at the insistence of a film producer in 1939;[204] in the year in which the film adaptation of *Gone with the Wind* was released, that surname was the *sine qua non* of Irishness.[205] O'Hara's first film to be shot in Technicolor, the colour process associated with the zenith of Hollywood's Golden Age, was *To the Shores of Tripoli* (1942), as she describes in her memoir:

> Apparently my features – red hair, hazel-green eyes, and a fair complexion – had photographed so well in Technicolor that...Dr. Herbert Kalmus, who had invented the Technicolor process, was so pleased that he started saying, 'Maureen O'Hara is *my* "Queen of Techicolor"', and since he owned the technology, I became known as *the* Queen of Technicolor.[206]

Technicolor's amplification of O'Hara's pale colouring allowed her to be packaged as both unethnicized American and 'fiery' ethnic, depending on the part. She performs the latter in her role as feisty bride Mary Kate Danaher in John Ford's *The Quiet Man* (1952),[207] probably the most written-about film with an Irish setting. As this study's theorization of Irish paleness as racial liability in the historical Caribbean context suggests, O'Hara's colouring could signal both white and 'off-white', a flexibility that yields racial ambiguity when her casting as a red-haired Odile in the *Foxes* adaptation is considered. In the absence of Yerby's insinuating descriptions of Etienne as 'swarthy' (and the like), the 'red Irish' actress inadvertently lets some of the racial ambiguity cut by the screenplay back in.

In many European colonial contexts, 'Creole' may signal mixed-race identity, and the Italian and French translations of the film adaptation's title ('La Superba Creola' and 'La Fière Créole', respectively) foreground that term. Moreover, although *The Foxes of Harrow* was shot in black and white, O'Hara had been known in her Technicolor glory since 1942's *To the Shores of Tripoli*, and the artwork for promotional posters in various language markets endows Odile/O'Hara with a vivid shade of red hair and/or pale skin.[208] In Yerby's novel, Stephen possesses red hair, blue eyes, and freckled skin, all the hallmarks of an extreme paleness appropriate to his low caste Irish origins. In the adaptation, however, Harrison's hair is dark, so the markers of 'red Irishness' are carried by O'Hara's iteration of Odile alone. Indeed, O'Hara's red-haired Odile challenges Mitchell's positioning of a dark-haired Irish colleen (Scarlett O'Hara) as the pretty face of Southern white supremacy, since pale Irish colouring is associated with 'off-whiteness' in *GWTW*: 'common red-haired' *nouveau riche* Irish carpetbagger and former chambermaid Bridget Flaherty also possesses extremely pale skin, both of which mark her as deportee-class, while more 'common' again is Belle Watling, who 'stood out' among wartime Atlanta's many prostitutes 'due to her flaming hair'.[209] In short, in *GWTW* red hair in a woman signals vulgarity and a dangerous excess of taste or sexuality.[210] The Irish redhead actress exceeds Dyer's schema that extreme female paleness onscreen (as amplified by lighting) invariably codes high class.[211] This renders O'Hara as the seeming antithesis of the icy Irish blonde considered presently. O'Hara's success in Hollywood opened the door for other performers of Irish connection, and not even a generation later, that Irish blonde, Grace Kelly, became central to Irish America's final arrival at uncontested whiteness.

5
White Wedding
Grace Kelly, Spectacle, and Irish Assimilation

Grace Kelly (1928–82) was a film actress of Famine-era Irish Catholic descent who was born in Philadelphia, Pennsylvania. Awarded an Oscar in 1955 for *The Country Girl* (1954), between 1951 and 1956 she appeared in eleven films, most notably *High Noon* (1952), *High Society* (1956), and Alfred Hitchcock's *Rear Window*, *To Catch a Thief*, and *Dial M for Murder* (1954–55). Kelly received the title of Princess Grace of Monaco upon her marriage to Prince Rainier III of Monaco in his principality's Catholic cathedral on 19 April 1956 (Figure 5.1).

In recent decades, Kelly has been popularly understood to be the kind of American bride portrayed in Henry James's novels: the upper-class, monied American woman—somehow simultaneously natural and sophisticated—who marries the worldly, titled European groom. But in the 1950s, there was yet to be an American president who shared Kelly's descent and certain exclusive roles were still not accessible to Catholic Irish Americans. Kelly's wedding was one of the largest international media events of that decade: broadcast live on television by Metro-Goldwyn-Mayer, it was watched by 30 million people.[1] This chapter concludes that the bride's globally visible ascent to the highest social echelon paved the way for America's 'royals', the Kennedy dynasty, as well as for broader Irish America's attainment of unconditional whiteness. Therefore, this rise was also related to the ebbing away of the differentiating term 'Scots-Irish' in the northeast. However, such connections have gone unrecognized in 'serious' historiography of Irish America, perhaps because the event is remembered as the 'frivolous' stuff of women's magazines. Donald Spoto, a recent biographer of Grace Kelly, complains that her story has not been well served by writers.[2] Although Spoto refers to her biographers, this is also true in the case of the scholarship of Irish America, in which there is a startling absence of work on an impactful and cultured woman whose deep interest in her heritage led her widower to endow the Princess Grace Irish Library of Monaco in her honour.[3]

Philadelphia's racio-ethnic politics shaped both Kelly's self-presentation and the persona created for her by film studio executives, but the role her beauty and its marketing played in the evolution of Irish 'whiteness' remains unexamined.[4] In the opening decades of the twentieth century, the increasingly lucrative though still segregated business of beauty was still new and *outré* enough to allow Black and 'off white' immigrant women to make fortunes and rise socially, from Madam

Race, Politics, and Irish America. Mary M. Burke, Oxford University Press.
 DOI: 10.1093/oso/9780192859730.003.0006

Figure 5.1 Prince Rainier III of Monaco and Grace Kelly during their 1956 wedding ceremony. Courtesy of ALAMY.

C.J. Walker and the Polish-Jewish Helena Rubinstein, to the Dublin-born Kathleen Mary Quinlan (1887–1957).[5] Precisely because the business and practice of beauty and fashion have been associated primarily with women and queer people, they are overlooked in surveys of Irish-American history and assimilation.[6] Such works have traditionally focused on male-dominated business, political, and Catholic Church spheres. Moreover, even these often fail to incorporate significant women politicos, activists, and religious leaders of Irish connection (such as Rachel Carson, Mary Elizabeth Lease, and Katharine Drexel),[7] never mind women who made their names in 'frivolous' fields. The lack of consideration of the meaning of Kelly's beauty in relation to her ethnicity and gender and its history of simianized images (see Figure I.1) is an extraordinary omission when one considers the overlaps between dermal whiteness and images used to sell beauty, film, and fashion products. Irish-American Studies has traditionally been preoccupied with narratives of historical suffering. These do not gel with the story of an exceedingly photogenic woman from an immediate background of some privilege who rose into the ranks of both major Hollywood stardom and minor European royalty. Nevertheless, Kelly's veneer of glamour is the end-point of a multi-generation story that follows the broad contours of post-Famine Irish experience, though in the specific context of Philadelphia, a highly stratified city that Judith Ridner has termed the 'cradle' for Scots-Irish culture. Ana Salzberg and Stella Bruzzi have beautifully theorized Grace Kelly the celluloid goddess, but the emphasis in this chapter is on the undertheorized meaning of her image in relation to her ethnic heritage. However, before turning to the impact of this background on Grace's film career and the transformation of Irish America initiated by her wedding spectacular, the chapter first examines the broader canvas of her family roots, including the inner history of Irish Pennsylvania in the period of her childhood in the work of John O'Hara and that of her playwright uncle, George Kelly.

The Kellys: 'Off-white' in a Scots-Irish City

Born in 1928, Grace was the daughter of John B. Kelly (1889–1960), a self-made millionaire. She was raised in a large home in East Falls, a residential Philadelphia neighbourhood on the banks of the Schuylkill River. This waterway divided the *nouveau riche* from the Anglo-Protestant social elite on the opposite bank, families who constituted Philadelphia 'society' because they often traced their origins to the colonial period when English Quaker William Penn (1644–1718) founded the colony of Pennsylvania and developed plans for the city of Philadelphia. Spoto notes that the 'most respected, established families—Protestants with "old money" like the Drexels, Biddles, Clarks, Cadwaladers and Wideners—lived across the river [from the Kellys], in western suburbs along the so-called Main Line'.[8] '[A] realm of a sort' that lay northwest of Philadelphia, the Main Line had 'its own class system based on one's lineage and listing in *Philadelphia's Social Register*'.[9] The Kelly home was a fine one, consisting of seventeen rooms and set on lovely grounds, but in the eyes of 'old money' Main Liners, this picture of gentility would have been punctured by the fact that it had been newly built in the late 1920s with bricks from the family firm, Kelly for Brickwork.

John B.'s father, John Henry (d. 1917), had been born in a village called Drimurla in the hinterland of Newport, County Mayo in the Famine year of 1847, immigrating to Pennsylvania twenty years later. This region was particularly hard hit during the catastrophe, though Alexis de Tocqueville suggests that even in the decade before, Newport was already a byword for destitution.[10] Unsurprisingly, the locale became a centre for agrarian agitation in the post-Famine era.[11] John Henry's wife-to-be, Mary Costello (1852–1926), emigrated from Mayo at the age of thirteen, and married the labourer four years later. In an indication of family memory of Newport, an audit of the core Irish literature collection of the Princess Grace Library suggests Grace's politics leaned Irish nationalist, pro-Home Rule, and self-consciously 'Gaelic'.[12] Her interest in Irish culture ran deep: in a 1978 benefit poetry performance, the princess included the work of three poets of Irish connection, James Stephens, Seamus Heaney, and Gerard Manley Hopkins.[13] Grace stopped at John Henry's former home on her official state visit to Ireland in 1961, and in 1976, she purchased the small cottage and the surrounding smallholding.[14]

Due to the modesty of this background, mere wealth was not enough in the case of the highly successful children of immigrants John Henry Kelly and Mary Costello. The assumption, commonplace in Philadelphia right into the midcentury, that the post-Famine Irish could not convincingly occupy echelons reserved for those of 'old' WASP/Scots-Irish family, is explored by realist author (and Fitzgerald's erstwhile correspondent) John O'Hara (1905–1970). Born in the Pennsylvania coal town of Pottsville to a middle-class Irish Catholic family, O'Hara leapt to immediate prominence with his nihilistic debut novel, *Appointment in Samarra* (1934), set in the fictional town of Gibbsville, Pennsylvania. The novel tracks the inexplicable downward spiral of a suave Pennsylvania businessman after he assaults a loudmouth Irish-American Catholic on the rise called Harry Reilly, whose 'good clothes' do not mask his gaucheness.[15] ('Dressing', as sometime *Vogue* contributor Elizabeth Bowen noted with seeming anxiety, 'is the one art the unqualified must practice'.[16]) O'Hara's second novel, *BUtterfield 8* (1935), was set in Manhattan during the Depression, but the ethno-religious divisions of O'Hara's home state hover. In the novel, a minor Catholic Irish-American character named Jimmy Malloy delivers a diatribe that parses the hierarchy of whitenesses in the northeast in an angry response to being described by debutante Isabel Stannard as 'upper crust':

> I am a Mick [derogatory American slang for 'Irishman']. I wear Brooks [Brothers] clothes and I don't eat salad with a spoon and I probably could play five-goal polo in two years, but I am a Mick. [...] I suppose I could walk through Grand Central at the same time President Hoover was arriving on a train, and the Secret Service boys wouldn't collar me on sight as a public enemy. That's because I dress the way I do [...]. I am pretty God damn American, [...] and yet we're not American. We're Micks, we're non-assimilable, we Micks. [...] The people who think I am a Yale man aren't very observing about people.[17]

An 'icon of class and power' with a 'bland, smug, and conformist' image, New York's Brooks Brother (f. 1818) has supplied 'dark blue pinstriped suits, linen handkerchiefs, and regimental striped ties to generations of the American power elite'.[18]

Fitzgerald gave the label a product placement in two instances in *This Side of Paradise*, which, as O'Hara notes with relish, riled critics.[19] Jimmy concludes his rant by noting that he could never be 'upper crust' because he had once been too broke to eat for a couple of days until '"the n***** woman that cleaned up"' brought him food without prompting. '"She was swell"', he concludes, to which the incisive Isabel retorts, '"I should think she was swell enough for you to call her a colored woman instead of a n*****".'[20] As Fanning notes, Jimmy's outburst remains oft-quoted,[21] and is generally deployed to bolster Irish-American grievance regarding past 'off-white' status.[22] However, Isabel's closing retort is *never* excerpted in such contexts, though her words suggest that O'Hara *critiques* rather than endorses the desire for unambiguous 'whiteness', since she points up how Jimmy's toneless sense of grievance is entangled with his racism.

Spoto spells out that the Main Line divide was ethnic, religious, and political: 'The Kellys were Irish, Roman Catholic and Democrats; Philadelphia society was English, Episcopalian and Republican.'[23] Kelly's mother was quoted as saying that the family could have been listed in the city's *Social Register* if 'we'd wanted to', which Spoto calls an 'astonishingly naïve' statement.[24] Spoto conflates 'Episcopalian' and 'Protestant' when writing of the elite that barred the Kellys, although the aforementioned Biddles and Cadwaladers, for instance, were of English and Welsh Quaker origin, respectively, the denomination at the top of the white pile in Philadelphia due to the Quaker tenor of Penn's colony.[25] However, the Protestants with which Irish-Philadelphian Catholics were most familiar (for better or ill) were Irish-American Protestants, a cohort that, in Philadelphia, were often of non-conformist Ulster origin. Thus, although accounts of the Kelly family's social status measure it against some undifferentiated Anglo-Protestant elite, the history of inter-Irish sectarian tensions in Philadelphia means that the Protestantism that *mattered* to the Irish-Philadelphian Catholic who perceived a sectarian slight was that which originated in Ulster.

In the Ulster-Scots Adam Douglass's *The Irish Emigrant* of 1817, Philadelphia appears to be a kind of Eden to the newly arrived Irish.[26] Pennsylvania had been the 'preeminent destination' for eighteenth-century Ulster immigrants, being almost certainly the disembarkation point of Andrew Jackson's parents when they came to the colonies in the 1760s.[27] Ridner notes that by 1790, the increasingly influential Scots-Irish composed approximately 25 per cent of Philadelphia's population. They also comprised 15 per cent of Pennsylvania's population, since the state's pluralism and commercial opportunities had much to offer a cohort fleeing economic downturns and religious persecution in Ireland, not least that Philadelphia was the headquarters of the Presbyterian Church in America,[28] which had effectively been founded by a Scots-Irish immigrant.[29] Although Pennsylvania had been ground zero for the not uniformly positive image of the wild frontier Scots-Irishman, Philadelphia was the later birthplace of the 'ethnic pride' Scotch-Irish Society (f. 1889), which ameliorated the cohort's 'buffer' role on the colonial frontier by inserting them into Anglo-America's myth of founding. Spoto speaks broadly of Anglo-Protestant Philadelphia, but the Catholic Irish could not make the *Social Register* in part because the initially 'off-white' Ulster Irish had integrated earlier and had done so by differentiating themselves from the 'new' Irish. The increasing numbers of 'impoverished, unskilled, and Catholic' Irish immigrants in Philadelphia in the immediate pre-Famine period led to the emergence of the Protestant fraternal Orange Order in that location in the 1830s; the Scots-Irish, eager to protect their 'in' status in that city, 'were ready, eager, and able to renew the political, economic, social, and religious feuds of the old country'.[30]

In the early nineteenth century, Philadelphia's location a few miles north of the Mason-Dixon line led to a huge influx of freed and fugitive slaves,[31] and toxic inter-Irish relations were outpaced by toxic relations between the 'new' Irish and African Americans. Irish Catholics competed with Black Philadelphians for the lowest-paying jobs, and the former rioted for three days in August 1842, targeting the home of mixed-race abolitionist Robert Purvis as well as the African-American Second Presbyterian Church.[32] A contemporary marker of the riot on Lombard Street that memorializes the attack on a Jamaican Emancipation Day parade that prompted the riots—enslaved Jamaicans had received full freedom only four years earlier—robs this history of some of its ethnic specificity in referring only to 'a mob of whites'.[33] The soon-to-follow so-called 'anti-Catholic riots' in 1844 in Philadelphia were really 'anti-Irish riots',[34] and a similar 'de-ethnicization' of this fraught history is that 'Irish-born Protestants' rather than some undifferentiated Anglo-American cohort led the charge.[35]

Thus, although the cultural historiography of whiteness and Irishness tends to consider the nineteenth-century Catholic cohort alone, their drive for status was often most vehemently opposed by the earlier, predominantly Protestant immigrants out of Ireland who had first claimed unconditional whiteness. The Pennsylvania governor in the decade following the riots, James Pollock, 'a devout Presbyterian of Scotch-Irish ancestry', was elected in 1855 in part because of the support of the 'Know Nothing' political constituency.[36] Inter-Irish tensions erupted at street level again in Philadelphia in 1912, the crucial year for Unionist Belfast's monumental anti-Home Rule rally, as a result of which, mass demonstrations of support occurred in American cities with large and socially prominent Ulster-Irish populations.[37] To rewrite the celebrated opening of *A Tree Grows in Brooklyn*: 'Serene was not a word you could put to Philadelphia. Especially in the summer of 1912.'[38] Indeed, the rancour of that year for all factions of Irish America may well have influenced the late summer 1912 setting of O'Neill's *Long Day's Journey into Night*.[39]

Just as the Wilde–Carson antagonism may be seen as a clash of politics as much as a clash of *mores*, consideration of the Home Rule debate also makes for a more nuanced reading of the disturbances that greeted the Abbey Theatre's touring production of J.M. Synge's *The Playboy of the Western World* in January 1912 in

Philadelphia. This event has tended to be read as nothing more than a contagion caught from the riotous New York City response to that production two months earlier,[40] where it was perceived as a slight against Catholic rural Ireland by an upper-class Irish Protestant dramatist. The instigator in the Philadelphia *Playboy* disturbance was one Joseph McLaughlin, a Donegal-born Vice President of the Ancient Order of Hibernians who would go on to become a member of the US House of Representatives from Pennsylvania.[41] The AOH was an Irish Catholic fraternal organization created in mid nineteenth-century New York in response to nativist mobilization that had, by the opening decade of the twentieth century, also emerged strongly in Ulster as a Catholic response to the Orange Order's sectarian shows of Protestant strength at its parades. The AOH organized counter parades that sometimes ended in sectarian violence.[42] When seen in the light of that same year's mass demonstrations in Philadelphia of support for Belfast's Carson-led anti-Home Rule movement, the AOH officer's protest can be contextualized in the Irish sectarian tensions of *both* Belfast and Philadelphia. Lucy McDiarmid's suggestion that McLaughlin's confrontation with consumers of what he perceived to be 'anti-Irish high culture—the Wisters, Rodmans, Biddles, and so forth' implies that the tussle arose out of very local tensions for the Donegal man.[43] McLaughlin had the players arrested on a soon-dismissed charge of immorality. However, his impression of a trans-Atlantic elite Protestant conspiracy to insult Catholic Gaels would have seemed to have been confirmed by the fact that one of the lawyers representing the Abbey actors was a Philadelphia Biddle![44]

Comparing Philadelphia to New York and Boston, where the Irish dominated the urban machine, Clark suggests that the denial of commanding political power to the city's Irish cohort lasted until the mid-twentieth century, at about the time Grace Kelly rose to prominence: 'It consigned the Irish Catholics either to political futility in the ranks of an ineffectual Democratic Party or to the status of permanent minority stepchildren within the ranks of a Republican organization dominated locally by Anglo-Saxon businessmen and statewide by Scotch-Irish political bosses.'[45] Clark's suggestion that the pre-war Catholic Irish were always only ever on the cusp of where true power lay illuminates the defanged nature of John B. Kelly's role as Chair of the Philadelphia County Democratic Party as of 1937. As Grace's biographer Robert Lacey concludes, '[w]ith his charisma, wealth, and political connections, Jack Kelly would have made it to the top of almost any other city in North America.'[46] By the period of Grace's father's birth in 1889, the legacy of the Catholic Irish being overshadowed by an earlier and by now British-American Ulster cohort is that Philadelphia does not 'enjoy the reputation of other urban centers as a location of Irish awareness in America.'[47] This, despite the fact that by 1880 the Irish constituted 60 per cent of the foreign-born population of Philadelphia and 33 per cent of that cohort by 1900.[48]

The Belfast sectarian agitation that was echoed on the streets of Philadelphia in 1912 would doubtlessly have had a strong impact on John B. Kelly, who was then a young man. The youngest of the ten children born to John Henry and Mary, none of whom were schooled beyond the eighth grade,[49] his later success in the fields of rowing and business made John B. into one of the best-known Philadelphians of his day. After quitting school early, John B. joined his brothers' bricklaying firm and became a champion boxer during his army service in World War I. Afterwards he founded Kelly for Brickwork, and the building boom of the 1920s made him a millionaire. President Franklin Roosevelt, who once called John B. Kelly the handsomest man he had ever met,[50] later appointed him as National Director of Physical Training,[51] and in the 1950s, Kelly authored an article entitled 'Are We Becoming a Nation of Weaklings?'[52] Kelly, notes Spoto, 'had little interest in cultural or intellectual matters'[53] and was puzzled by the theatre interests of his brothers Walter and George, a vaudevillian and a playwright, respectively. Altogether, John B. fit the American stereotype of the Irishman as physical and no-nonsense rather than cerebral and urbane. It is striking, in light of the usual emphasis on the near-naked female body in celebrity culture, that numerous images of Grace Kelly's sculling [river rowing]-champion brothers and father dressed only in bathing suits that highlight their peak physical condition circulate online.[54]

In 1920, Kelly applied to race in the Diamond Sculls at the Henley Royal Regatta, rowing's most prestigious event held annually on the Thames in Henley, England. At the time, Kelly had won six US National Championships, but his Henley application was rejected, purportedly because he had done manual labour as a bricklayer. This contravened the regatta's definition of an amateur, in place as of 1894, which was anyone who had ever been employed as 'a mechanic, artisan or labourer, or engaged in any menial duty'.[55] The incident was seized upon as an egregious instance of anti-Irish sentiment, and Spoto echoes numerous previous declarations in claiming that the 'true reason' for Kelly's rejection 'was that the English did not want to risk giving a prize to an Irish-American Catholic'.[56] However, a recent biographer stresses that what the oarsman perceived to be a snub had less to do with 'lineage' than with the simple fact that he had worked with his hands.[57] What is interesting is that the reason for the decision is clearly up for interpretation, but it has been unequivocally stated to have been the result of anti-Irish bias in every popular account of John B.'s life.

Sports in the 1890s and early 1900s among the Irish in Philadelphia aided in the construction of a more 'assertive' and 'militant' 'Irish Catholic masculinity',[58] illuminating the challenge to ethnic pride that Kelly felt in being barred from proving his prowess in the most upper-class English of sporting events. Stung by this perceived insult, the highly motivated Kelly went on to win two gold medals in sculling in the 1920 Olympics at Antwerp, Belgium. Philadelphia folklore holds that Kelly subsequently mailed his racing cap to King George V with the message, 'Greetings from a bricklayer'.[59] Finally, a third theory that only emerged in John B.'s *Times* obituary claims that he was barred because of a 1905 resolution that no member of his Philadelphia boat club was permitted to compete at Henley due to its previous infringement of the rowing event's rules.[60] At any rate, and in light of the sense of ethnic slight that the debacle has always facilitated in Irish America, it is ironic that a year before Princess Grace's death in 1982, she was invited to present the prizes at the Royal Regatta. Moreover, in 2003, the Henley Royal Regatta renamed its women's quadruple sculls rowing event the Princess Grace Challenge Cup.

Ignatiev influentially traces the manner in which the oppressed became the oppressors: post-Famine Irish immigrants began the process of achieving acceptance among an initially hostile population by being more pitiless in their dealings with African Americans than even the nativists. This narrative illuminates the vaudeville career of Grace's uncle Walter Kelly (1873–1939), who became a headliner by 1905 with his 'Virginia Judge' act, which was a success throughout America and even the Anglophone world.[61] This comedy monologue was based on the belittling sentencings of a police court judge in Walter's adopted city of Newport News, Virginia, who 'dispensed assembly-line justice to the city's poor blacks who had run afoul of Jim Crow law', and Walter's routine also made comedy from uneducated defendants' artless statements in court. Though 'comically folksy', the act, in which Kelly played all the parts, 'was essentially racist',[62] partaking of both the receding minstrelsy form and the ascendant vaudeville mode. If, as Roediger argues, 'blackface minstrels were the first self-consciously *white* entertainers in the world',[63] then Walter's vocal movement from 'Black' to 'white' voice/character was an attempt by the Irish Catholic son of a poor immigrant to assert unassailable whiteness. This, as Roediger notes of earlier Irish minstrel performers who projected onto Black characters the very stereotypes of naivety and laziness to which their own community was subject, 'only made for greater psychic investment'.[64] Off-stage, Walter 'referred to blacks as "darkies" and their offspring as "pickaninnies"', and refused to share a stage with a Black song-and-dance act in 1909.[65] A cross-generational graph spanning half a century of Kelly showbusiness careers would move from Walter's successful career in what could, at times, be the *déclassé* world of vaudeville, to the subsequent and more 'respectable' success of his dramatist younger brother, George, and later still, to the worldwide adulation of their Oscar-winning niece, Grace. This trajectory maps neatly onto the broad graph of post-Famine Irish-American upward mobility, and it is especially striking that both graphs begin with initial success achieved through the depreciation of African Americans.

This is *not* to suggest that Grace herself was prejudiced against any minority identity. Indeed, she actively defended sexual and racial minorities when this stance was neither profitable nor popular in most mainstream white-dominated spheres. She was accepting of her Uncle George's sexuality and championed his work to the indifferent Kelly clan.[66] Moreover, when still trying to make her name as an actor in 1951, she took the risk of staging a very public walk-out with Josephine Baker's party because that storied performer, French Resistance agent, and Civil Rights activist had been demeaned by the staff of Manhattan's Stork Club.[67] Baker and Kelly remained friends after the incident, perhaps not least because of a recognition that they both self-consciously responded to normative white aesthetics in their self-presentation, albeit in different ways.[68] In 1975, Grace backed Baker's triumphant Paris comeback and later paid her burial expenses[69] (see Figure 3.7). Furthermore, in her role as Princess of Monaco, Grace was continually inundated with requests for endorsements, the bulk of which she declined. Therefore, her choice to provide an introduction for a whimsical 1980 children's book about a tiger who insists on being in love with a red flower instead of a 'white tigress'—a fable that seemingly calls for acceptance of queer and interracial relationships—testifies to her life-long commitment to equality: 'Love can open eyes', she writes in the preface, 'Love lifts barriers that have shut out understanding and compassion.'[70] This tolerance regarding racial and sexual diversity were not useful attributes in the aspirational 1920s Irish Catholic Philadelphia of Grace's birth, in which full acceptance into elite, conservative WASP heteronormativity was the prize for which to aim. The oeuvre of a once-prominent dramatist of middle-class Philadelphia of that period makes for a particularly interesting source for this inner social history, and that Pulitzer Prize-winning dramatist was Grace's beloved paternal uncle, George. The distrust of both mandatory heterosexuality and middle-class suburbia in his drama reveal a man uneasy with both his closeted sexuality and effaced humble immigrant roots. George's inter-war drama explores the anxiety of implicitly 'non-WASP' white Philadelphians and the ethnic hierarchy that shaped Pennsylvania in the early decades of Grace's life. In short, he was perfectly placed to portray the Irish ethnic world that his niece would later transform.

America's 'Queerest Writer': George Kelly in the Ethnic Closet

Sexuality is one of the great evasions of the Catholic Irish-American narrative: into this century, 'ethnic pride' celebrations of the Kennedy administration in mainstream liberal Irish America avoid references to the president's well-documented sexual peccadillos,[71] and such were unmentionable in the public discourse of buttoned-up 1960s Ireland.[72] Nevertheless, although robust heterosexuality was not openly discussed, it was understood to exist, but homosexuality was so little understood among some of the Irish Catholic laity that it could hide in plain sight. In *To the Shores of Tripoli*, her 1942 breakthrough in Technicolor, Maureen O'Hara's nurse character Mary Carter pulls rank when a leatherneck (military slang for a member of the US Marine Corps) tries to seduce her: 'As a navy nurse', she reprimands the young recruit in the vaguely Irish accent she uses in the film,

'I hold rank equal to a lieutenant.' After they kiss in a later scene, the marine declares, 'I'll bet I'm the first leatherneck in history that ever kissed a lieutenant.' Queerness is readable—if unread—in this O'Hara vehicle as it has often been in the cultural productions of Irish America. This reticence regarding homosexuality is also apparent in the resistance of his own family and certain earlier critics to using that lens to read the life and work of George Kelly.[73] The playwright's sexuality is considered in the following, but the deeper interest is in deploying 'queer' in its broader gloss of looking askance at received ideas, a useful lens for interpreting Kelly's take on Irish Catholic Philadelphia.

George Edward Kelly (1887–1974), the ninth of John H. and Mary's ten children, is today largely forgotten by scholars of American drama, though he achieved considerable popular and critical success in the 1920s. Victorian-era Philadelphia was the site of numerous textile mills that employed many unskilled Irish workers,[74] and after a short education, one by one the five Kelly boys—including George—went out to labour at the Dobson Mills, a huge Falls area employer.[75] After George took a night course in drama at a local school, he moved to New York, where he secured his first acting job with a touring company by his early twenties, and was writing one-act sketches a few years later. After his 1920s heyday, George worked as a screenwriter in Hollywood for MGM. He had a minor second flowering in the 1940s, during which his aspiring actress niece, Grace, made her professional stage debut in a July 1949 production of his 1922 play, *The Torch-Bearers* (Figure 5.2).[76] Just as Wilde, in celebrated Irish-American critic Mary McCarthy's summary, could not pass as a gentleman because 'he dressed too well and his manners were too polished',[77] Kelly's upper-class elegance was a pose. Beautifully spoken and presented, Kelly also self-consciously rejected the politics and the exemplars of Irish-American culture and his own Democrat family, evincing a strong dislike of John F. Kennedy in later life.[78] Kelly's early family background is probably most accurately described as striving immigrant on the cusp of prosperity, but he would later falsely claim to have been privately educated by tutors. Moreover, Kelly destroyed any personal documents that could be of use to future biographers.[79] This guardedness is a response to the precarious social position of the Catholic Irish in the Philadelphia of his youth and to having to live as a closeted gay man. Kelly has received some relatively recent Queer Studies attention, but as with James, his closeted Irishness is difficult to disentangle from his hidden sexuality. Although the question of George's sexuality was first addressed in print as early as Arthur Lewis's 1977 biography of the Kelly family, he has yet to be outed as a Philadelphian-Irish dramatist.

Kelly had a life-long partner named William Weagley (or Weagly), and the Kelly family's refusal to acknowledge him as anything other than George's valet arose from the entwinement of their Catholicism with a keen desire to be socially respectable. When he visited the family home with George, Weagley ate in the kitchen with the help and a neighbour later recalled that '"the family would not

Figure 5.2 Grace Kelly on 25 July 1949 (opening night) at the Bucks County Playhouse, Pennsylvania, in her stage debut as Florence McCrickett in *The Torch-Bearers* (1922), her uncle George Kelly's play. Photo by Richard W. Cauffman and courtesy of Jeff Cadman.

accept him in any other way. That was in Philadelphia. Elsewhere, it was different.'"[80] Indeed, in light of what will be demonstrated to be the role played by the recurring character of an Irish maid in Kelly's plays, there is premediated social slight in the insistence of George's family that Weagly was his valet. (This, in an era in which same-sex partners could be described with respectful and egalitarian euphemisms such as 'companion' or 'friend'.[81]) Poignantly, in a display of the need for social decorum of the Irish Catholic family that has risen through the ranks, the Kellys did not even invite Wegley to George's funeral, so he was forced to creep into the back pew of the church.[82]

Certainly, something undercuts the seemingly heteronormative WASP middle-class surfaces of Kelly's works, a sense of refusal to which he gives voice in advice to would-be playwrights: '"Avoid the obvious. Don't say the thing they want you to say."'[83] Queer theorists have found McCarthy's declaration that Kelly was 'the queerest writer [...] in America' irresistible.[84] However, the closest he ever came to peeking out of the closet was in an early career vaudeville one-act, *The Flattering Word,* staged in New York in 1922. The dramatist himself played the role of travelling actor Eugene Tesh and also directed the production. While on tour near the home of his old friend, Mary, who is now married to a Protestant man of the cloth, Tesh visits her house, which is sited next to her husband's church, and the following exchange ensues:

> MARY: I suppose you never go to church, do you, Gene? [...]
> TESH: No, but I have a very intimate friend who has been there. Is this your church out here?
> MARY: Yes; [...] we had three weddings in it last month.
> TESH: (*casually*) It isn't so innocent as it looks, is it?
> MARY: Are you married, Gene?
> TESH: What?
> MARY: I say, are you married?
> TESH: Why, not this season. [...]
> MARY: Aren't you really married, Gene?
> TESH: No, really, I'm not, Mary. [...] I have played husbands so often that I am quite disillusioned.[85]

Eugene's flippancy regarding marriage, his framing of heterosexuality as a literal performance, his evasiveness regarding his bachelorhood, his reference to an 'intimate friend' that avoids the use of any pronoun, and his sustained friendship with a woman that involves no hint of romantic history all nudge toward a reading of him as a gay man. Despite this, what McCarthy labelled Kelly's possible 'queerness'—if, indeed, non-normative sexuality was what she was trying to convey with the phrase in a mainstream 1947 publication[86]—is only partially rooted in his sexuality. The displaced meanings so many astute critics of the past sensed in Kelly's words arise from a complex interplay between the 'queerness' of being Irish Catholic in early twentieth-century WASP Philadelphia with the 'queerness' of being queer in that *milieu*.

James's work is illuminated when we accept Tóibín's premise that the American's reticence regarding his sexuality entwines with his (James's) perception that Irish roots were a social liability in elite circles. It is equally interesting to link Kelly's fear of public knowledge of his sexuality with his life-long quest to efface his family's modest origins. Under the inane chit-chat and attention to seemingly meaningless props of the typical Kelly drama, McCarthy suggests, things unsaid and unsayable throb silently.[87] Foreshadowing Pinter and Beckett, Kelly's well-made plays take the dramatic devices of mundane gestures and everyday speech beyond realism: characters chat about the weather, ask each other the time, or seek clarifications of insignificant points, though such exchanges never forward the plot. (The *Times* review of the 1929 London production of Kelly's *Craig's Wife* misread the technique as a failing.[88]) Much of the seemingly meaningless theatre business of Kelly's drama involves the tasks and directions carried out by a recurring character across decades of his plays: the maid whose speech patterns imply her Irishness.[89]

Like many Kelly plays, *Craig's Wife*, his 1925 drama of a middle-class marriage slowly soured by a controlling wife, opens with a well-appointed interior in which the implicitly Irish servant is at work, and she bustles in and out and converses throughout the action. This foregrounding contrasts with the dominant strain of 'classic' Anglo-American literature, in which the quotidian proceeds seemingly effortlessly through the mostly unseen and silent work of protagonists' servants. The actor as well as the character repeated: Broadway entertainer Mary Gildea (c. 1897–1957) took on the role of maid in numerous Kelly productions.[90] There is an unsettling insistence on the simultaneous ubiquity and invisibility of working-class Irish labour in a stock character repeatedly performed by *the same actor* across Kelly's oeuvre that speaks to the playwright's consciousness regarding his origins. The sense that Kelly identified on some level with the servant rather than the householder is arguably indicated by his choice of partner: Weagly was a New York hotel bellhop when he met Kelly in the 1920s. For someone of Kelly's descent, the Irish maid would have evoked a complex response that encompassed both resentment of WASP stereotypes and ethnic memory.[91] Margaret Lynch-Brennan's survey of the lives of such immigrants in the private homes of the northeast explicitly connects the jokes representing 'Bridget' (the Irish maid) as stupid or lacking domestic skills to wider nativist mid-nineteenth-century anti-Catholic bigotry.[92] Henry James's sister, Alice, who lived in a household with five Irish-born servants in the 1850s, later recalled with embarrassment that as a child she had been raised to believe that 'our servants lie because they are Catholics [...]'.[93] A further strain of ridicule mocked 'Bridget's' desire to dress 'above her station'.[94] The stereotype's fixed title of 'Bridget' conveyed the interchangeability of one Irish maid with the next.[95] As such, the bitter cultural in-joke of Gildea's repeated answering of the phone or door in various Kelly plays becomes apparent.

Ironically, the tradition of representing the Irish servant on the Philadelphia stage had been established for so long that it stretched back to a period in which to be 'Irish' was probably to be of Ulster Presbyterian stock, as in John Murdock's *The Triumphs of Love*. This 1795 Philadelphia play stages the 'whitening' of indentured servant Patrick by contrasting him with the enslaved Sambo, who is a grotesque and vain figure.[96] By Kelly's lifetime, however, the 'Stage Irish Servant' figure is always understood to be of post-Famine Catholic Irish origin,[97] even if various other nationalities and Black migrants from the South increasingly took on such employment in the northeast in that period. Kelly himself expresses disdain regarding the hackneyed nature of the 'Stage Irish Servant' in *The Flattering Word*. Lena, an amateur actor, is prompted by her 'stage mother', Mrs Zooker, to show off her skills to Eugene.

> MRS. ZOOKER: Don't you remember that Irish piece you used to do, about the cook? (*Lena shakes her head negatively*) She used to do one of them pieces where she had to take off the Irish brogue,—and she'd have you dyin' in it.[98]

Mrs Zooker discusses the portrayal of a presumably amusingly uneducated Irish servant in ungrammatical English, and mockingly mimics the Hiberno-Irish syntax that Kelly's own uneducated immigrant parents were likely to have used. Altogether, the use of the adjective 'Irish' in the critically neglected *The Flattering Word* is fascinating in being the only time Kelly peeps out of the *ethnic* closet.

The pinnacle of a career that lost steam in the 1930s, not least because his stylish sets did not fit with the social realism that dominated the American stage in the Depression years, Kelly's *Craig's Wife* ran at New York's Morosco Theatre from October 1925 into August of the following year for 360 performances and was adapted for the screen three times. It was awarded the 1926 Pulitzer Prize in Drama in response to a controversy surrounding the 1925 winner, *Hell-Bent for Heaven*; in an echo of the seeming closing of ranks that George's father had suffered at Henley, Kelly's comedy hit, *The Show-Off*, had actually been recommended for the drama prize by the Pulitzer jury of 1924, but was overruled by that year's administrator, Columbia University. Shockingly, that institution insisted on awarding it to *Hell-Bent for Heaven*, a 'hillbilly drama' centred on white Protestant Appalachian folk by Hatcher Hughes, a Columbia professor of similar background.[99]

At one point in the action of Kelly's *Craig's Wife*, the title character asks her implicitly Irish servant, Mrs Harold, to dust the tree in front of her dining room window;[100] the received critical view is that the householder is an unsympathetic character whose pathological need to control her home, husband, and household staff is rooted in a domineering nature. However, *Craig's Wife* may be read as an inner history of the problems that attended the social rise—or desire for such—of the Catholic Irish in Philadelphia. Ester Bloom pithily describes the stark socio-economic demarcation that divided American women right up to World War II: 'For centuries, a woman's social status was clear-cut: Either she had a maid or she was one.'[101] Because of America's particular racial and immigrant make-up, this unambiguous divide was one that differentiated 'native' or WASP women from Black and white immigrant women. Harriet Craig is not neurotically house proud because she is of flawed character but because she is a woman determined to never again have to return to the employee side of the maid-householder divide. Like O'Neill's Mary Tyrone in *Long Day's Journey into Night*, who alternates between seeing herself as a class above her Irish cook and maid and fraternizing with them, Mrs Craig is insecure in her middle-class American status because it is new to her ethnic cohort. What throbs beneath the surface of *Craig's Wife* is that homeowner and maid *are both* working-class Irish by origin.

The emphasis in *Craig's Wife* on the emptiness of white middle-class marriage is a thread that runs through Kelly's triumphs *The Torch-Bearers* (1922), *The Show-Off* (1924), and his two later minor Broadway successes, *The Deep Mrs. Sykes* (1945), and *The Fatal Weakness* (1946). Mrs Craig's niece is engaged to a man of great culture but little money, and the older woman's warning regarding 'romantic illusions' is not so much feminist as an expression of the 'off-white' working-class immigrant woman's mindset when strategizing a rise into the proprietor class:

> MRS. CRAIG: I saw to it that my marriage should be a way toward emancipation for *me*. I had no private fortune [...]. Mr. Craig wanted a wife and a home; and he has them. [...] And my share of the bargain was the security and protection that those conditions imply. And I have *them*. But, unlike Mr. Craig, I cannot be absolutely sure of them; because I know that, to a very great extent, they are at the mercy of the *mood* of a *man*.[102]

When Craig later winces at his wife's description of their marriage as a 'bargain', the transactional nature of conventional heterosexual marriage is laid bare:

> CRAIG: I never regarded this thing as a bargain.
> MRS. CRAIG: Did you expect me to go into a thing as important as marriage with my eyes shut. [...] [*Almost crying*] I've been trying to preserve my home.
> CRAIG: That's all I've heard from you since the day I married you.
> MRS. CRAIG: Well, what else has a woman like me *but* her home?[103]

Mrs Craig's flintiness is rooted in her class and—by extension, if we attend to his surname—her denominational and ethnic difference from her husband. Craig is a topographical surname of Scottish origin,[104] and in Pennsylvania it was the name of a prominent family of eighteenth-century Ulster-Irish origin, as well as being a founding name of the Scottish colony of Ulster.[105] The play is not, as claimed, 'curiously unlocalized',[106] but very specifically of a time and place in which the cachet of a Scottish name is very much understood by a Catholic Philadelphian-Irish playwright. Mrs Craig may be in possession of a pedigreed Pennsylvanian Scots-Irish surname, but it is one that she has, like much else she possesses, acquired through her marriage. All in all, in order to understand the specific tensions of the ethnic world into which Grace Kelly was born in Philadelphia in 1928, one of the most illuminating sources is the work of her own uncle.

WASP Performance: Grace Kelly, White Gloves, and Alfred Hitchcock

In a 1906 'ethnic humour' verse by the popular Philadelphian-Irish Catholic author T.A. Daly, an Irish father spares no expense on his daughter's American high school graduation finery in order to signal his whole family's social aspirations:

> Now, this Casey loved his daughther in a most indulgent
> way,

An' he spent his gold like wather for her graduation day.
Sich a dale of great preparin'! Shure, ye'd think she was a bride;
Sorra hair was Casey carin' for a blessed thing beside.
For whin Casey once comminces, faith, he niver stops at all,
An' he dressed her like a princess at a Coronation Ball.[107]

Daly's use of 'Oirish' dialect suggests that Miss Casey's visual aping of WASP style is undermined by the 'shanty Irishness' that will become apparent when she opens her mouth. The verse's assumption that the aspirational Philadelphia-Irish girl cannot quite make the cut is also subtly present in the press coverage of Grace Kelly the emerging movie star half a century later. *Collier's* magazine described Grace Kelly as 'the white-gloved Philadelphia Main-Liner' in 1955.[108] However, in the same year and in an article titled 'The Girl in White Gloves,' *Time* magazine pinpointed the fine—but for Philadelphia—*crucial* distinction that although publicists tagged 'Miss Kelly as "a Main Line debutante"', she was 'neither Main Line nor a debutante, but she is the next thing to both.'[109] The phrase 'next thing to both' suggests that Kelly *nearly passes* for WASP, a sociological term popularized by a postwar University of Pennsylvania scholar.[110] Strikingly, the early stage and television roles in which Kelly was cast as a privileged WASP are all the creations of aspirational Irish-Americans. During the 1949 summer season at the Bucks County Playhouse in Pennsylvania at which she made her stage debut as the decorative Florence McCrickett in Uncle George's *The Torch-Bearers*, Grace was also cast as the elegant Marian Almond in *The Heiress*, a 1947 play based on James's *Washington Square* (1880). In addition, she later appeared in a 1951 television adaptation of the play *Berkeley Square* (1929), based on the same author's *The Sense of the Past*, while in the following year she played socialite Paula Legendre in the television adaptation of Fitzgerald's *Gatsby*-esque story, 'The Rich Boy.'[111]

As was typical of the studio system, publicists attempted to exert huge control over Kelly's image in the early to mid-1950s. Grace rarely spoke to reporters, and her silence, the very antithesis of the very old stereotype of Irish garrulousness, played a huge role in the creation of her slightly icy but elegant public persona, as Alexis Schwarzenbach suggests:

> it was Grace Kelly's [male] co-stars who kept on praising her, while the actress herself almost never made a statement about herself. The aim of this publicity strategy was, of course, to show that Grace Kelly was a real lady and as such far too well educated and reserved to make public statements about private matters.[112]

White gloves were an intrinsic part of the arsenal of the 'super-elite task force of lethally disciplined femininity' of Southern belle culture,[113] as critiqued in the performances of Jamaican-American guerrilla artist Lorraine O'Grady (1934–), in which the role of the whip in maintaining 'gentility' is made explicit (Figure 5.3).[114]

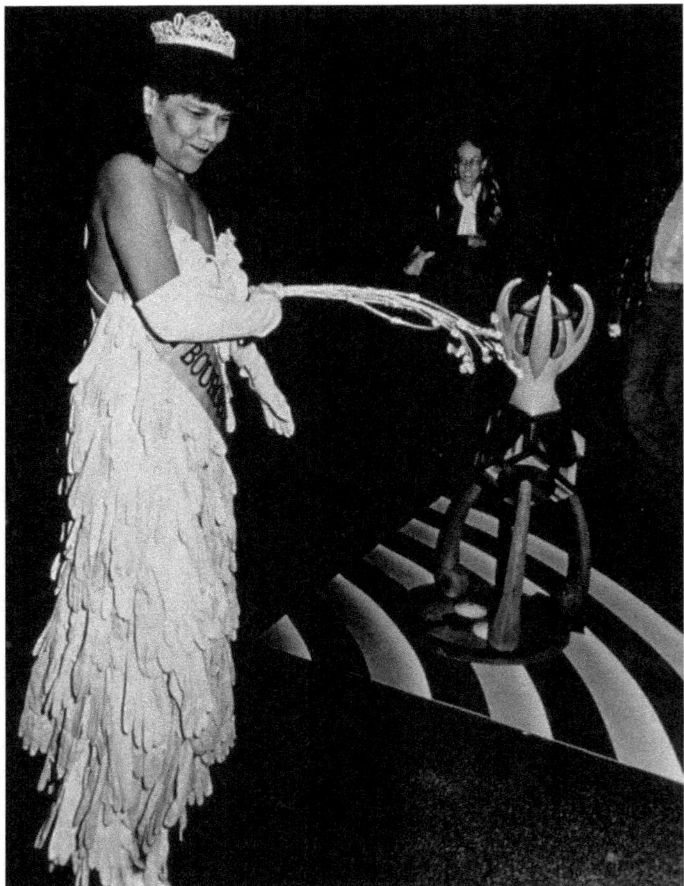

Figure 5.3 Lorraine O'Grady (in a dress hand-stitched from 180 pairs of white gloves), 'Mlle Bourgeoise Noire Beats Herself with the Whip-That-Made-Plantations-Move' from *Untitled (Mlle Bourgeoise Noire)*, 1980–83/2009. Silver gelatin fibre, part 10 of 14, 10.13×7.5 inches, *Edition 20 + 2AP*. Courtesy of Alexander Gray Associates, New York ©2022 Lorraine O'Grady/Artists Rights Society (ARS), New York.

Thus, the white gloves with which Kelly was associated in the press were meant to signal 'whiteness', and it is no coincidence that this fashion disappeared in the 1960s, a period of street battles over desegregation. A seminal 1957 analysis spells out the promotion strategies through which the MGM Studio constructed Kelly's image: 'Terms like "cool", "lady", "genteel", "elegant", "reserved", "patrician" are as frequent in the features and reviews of her film roles as they are in her personal publicity'.[115] Even a cursory acquaintance with James's depictions of the American elite would suggest that 'lady' is a stand-in for 'wealthy WASP',[116] so these emphases were meant to diminish the usual associations of an Irish Catholic background in mainstream America.

This carefully curated public image was amplified by Kelly's onscreen appearance. Peiss notes that the conventions around very early American photographic technology created a standardized female beauty that was pale and fair,[117] and Dyer argues that in the visual cultures of the global north, exposures, lighting, make-up, and developing processes evolved with the presumption that white skin was the default.[118] In addition, women's faces have traditionally been lit to look whiter ('more ethereal') than those of men and higher-class women are presented as 'whiter' than lower-class women.[119] When backlit in film, blond hair intensifies what Dyer calls the 'effulgent dazzle' of the shadowless lit white woman's face.[120] Thus, Kelly's natural fairness was amplified so as to further signal high status. This shaping of her image through clothing and lighting is not to imply that she was passive: she collaborated with Howell Conant on publicity photographs that broke the mould of studio publicity shots in their arch 'naturalness'. Moreover, as a relative unknown she had, on the advice of old MGM hand, Uncle George, insisted upon favourable terms before signing with that studio in 1952.[121] Nevertheless, she could only control her image to a certain degree in the face of the studio system juggernaut.

Despite the attempted construction of Kelly as a WASP blonde by Hollywood, the Philadelphia caste system arguably impacted her film roles in subtle ways. For instance, Main Line socialite Helen Hope Montgomery Scott (1904–95) inspired the character of Tracy Lord in the 1939 Broadway comedy of manners, *The Philadelphia Story*. The self-consciously Scottish Montgomerys had originated in Ardrossan, an origin of such social *cachet* in Philadelphia that the family named its built-from-scratch early twentieth-century American estate after that Scottish town.[122] *The Philadelphia Story* was filmed under that title one year later and remade as the film musical *High Society* in 1956. Although Tracy Lord had been played by the patrician Katherine Hepburn in both the 1939 stage production and the 1940 movie adaptation, Grace Kelly was chosen for the film remake some sixteen years later. In his consideration of *High Society*, the author of a study of the so-called 'Philadelphia aristocracy' describes Kelly as having 'passed' as upper-class Philadelphian to obtuse Hollywood *precisely because*, to use James's phrase, she was not 'the real thing'.[123] (In comparing Kelly unfavourably with Hepburn in his *New York Times* review of the 1956 film, the Princeton-educated Bosley Crowther implied as much.[124]) Even Hollywood, however, may have realized that the Irish Catholic actress could not convincingly convey the subtle particulars that, even into the 1950s, continued to differentiate Main Line WASPs from the merely wealthy and unpedigreed Philadelphian: Tracy Lord's background in *High Society* was switched from Philadelphia to the upper-class enclave of Newport, Rhode Island, then long past its Whartonian Gilded Era relevance as a playground of the elite.[125]

A further unexamined manner in which Kelly's film persona was shaped by her ethnic background emerges in her relationship with English director, Alfred Hitchcock, which has overwhelmingly been analysed within a framework of the 'Hitchcock Blonde', the cool, patrician look that the director favoured in leading ladies. However, this leaves the surprising source of their *simpatico* relationship unexplored. Maureen O'Hara's first film role was in Hitchcock's *Jamaica Inn* (1939), but he was even more central to the success of Kelly, who starred in three of his films, though only the crime mystery, *Dial M for Murder* (1954), is considered here. François Truffaut's influential take on the Hitchcock–Kelly relationship suggests that 'the former cockney lad was rather awed by the title of Princess the beautiful Philadelphia society girl acquired when she left Hollywood for the cliffs of Monaco'.[126] However, this distracts from the fact that, in terms of background, actor and director had much in common and were close: in a preface for Spoto's 1976 book on Hitchcock, Princess Grace describes the subject as a 'warm and understanding human being'.[127] Hitchcock was a Cockney tradesman's son, but his deep ancestry was as Irish as Kelly's. His mother was the daughter of an Irish immigrant called Whelan, whose birth year in Ireland (1838) may suggest that his family had lived through or fled the Famine.[128] Thus, both Hitchcock and Kelly were descended from an Irish Catholic immigrant grandfather, both were educated in Catholic schools, and both were quite culturally Catholic in outlook.[129] When discussing *I Confess*, his 1953 film centred on a priest, Hitchcock speaks in tribal tones of his ethno-religious minority: 'We Catholics know that a priest cannot disclose the secret of the confessional, but the Protestants, the atheists, and the agnostics all say, "Ridiculous!"'[130] An anecdote the princess told Spoto suggests the shared bond of the Anglo-American subculture of the Catholic school education that older director and young actress had in common:

> 'One time he turned to me after telling [*Dial M for Murder* co-star] Ray Milland a very raw joke, and he said, "Are you shocked, Miss Kelly?" I smiled and replied, "Oh no, Mr. Hitchcock, I went to a girls' convent school—I heard all those things when I was thirteen." He loved that answer.'[131]

Moreover, it was Kelly's performance of immigrant Irishness that produced her first leading role in *Dial M for Murder*, before which she had won only minor film roles or parts on television plays or in theatre productions. In 1952, Kelly had unsuccessfully auditioned for the role of an Irish immigrant mother in the film *Taxi* (1953) because she '"wanted to try an Irish accent"',[132] and could, presumably, do a passable one, given her roots. Although studio executives saw no promise in Kelly's screen test, Hitchcock did, as did another director of Irish immigrant ancestry, John Ford, who gave Kelly her breakthrough support role in *Mogambo* (1953).[133]

Although Britain did not have the same racial history as America since its slave trade had never operated on home soil, L. Perry Curtis's seminal *Apes and Angels* (1971) intimates that a racialized simian Irishman nevertheless evolved in Victorian British lampoon and contributed to the American stereotype of Irish Catholic cultural 'off-whiteness'. Since the child or grandchild of minority culture or minority religion immigrants self-consciously *performs* dominant identity to a certain degree, Hitchcock would have been knowing about Kelly's assembly by studio executives and voice coaches into an Anglo-American 'lady'; Grace's voice training by coaches Aristide d'Angelo and Englishman Edward Goodman at the private New York American Academy of Dramatic Arts in the late 1940s had endowed her with the 'correct' (i.e., upper-class British-sounding) accent and intonation.[134] Thus, it must have been a kind of in-joke for Hitchcock to further coach Kelly in performing elite Britishness in *Dial M for Murder* since the self-made director, too, would have undergone this very transformation in his journey from working-class fishmonger's son to Sir Alfred Hitchcock KBE.[135] In *Dial M for Murder* Kelly performs a woman who duplicitously *performs* the role of a proper upper-middle-class English wife: In the opening montage, Margot Mary Wendice (Kelly), dressed in a quietly sophisticated cream silk dressing gown, contentedly breakfasts with her husband (Milland). Reading the *Times*, Britain's newspaper of the establishment, Margot spots a notice of the arrival in London of an American writer, at which point her mask of pleasantness slips to reveal the face of a dead-eyed schemer.[136] Costumed in a revealing and almost garish red dress in the next scene, we learn that she is conducting a long-distance affair with the novelist, whom she embraces in the apartment in which she had earlier breakfasted with her husband, a sharp transition that transforms Margot from fake 'lady' to genuine 'harlot'.

Hitchcock links himself to Margot/Kelly subliminally in *Dial M for Murder*. It was based on a 1952 teleplay for BBC Television by Frederick Knott, who also wrote the stage adaptation performed in the same year in London's West End and New York's Broadway. The teleplay and London production playscript give Kelly's character's name as 'Sheila Wendice',[137] which becomes 'Margot Wendice' in the New York production. However, in the film adaptation, Margot is given the middle name 'Mary'. This is revealed in the closing credits as well as in a courtroom scene in which her full name is read aloud, a scene that is in the film alone. Irish-American scholar Patrick McGilligan considers the significance of Hitchcock's surname, first name and *middle* name: 'His name was as English as trifle. The "Alfred" stood in honor of his father's brother. The "Joseph" was a nod to the Irish Catholicism of his mother—the name of the carpenter of Nazareth and husband of Mary.'[138] The 'husband of Mary' suggests some submerged attempt on Hitchcock's part at connection to a character to whom that very name had been quietly gifted. Moreover, in endowing Kelly's character with the name of Catholicism's ultimate unobtainable woman, Hitchcock provides evidence for the well-documented nature of his complicated obsession with the actress. Nevertheless, it is also evidence of something less discussed, which is his identification with her as a fellow Irish Catholic. Indeed, both resonances cannot be disentangled if considered in the context of Hitchcock's much-discussed Madonna-whore complex. Hitchcock used a sequence of 'icy blonde' leading ladies in his work, famously saying that the 'the perfect "woman of mystery" is one who is blonde, subtle and Nordic'.[139] This last term is an early twentieth-century synonym of 'WASP', and critics generally assume that Kelly is encompassed under this rubric, but Hitchcock must have been aware that the *performance* of being 'Anglo-Saxon' and elite was a daily one in his own case and in that of his Irish-American leading lady.

Haunted by History: Princess Grace of Monaco's Wedding Gown

A very woman-dominated fashion industry is an overlooked aspect of the midcentury transformation of the image of Irishness: that era's fashion export business in Ireland, like the early cosmetics industry in the US, was a rare sphere in which female entrepreneurship thrived. From the 1950s and into the 1960s, and due to improved transportation links, high-end clothing exports utilizing native fabrics and needlecraft traditions were shrewdly marketed in America and to American tourists in the Irish motherland with the aid of Irish state agencies. Moreover, for all their calls to 'tradition', these offerings functioned as a shop-window for a government eager to advertise Ireland's economic modernization.[140] Such increased postwar contact with the motherland is part of what generated 'a turn towards Ireland within American modernist literature', in Tara Stubbs's view.[141] Indeed, it even generated novels belonging *equally* to Ireland and America, as in the case of J.P. Donleavy's *The Ginger Man* (1955). Transatlantic film production contributed to this scene too: the Technicolor-enhanced landscape of the Maureen O'Hara and John Wayne vehicle, *The Quiet Man* (1952), disseminated the image of a colour-saturated rural Ireland to American consumers. In response to what were called 'American needs', the contemporaneous Irish textile industry began experimenting with more vibrant colours,[142] which were subsequently marketed as 'traditional' Irish landscape-inspired hues. In this context, a symbiotic relationship developed between female Irish-American celebrity and quality Irish garments made by Irish women designers and workers in which the *cachet* of one reinforced that of the other. To wit: a young Princess Grace of Monaco was photographed more than once in an Aran sweater, and commissioned Irish lace gowns from Tipperary designer Irene Gilbert.[143] 'Ireland' was briefly so recognizably a signifier of upmarket style that it was appropriated by 1950s American designer-manufacturers.[144] In addition, iconic Pittsburgh department store Joseph Horne hosted an Irish goods promotion that featured a display on 'the Irish ancestry of prominent early Pittsburgh families'.[145] Thus, the once differentiated histories of Pennsylvania's pre- and post-Famine Irish were breezily melded in the service of selling nice linen frocks. Indeed, the event saw the Horne interior transformed into a replica of recently renovated tourist attraction Bunratty Castle, the O'Brien stronghold that William Penn's father besieged in 1646 when he served under Cromwell in Ireland.[146] However, this was not the kind of link between Pennsylvania and Ireland that the department store wished to highlight. The Princess's modish engagement with and promotion of things *haute* Irish is suggested in the detail that her delivery room in the royal palace was 'draped in Irish green silk for luck' in preparation for her daughter Caroline's birth in 1957.[147] However, Kelly's most impactful sartorial choice is the magnificent handmade gown gifted to her by MGM for her wedding and on which she collaborated with the studio designer.[148] It is to the cultural and ethno-racial meanings of this iconic dress in Irish Philadelphia and far beyond that this chapter now turns.[149]

In *The White Rose of Memphis*, an 1881 best-seller by Faulkner's paternal great-grandfather, an unnamed Irish maid's 'inappropriately' refined clothing is ultimately revealed to have been stolen from her employer.[150] There is an echo of this 'passing' in the intimation that the subdued elegance for which Kelly was famous in her film star days was her attempt to dress in the manner of the Philadelphia elite.[151] That city had long used fashion to reinforce its ethno-racial divides: Kate Haulman notes that by the early 1770s and marked by 'increasing socioeconomic stratification', Philadelphia 'stood as the largest, most refined, and most fashionable city in the colonies, its position signified by the rise of conspicuous consumption and high style'.[152] Needless to say, the images of idealized white people used to sell fashion rendered it a weapon for enforcing ethnic and racial boundaries: the lithographed series *Life in Philadelphia* (after the work of Clay) includes a racist *c.* 1830 lampoon entitled 'Have you any flesh coloured silk stockings...?' that depicts an overdressed African-American woman oblivious to the fact that 'flesh-coloured' means solely the tones of white flesh.[153] Likewise, a *c.* 1831 *Life in New York* lithograph series features an image in which an overdressed African-American couple and a bedraggled Irishman are lampooned equally for their clothing (Figure 5.4).

A similar conjunction hovers in a poem by foremost 'Rhyming Weaver' James Orr (1770–1816) on the emigrant ship he took with other 1798 Rebellion exiles toward his ultimate destination of Philadelphia. The Ulster-Scots dialect voice implies that the disembarking Ulster immigrants are conscious of their unimpressive clothes, not just in comparison to prosperous native whites but also, possibly, in comparison to African Americans: 'Creatures wha ne'er had seen a black, / Fu' scar't [full scared] took to their shankies [legs]; / Sae [so], wi' our best rags on our back, / We mixt amang the Yankies [...]'.[154]

Figure 5.4 Overdressed African-American steam laundry owners are importuned by a bedraggled Irishman with a dirty coat. *c.* 1831 lithograph in lampoon series *Life in New York.* Courtesy of Library Company of Philadelphia.

The subliminal concern with race of the fashion industry suggests that there is an aptness to the venue in which 'Désirée's Baby' first appeared: Chopin's fable of miscegenation revealed by the sudden absence of fine clothes was published in the very first issue of American *Vogue* in 1893.[155] Farther back again, *Godey's Lady's Book*, the first successful women's magazine and the most widely circulated magazine in pre-Civil War America, was founded in Philadelphia in 1830. Its hand-tinted fashion plates promoted what it initially labelled 'Philadelphia Fashions' in a nod to the city's reputation for modishness. *Godey's* influence and the racial contexts of fashion in the period is suggested by the fact that it successfully promoted the fashion for white wedding dresses in the United States.[156] This trend ostensibly signalled sexual purity,[157] but in the racialized American context it also signalled privileged whiteness, since such a garment required the attentions of 'a laundress, seamstress, and ladies' maid' in order to remain 'pristine'.[158] As such, it is no accident that Scarlett O'Hara wears a frou-frou white gown in the opening antebellum scene of the film adaptation of *Gone with the Wind.* When viewed within American contexts of race, the title of the 1849 *Godey's* article that insists on white as the only feasible hue for a wedding gown is hair-raising: 'Description of Uncolored Fashions'. Thus, in America, particularly, the white wedding dress signalled, quite simply, whiteness. In an interesting addendum to his claim that, in visual culture, idealized white women 'are bathed in and permeated by light', Dyer suggests that bridal wear particularly endows this glow:

> Weddings are the privileged moment of heterosexuality, that is, (racial) reproduction, and also of women, since they are glorified on what is seen as their day. The ubiquity of white as the colour for wedding dresses [,] [...] the veil and the use of lace [...], all facilitate a radiant look. Dark-skinned brides may wear white as well, of course, but not only do they seldom have fair hair but their skin colour is likely to contrast strongly with their bridal wear, whereas white women's complexions, especially in wedding photography, can seem like the apotheosis of the clothing's whiteness and glow.[159]

The image of the radiant Grace Kelly on her wedding day has been endlessly disseminated (see Figure 5.1). In her case, it was not so much a moment of 'racial reproduction' as one in which her ethnic cohort's racial whiteness was finally unequivocally confirmed. Raka Shome's study of Princess Diana's global fame and whiteness leads to the crucial distinction between the two most famous princesses of the twentieth century: Lady Diana Spencer was born into the British aristocracy, so her whiteness was never in doubt, but Miss Grace Kelly *secured* her ethnic cohort's whiteness when she became Princess of Monaco.

Kelly's wedding had implications for Irish women's self-fashioning too: her gown appears to have created the template for subsequent royal dresses into the next century,[160] but it also changed wedding fashions overnight in Ireland, where the event was followed with possessive pride. In Teresa Deevy's present-tense short play, *The King of Spain's Daughter* (1935), starry-eyed Irish countrywomen variously describe the wedding attire of an aristocratic bride of the locale as 'red', 'green', and 'gold'. Caitriona Clear notes that into the early 1950s, the wedding outfit of ordinary Irish women was a formal day dress or suit and that the white dress and veil was more typically worn by young and first-time brides from elite backgrounds. The transition to white 'seems to have happened fairly quickly in the 1950s' so that by 1957, 'the colour' of wedding dresses is 'so taken for granted' that it goes unmentioned in newspaper accounts.[161] Given the impact of the sudden rise of an Irish-American woman to the status of European princess and the fawning coverage of her nuptials in the home of her paternal ancestors,[162] the bathos of the outfitting of the 'daughther' 'like a princess' in Daly's 1906 poem had suddenly deflated. Altogether, it is safe to surmise that Kelly influenced this sudden change in Irish wedding gown fashions and that her modest Irish roots allowed ordinary Irish women to subsequently find white wedding attire approachable.

Grace's gown was donated to the Philadelphia Museum of Art's permanent collection after the wedding and has been on permanent exhibition at that venue since 2006. A 1961 description of the holdings of the museum's Fashion Wing as running from 'the wedding gown of an eighteenth century [sic] Quaker lass to that of Princess Grace of Monaco'[163] conveys the role that wedding attire played in signalling status in Philadelphia. The new Princess's donation indicates how the growing social confidence of the post-Famine Irish in this old Scots-Irish and well-established fashion industry city could be expressed through finery. The donation had been arranged in advance of the royal wedding, and in June 1956, two months after the event, it is striking that it was Mr and Mrs John B. Kelly who presented the gown to the Philadelphia Museum of Art. The donation 'acknowledged that many had hoped the ceremony would take place, not in Monaco, but in the Kelly family's "home town" of Philadelphia'.[164] The donation turned the gown 'into a work of art',[165] but also transformed it into a talismanic object for the family's ethnic community.[166] Grace's wedding spectacular came only three years after the coronation of Queen Elizabeth II, a momentous televisual event whose public aspects were covered by more than 2,000 journalists. For those of Irish nationalist persuasion in Ireland and America, the 1956 wedding would have seemed an Irish Catholic riposte to the crowning of the photogenic new British monarch at Westminster Abbey in June 1953, which was watched by 27 million people in the United Kingdom alone through the relatively new medium of television.[167] As though to reinforce the new social significance of Irish Catholic Philadelphia in the wake of their daughter's wedding, the Kelly family effectively re-enacted her April 1956 spectacular for the eyes of a local audience and on a local scale: At the opening event to honour the donation, a mannequin designed to look like Grace and surrounded by flowers was dressed in the talismanic wedding gown, now charged with the magical aura of its newly ennobled and racially transformed wearer. This simulacrum was the centerpiece of 'a surrogate wedding reception; museum visitors could perhaps imagine they were guests at the wedding'.[168] If the scene comes across as oddly similar to an open-casket funeral, then it might be said to mark what the Kelly family apparently hoped to be the final expiration of probationary whiteness for the post-Famine Irish in Philadelphia, very much a 'white wedding' in multiple registers. Tara Harney-Mahajan's examination of the persistently negative depiction of the wedding dress by writers such as Marina Carr, Edna O'Brien, and Eugene O'Neill concludes that the wedding dress is 'a distinct scene of haunting' in the Irish and Irish-American imagination that 'carries the weight of the historical past'.[169] To that list one might add George Kelly's Mrs Espenshade in *The Fatal Weakness*, who copes with her imploded marriage by lurking in churches to admire the gowns of brides she does not know, or Bowen's 1952 depiction of a spectacularly haunted old bridal veil belonging to the widow of an Anglo-Irish officer who had committed suicide in colonial India.[170] In contrast to such heavy history, Grace Kelly's wedding gown appeared—at least in 1956—to gesture towards a fairytale future for Irish America from which all ghosts had been exorcised.

This chapter concludes by pivoting to a possible trace of Grace Kelly's impact upon Irish-American self-fashioning in a seminal cult novel that belongs equally to the Irish and American canons. Her movie stardom was peaking at the time of publication of Irish-American novelist J.P. Donleavy's *succès de scandale, The Ginger Man* (1955), which features the strikingly named Constance Kelly.[171] The novel opens with two GI Bill Trinity College Dublin undergraduates, Sebastian Dangerfield and his compatriot Kenneth O'Keefe, the first a reprobate WASP and the latter a *soi-disant* Irish-American Catholic 'mick'. Dangerfield and O'Keefe are a Janus-faced composite of the past and future of the ethnic Irish in a novel published at the very point at which mainstream America understood them to be leaving the slums for the lily-white suburbs.[172] The novel repeatedly turns to the men's fantasies of future status, and in the following passage, O'Keefe imagines a fate he wishes for Constance, who had 'strung [him] along' as she held out 'for wealth on Beacon Hill' (an elite Boston neighbourhood):

> I would have married her but she didn't want to get stuck at the bottom [...] with me. One of her own kind. Jesus, she's right. But do you know what I'm going to do? When I go back to the States when I'm fat with dough, wearing my Saville Row suits, with black briar, M.G. and my man driving, I'm going to turn on my English accent full blast. Pull up to some suburban house where she's married a mick, turned down by all the old Bostonians, and leave my man at the wheel. I'll walk up the front path knocking the kid's toys out of the way with my walking stick and give the door a few impatient raps. She comes out. A smudge of flour on her cheek and the reek of boiled cabbage coming from the kitchen. I look at her with shocked surprise. I recover slowly and then in my best accent, delivered with devastating resonance, I say Constance...you've turned out... just as I thought you would.[173]

O'Keefe's desire for fine clothes that would enable him to 'pass' is a staple of Irish-American fiction, but the rarely discussed Constance Kelly is of interest also. Constance, too, is a Janus-faced figure, capable of regressing to fecund cabbage-boiling slum Irish type or, with the right marriage, of ascending to WASP glory. Grace's engagement to a European prince in the spring of 1955 outdid even O'Keefe's wildest fantasies of grandeur. Since he later comes out of the closet in *The Ginger Man*, it is not Constance that O'Keefe desires but her ability, as a heterosexual woman, to obtain sudden social and ethno-racial transformation through the 'right' marriage, which cannot be to 'one of her own'. Constance Kelly is the glorious Irish-American future in the castle, O'Keefe the Irish past in the slums. However, centuries of Gothic narratives hold that power begets corruption, corruption begets punishment, and where there is a castle, horror will soon emerge. The glitter of Kelly's fairytale 'white' wedding was tarnished by the subsequent and ongoing tabloid narrative that she found palace life stifling and that her millionaire father had sold her into royalty with an enormous dowry. This suggests that George Kelly's portrayal of the transactive nature of the heteronormative WASP marriage predicts the cold calculation of Irish America on the rise. The Gothicizing of the Kennedy-era new Irish elite as a result of the souring of the fairytale is the focus of the epilogue.

Coda: Remembering Ann Lowe (1898–1981)

Among the 2,000 journalists who covered the coronation in London in June 1953 were two women of relevance to this study. One was a remnant of Ireland's Anglo-Irish elite, novelist Elizabeth Bowen, whose account for the July 1953 issue of *Vogue* suggests how attitudes to the event broke down along caste lines in the Irish context. The mood of the massive throng that lined Elizabeth II's procession from the Palace to Westminster Abbey is conveyed in Bowen's highly evocative description of the hushed, expectant atmosphere in London that morning, and its closing salutation to the just-crowned Queen is unambiguously royalist.[174] Another and much more prosaic account was written by a younger and less experienced journalist with the *Washington Times-Herald*.[175] She likely did not guess that an equally bright global spotlight would be upon her within a decade. Her name was Jacqueline Bouvier and within two months—wearing a silk taffeta gown by designer Ann Lowe (1898–1981), the granddaughter of an enslaved woman—she would wed a young senator from Massachusetts. In a reflection of the foundational American divide that would begin to come to a head in the tumultuous Kennedy-dominated decade to come, the African-American designer's name was unmentioned in the press release and in newspaper accounts of the splashy Bouvier–Kennedy wedding.[176]

Epilogue

Kennedy Gothic

The decisive shift in Irish-American status inaugurated by Grace Kelly's 1956 wedding could not have occurred without prior stirrings. 1952 seems to be about the moment in which 'green' blood begins to upgrade to 'blue' in a variety of American registers and locations. Democrat John F. Kennedy, the great-grandson of a Famine-era immigrant, began his rise to power late that year by defeating a member of the 'Boston Brahmin' (Yankee blueblood) Lodge family in the United States Senate election in Massachusetts. As a result, Kennedy earned the title 'first Irish Brahmin'.[1] Beth O'Leary Anish inventively categorizes John Steinbeck's novel of that year, *East of Eden*, as midcentury Irish-American ethnic fiction, but the work is also marked by the concurrent fudging of old distinctions between Irishnesses.[2] To wit: *East of Eden*'s spiritual centre, Samuel Hamilton, is explicitly based on Steinbeck's own Ulster Presbyterian grandfather of that very name, yet the fictionalized Hamilton codes 'Gaelic'.[3] Likewise, in a landmark televised speech during Richard Nixon's Republican Vice-Presidential campaign in 1952, his wife, Pat, was described as 'Irish', but it was not 'revealed whether she was a Protestant or a Catholic',[4] a canny play for the widest possible Irish vote. (Nixon was himself of Irish Quaker ancestry.[5]) Moreover, the Immigration and Nationality Act of 1952 encouraged unrestricted emigration from the Western Hemisphere, leading to a new influx from Ireland, which is the context of Tóibín's 2009 novel, *Brooklyn*. Although the Act symbolically gestured to racial egalitarianism, 85 per cent of immigration quotas were allocated to western and northern Europe,[6] and Ireland's inclusion in that category indicated that the Irish were being enfolded into America's imaginary of the 'Nordic'/'Saxon' sphere. In the European context, Saxonist terminology and its euphemisms were tainted after the catastrophic consequences of Nazi theories of Aryan superiority for Jewish people, Romanies, and other minorities were revealed. However, the Immigration and Nationality Act suggests that in postwar America the category of uncontestably white arguably merely *expanded* to include the Irish rather than being seriously queried.

Kennedy himself played an active role in the process of fudging old distinctions between Irish cohorts: in his book, *A Nation of Immigrants*, mostly written in 1958, the Ulster Irish do not appear to be enfolded in *either* the British or Irish immigration waves described.[7] Indeed, the perceived effacement of the long history of Scots-Irish presidents in the labelling of Kennedy as the 'first Irish president' led to push-back from Ulster Unionist leader Ian Paisley.[8] A further factor in the seeming

Race, Politics, and Irish America. Mary M. Burke, Oxford University Press.
 DOI: 10.1093/oso/9780192859730.003.0007

ebbing away of Scots-Irishness as a named identity in the northeast is Michael Harrington's Kennedy-era sociological work, which inspired the War on Poverty of that president's successor, Lyndon B. Johnson.[9] Targeted particularly at historically Scots-Irish areas, the policy transformed 'Appalachian', a quasi-ethnicized term that had often been understood to encompass the Ulster Irish, into a geographical and administrative category that implied an undifferentiated and unethnicized 'poor white' identity.[10] In short, the War on Poverty rendered the Scots-Irish, in the title of a study of the era, 'Yesterday's People'.[11]

1952 was also the year that a 'fighting Irish' pairing of self-styled 'Scotch-Irish' boy (John Wayne) and red-headed colleen (Maureen O'Hara) sparred their way to the altar as Sean Thornton and Mary Kate Danaher in John Ford's marriage-as-Union film, *The Quiet Man*.[12] Born Marion Morrison of Antrim Presbyterian stock in 1907, the actor took his stage name from 'Mad' Anthony Wayne, the military officer of settler-colonial Irish origin given as Dick's ancestor in Fitzgerald's *Tender Is the Night*.[13] Wayne was known for his many roles as cowboys in Westerns that celebrated frontier violence against Native Americans. Thus, for Roger Ebert, the actor's 1956 revisionist Western with Ford, *The Searchers*, finally exorcised the ghost of Andrew Jackson from the Irish-American imaginary in 'nervous[ly]' acknowledging the traumatic afterlife of the latter's genocidal actions.[14] Though a romantic comedy-drama, *The Quiet Man*, too, attempts to process unfinished Irish-American history. It centres on a Pittsburg-Irish boxer (Wayne) who moves to rural Ireland and marries a feisty local (O'Hara), and the tense history of inter-Irish relations in America hides in plain sight: unusually for a feel-good romance, promotional images show the couple physically struggling rather than embracing. Indeed, the original trailer and some of the film's most heavily distributed stills frame the courtship and marriage as a drawn-out boxing match (Figure E.1).[15] Nevertheless, within a well-established political logic of the Irish marriage plot, the couple's union, however fraught, represents the healing of enmities. This was reinforced thematically by the cooperative relationship between the film's Catholic priest and Protestant vicar. In short, by 1952, the inter-Irish hostility that had once led to riots in the urban northeast could be played for laughs in the movie theatres of the same cities. The time for the Famine Irish to claim uncontested whiteness and all of its spoils appeared to be nearing. The future seemed bright.

Bouvier Gothic: *Grey Gardens*

In the eventful year of 1952, a woman of thirty-five returned home forever to her large nineteenth-century ocean-front family home on the southern tip of Long Island, New York after an unsuccessful career as a performer and model. The grand house and its land had been acquired in the mid-1920s by her parents, Phelan and Edith Beale, a successful lawyer and his socialite wife. This was about the time

Figure E.1 John Wayne (as Sean Thornton) and Maureen O'Hara (as Mary Kate Danaher) in John Ford's *The Quiet Man*, 1952. Courtesy of ALAMY.

that the F. Scott Fitzgeralds were making summering on the beach fashionable. Phelan's wealth was reduced by the 1929 stock market crash and his wife was wildly bohemian, a combination that ultimately led to his quitting the house. As Edith did not have the financial means to maintain the estate, it fell into disrepair. The garden reverted back to untamed nature and the house became almost entirely hidden behind sprawling overgrowth. An old black Cadillac sat abandoned at the front, its door left open for so long that nature colonized the interior. The house fell into disorder too, and numerous animals took up residence with Edith and her equally non-conformist daughter, also named Edith. The pair blithely maintained their dated patrician manners, accents, worldview, and songs amid the growing squalor, changing *mores*, and lengthening century. They did not possess a clock, and the unfinished business of the past continually erupted during their bickering, which often centred on the social status of the younger Edith's former beaus. The women hardly ever left the house or received outsiders other than handymen. Out of a mixture of creativity and necessity, daughter Edith, who sometimes matter-of-factly discussed the kitchen's resident ghost, enjoyed improvising old finery: cardigans were worn as skirts, a bathing suit became a dance leotard, tops were used as turbans, and dark lace stockings were paired with pale heels. She fed the countless cats who had the run of the house, as well as the wild mammals inhabiting the attic.[16] Online photos of the state of the interior by the 1970s show traces of former elegance amid dirt, decrepit furniture, peeling wallpaper, cracked windows, and hoarded chaos.[17] Altogether, this transformation rendered what had once been a sunny summer playground into a dilapidated Gothic pile that now better reflected the home's name of 'Grey Gardens'.

Mother and daughter Edith 'Little Edie' Bouvier Beale (1917–2002) and Edith 'Big Edie' Bouvier Beale (1895–1977), the once-shining names on New York's Social Register who became eccentric and co-dependent recluses, were the first cousin and paternal aunt of Jacqueline Bouvier Kennedy Onassis. The Beales became cult figures after they were the focus of the critically acclaimed *Grey Gardens*, a 1975 documentary that explored their peculiar lives and home (Figure E.2). Jackie had spent childhood summers at Grey Gardens and all three kinswomen had attended the elite Connecticut girls' school, Miss Porter's. As their relation became a society bride, a mother, the wife of a president, and then his widow, the Beales existed in a vacuum reminiscent of Gormenghast Castle.[18] Perhaps the only way in which the arrival of second-wave feminism during the period of their suspension from history leaves a trace is that the *doppelganger* trope that has generally only enfolded men within a lineage could now incorporate the two Edie Bouvier Beales. The unease invoked by the shared name gives Gothic resonance to the fact that Big Edie, who seems to have forced Little Edie to remain at Grey Gardens, may have thwarted her namesake.

It may be argued that President John F. Kennedy's wife was not Irish, given that she was born Jacqueline Bouvier into a prominent Catholic family of French descent on her father's side. However, she was of wholly Famine-Irish immigrant maternal descent,[19] though her mother, like F. Scott Fitzgerald, presented the family background as prosperous pro-Confederate Maryland,[20] preferring the apparent *cachet* of being pro-slavery to the stigma of famine. Moreover, and in a period in which a wife invariably took her husband's surname upon marriage, in Ireland and Irish-America Jackie Kennedy was—and remains—'Irish'.[21] Nevertheless, and though it represented 'only one-eighth of her ancestry', she was identified as 'French' by her husband's presidential campaign managers, who justifiably feared anti-Irish bigotry among voters.[22] An occupational surname, 'Bouvier' means 'cowherd', but Jackie's social-climbing paternal grandfather falsely claimed that the Bouviers had descended from the French nobility.[23] (Little Edie later upgraded the Bouvier origins to the French royalty.[24]) The noble origin

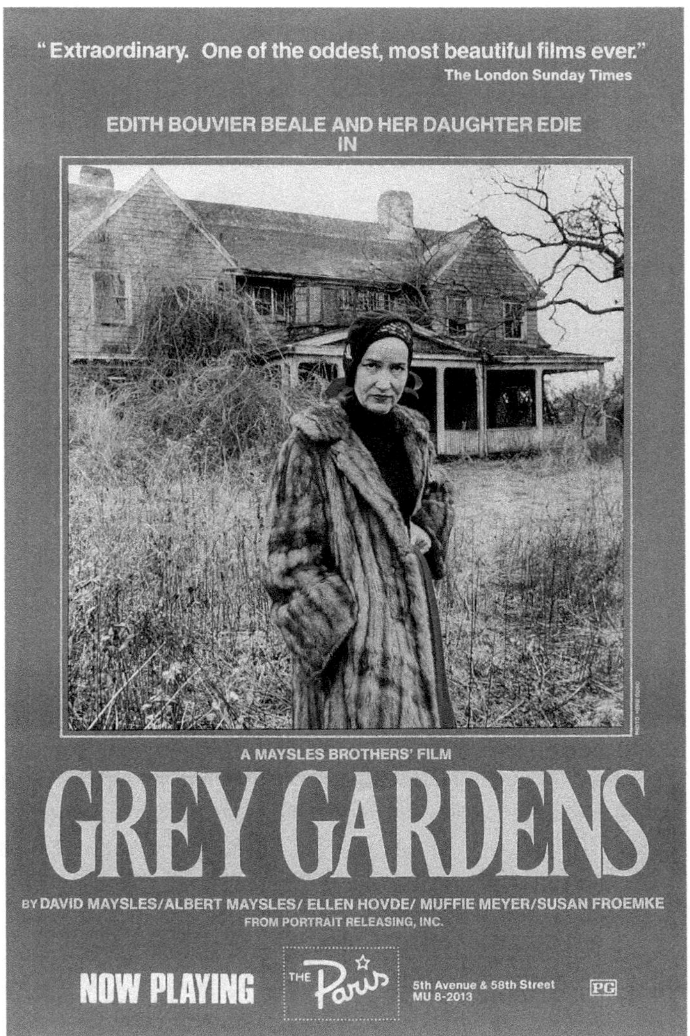

Figure E.2 Edith 'Little Edie' Bouvier Beale on the poster for the 1975 documentary, *Grey Gardens*. Courtesy of ALAMY.

was trumpeted in the press upon Jackie's marriage to JFK in 1953, though in her girl-about-town days Bouvier was, in the words of a former *Vogue* editor, a conspicuously 'Catholic ethnic' among the 'purely WASP' elite.[25] Thus, by association, the Bouvier Beales may be considered to have been enfolded within the post-Kennedy Irish Catholic elite, not least because their connection to Mrs Kennedy formed the basis of the lurid and sustained attention that *Grey Gardens* has received.[26]

As framed in *Grey Gardens*, whose non-linear narrative is dictated by its subjects' bickering, anecdotes, and old photographs, the Beales possess the eccentricity tolerated only in the very rich or the aristocratic, while their dilapidated home is shot as a Gothic manse. As both Henry James and George Kelly depict, only strivers and 'new money' wear impeccable clothing and live in immaculate new houses. Like Dickens's jilted Miss Havisham in *Great Expectations* (1861), fading away in her inherited mansion while clad in a rotting wedding gown, eccentric 'old money' cares nothing for *bourgeois* opinion. Dickens's utilization of mouldering lace to symbolize Havisham's social retreat is suggestive in the case of an ethnic cohort pejoratively called 'Lace Curtain Irish' on their upward trajectory, a *milieu* examined in the 1948 novel *Lace Curtain* by Ellin Berlin, who had been born into the wealthy Irish Catholic Mackay mining dynasty.[27] Gothic is the vampire of genres, able to renew and re-emerge in novel locations and contexts in order to incorporate new power elites. As such, *Grey Gardens* may be read as an instance of what will be termed the 'Kennedy Gothic' mode, though it is a softer iteration than that to which core members of the Kennedy dynasty were generally subject.

John F. Kennedy Gothic: Conspiracy

John F. Kennedy (1917–1963), America's first president of Famine-Irish Catholic descent, died by an assassin's gun three years after his election in 1960, and the national mood further darkened due to the ongoing crises of the Vietnam War and Civil Rights. Consequently, historians were initially at loggerheads over the seeming lack of major legislation during Kennedy's term, leaving room for divergent readings of his presidency.[28] It is generally claimed that the legislative and executive support of Civil Rights during JFK's presidency were, to a huge extent, the result of the resolve of his brother, Attorney General Robert Kennedy.[29] (This momentum culminated in Johnson's Civil Rights Act of 1964.) Bobby's electrifying speech during his 1968 presidential campaign in response to Civil Rights leader Martin Luther King Jr's assassination in April of that year intimates that he, more than his brother, was the great 'what might have been' of Black-Irish relations in America:

> For there is another kind of violence, slower but just as deadly destructive as the shot or the bomb in the night. This is the violence of institutions: indifference and inaction and slow decay. This is the violence that afflicts the poor, that poisons relations between men because their skin has different colors.[30]

Two months after that speech, Bobby was assassinated.

Numerous biographies of the Kennedy dynasty detail how the wealthy *paterfamilias*, Joe Sr, had originally strategized that his first-born, Joseph Jr, would run for president before the latter was shot down during WWII. After Bobby died, yet another Kennedy, Edward, attempted to run in 1980. In turn, speculation regarding such ambitions followed the next generation of Kennedys, especially John and Jackie's son, John Jr, before he met his death in a 1999 airplane crash. The family's seeming ambitions to hereditary rulership were discussed as early as Richard J. Whalen's 1960s biography of Joe Sr, which allowed the terms 'American aristocracy' and 'American royalty' to attach to the Kennedys with his children's generation. In foundational eighteenth-century English Gothic set in continental Europe, from British Whig politician and author Horace Walpole's *The Castle of Otranto* (1764) onwards, elements of excess, corruption, or illegitimacy are often linked to the Catholicism of the all-powerful patriarch or elder.[31] As the Kennedys were increasingly slotted into a Gothic narrative in America, accusations of sharp business dealings made against Joe Sr.—the more lurid of which have been disputed—[32] allowed him to come to fit that ready-made mould. In addition, Gothic literature tends towards many of the following elements: a non-linear narrative into which the past repeatedly erupts and in which facts are difficult to ascertain; a setting in a hereditary family seat; a long-standing prophecy, secret, or curse linked to a particular and usually corrupt hereditary bloodline; sexual excess or perversity; an endangered beautiful woman; a series of deaths or disruptions to inheritance or inheritors. Most of these elements will be seen to have correspondences in Kennedy Gothic narrative.

The Gothicization of the Kennedys suggests that the power of the Irish in America had become a given, and in the decades after the assassinations of JFK and RFK, the moral compromises that various family members had made in order to gain and maintain power were increasingly discussed. Since the dynasty's rise and legacy could be interpreted in divergent ways, however, it was Gothicized differently by both sides of America's political divide. The Kennedy Gothic of conservatives and Irish-American voters abandoning hereditary Democratic Party allegiance portrayed 'America's royals' as being enmeshed with the moral decay at the heart of power, a central theme of Gothic since its inception. By contrast, the liberal and Democrat iteration of Kennedy Gothic held that family members were *themselves* the innocent victims of sinister conspiracies. I will begin with the latter cultural narrative as it posthumously evolved in relation to JFK, before turning to the differing Gothic narratives that attached to Jackie Kennedy and Ted Kennedy.

For those who had looked to the Kennedy administration to move forward on Civil Rights and other progressive policies, the president's assassination in Dallas, Texas on 22 November 1963 as he and his wife sat waving at crowds from their open car was a conspiracy of dark and unknown powers. The car sped off to a nearby hospital immediately after the attack, but Kennedy could not survive the catastrophic wounds caused by three bullets. His body was loaded onto Air Force One for the return to Washington after he was declared dead. In the presence of Jackie, Vice-President Johnson, who had, with his wife, Lady Bird, accompanied the Kennedys to Texas, was sworn in as president aboard the plane. Lee Harvey Oswald, a Marxist-leaning employee of the Texas School Book Depository, from the sixth floor of which the deadly bullets were initially believed to have come, was charged with the murder on the following day. The day after that, Oswald was fatally shot live on television, but not before he had claimed to media that he was a front for a bigger conspiracy ('I'm just a patsy').

Amateur footage shot on 22 November was viewed by the official investigation of the assassination ordered by President Johnson, which concluded that a lone gunman had assassinated Kennedy. However, seen within the constellation of the subsequent assassinations of Dr King (April 1968) and Bobby Kennedy (June 1968), progressive America appeared to be under sustained attack, a looming future predicted in 'November 26, 1963', Wendell Berry's elegiac 1964 poem on JFK's death. Moreover, the official narrative of the lone gunman was undermined when this amateur footage became public in 1975, and the subsequent massive public disquiet led to a further official investigation in 1976 into the killings of both Kennedy and King. This concluded that there was a high probability of a second gunman—and thus, of a conspiracy—in the case of the assassination of the president. This unsettling U-turn in the official narrative fed the many theories of sinister and even insider forces arraigned against the president: he was murdered by Johnson, whom JFK may have been intending to replace as Vice President; by the CIA because of the softening of his Cold War rhetoric; by the mafia because RFK was planning to investigate organized crime; by the USSR after its humiliation in the superpower stand-off that was the previous year's Cuban Missile Crisis.[33]

Ted Kennedy Gothic: The Family Curse

The transformation of the Kennedys from an association with the Arthurian legend of benign rule ('Camelot') in the immediate aftermath of the 1963 assassination to the dark literary mode of Gothic is entangled with the gradual move to the political right of the Irish-American voter base after the 1960s. Jacqueline Kennedy used the phrase 'Camelot' to a *Life* magazine reporter in the days after the assassination to denote the idealism of her husband's administration.[34] However, the picture of a morally complex JFK emerged in the years after with growing scrutiny of his personal life and political decisions. In foundational English Gothic, the corruption or perversity of the Catholic patriarch is unmasked at the close, a manoeuver repeated in the trajectory of the Kennedys from beacon of Irish-American arrival to personification of corruption.[35] The Kennedy family's multi-home summer compound at Hyannais Port, Massachusetts plays the role of Gothic pile in this narrative, a fulcrum of dynastic power that was the base from which the 1960 presidential race was plotted and the scene of much dissipation during the presidency.[36]

As the Irish moved to the Republican Party, the Kennedy family became a byword for the soured dream, not despite but *because of* their liberal politics, which, for conservative Irish-American Catholics, became muddled with the reputation of many of the male Kennedys for 'liberal' behaviour with attractive women. This coalesces in the gruesome case of the 1969 death of a young woman in the company of the married Ted Kennedy, the family's last hope for Restoration in that generation. A year after RFK was assassinated, Ted drove off a bridge in Chappaquiddick, Massachusetts and his passenger, named Mary Jo Kopechne, drowned after Kennedy left her in the water and did not report the accident for ten hours. He subsequently pleaded guilty to a charge of leaving the scene of an accident and later received a two-month suspended sentence. Ted served as a US Senator from Massachusetts for nearly half a century, from 1962 until his death in 2009, and was hugely successful in translating his progressive policies into law. Nevertheless, the Chappaquiddick death tainted his reputation and, arguably, that of his party: Neal Gabler's biography records that it was said at the time that when Ted went over that bridge, he took the moral authority of the Democrats with him.[37] The Gothic trope of the endangered young woman finds further iteration with the emergence of a conspiracy theory that Bobby Kennedy had played some murky part in the coverup of the 1962 death of Marilyn Monroe, whose affair with his president brother is well documented.[38] The persistence of the rumour that Monroe also had an affair with the very religious and family-oriented Bobby appears not to hold water,[39] but attests to the ability of lurid detail to adhere to members of the dynasty.

'I used to wonder what our father or his father could have done', muses Rosa in *Absalom, Absalom!*, 'what crime committed that would leave our family cursed'.[40] In a subsequent public response to the Chappaquiddick death, Ted referred to 'some awful curse' upon his family,[41] deploying the phrase through which the sprawling dynasty's mishaps have been Gothicized ever since. The concept of a 'Kennedy curse'—with its Faulknerian implication of originary crime—has been repeatedly invoked in accounts of the numerous premature deaths of family members over the past century. (They do, when tallied, seem to be statistically improbable.[42]) Belief in the Kennedy curse is deep and persistent: The adult daughter of Jackie's second husband from 1968 to 1975, Greek magnate Aristotle Onassis, convinced her father to disinherit his wife when the family endured much ill fortune after the widow's arrival on the scene, including the death of the Onassis heir in a 1973 plane crash.[43] Tragically, the Kennedy Compound has itself been the scene of what the *New York Times* covered as the most recent strike of the family curse, when Bobby's young granddaughter, Saoirse Kennedy Hill, died at that location of a drug overdose in 2019.[44]

Jackie Kennedy Gothic: Blood and Red Roses

From her forties onwards, Jacqueline Kennedy Onassis became an impactful conservationist and a well-regarded book editor. She led the charge to save New York's Beaux Arts Grand Central Railway Station in 1975 when it was threatened, and deployed her former First Lady soft power to negotiate the loan of valuable artifacts from the Soviet government for a MOMA exhibit organized in conjunction with her publishing house.[45] Nevertheless, history generally records her as the decorative appendage of her husband, and even Rosalind Miles's important survey of women's history dismisses Jacqueline (as well as Diana, Princess of Wales) in this manner.[46] McMillan Cottom notes in relation to the image-control of today's most visible American female politicians: 'a dress is never just a dress. It is always strategy.'[47] Thus, far from being a passive clothes horse, even in the days of her traditional political wifehood Jackie communicated with clothing: during the 1960 presidential run, and in response to relentless chatter that the candidate's wife spent too much on French *couture*, the pregnant Mrs Kennedy showed reporters her inexpensive American-made maternity dresses.[48] In the manner of Princess Grace, Jacqueline, too, went on to use *couture* to create a complex message that simultaneously signalled 'elite' and 'Irish': In her official White House portrait, Mrs Kennedy is beautiful but unsettlingly wraith-like in a pale Ulster linen gown by Sybil Connolly, the most successful *couturière* in midcentury Ireland's female-dominated fashion industry (Figure E.3). Poignantly, however, Mrs Kennedy's most visceral use of clothing-as-message was unplanned.

In the dark days after Jackie had buried her assassinated brother-in-law, Robert, she compared the family disarray at Hyannis Port—where she, Ted, and all the fatherless children of Jack and Bobby had fled—to 'the milieu of the White Russians in Paris, grand dukes who drank and despaired all day [...].'[49] To sympathizers for whom JFK became America's slain king, Mrs Kennedy became an unjustly defiled queen when stills of her crawling in the besieged presidential car in Texas in a bloodied pink Chanel-style suit were seen around the world. The image invokes both Gothic's endangered beautiful woman trope and Edmund Burke's much-quoted description of the historical rupture caused by a dishevelled Marie Antoinette fleeing blood-spattered would-be assassins.[50] (The supposed Bouvier connection to French royalty plays out in this moment, though in the most nightmarish way.) If Grace Kelly's pristine white bridal gown signified the Irish-American fairytale, then its Gothic inverse is the First Lady's white leather gloves, so stiff with her husband's dried blood in the wake of his assassination that she had to be assisted in their removal.[51] Deeply cognizant of the power of image from her years as one of the most photographed women in the world, Jacqueline's refusal to change out of the bloodied pink suit as soon as the opportunity arose was a conscious choice: Barbara Leaming details how a white dress into which to change had been laid out in the presidential quarters of Air Force One when

Figure E.3 Official portrait of First Lady Jacqueline Bouvier Kennedy by Aaron Shikler (1970) depicts her wearing a pleated Ulster linen gown by her personal friend, Irish designer Sybil Connolly. Courtesy of the White House Collection/White House Historical Association.

Jackie boarded after the assassination, a colour meant to mitigate the horror. However, when Mrs. Kennedy reappeared for the hurried swearing-in of Johnson, 'she was still defiantly wearing the bespattered suit', and her stockings remained '"saturated with blood"'. When Lady Bird Johnson urged the new widow to change, Jackie refused by saying, '"I want them to see what they have done to Jack."'[52] (This

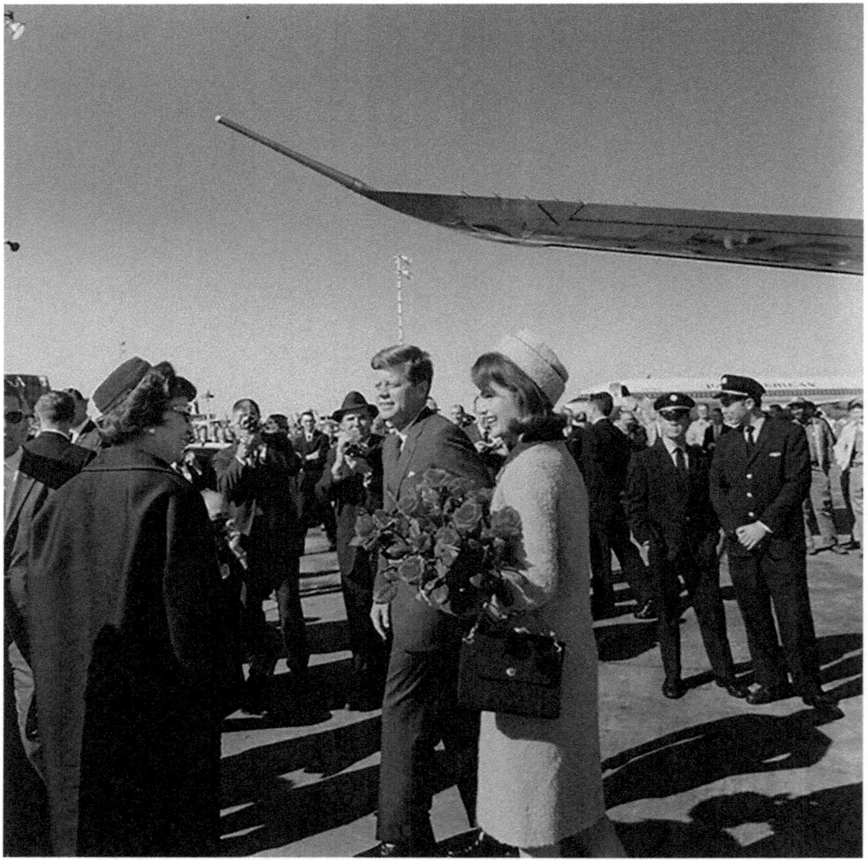

Figure E.4 President and Mrs. Kennedy arrive in Dallas on 22 November 1963. Courtesy of ALAMY.

'they' is the first inkling of the theory that a plurality of conspirators rather than a lone gunman was to blame for her husband's murder.) The deeply traumatized Jackie appears to have framed the assassination through a Gothic lens in the interview granted to *Life* magazine soon after the event, ruminating on the portent of having been presented with red roses on arrival in Dallas (Figure E.4): 'Three times that day in Texas they had been greeted with the bouquets of yellow roses of Texas. Only, in Dallas they had given her red roses. She remembers thinking, how funny—red roses for me; and then the car was full of blood and red roses.'[53]

Jacqueline's quieter third act, after her two internationally documented marriages, was her successful career as a book editor in New York from 1975 onwards, a city that took her to its bosom. In 1994, the year of her death, the Central Park Reservoir, which had been decommissioned and turned over for future recreational use, was renamed the Jacqueline Kennedy Onassis Reservoir. A long-dedicated granite, slate, and gilded bronze monument to John Purroy Mitchel is located on the reservoir's eastern embankment at 90th Street.[54] (See Figure 2.5.) It is safe to assume that contemporary Manhattan tourists and residents are generally much more familiar with the name of the former First Lady than that of the former mayor, but the coupled monuments speak to the ubiquity of New York's Irish ghosts. This is to say nothing of the city's African ghosts: the 1991 discovery of the Negroes Burial Ground in lower Manhattan drew attention to the neglected history of enslaved people in early New York.[55] It may seem odd to use Gothic vocabulary to discuss monuments and historical remnants in the urban northeast, since Gothic, like slavery, has been popularly represented as belonging only to the South. However, every inch of American soil—just like every inch of Irish soil—is haunted, and the long-neglected intertwined histories of Irish, Native, and African in the Americas, both good—the AAIDN—and bad, are still materializing.[56]

Coda: Irishness, the US Presidency, and Black Lives Matter

In this one-act play, a marginalized Black man, though warned that some white policemen are coming for him, refuses to leave his beloved grandmother's deathbed. When the final curtain drops, he is waiting, door barricaded, clasping his grandmother with his left hand and his revolver with his right as the approach of the police can be heard in the hallway. This seemingly up-to-the-minute depiction of a man of colour that challenges dehumanizing constructions of Black men was not written in response to the murder of George Floyd in May 2020. It is, in fact, O'Neill's *The Dreamy Kid* (1918), a play that testifies to an often-effaced history of solidarity and allows this conclusion to pivot to the Black Lives Matter movement's meanings in the Irish and Irish-American present.

There is an increasing chasm between a contemporary Ireland that found it uncontroversial to have a mixed-race (and openly gay) prime minister in recent years,[57] and an America in which the election of Barack Obama, its first Black president, revitalized the 'dog whistle' Saxonist discourse that reemerged during the Trump administration. The Trump family had claimed Swedish origins for three generations after their arrival in America in the 1880s,[58] a period in which the American hierarchy of immigrant whitenesses privileged those perceived to have both recent and deep Scandinavian ('Viking'/'Nordic'/'Anglo-Saxon') roots. In fact, like Fitzgerald's Gatsby, Trump's father was the son of German Lutheran immigrants, and Trump latterly claimed his German ancestry.[59] Ironically, however, in contrast with his paternal origins, both real and assumed, Trump's Gaelo-American mother's ancestry might have been less coherent within the earlier immigrant hierarchy. Mary Anne MacLeod (1912–2000) was born into a humble Gaelic-speaking Presbyterian family on Scotland's Isle of Lewis, some of whose antecedents were supposedly dispossessed by landlords during the Highland Clearances.[60] The combination of MacLeod's linguistic culture (Scottish Gaelic) and denominational allegiance (Presbyterianism) would not have always cleanly aligned within the fixed binary of 'Anglo-Saxon' Protestant Scots/Scots-Irish and Gaelic Catholic Irish that emerged strongly in nineteenth-century America. Indeed, it was her son who revived the old vocabulary of 'preferred' immigrants: Trump proclaimed in 2018 that he wished that more immigrants to America could come from 'places like Norway' rather than the 'shit-hole countries' from which Haitians, Salvadorans, and Africans originated.[61] The roots of this racial hierarchy in Emerson's theory of Scandinavian Ur-whiteness became visible during the storming of the US Capitol (a federal government seat) in Washington, DC on 6 January 2021: the event's most widely disseminated immediate image was of a participant costumed as a Viking-cum-shaman. Thus, Sweden and Norway were not arbitrary choices in the Trump lexicon, nor indeed, given the threat of Black resistance that it represents in cultural memory, was Haiti.

The Catholic Famine-Irish have hitched themselves to a 'whiteness' that once more readily accommodated the Scots-Irish, and both Irishnesses are now enfolded within the contemporary white Christian constituency for which Trump claimed to speak. Indeed, some of the most prominent members of the Trump administration stressed their Catholic Irish-American roots.[62] It is one of the many ironies of the convoluted history of Irishnesses in America that, while still stressing historical victimization in the colonial motherland,[63] Catholic Irish America now converges with the Scots-Irish-inflected conservative Protestant America from which it once so strongly strove to distinguish itself. Altogether, in a contemporary America in which native Irish surnames now code 'white',[64] the critical question today is not, as Liam Kennedy recently noted, how the Irish became white, but how white people in the US became Irish.[65]

A recent translation controversy that arose in the context of Black Lives Matter symbolizes the manner in which Irishness is now used as a stand-in for 'white'. 'Red' has been repeatedly discussed as a racialized colour term in reference to the descendants of white indentured servants and convicts from the social, linguistic, and political margins of Ireland and Britain. However, at this late juncture, a fourth such term is required, and that is 'blue' (*gorm*). 'Gorm' has traditionally been used in Irish and Scottish Gaelic to refer to Black people, though medieval usage implies 'swarthy' rather than 'blue'.[66] In it important to stress that it is incorrect to use the Scottish and Irish Gaelic colour term *dubh* ('black') in reference to people of African descent. The long existence of a specific term in Irish to denote Black skin reflects historical contact between Irish and African within multiple contexts.[67] There is also a long history of Black characters in Irish settings in literature from Ireland in both Irish and English, from Le Fanu to the late modernist novel, *Cré na Cille* (Graveyard Soil; 1949).[68]

The Irish-language 'Black Lives Matter' Wikipedia page offers the following translation of the movement's name: '*Mór Againn Beatha Daoine Gorma*'. Translated nearly word for word, this means, 'We Respect the Lives of Blue [i.e., Black] People', The pro-police slogan 'Blue Lives Matter' arose in opposition to the summer 2020 'Black Lives Matter' demonstrations against police killings of civilians in response to the George Floyd case. In rejoinder, one amateur American translator—apparently certain that their politics reflected twenty-first-century Irish values—rendered 'Blue Lives Matter' as *Gorm Chónaí Ábhar*. As Audrey Nickel notes, this approximate translation was actually closer to meaning 'Black Lives Matter'.[69] In 2021, Nigerian-Irish broadcaster and Irish-language activist Ola Majekodunmi successfully petitioned to have the coinage *duine de dhath* ('person of colour'), an alternate to the increasingly hijacked *gorm*, entered in the government-sponsored National Terminology Database for Irish,[70] suggesting that the ripples of the George Floyd case continue to reach Irish shores. Similarly, and due to debates sparked by BLM mobilization, the often uncritical celebration of Irish-American material success is being reassessed: an heroic statue of novelist Ellin Berlin's Dublin-born father, mining magnate John W. Mackay (1831–1902), may soon be removed from a Nevada campus because his fortune was 'made largely off the backs of black and indigenous people in America'.[71] In the end, the American history of exploitation indicted in Fitzgerald's 'The Diamond as Big as the Ritz' turns out to be Irish-American history too.

The increasing abandonment of the Democratic Party by the Catholic Irish after its embrace of Civil Rights has not reversed. Although JFK's election enjoyed huge support among Irish and Irish-American Catholics as a welcome signal that they were finally fully part of the white mainstream, the current presidency (at time of writing) of what is America's second only Catholic leader of Famine-Irish origin divides his co-religionists. An ever-growing political chasm among American Catholics means that President Biden—who skews liberal on the divisive issues of more recent decades of abortion and gun control—does not enjoy the support of Catholics and their bishops on the American right.[72] Fintan O'Toole recently named Biden the 'most gothic figure in American politics'. This Gothicizing does not bode well for the legacy within Irish America of this 'revenant' from the Kennedy era, nor for the pact that the earlier administration attempted to forge between progressive politics and Irish-American Catholicism.[73] In addition, the Famine-era immigrant origins of both Obama and Biden challenge conservative Catholic Irish America's reading of that catastrophe as involving a clear-cut binary of Catholic/colonized victim and Protestant/colonizer perpetrator: Biden's Mayo ancestor was a workhouse overseer during the Famine,[74] while Obama's Irish ancestry on his white mother's side leads to a family of Protestant affiliation.[75] This book has repeatedly circled upon the white Scots-Irish, Famine Irish, and even, latterly, the Scottish Gaelic origins of numerous US presidents. It has also

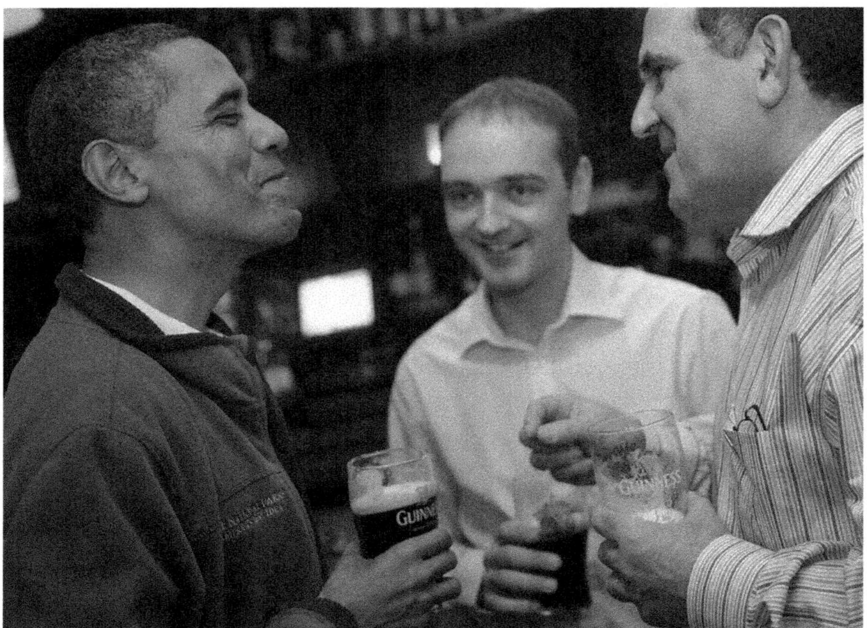

Figure E.5 President Barack Obama celebrates St Patrick's Day in Washington in 2012 with his distant Irish cousins, Henry Healy and Ollie Hayes. Courtesy of ALAMY.

considered an alternative American history of African-Irish solidarity, as imagined by Black and white Irish Americans such as Yerby and O'Neill. Therefore, it closes by naming Barack Obama for what he could have been called had the term not been long-ago hijacked by the cultural history of race and Irishness that this book has outlined, which is America's first Black Irish president (Figure E.5).

Endnotes

Introduction

1. Quoted in Geraldine Higgins, 'Tara, the O'Haras, and the Irish *Gone with the Wind*'. *Southern Cultures* 17.1 (2011): 42.
2. Peter D. O'Neill, *Famine Irish and the American Racial State* (London; New York: Routledge, 2019), 5.
3. Kerby Miller, *Emigrants and Exiles: Ireland and the Irish Exodus to North America* (Oxford: Oxford University Press, 1988).
4. I respectfully acknowledge that although 'Scots-Irish' is the predominant contemporary usage among scholars and journalists, for those for whom it is a lived identity the older term 'Scotch-Irish' is sometimes still preferred. My thanks to Bill McGimpsey for this discussion.
5. Maldwyn A. Jones, 'Scotch-Irish', in Stephan Thernstrom (ed.), *Harvard Encyclopedia of American Ethnic Groups*. Harvard UP, 1980, 895.
6. Some of the earliest post-Famine Irish self-ascription as 'white' is generated by this context: in August 1862, and in response to the many formerly enslaved people making their way North as a result of escape or being freed by the Union Army, the *Boston Pilot*, a Catholic-Irish newspaper, complained: 'These *wretches* crowd our cities, and by overstocking the market of labor, do incalculable injury to *white* hands' (latter italic added). Quoted in Stephen Steinberg, *The Ethnic Myth* (Boston: Beacon Press, 1981), 177. The Black press could give as good as it got, as suggested by a reference to white immigrants in a 1907 Black magazine: 'Already the day is upon us, when the scum of Europe is with us, her paupers, her convicts, her socialists, [and] her anarchists...' S.R.S., 'The Negro and the Chinese', *The Colored American Magazine* 13.2 (August 1907): 113. (The article appears to be a reprint from an 1891 *Boston Courant* issue, an early and short-lived African-American newspaper founded by George Washington Forbes.)
7. Margaret Mitchell, *Gone with the Wind*. Preface by Pat Conroy (New York: Scribner, 2011), 565.
8. Joe Cleary, 'Irish American Modernisms', in Joe Cleary (ed.), *The Cambridge Companion to Irish Modernism* (Cambridge University Press, Cambridge, 2014), 190, footnote 7.
9. Gail Sheehy, 'Inside Grey Gardens' *New York Magazine*, 10 January 1972, 25. https://nymag.com/news/features/56102/.
10. Tressie McMillan Cottom, 'Why We Should Talk about What Kyrsten Sinema Is Wearing', *New York Times*, 29 October 2021.
11. See Christopher Dowd, *The Irish and the Origins of American Popular Culture* (New York: Routledge, 2018).

12. 'Jim Crow' were post-Civil War state and local statutes that legalized racial segregation and disenfranchisement. They were undone with the Supreme Court declaration that separate was unequal in its 1954 *Brown v. Board of Education* ruling.
13. André Leon Talley in conversation with Alexis Boylan. University of Connecticut Humanities Institute (online), 12 November 2020.
14. See Emma Dabiri, *Twisted: The Tangled History of Black Hair Culture* (New York: Harper Perennial, 2020).

Chapter 1

1. J.D. Vance, *Hillbilly Elegy* (New York: Harper, 2016), 3.
2. Cameron Joseph, 'The Scots-Irish Vote', *Atlantic,* 6 October 2009. Online: https://www.theatlantic.com/politics/archive/2009/10/the-scots-irish-vote/27853/.
3. Nicholas Carnes and Naom Lupu. 'It's Time to Bust the Myth: Most Trump Voters Were Not Working Class'. *Washington Post,* 5 June 2017. Online.
4. Razib Khan, 'The Scots-Irish as Indigenous People', *Discover*, 22 July 2012. Online: https://www.discovermagazine.com/mind/the-scots-irish-as-indigenous-people.
5. Within a generation of arrival, the Scots-Irish who had first settled in New Hampshire and Maine had begun moving down along the Appalachian spine, from western Pennsylvania and southeastern Ohio down into Virginia, North Carolina, northern Georgia, Mississippi, Alabama, South Carolina, Kentucky, and Tennessee. Many moved further south and west, down to the Gulf Coast and out to Oklahoma, Arkansas, East Texas, and beyond. Eventually they migrated out to the Bakersfield region of California, and up the Great Plains to parts of Michigan, Kansas, Nebraska, and Colorado. Joseph, online.
6. Roxanne Dunbar-Ortiz, *Red Dirt: Growing Up Okie* (Norman, OK: University of Oklahoma Press, 2006), 46.
7. https://thehermitage.com/learn/mansion-grounds/slavery/.
8. Ta-Nehisi Coates, 'The First White President: The Foundation of Donald Trump's Presidency is the Negation of Barack Obama's Legacy'. *Atlantic,* 15 October 2017. Online.
9. Jenna Amatulli, 'Rudy Giuliani: Trump Is "Greatest Victory for People of America since Andrew Jackson"'. *HuffPost,*9 November 2016. Online.
10. Alan Rappeport, 'Harriet Tubman $20 Bill Is Delayed Until Trump Leaves Office, Mnuchin Says' *New York Times,* 22 May 2009. Online. The Underground Railroad was a secret network in nineteenth-century North America used by enslaved people for escape.
11. Michael Kazin, *The Populist Persuasion: An American History* (Ithaca, NY: Cornell University Press, 1998), 21.
12. Presidents in this period of direct Scots-Irish descent are as follows: Andrew Jackson (1829–37), James K. Polk (1845–49), James Buchanan (1857–61), Andrew Johnson (1865–69), Ulysses S. Grant (1869–77), Chester A. Arthur (1881–85), Grover Cleveland (1885–89 and 1893–97), Benjamin Harrison (1889–93), William McKinley (1897–1901), and Woodrow Wilson (1913–1921). See George McBride, *American*

Presidents of Ulster Descent: A Guide to Their Family Origins and the Locations of Their Ancestral Homesteads in Northern Ireland (Lisburn, Co. Antrim: G. McBride, 1969).

13. William J. Clinton, 'Remarks to Mackie International Employees in Belfast, Northern Ireland, November 30, 1995', in *Public Papers of the Presidents of the United States: William J. Clinton: 1995*, 2 vols (Washington: United States Government Printing Office, 1996), vol. I, 1806.
14. Mike and Biddy Bogan emigrate from Ireland with their baby son, Danny, who is given every advantage of education that his hard-working parents can provide. Arrogant regarding the sparkling future ahead, Danny complains that had he not been born before his parents emigrated, '"maybe I'd be prisident."' (The United States Constitution stipulates that only a natural-born citizen may hold the office of president or vice president.) Depicted as being increasingly over-reaching, young Danny begins to keep rough company and eventually dies in a brawl. Sarah Orne Jewett, 'The Luck of the Bogans', *Scribner's Magazine* 5.1 (January–June, 1889): 106.
15. Fitzgerald, *This Side of Paradise* (New York: Charles Scribner's Sons, 1921), 140.
16. Theodore Roosevelt, *The Winning of the West* (New York: Review of Reviews Company,1889), vol. I, 127.
17. Richard Blaustein. *The Thistle and the Brier* (Jefferson, NC: McFarland, 2003), 31.
18. Patrick Griffin, *The People with No Name: Ireland's Ulster Scots, America's Scots Irish, and the Creation of a British Atlantic World, 1689–1764* (Princeton, NJ: Princeton UP, 2001), 105; 162.
19. See Michael A. Lofaro, 'David "Davy" Crockett', in *Tennessee Encyclopedia,* 7 March 2018. Online.
20. Western Literature Association, *A Literary History of the American West* (Fort Worth: Texas Christian University Press, 1987), 171–2.
21. Frederick Jackson Turner, *The Frontier in American History* (New York: Henry Holt, 1921) 22.
22. See a work such as Charles Knowles Bolton, *Scotch Irish Pioneers in Ulster and America* (Boston: Bacon and Brown, 1910), whose tone is typical of a rash of 'booster' histories of the Scots-Irish in the period.
23. Jane H. Corwin, 'A Dialogue between Mr. Native and Mrs. Foreigner, on Literary Subjects', in *The Harp of Home; or The Medley* (Cincinnati, OH: Moore, Wilstach, Keys, and Co., 1858), 15–32.
24. Anatol Lieven, 'Clinton and Trump: Two Faces of American Nationalism', *Survival* 58.5 (2016): 13.
25. James, 'The Ghostly Rental', *Scribner's Monthly* 12.5 (September 1876): 678.
26. James, 'The Ghostly Rental', 666.
27. This is a new version published in 1993. It was originally published as *The Last Tycoon* in 1941.
28. Fitzgerald, *The Love of the Last Tycoon: A Western.* Matthew J. Bruccoli, ed. (Cambridge: Cambridge University Press, 1993), 9. See Jessica Adams, *Wounds of Returning: Race, Memory, and Property on the Postslavery Plantation* (Chapel Hill, NC: University of North Carolina Press, 2007).
29. Fitzgerald, *The Love of the Last Tycoon*, 13.
30. Clukey, 'White Troubles: The Southern Imaginary in Northern Ireland 2008–2016', *Arizona Quarterly: A Journal of American Literature, Culture, and Theory* 73.4 (2017):

61–92. Peter Moloney has posted a visual record of a mural depicting Jackson and his ancestral Ulster homestead that was located off the Shankill Road, Belfast, between *c.* 2006 and 2015. https://petermoloneycollection.wordpress.com/2007/08/31/andrew-jackson/.

31. Jackson also haunts the action of Fitzgerald's 1923 political satire, *The Vegetable*, a play about an incompetent US President.
32. Eugene O'Neill, quoted in Croswell Bowen, 'The Black Irishman', in *Conversations with Eugene O'Neill*, ed. Mark W. Estrin (Jackson, MS and London: University Press of Mississippi, 1990), 221; 222.
33. William Faulkner, *Absalom, Absalom!* (New York: Modern Library, 1951), 21.
34. David H. Fischer, *Albion's Seed: Four British Folkways in America* (New York: Oxford University Press, 1989), 605–782.
35. Abbott Emerson Smith, *Colonists in Bondage: White Servitude and Convict Labor in America, 1607–1776* (Chapel Hill, NC: University of North Carolina Press, 1947), 154.
36. Steven Ellis, *The Making of the British Isles: The State of Britain and Ireland, 1450–1660* (London: Routledge, 2014), 296.
37. A.J. Aitken, 'Scots', in Tom McArthur and Roshan McArthur (eds), *The Concise Oxford Companion to the English Language* (Oxford: Oxford University Press, 1998), 687.
38. Miller, *Emigrants and Exiles*, 137; 149–50.
39. Miller, *Emigrants and Exiles*, 159.
40. Maldwyn A. Jones, 'The Scotch-Irish in British America', in BernardBailyn and Philip D. Morgan (eds), *Strangers Within the Realm: Cultural Margins of the First British Empire* (Chapel Hill, NC: University of North Carolina Press, 1991), 291–2.
41. James Anthony Froude, *The English in Ireland in the Eighteenth Century* (London: Longmans & Green, 1872), vol. I, 393.
42. Jones, 'Scotch-Irish', 895.
43. Fanning, 39.
44. Jason King reads *The Irish Emigrant* as both an historical novel about the United Irish Uprising of 1798 (in which the author's father participated) and a romance centred on a union symbolizing the shared republicanism of Ireland and America. Jason King, '*Reading the Fenian* Romance: Irish-American and Irish-Canadian Versions of the National Tale', in Marguérite Corporaal and Christina Morin (eds), *Traveling Irishness in the Long Nineteenth Century* (Cham, Switzerland: Palgrave Macmillan, 2017), 210.
45. David 'Davy' Crockett (with Thomas Chilton), *A Narrative of the Life of David Crockett of the State of Tennessee* (Philadelphia: Carey & Hart; Boston: Allen & Ticknor, 1834), 68.
46. Peter Gilmore, *Irish Presbyterians and the Shaping of Western Pennsylvania, 1770–1830* (Pittsburgh, PA: University of Pittsburgh Press, 2018), xx.
47. Samuel Thomson, 'To Captain M'Dougall, Castle Upton', in *Simple Poems on a Few Subjects* (Belfast: Smyth & Lyons, 1806), 37.
48. See David Noel Doyle, 'Scots Irish or Scotch-Irish', in Joseph Lee and Marion R. Casey (eds), *Making the Irish American: History and Heritage of the Irish in the United States* (New York University Press, 2006), 151–70; Marilyn J. Westerkamp, *Triumph of the Laity: Scots-Irish Piety and the Great Awakening, 1625–1760* (New York: Oxford

University Press, 1988); Grace Elizabeth Hale, *Making Whiteness: The Culture of Segregation in the South, 1890–1940* (New York: Pantheon Books, 1998); James G. Leyburn, *The Scotch-Irish: A Social History* (Chapel Hill, NC: University of North Carolina Press, 1962), 236; 306; Bernd Weisbrod, 'Theatrical Monarchy: The Making of Victoria, the Modern Family Queen' in Regina Schulte (ed.), *The Body of the Queen: Gender and Rule in the Courtly World, 1500–2000* (New York and Oxford: Berghahn, 2006), 243.

49. A turn-of-the-century Irish-born New Hampshire author argued that the belief that Ulster Scot and Irishman did not share blood was a fallacy rooted in anti-Catholic prejudice. See John C. Linehan, *The Irish Scots and the 'Scotch-Irish'* (Concord, New Hampshire: American-Irish Historical Society, 1902), 6; 7.
50. See, for example, Rev. Samuel Cotton, 'The Foundling', in *The Three Whispers and Other Tales* (Dublin, 1870), 149–218.
51. See John Carlos Rowe, 'Religious Transnationalism in the American Renaissance: Susan Warner's *Wide, Wide World*'. *ESQ: A Journal of the American Renaissance* 49.1 (2003): 48–50. *Project MUSE*, doi:10.1353/esq.2010.0009.
52. See Eileen Sullivan, *The Shamrock and the Cross: Irish American Novelists Shape American Catholicism* (Notre Dame, IN: University of Notre Dame Press, 2016).
53. Noel Ignatiev, *How the Irish Became White* (New York: Routledge, 1995), 41.
54. Henry David Thoreau to Emerson, 12 January 1848 in *The Correspondence of Henry David Thoreau*, ed. Walter Harding and Carl Bode (New York: New York University Press, 1958), 203–4.
55. Edmund Burke [and William Burke], *An Account of the European Settlements in America* (Boston: Wilkins and Hilliard & Gray, 1835), 285.
56. Hector St John de Crèvecoeur, *Letters from an American Farmer* (London: Printed for Thomas Davies, 1783), 78–9.
57. Griffin, 3.
58. Samuel Blunston to Thomas Penn, 13 August 1734, qtd in Griffin, 105.
59. Leyburn, 176.
60. Richard Hooker (ed.), *The Carolina Backcountry on the Eve of the Revolution: The Journal and Other Writings of Charles Woodmason, Anglican Itinerant* (Chapel Hill, NC: University of North Carolina Press for the Institute of Early American History and Culture at Williamsburg, VA, 1953), 60, 52.
61. Benjamin Franklin, *A Narrative of the Late Massacre in Lancaster County* (Philadelphia, 1764), qtd in Griffin, 170. Kevin Kenny's account, *Peaceable Kingdom Lost,* attends to the role played by the Paxton Boys' Ulster Irish heritage in the perception of the event and its aftermath.
62. Ian R. McBride, 'When Ulster Joined Ireland': Anti-Popery, Presbyterian Radicalism and Irish Republicanism in the 1790s', *Past & Present* 157 (Nov., 1997): 68–71; 66.
63. Jared Gardner, 'Alien Nation: Edgar Huntly's Savage Awakening', *American Literature* 66.3 (1994): 430.
64. Terri D. Halperin. *The Alien and Sedition Acts of 1798: Testing the Constitution* (Baltimore, MD: Johns Hopkins University Press, 2016), 44. Strikingly, 'wild Irish' was an old Elizabethan category for the native Irish.
65. Gardner, 436.

66. Piers Wauchope, *Patrick Sarsfield and the Williamite War* (Dublin: Irish Academic Press, 1992), 4; 119. Sarsfield's association with unfinished trauma illuminates his seemingly incongruous name-check in the opening of J.S. Le Fanu's disturbing 1870 Gothic story, 'The Child that Went with the Fairies'.
67. Gardner, 450.
68. Philip Barnard and Stephen Shapiro, Introduction to Charles Brockden Brown, *Edgar Huntly, Or, Memoirs of a Sleep-walker; with Related Texts* (Indianapolis, IN: Hackett, 2006), xxii.
69. See Christopher Stampone, 'A "Spirit of Mistaken Benevolence": Civilizing the Savage in Charles Brockden Brown's Edgar Huntly', *Early American Literature* 50.2 (2015): 415–48; Luke Gibbons, 'Ireland, America, and Gothic Memory: Transatlantic Terror in the Early Republic', *boundary 2*, 31.1 (2004) 32. muse.jhu.edu/article/5426
70. Diana Loercher Pazicky, *Cultural Orphans in America* (Jackson, MS: University Press of Mississippi, 2008), 90.
71. See Jarlath Killeen, *Gothic Ireland: Horror and the Irish Anglican Imagination in the Long Eighteenth Century* (Dublin: Four Courts Press, 2005).
72. These are the celebrated opening words of L.P. Hartley's 1953 novel, *The Go-Between.*
73. Robert Smart, 'The "Vital Blood" of Irish Colonials in America and the Formation of the New Nation', in Christine Kinealy and Gerard Moran (eds), *Irish Famines Before and After the Great Hunger* (Cork: Cork University Press, 2020), 49–60.
74. Due to the fact that representations of the Scots-Irish have not been made visible in discussions of Gothic literature and because the actual Scots-Irish are often undifferentiated within discussions of Irish Protestant America, this study attends mostly to this grouping above other Irish-American Protestant cohorts.
75. A search within a relatively recent resource such as the multi-volume *Greenwood Encyclopedia of Multiethnic American Literature* (2005) contains not one reference to Scots-Irish or even Scottish literature or identity.
76. *Barren Ground* lays out how class and denominational differences in the town of Pedlar's Mill, Virginia between those of Ulster Presbyterian heritage and the more culturally dominant Anglicans leads to the former's invisibility: 'The good families of the state have preserved, among other things, custom, history, tradition, romantic fiction, and the Episcopal Church. The [Scots-Irish], according to the records of clergymen, which are the only surviving records, have preserved nothing except themselves. Ignored alike by history and fiction, they have their inconspicuous place in the social strata midway between the lower gentility and the upper class of "poor white"...', 5.
77. Lorna Carson, *Ulster Scots: Language Movement and Speech Community.* TCD M.Phil in Applied Linguistics Thesis, 2002.
78. Edmund Thomas Bewley, *The Origin and Early History of the Family of Poë or Poe* (Dublin: Printed for the author by Ponsonby & Gibbs, 1906), 49; 51.
79. Bewley, 56; 64.
80. Killeen, *The Emergence of Irish Gothic Fiction* (Edinburgh: Edinburgh University Press, 2013), 46.
81. Madeline McCully, *Haunted Donegal* (Dublin: History Press Ireland, 2016), 43. The use of Gothic to obtain 'poetic justice' seems to be a feature of Irish Gothic in the colonial period: Thomas Furlong's Maturin-influenced and posthumous Catholic

Emancipation-era long poem, *The Doom of Derenzie* (1829), which centres on the murder of a pregnant labouring-class girl by a member of the local gentry, was inspired by real events in Wexford. See Sean Mythen, *Thomas Furlong, the Forgotten Wexford Poet* (Ferns, Co. Wexford: Clone Publications, 1998), 160–85.

82. Cecil Frances Alexander, 'The Ballad of Stumpie's Brae', in *The Legend of the Golden Prayers: And Other Poems* (London: Bell & Daldy, 1859), 54, lines 125–26.
83. Arthur Hobson Quinn, *Edgar Allan Poe: A Critical Biography* (Baltimore: The Johns Hopkins University Press, 1998) 75.
84. Edgar Allan Poe, 'William Wilson', in J.Gerald Kennedy (ed.), *The Portable Edgar Allan Poe* (New York: Penguin, 2006), 176.
85. Faulkner, *Absalom, Absalom!*, 261.
86. William III of England's 1690 victory at the Boyne over James II secured Protestant Ireland. King William's victory continues to be celebrated on 12 July in loyalist (pro-British) Northern Ireland, the date of the Battle of the Boyne.
87. Poe, 'William Wilson', 186.
88. Bewley, 64–8.
89. Walt Whitman, 'Edgar Poe's Significance', *The Critic* 2 (1882): 147.
90. James, in an 1876 review of Baudelaire's *Les Fleurs du Mal*, quoted in Burton R. Pollin, 'Poe and Henry James: A Changing Relationship', *The Yearbook of English Studies* 3 (1973): 233.
91. James, 'Owen Wingrave', in *Henry James: Complete Stories, 1892–1898* (New York: Library of America, 1996), 275.
92. James, 'Owen Wingrave', 273.
93. Owen's father dies by 'Afghan sabre' and a family connection 'had fallen in the Indian Mutiny'. James, 'Owen Wingrave', 262; 263.
94. James, 'Owen Wingrave', 279; 280.
95. James, 'Owen Wingrave', 271.
96. James, 'Owen Wingrave', 275.
97. This description of a 'relic' who resembles the ancestor who haunts his abode recalls the description of the ghost-to-be/Andrew Jackson double in 'The Ghostly Rental' as an 'old soldier', suggesting that Jackson hovers in this story too. James, 'Owen Wingrave', 262.
98. James, 'Owen Wingrave', 278.
99. James, 'Owen Wingrave', 290.
100. James, *The Sense of the Past* (New York: Scribner, 1917), 87; 88.
101. James, *The Sense of the Past*, 87.
102. Edel and Lyall H. Powers (eds), *The Complete Notebooks of Henry James* (New York and Oxford: Oxford University Press, 1987), 502–8.
103. Jane O'Reilly, *The Girl I Left Behind* (New York: Collier, 1980), 156.
104. Bryan Giemza, *Irish Catholic Writers and the Invention of the American South* (Baton Rouge, LA: Louisiana State University Press, 2013), 85–97.
105. The bride of the title gives the following reason for leaving Cazeau, her perfectly kind husband: 'No, I don't hate him. [...] I hate being Mrs. Cazeau, an' would want to be Athénaïse Miché again.' Kate Chopin, 'Athénaïse', in *Kate Chopin: Complete Stories and Novels* (New York: Library of America, 2000), 358.

106. Brian McEvoy and Daniel G. Bradley, 'Y-chromosomes and the Extent of Patrilineal Ancestry in Irish Surnames', *Human Genetics* 119.1–2 (2006): 212
107. Micheál Ó Siochrú, 'The Curse of Cromwell?' *History Ireland* 5 (Sept/Oct. 2008). https://www.historyireland.com/early-modern-history-1500-1700/the-curse-of-cromwell-2/.
108. Le Fanu's Huguenot (French Protestant refugee) origins arguably allowed him to look askance at normative Anglo-Ireland.
109. Presbyterian immigrants readily switched nonconformist Protestant allegiance after the Great Awakening. Kevin Kenny, *The American Irish* (London: Longman, 2000), 34–6.
110. The *Colored American Magazine* noted with obvious relish that a Black postal service employee named Murphy applied for and was granted a promotion in a new location sight-unseen because he was presumed to be white. '"Africanizing" the Postal Service', *The Colored American Magazine* 13.4 (October 1907): 137.
111. See Richard Alba, *Ethnic Identity: The Transformation of White America* (New Haven, CT: Yale University Press, 1990).
112. See Herbert J. Gans, 'Symbolic Ethnicity: The Future of Ethnic Groups and Cultures in America', *Ethnic and Racial Studies* 2.1 (1979): 1–20, and Alba, 'Social Assimilation among American Catholic National-Origin Groups', *American Sociological Review* 42 (1976): 1030–46.
113. James, 'The Chaperon', in *'The Real Thing' and Other Tales* (New York: Macmillan, 1922), 221; 219.
114. In the sectarian Belfast-alike of *Milkman*, the old 'Saxon' and 'Celtic' categories are still not history when it comes to names and naming: a Catholic couple maintain a list of 'banned' British first names. Anna Burns, *Milkman* (London: Faber and Faber, 2018), 23.
115. By contrast there is a knowingness to 'Lily-White', contemporary Irish artist Gemma Brown's title for her 2006 solo show of portraits of Irish teen girls. https://www.gemma-browne.com/lily-white.html.
116. M. H. Abrams, *The Mirror and the Lamp: Romantic Theory and the Critical Tradition* (New York: Oxford University Press, 1953); James Joyce to Grant Richards, 23 June 1906, Stuart Gilbert (ed.), *Letters of James Joyce*, 3 vols (New York: Viking, 1957) I, 64.
117. Poe, 'William Wilson', 186.

Chapter 2

1. See Paul Jerome Croce, 'Money and Morality: The Life and Legacy of the First William James, 1771–1832', *New York History* 68.2 (1987): 174–90.
2. Henry Jones Ford, *The Scotch-Irish in America* (Princeton, NJ: Princeton University Press, 1915), 256.
3. Alfred Habegger, *The Father: A Life of Henry James, Sr.* (New York: Farrar, Strauss, and Giroux, 1994), 12.
4. Jerome Karabel. *The Chosen: The Hidden History of Admission and Exclusion at Harvard, Yale, and Princeton* (Boston & New York: Houghton Mifflin, 2005), 58.

5. Habegger, 151–3.
6. A turn-of-the-century New York 'rich boy' in Fitzgerald spoke in an English-sounding accent 'that is peculiar to fashionable people in the city of New York', Fitzgerald, 'The Rich Boy', in James L. W. West III (ed.), *All the Sad Young Men* (Cambridge and New York: Cambridge University Press, 2007), 5.
7. S.S. McClure (with Willa Cather), 'My Autobiography', *McClure's Magazine*, 41.6 (October 1913): 33.
8. James, *A Small Boy and Others*, 6.
9. Paul Grondahl. 'James Family Plot (1771–1832): Patriarch William James and Relatives of Novelist Henry James', *Times Union*,5 December 2013. Online.
10. In 'The Jolly Corner', a New York-born European is haunted by the spectre of the successful businessman he might have been when he returns to his birthplace.
11. James, *The American* (Boston: Osgood, 1877), 48
12. James, *The American*,49.
13. 'The Irish Question', in Eric L. Haralson and Kendall Johnson (eds), *Critical Companion to Henry James: A Literary Reference to His Life and Work* (New York: Facts on File, 2009), 398.
14. Henry James, Author Note, *The Portable Henry James*, ed. John Auchard (New York: Penguin, 2004), unpaginated.
15. William Dean Howells, 'Henry James Jr.', *The Century* 25 (Nov. 1882): 25.
16. George Monteiro, *Reading Henry James: A Critical Perspective on Selected Works* (Jefferson, NC: McFarland, 2016), 79.
17. John Kaag, 'William James's Varieties of Irish Experience', *New York Times*, 16 March 2020. Online.
18. J. Chris Westgate, *Staging the Slums, Slumming the Stage: Class, Poverty, Ethnicity, and Sexuality in American Theatre, 1890–1916* (New York: Palgrave Macmillan, 2014), 35.
19. James, *A Small Boy and Others* (New York: Scribner, 1913), 100; James, *Washington Square* (Oxford; New York: Oxford University Press, 2008). 73.
20. Robert Emmet (1778–1803) was born into a wealthy Dublin Anglican family who supported the American Revolutionary War. After 1798, the Rising of 1803, which he strategized, comprised the first attempt of the republican United Irishmen to sever the Act of Union by armed force. Emmet was subsequently executed for high treason. See Ruán O'Donnell, *Robert Emmet and the Rebellion of 1798* (Dublin: Irish Academic Press, 2003). His equally radical brother, Thomas Addis Emmet (1764–1827), fled to the United States, where he became a prominent New York lawyer and politician and a close friend of Henry James's grandfather. Three of Henry Jr's first cousins married men of this Emmet branch. Habegger, 12; James, *A Small Boy and Others*, 40.
21. This was Sarah, daughter of pro-abolition orator John Philpot Curran. See Douglass, *The Speeches of Frederick Douglass: A Critical Edition*. Eds. John R.McKivigan *et al.* (New Haven CT: Yale University Press, 2018), 50, and Washington Irving, 'The Broken Heart' in *The Sketch Book of Geoffrey Crayon, Gent.* (Chicago & New York: Belford, Clarke & Co., 1884), 73–78.
22. James, *A Small Boy and Others*, 40. See also Habegger, 150–3.
23. Mitchell, 206. The lament closes Irving's 'The Broken Heart'.
24. Guy Beiner, 'Disremembering 1798? An Archaeology of Social Forgetting and Remembrance in Ulster', *History & Memory* 25.1 (2013): 9.

25. Colm Tóibín, 'Henry James in Ireland', in Susan M. Griffin (ed.), *All a Novelist Needs: Colm Tóibín on Henry James* (Baltimore: Johns Hopkins University Press, 2010), 16.
26. Tóibín, *The Master* (New York: Scribner, 2004), 15.
27. This phrase was the title of a talk given by Terry Eagleton at the University of Oxford to the Royal Society of Literature in November 2000.
28. Daniel Mendelsohn, 'The Passion of Henry James', *New York Times*,20 June 2004, section 7, p. 10.
29. Tóibín, *The Master*, 66.
30. Tóibín, *The Master*, 72.
31. Tóibín, *The Master*, 34–5.
32. This was Tom McHale's debut novel challenging the pieties of post-war Irish Catholic Philadelphia.
33. Julian Moynihan, 'Hyphenated Americans in Old Philadelphia', *New York Times*, 9 August 1970, 7. James records that he was exempted from Civil War military service due to an 'obscure hurt', which has led to lurid speculation. James, *Notes of a Son and Brother* (London: Macmillan, 1914), 277.
34. Mitchell, 397. Emmie suggests an ethnic memory of the synonymity with contagion of Irish immigrant domestic 'Typhoid Mary'. As a healthy carrier of *Salmonella typhi*, domestic Mary Mallon was forcibly quarantined for a total of twenty-six years. Marineli, Filio et al., 'Mary Mallon (1869–1938) and the History of Typhoid Fever', *Annals of Gastroenterology* 26.2 (2013): 132.
35. Mrs Grose reveals to the narrator governess that Quint, the manservant who has been lurking about, wears his master's clothes because the latter is dead, only to matter-of-factly add that Quint, too, is dead. James, *The Turn of the Screw* (1898) in *The Portable Henry James*, 156–7. Quint's red hair 'clinch[es]' the reading of this character as Irish. Rowe, 'Henry James in a New Century', in John C. Rowe and Eric Haralson (eds), *A Historical Guide to Henry James* (New York: Oxford University Press, 2012), 209. Haralson adds a further layer of Irish resonance in suggesting that Wilde's trials inflect the story's unease regarding sexuality and sexualization. Haralson, *Henry James and Queer Modernity* (Cambridge: Cambridge University Press, 2003), 91.
36. James, *Daisy Miller: A Study* (New York: Harper & Bros, 1879), 32.
37. The de Nangle family was the first Norman family in Ireland to assume a 'Mac' prefix in an attempt to integrate with the Gaelic elite, becoming *Oisdealbh* and then *Mac Oisdealbhaigh*, which was later Anglicized as *(Mac) Costello*. Edward MacLysaght, *The Surnames of Ireland* (Dublin: Irish Academic Press, 1991), 60.
38. J.M. Synge, *When the Moon Has Set* (TCD MS 4382, Trinity College, Dublin, Ireland, unpublished playscript, *c.*1900–01).
39. *Encyclopedia of American Biography* (New York: American Historical Society, 1918), vol. IV, 269.
40. See George Eustis Corcoran, *Daisy Miller*. Harvard Theatre Collection, MS Am 1237.19, Houghton Library, Harvard University, Cambridge.
41. See Hugh Thomas, *The English and the Normans*(Oxford: Oxford University Press, 2003), 105–37.
42. Jonathan Swift, 'An Abstract of the History of England', *Prose Works* (London: Bell, 1900), XI, 225.

43. Domhnall Ó Néill, *Remonstrance of the Irish Chiefs to Pope John XXII*. CELT/Corpus of Electronic Texts: A Project of University College, Cork, 2005–2010. ucc.ie/celt
44. 'The Munster Bards', *Ulster Journal of Archæology* 7 (1859): 102.
45. See Gearóid (Iarla) Mac Gearailt [Gerald (Earl) Fitz Gerald], 'Mairg Adeir Olc Ris na Mnáibh' (Woe to Him Who Slanders Women), in Angela Bourke et al., *Field Day Anthology of Irish Writing: Volume IV: Irish Women's Writing and Traditions* (New York University Press, 2002), 324–5.
46. Edmund Spenser, *A View of the Present State of Ireland*, ed. W L. Renwick (London: Partridge at the Scholartis Press, 1934), 86.
47. The Keating text concerned was *History of Ireland/ Foras Feasa air Éirinn* (1634). Bernadette Cunningham, *The World of Geoffrey Keating* (Dublin: Four Courts, 2000), 26.
48. Douglas Hyde, 'The Necessity for De-Anglicising Ireland', a talk delivered to the Irish National Literary Society in Dublin on 25 November 1892.
49. See Stephen Collins, 'FF and FG Tribal Split Traced Back to 12th Century', *Irish Times*, 27 June 2011. Online. This article cites a 2011 study of the surname patterns among Ireland's post-independence parliamentarians from the country's two dominant centre-right parties, Fianna Fáil and Fine Gael, suggested a bias in affiliation toward Fianna Fáil representatives having Gaelic surnames and the historically more pro-British Fine Gael politicians having 'Old [Norman] and New [post-Williamite] English' surnames.
50. *The Letters of William James*, ed. Henry James [II] (Boston: Atlantic Monthly Press, 1920), vol. 1, 8.
51. James, *The Complete Notebooks* of *Henry James*, eds Leon Edel and Lyall H. Powers (New York: Oxford University Press, 1987), 229.
52. MacLysaght, 296.
53. Mitchell, 66; 206.
54. John O'Sullivan, 'Annexation', *The United States Magazine and Democratic Review* 17 (July–August 1845): 5–6; 9–10.
55. This was an Irish Catholic uprising challenging the Plantation of Ireland. Modern research calculates the number of deaths to have been 12,000 out of a total Protestant population in Ulster at the time of 40,000. As a result, the event gained an aura of Gothic horror in Protestant Irish lore in the manner of Cromwell's depredations a decade later in Irish Catholic memory.
56. Melville Henry Massue, *The Jacobite Peerage, Baronetage, Knightage and Grants of Honour* (Edinburgh and London: Jack, T.C. & E.C. Jack, 1904), 17–18. Massue is a rare though unreliable source on the topic, but his information on the O'Sullivans is accurate.
57. See Robert J. Miller, *Native America, Discovered and Conquered: Thomas Jefferson, Lewis & Clark, and Manifest Destiny* (Westport, CT: Praeger, 2006), 119.
58. After James II and VII was deposed and replaced by his daughter Mary II and her husband, William III of Orange, between 1688 and 1689, he and subsequent Jacobite pretenders granted titles to exiled prominent supporters. See Massue.
59. See L. Perry Curtis, *Apes and Angels: The Irishman in Victorian Caricature* (Washington, DC: Smithsonian Institution Press, 1997).

60. Mark Twain and Charles Dudley Warner, *The Gilded Age: A Tale of Today* (Hartford, CT: American Publishing Company, 1874), 302; 304.
61. James, *Daisy Miller*, 13.'[...] the insistence on whiteness prods blackness, in effect, into the text. [...] This iterative whiteness, traditionally read as an affirmation of her virtue, is also simply – complicatedly – whiteness'. Bryan R. Washington, *The Politics of Exile: Ideology in Henry James, F. Scott Fitzgerald, and James Baldwin* (Boston: Northeastern UP, 1995), 36; 40.
62. See Matthew Frye Jacobson. *Whiteness of a Different Color: European Immigrants and the Alchemy of Race* (Cambridge, MA: Harvard UP, 1999).
63. Jennifer Guglielmo and Salvatore Salerno, *Are Italians White?: How Race Is Made in America* (New York: Routledge, 2003), 33.
64. Henry James, 'The Last of the Valerii', in Michael Swan (ed.), *Henry James: Selected Short Stories* (Harmondsworth, Penguin, 1975), 13 [13–42].
65. James, 'Valerii', 13.
66. James, 'Valerii', 16.
67. James, 'Valerii', 14.
68. James, 'Valerii', 23.
69. James, 'Valerii', 29.
70. James, 'Valerii', 31; 32.
71. James, 'Valerii', 36.
72. James, 'The Real Thing', in *The Portable Henry James*, 88.
73. James, 'The Real Thing', 97; 101; 97.
74. James, 'The Real Thing', 83.
75. James to Edwin Lawrence Godkin, 22 January 1882, in Philip Horne (ed.), *Henry James: A Life in Letters* (New York: Viking, 1999), 135.
76. 'Colin Clout and the Faëry Queen', *Atlantic Monthly* 2: 13 (1858) 688.
77. Bewley, 51–4.
78. Nell Irvin Painter, *The History of White People* (New York: Norton, 2011), 160.
79. Ralph Waldo Emerson, *English Traits* (Boston: Philips and Samson, 1856), 176; 48.
80. Emerson, 72.
81. 'The boy was of that fair and ruddy complexion and that athletic mould which in those days (as in these) were the sign of genuine English blood [...]'. James, 'The Romance of Certain Old Clothes', *Atlantic Monthly* 21.124 (February 1868): 209.
82. Emerson, 59.
83. Oliver Wendell Holmes to Frederick Pollock, 25 April 1920 in *Holmes-Pollock Letters: The Correspondence of Mr. Justice Holmes and Sir Frederick Pollock, 1874–1932* (Cambridge, MA: Belknap Press of Harvard UP, 1961), 40; Oliver Wendell Holmes wrote the 8–1 majority opinion in *Buck v. Bell*, a 1927 Supreme Court case upholding a Virginia law that authorized the state to forcibly sterilize 'mental defectives'. See Adam Cohen, *Imbeciles* (New York: Penguin, 2016), 1–2.
84. Edward Waldo Emerson, *The Early Years of the Saturday Club: 1855–1870* (New York: Houghton Mifflin, 1918), 328.
85. 'Carson, Edward Henry – 1822–1881', *Dictionary of Irish Architects 1720–1940*. Online at https://www.dia.ie/.

86. Wilde's implicit reference to Carson as a 'Philistine' under cross-examination may be partly contextualized within the oppositional stereotypes of an industrialized, Unionist north and a culturally rich, nationalist south that galvanized the Home Rule divide. Merlin Holland, *The Real Trial of Oscar Wilde* (New York: Perennial, 2004), 81.
87. Janice Helland, 'A Gift of Lace: Queen Mary's Coronation Train, 1911', *Textile History* 49.1 (2018): 92–111.
88. Eugene O'Neill, *The Long Journey Home*, in *The Moon of the Caribbees and Six Other Plays of the Sea*. Intro. by George Jean Nathan. (New York: Boni and Liveright, 1923), 65.
89. Nelson McCausland, introduction to Whitelaw Reid, *The Scot in America and the Ulster Scot* (Down, Northern Ireland: Books Ulster, 2005), 23.
90. See David Fitzpatrick, *Descendancy: Irish Protestant Histories since 1795* (Cambridge: Cambridge University Press, 2014), 136–45.
91. Rory Fitzpatrick, *God's Frontiersmen: The Scots-Irish Epic* (London: Weidenfeld and Nicolson, 1989), 261.
92. Joseph Conrad, 'Henry James: An Appreciation'. *The North American Review* 180.1 (January 1905): 106.
93. The one-line and paragraph-long synopses are taken from http://www.henryjames.org.uk/modernw/synop.htm. Accessed 3 November 2018.
94. Denis Flannery, 'Irish Strands and the Imperial Eye: Henry James's "The Modern Warning"', *Henry James Review* 31.1 (2010): 42.
95. The Mac Cárthaigh Mór (senior branch) reigned for centuries in current-day Cork and Kerry. Florence MacCarthy (1560–1640) was the last credible MacCarthy Mór claimant before its suppression by the Crown. See Daniel MacCarthy, *The Life and Letters of Florence MacCarthy Reagh: Tanist of Carbery, MacCarthy Mor* (London: Longmans, Green, Reader, and Dyer, 1867).
96. Percy H. Reaney, *The Origin of English Surnames* (London: Routledge & K. Paul, 1967), 237.
97. MacLysaght, 110.
98. James, 'The Modern Warning', 393–4.
99. Flannery, 43–44.
100. See the film *The Quiet Man* (1952) and writings such as J.P. Donleavy's *The Ginger Man* (1955), John B. Keane's *The Field* (1965), and Mary Lavin's 'Tom' (1973). The theme became hackneyed enough that Roddy Doyle reveres it in 'Home to Harlem', a story about a mixed-race Irish student who travels to New York to track down his African-American GI grandfather. For an overview, see Sinéad Moynihan, *Ireland, Migration and Return Migration: The 'Returned Yank' in the Cultural Imagination, 1952 to Present* (Liverpool: Liverpool University Press, 2019).
101. *Peg o' My Heart* features a poor Irish lass sent to England under the care of her scheming British upper-middle class aunt. Peg ultimately escapes her kinswoman's clutches by marrying a titled neighbouring landowner, readable as a covert plea for Union despite the history of 'family' squabbling. https://www.ibdb.com/broadway-production/peg-o-my-heart-7544. Ironically, the film adaptation of 1922 was released in the very period in which Ireland was partitioned.

102. James, 'Some Notes on the Theatre' in Montrose Jonas Moses and John Mason Brown (eds), *The American Theatre as Seen by its Critics, 1752–1934* (New York: Norton, 1934), 122–6.
103. Claire Connolly, 'Writing the Union', in Dáire Keogh and Kevin Whelan (eds), *Acts of Union: The Causes, Contexts, and Consequences of the Act of Union* (Dublin: Four Courts Press, 2001), 180.
104. Mary Jean Corbett, *Allegories of Union in Irish and English Writing, 1790–1870: Politics, History, and the Family from Edgeworth to Arnold* (Cambridge: Cambridge University Press, 2000) 6.
105. James, 'The Modern Warning', in *Complete Stories, 1884–1891* (New York: Library of America, 1999), 386.
106. James, 'The Modern Warning', 398.
107. James, 'The Modern Warning', 420.
108. James, 'The Modern Warning', 424.
109. Fred Kaplan, *Henry James: The Imagination of Genius: A Biography* (New York: Morrow, 1992), 293–4.
110. Henry James to Grace Norton, 7 February 1886, quoted in Kaplan, 294–5.
111. Sara Blair, *Henry James and the Writing of Race and Nation* (Cambridge: Cambridge University Press, 2009), 44.
112. Flannery, 'Irish Strands and the Imperial Eye', *Henry James Review* 41.
113. James, *A Small Boy and Others*, 366.
114. Henry James to William James, 29 October 1888 in Horne, ed. *Henry James: A Life in Letters*, 213.
115. Duncan Bell, 'The Dream Machine: On Liberalism and Empire', in *Reordering the World: Essays on Liberalism and Empire* (Princeton, NJ: Princeton University Press, 2016), 37.
116. Daniel J. Kuntz, 'Stewart, Charles (1778–1869)', in Michael Glazier (ed.), *The Encyclopedia of the Irish in America*(Notre Dame, IN: University of Notre Dame Press, 1999), 881.
117. Monteiro, 'Americanism in Henry James "The Modern Warning"', *American Literary Realism* 43.2 (2011): 169–74.
118. Lepel H. Griffin, *The Great Republic* (London: Chapman & Hall, 1884), 128–34.
119. Lepel H. Griffin, 136.
120. See Hugh Stevens, *Henry James and Sexuality* (Cambridge: Cambridge University Press, 2008).
121. James, *The American*, 235. His Irish line, Finucane, was the name of a native Irish family with an estate in Clare. See http://landedestates.nuigalway.ie/LandedEstates/jsp/estate-show.jsp?id=2150.
122. John Mitchel, *The Last Conquest of Ireland (Perhaps)*, Author's Edition, (Glasgow: R. & T. Washbourne, 1876), 126.
123. For instance, the 1728–29 food crisis in Ireland created 15,000-person wave of Scots-Irish emigration to western Pennsylvania. Benjamin Bankhurst, *Ulster Presbyterians and the Scots Irish Diaspora, 1750–1764* (Basingstoke: Palgrave Macmillan, 2013), 14.
124. Mary Daly, 'Revisionism and Irish History: The Great Famine', in George Boyce and Alan O'Day (eds), *The Making of Modern Irish History: Revisionism and the Revisionist Controversy* (London & New York: Routledge, 1996), 71.

125. Anthony G. Russell, *Between Two Flags: John Mitchel & Jenny Verner* (Kildare, Ireland: Merrion Press, 2015), 32–3; 54; 61; 41–3; 159–60.
126. Betty Smith, *A Tree Grows in Brooklyn* (New York: Harper Perennial, 2018), 192; 193.
127. To be precise, because Gaynor died in office during the final weeks of his term, it was finished by Acting Mayor Ardolph Loges Kline.
128. John F. McClymer, 'Of "Mornin' Glories" and "Fine Old Oaks": John Purroy Mitchel, Al Smith, and Reform as an Expression of Irish-American Aspiration', in Ronald H. Bayor and Timothy J. Meagher (eds), *The New York Irish* (Baltimore, MD: Johns Hopkins University Press, 1996), 380–1.
129. McClymer, 376.
130. Footage of the funeral is available online at https://videopress.com/v/jN20KixT.
131. F. Scott Fitzgerald, *The Beautiful and Damned* (New York: Signet Classics, 2007), 301.
132. The full text of the letter is in Jeremiah's memoir. See Jeremiah A. O'Leary, *My Political Trial and Experiences* (New York: Jefferson, 1919), 488.
133. 'O'Leary Gives Story of Truth Society', *New York* Times, 16 July 1918: 6.
134. Peter D. O'Neill, 'Memory and John Mitchel's Appropriation of the Slave Narrative', *Atlantic Studies: Global Currents* 11.3 (Fall 2014): 338.
135. William Lloyd Garrison, Preface to Frederick Douglass, *Narrative of the Life of Frederick Douglass* (Boston: The Anti-Slavery Office, 1845), vii.
136. The cartoon, titled 'American sympathy and Irish blackguardism', depicts responses to O'Connell's condemnation of US slavery. It features a caricatured African-American man, John Tyler (US President, 1841–45), Tyler's son, Robert, a minor poet who visibly carries his pro-Robert Emmet composition, a thuggish O'Connell, who condemns Tyler as a slaveholder in a caricatured brogue, and abolitionist William Lloyd Garrison. It may be viewed on the Library Company of Philadelphia website: https://digital.librarycompany.org/islandora/object/Islandora%3A65069.
137. For an examination of the interactions between Irish and American abolitionists and Irish nationalists, see Angela F. Murphy, *American Slavery, Irish Freedom: Abolition, Immigrant Citizenship, and the Transatlantic Movement for Irish Repeal* (Baton Rouge, LA: Louisiana State University Press, Press, 2010).
138. Russell, 30–1, 119.
139. Kieran Quinlan, *Strange Kin: Ireland and the American South* (Baton Rouge: Louisiana State University Press, 2005), 72–3.
140. For all of the shameless peddling to anti-Native American and sectarian sentiment in his western novels, the Ulster transplant also wrote the abolitionist *The Quadroon* (1856), in which the 'Britisher' hero (rumoured to be 'English, Irish, or Scotch') falls in love with and rescues a mixed-race enslaved woman. Reid combined his frontier adventure and anti-slavery modes in the post-Civil War *The Yellow Chief* (1870), in which an escaped enslaved mulatto gains leadership over a Cheyenne tribe in a bid to wreak revenge upon the plantation owners who had abused him. Reid's depiction of Black characters is not unproblematic and his Native American characters are generally woefully problematic, but the anti-slavery message nevertheless triumphs in the two popular novels.
141. Having escaped north, Jacobs was threatened with recapture due to the Fugitive Slave Law just as Mitchel publicly proclaimed support for slavery. Harriet Jacobs, *Incidents*

in the Life of a Slave Girl, Written by Herself, ed. L. Maria Child (Boston: Published for the Author, 1861), 298.

142. John Mitchel, *Jail Journal* (New York: Office of *The Citizen*, 1854), 170.
143. Anthony R. Hale, 'Martyrs for Contending Causes: John Mitchel, David Walker, and the Limits of Liberation', in Peter O'Neill and David Lloyd (eds), *The Black and Green Atlantic* (Basingstoke: Palgrave Macmillan, 2009), 204.
144. 'It was as difficult for the Confederate Irish to understand why Yankees fought states seeking "independence"—a long-cherished goal of Ireland—as it was for the North's Irish to see why the South should split from a country that provided immigrants freedoms unattainable in Ireland'. Dennis Clark, *Hibernia America: The Irish and Regional Cultures* (Westport, CT: Praeger, 1996), 105.
145. Mitchel's old well-to-do Catholic brother-in-arms in 1840s Ireland, Thomas Francis Meagher, who ended up on the opposite ideological side of the Civil War, 'rarely' mentioned 'slavery or Lincoln' when organizing his fellow Irishmen to fight for the Union. Timothy Egan, *The Immortal Irishman* (Boston and New York: Houghton Mifflin Harcourt, 2016), 175.
146. Russell, 127; 135; 206–7.
147. The only full-length biography (that of Lewinson) was published in 1965. The biography by his secretary, William Brown Meloney (1878–1925), held in the Mitchel and Purroy Family Papers collection at Columbia University, remains unpublished.

Chapter 3

1. G.K. Peatling, 'Thomas Dixon, Scotch-Irish Identity, and "the Southern People"', *Safundi: The Journal of South African and American Studies* 9:3 (2008): 239.
2. What has become known to dermatologists as the Fitzpatrick phototyping scale rates so-called 'Celtic' skin as 1–2, that is, the palest possible tone. See T.B. Fitzpatrick, 'Soleil et peau' [Sun and skin]. *Journal de Médecine Esthétique* 2 (1975): 33–4.
3. An Irish dermatologist suggests that because 'the redness of Rosacea is made worse with alcohol intake some people have wrongly attributed the cause of this disorder to alcohol excess' causing 'additional social problems' for sufferers. This implies that the stereotype of the prevalence of Irish alcohol abuse and the presentation of rosacea in the pale Irish may be entwined. Frank Powell, *Rosacea: The Curse of the Celts: A Handbook for Patients and the General Public*. University College Dublin Charles Institute for Dermatology, n.d., 3.
4. Doris Alexander, *The Tempering of Eugene O'Neill* (New York: Harcourt Brace & World, 1962), 139–46.
5. O'Neill, quoted in Alexander, 145.
6. Alexander, 241.
7. Shannon Steen, *Racial Geometries of the Black Atlantic, Asian Pacific and American Theatre* (Basingstoke, Hampshire; New York: Palgrave Macmillan, 2010), 84.
8. In his youth, the flight to Philadelphia of the modest Ulster Presbyterian farming family of John McCullough (1832–1885) was expedited by a Famine-era eviction. Excelling in tragedies and melodramas, the self-taught theatre actor achieved eminence and wealth

in his heyday. See Liz Evers, 'McCullough, John Edward', *Dictionary of Irish Biography*, December 2019. https://www.dib.ie/biography/mccullough-john-edward-a10107.

9. O'Neill, quoted in Croswell Bowen, 'The Black Irishman' (1946), in *Conversations with O'Neill*, 204.
10. David Clare, quoted in Dan McGovern, 'Eugene O'Neill's Place in Irish Theater Today: Interviews with Irish Theater Scholars', *Eugene O'Neill Review* 39.1 (2018): 146.
11. Brenda Murphy, David Clare, and Jackson R. Bryer, 'Used Books: Travis Bogard *Contour in Time: The Plays of Eugene O'Neill*', *Eugene O'Neill Review* 43.1 (2022): 77. In an apparent *homage* to O'Neill's *The Emperor Jones,* Scott's *An Echo in the Bone*, whose first staging was in Mona, Jamaica with an all-Black cast, also utilizes an Afro-Caribbean dialect, a non-naturalistic style, and similar time jumps between the present in the Americas and race memory of enslavement in the African past.
12. For a wide picture of Irish dynasties in West India in the early modern Atlantic word, see Nini Rodgers, *Ireland, Slavery and Anti-Slavery, 1612–1865* (Basingstoke; New York: Palgrave Macmillan, 2007).
13. The explosion of this discourse appears to have been encouraged by Sean O'Callaghan's *To Hell or Barbados: The Ethnic Cleansing of Ireland* (New York: O'Brien Press, 2013), which is widely cited online.
14. Liam Hogan. 'The Unfree Irish in the Caribbean Were Indentured Servants, Not Slaves'. *thejournal.ie*,6 October 2015. https://www.thejournal.ie/readme/irish-slaves-myth-2369653-Oct2015/.
15. Hilary Beckles, *White Servitude and Black Slavery in Barbados, 1627–1715* (Knoxville TN: University of Tennessee Press, 1989), 5–6.
16. Abbott Emerson Smith, *Colonists in Bondage,* 171.
17. See Michael Malouf, *Transatlantic Solidarities: Irish Nationalism and Caribbean Poetics* (University of Virginia Press, 2009).
18. Sheena Jolley, 'The Irish of Barbados', *Irish America* magazine, October/November, 2015. https://irishamerica.com/2015/10/the-irish-of-barbados-photos/.
19. Lindsay Haines, 'Poor, Backward and White', *New York Times*, 25 February 1973, 5.
20. Haines, 5.
21. Richard Dunn, *Sugar and Slaves: The Rise of the Planter Class in the English West Indies, 1624–1713* (University of North Caroline Press, 1972), 57.
22. Peter Linebaugh and Marcus Rediker. *The Many-Headed Hydra* (Boston: Beacon, 2000), 123.
23. Peter Kolchin, *American Slavery: 1619–1877* (New York: Hill and Wang, 2003), 7; 8.
24. Kolchin, 9; 11; 16.
25. Kolchin, 5.
26. Nancy Shoemaker does not infer a link with the 'Redleg' phenomenon in detailing that, at the start of the eighteenth century, Indians and Europeans rarely mentioned the colour of each other's skins. However, by mid-century, and likely as a result of a heightened awareness regarding status *vis-à-vis* skin tone that emerges out of the transatlantic slave trade, 'remarks about skin color and the categorization of peoples by simple color-coded labels (red, white, black) had become commonplace'. Nancy Shoemaker, *A Strange Likeness: Becoming Red and White in Eighteenth-Century North America* (New York: Oxford University Press, 2004), 129. See the work of Indigenous

scholar-activist Sandy Grande for some of the many ways in which 'Red' has been claimed and theorized by some of that descent.

27. Beckles, 8.
28. Donald H. Akenson, *If the Irish Ran the World: Montserrat, 1630-1730* (Montreal: McGill-Queen's University Press, 1997), 48–9.
29. Beckles, 3.
30. Sheila S. Walker, 'Everyday Africa in New Jersey: Wonderings and Wanderings in the African Diaspora', in Sheila S. Walker (ed.), *African Roots/American Cultures: Africa in the Creation of the Americas.* Lanham, MD: Rowman & Littlefield, 2001), 57.
31. Beckles, 175.
32. Linebaugh and Rediker, 126.
33. Abbott Emerson Smith, *Colonists in Bondage*, 172.
34. Linebaugh and Rediker, 127.
35. Beckles, 10.
36. Beckles, 174–5.
37. Harvey O'Brien, 'The Final Fortress: The Redlegs and Bajan-Irish Abjection' in Alison Donnell, Maria McGarrity, and Evelyn O'Callaghan (eds), *Caribbean Irish Connections: Interdisciplinary Perspectives* (Kingston, Jamaica: University of the West Indies Press, 2015), 183; 175; 176.
38. O'Neill, quoted in Bowen, 'The Black Irishman', 221.
39. O'Neill, *Thirst* in Thirst *and Other One Act Plays* (Boston: Gorham Press, 1914), 7.
40. O'Neill, *Thirst*, 7–8.
41. O'Neill, *Thirst*, 8–9.
42. O'Neill, *Thirst*, 20–1. The play's ambivalent treatment of the *Titanic* disaster suggests O'Neill's socialist viewpoint that the behemoth was a product of Unionist-dominated Belfast's sectarian exclusion of Catholics from well-paid working-class jobs. Yank in O'Neill's *The Hairy Ape* shares this socialist solidarity with his oppressed international ship-worker brethren when he identifies a bullying overseer/engineer with sectarianism: 'Belfast bum [...] yellow mut of a Catholic-moiderin' bastard!' O'Neill, *The Hairy Ape* in *Early Plays* (New York: Penguin, 2001), Act III, 372.
43. O'Neill, *Thirst*, 9–10.
44. Édouard Glissant knowingly uses the language of commodity in describing this scenario: 'Whenever a fleet of ships gave chase to slave ships, it was easiest just to lighten the boat by throwing cargo overboard, weighing it down with balls and chains'. Édouard Glissant, *Poétique de la relation / Poetics of Relation*, trans. Betsy Wing (Ann Arbor, MI: University of Michigan Press, 1997).
45. Rivers Solomon with Daveed Diggs, William Hutson, and Jonathan Snipes, *The Deep* (New York: Gallery / Saga Press, 2020).
46. O'Neill, *Thirst*, 15.
47. O'Neill, *Thirst*, 38.
48. Ella Myers. 'Beyond the Psychological Wage: Du Bois on White Dominion'. *Political Theory* 47.1 (2019): 6.
49. Charles A. Merrill, 'Eugene O'Neill, World-Famed Dramatist' (1923) in *Conversations with Eugene* O'Neill, 39–40.

50. O'Neill, *The Moon of the Caribbees* in *The Moon of the Caribbees and Six Other Plays of the Sea,* 4.
51. See J.J. Hogan and Patrick C. O'Neill. 'A North-County Dublin Glossary', *Béaloideas* 17.1–2 (1947): 276. The same dialect slur is also used by an Irish 'Bridget' (maid) in *Gone with the Wind* and by Irish rioters attacking African Americans in a Frank Yerby novel, suggesting that it was depressingly familiar to American ears. Mitchell, 627; Frank Yerby, *McKenzie's Hundred* (Garden City, NY: Doubleday, 1985), 265; 266.
52. O'Neill, *The Moon of the Caribbees,* 12; 8; 13.
53. See Charles Carroll, *The Negro: A Beast* [1900] (Salem, NH: Ayer, 1991), 46.
54. English performer of Irish descent, Elvis Costello, records that the slur was used of his paternal grandfather while he served in the British Army's Royal Irish Regiment (1684–1922) during the First World War (roughly concurrent with the first staging of *The Moon of the Caribbees*). This family lore was controversially incorporated into Costello's song on the Northern Irish Troubles, 'Oliver's Army'. Tomas Doherty, 'Elvis Costello drops Oliver's Army over racist slur', *Irish Times* 12 January 2022.
55. O'Neill, *The Moon of the Caribbees,* 15.
56. Steen, 91.
57. Yerby, 'A Note to the Reader', *Speak Now* (New York: Dell Press, 1969), n.p.
58. Robert M. Dowling, *Eugene O'Neill: A Life in Four Acts* (New Haven, CT and London: Yale University Press, 2014), 276–80.
59. Jeffrey Meyers, *Edmund Wilson: A Biography* (Boston & New York: Houghton Mifflin, 1995), 84. Blair was Edmund Wilson's first wife.
60. Richard Brucher, 'O'Neill, Othello and Robeson', *The Eugene O'Neill Review* 18.1–2 (1994): 46.
61. Dowling, 276–7; editorial in *The Fiery Cross,* quoted in Dowling, 282.
62. Louis Kantor, 'O'Neill Defends his Play of Negro' (1924) in *Conversations with Eugene O'Neill,* 44.
63. Glenda Frank, 'Tempest in Black and White: The 1924 Premiere of Eugene O'Neill's *All God's Chillun Got Wings*', *Resources for American Literary Study* 26.1 (2000): 84–5.
64. The use of 'youse' (plural 'you') and the pronunciation of 'thanks' as 'tanks' mark the speech of young Ella and her white playmate as Leinster-region Hiberno-Irish. O'Neill. *All God's Chillun Got Wings,* 16; 18. See Dolan, 258.
65. O'Neill, *All God's Chillun Got Wings* in *All God's Chillun Got Wings and Welded* (New York: Boni and Liveright, 1924), 19.
66. O'Neill, *All God's Chillun Got Wings,* 40.
67. Brucher, 45.
68. Steen, 91.
69. Brucher, 47.
70. Donald C. Gallup, *Eugene O'Neill and His Eleven Play Cycle* 'A Tale of Possessors Self-Dispossessed' (New Haven, CT: Yale University Press, 1998), 260; 207–11.
71. O'Neill, *Long Day's Journey into Night.* Foreword by Harold Bloom (New Haven, CT: Yale University Press, 2002), 90.
72. Arthur and Barbara Gelb, *O'Neill: Life with Monte Cristo* (New York: Applesauce, 2000), 35.

73. Gelb and Gelb, xv–xvi. It was originally published in 1962 by Harper & Row as *O'Neill.* The title of the amended biography refers to James O'Neill's most famous role as the title character in the melodrama *The Count of Monte Cristo.*
74. See Mary C. Kelly, *Ireland's Famine in Irish-American History* (Lanham, MD: Rowman & Littlefield, 2016).
75. Gelb and Gelb, xv; 41.
76. Gelb and Gelb, 35.
77. O'Neill, *Long Day's Journey into Night,* 151.
78. O'Neill, quoted in E. Andrew Lee. 'The Image of Irish in the Life and Work of Eugene O'Neill'. *The Eugene O'Neill Review* 35.2 (2014): 139.
79. See John O'Connor, *The Workhouses of Ireland: The Fate of Ireland's Poor* (Dublin: Anvil Books, 1997).
80. Ben Brantley, 'A Mother's Haunting Presence In O'Neill's Unraveling Family' (review of 2003 Plymouth Theatre, New York production of O'Neill's *Long Day's Journey into Night*), *New York Times,*7 May 2003, E1.
81. See Cathal Póirtéir'. The Paupers and the Poorhouse', in *Famine Echoes* (Dublin: Gill & Macmillan, 1995), 116–31.
82. O'Neill, *Long Day's Journey into Night,* 153.
83. Gelb and Gelb, 660.
84. Aodh Mac Domhnaill, 'Milleadh na bPrátaí' (The Spoilage of the Potatoes), *Dánta Aodh Mac Domhnaill* (Poems of Hugh O'Donnell) Colm Beckett (ed.) (Dublin: An Clóchomhar/Dundalgan, 1987), 46, line 4.
85. Kevin Whelan. 'The Memories of "The Dead"', *Yale Journal of Criticism: Interpretation in the Humanities* 15.1 (2002): 87.
86. A belittling Hiberno-English term for a small landowner who aligns with the colonial order. The 'een' (*ín* in Irish) suffix is belittling when applied to an adult.
87. Gelb and Gelb, 88.
88. *The Life and Times of Aodh O'Neill, Prince of Ulster* (1845).
89. Alexander, 62.
90. Writers' Program of the Work Projects Administration in Northern California, *History of the San Francisco Theatre, Vol. XX: James O'Neill* (City and County of San Francisco, 1942), 105; 107.
91. Dowling, 281.
92. O'Neill to James T. Farrell, 28 July 1943 in Travis Bogard and Jackson R. Bryer (eds), *Selected Letters of Eugene O'Neill* (New Haven, CT: Yale University Press, 1988), 545.
93. *Catalog of Copyright Entries. New Series: 1942* (United States: Copyright Office, Library of Congress, 1942), 8299.
94. Nicholas P. Canny, 'The Ideology of English Colonization: From Ireland to America', *The William and Mary Quarterly* 30.4 (1973): 575–98.
95. O'Neill, *Desire Under the Elms* in *Plays: Desire Under the Elms; The Hairy Ape; Welded* (New York: Boni & Liveright, 1925), Part III, Scene 1, 80.
96. Wei H. Kao, 'Troubled Desires and Social Taboos in Eugene O'Neill's and Marina Carr's Dramas of the Land', *Journal of Irish Studies* 24 (2009): 51.
97. O'Neill, *Desire,* Part III, Scene 1, 82.
98. O'Neill, *Desire,* Part I, Scene 2, 21.

99. O'Neill, *Desire*, Part III, Scene 2, 84.
100. O'Neill, *Desire*, Part II, Scene 1, 54.
101. O'Neill, *Desire*, Part II, Scene 2, 60.
102. 'California was a Mexican province until 1848, and the residents [...] found their lands overrun during the gold rush. The flood of immigrants destroyed Indian villages, redirected waterways, and depleted food supplies'. 'To California by Sea' in *On the Water: Stories from Maritime America*. National Museum of American History, ongoing exhibition. https://americanhistory.si.edu/onthewater/exhibition/2_4.html.
103. Seamus Heaney, 'The Other Side', *Wintering Out* (London: Faber & Faber, 1972), 34–6, lines 11–12; 17; 7–8.
104. Interview with Annie Ryan (on Webex), 9 July 2021. Unless otherwise credited, the discussion of the Corn Exchange production of *Desire Under the Elms* derives from this interview.
105. Susan Conley, 'Dublin Theatre Festival: Desire Under the Elms'. *Irish Theatre Magazine*, 4 October 2013. http://itmarchive.ie/web/Reviews/Current/Dublin-Theatre-Festival—Desire-Under-the-Elms.aspx.html.
106. Hamilton Basso, 'Profiles: The Tragic Sense', in *Conversations with Eugene O'Neill*, 234.
107. Michael Hinds, 'Land'. Program note for the Corn Exchange *Desire Under the Elms* production directed by Annie Ryan at the 2013 Dublin Theatre Festival, 4–13 October 2013.
108. John Francis Taylor, *Owen Roe O'Neill* (London: T. Fisher Unwin, 1901), 108. 'Eugene' is the Latin variant of 'Owen'.
109. Gerald FitzGerald (c. 1456–1513), 8th Earl of Kildare, was Ireland's premier peer in his role as Lord Deputy of Ireland, a role continued by his son and namesake, the 9th Earl, while Thomas FitzGerald, the 10th Earl of Kildare (1513–1537) and Lord Edward FitzGerald (1763–1798) both led major rebellions in Ireland.
110. In a self-mocking genealogical chart sent to Edmund Wilson, F. Scott traced his family tree back to 'Duke Fitzgerald (Earl of Leinster)'. Fitzgerald to Edmund Wilson, late 1920 in *A Life in Letters*, 43. 'Duke of Leinster' was a title created in 1766 for the FitzGerald Earls of Kildare.
111. Images of the baptismal and burial records held at Gaithersburg's St Rose Catholic Church provided by Sarah Hedlund, librarian and archivist at Montgomery History museum and archive in Rockville, MD, confirm the dates for Michael, Cecilia, and Edward Fitzgerald, the author's grandparents and father. Michael and Cecilia's dates, as further provided on their gravestones, were also confirmed by Eileen McGuckian, a Montgomery County local historian and author with a deep knowledge of Fitzgerald family history. Personal email from Sarah Hedlund, 15 June 2021; personal email from Eileen McGuckian, 12 December 2021.
112. Foreword by Francis Scott Key Fitzgerald to Don Swann, *Colonial and Historic Homes of Maryland* (Baltimore: Etchcrafters Art Guild, 1939), n.p.
113. McGuckian and Lisa Greenhouse, *F. Scott Fitzgerald's Rockville: A Guide to Rockville MD in the 1920s* (Rockville, MD: Peerless Rockville Historic Preservation, Ltd, 1996), 55.
114. Bruccoli, Scottie Fitzgerald Smith, and Joan P. Kerr (eds), *The Romantic Egoists: A Pictorial Autobiography from the Scrapbooks and Albums of F. Scott and Zelda Fitzgerald* (Columbia, SC: University of South Carolina Press, 2003), 2.

115. Fitzgerald to Marie Hersey Hamm, 4 October 1934, in Matthew J. Bruccoli and Judith S. Baughman (eds), *F. Scott Fitzgerald: A Life in Letters* (New York, Simon and Schuster, 1994), 271.
116. Fitzgerald, 'May Day', in *Tales of the Jazz Age* (New York: Charles Scribner's Sons, 1922), 74.
117. Fitzgerald, 'The Camel's Back', in *Tales of the Jazz Age,* 17.
118. Fitzgerald, 'The Curious Case of Benjamin Button', in *Tales of the Jazz Age,* 197.
119. Fitzgerald, 'Curious Case', 197.
120. Fitzgerald, 'Curious Case', 209.
121. Fitzgerald, 'Curious Case', 221.
122. Mary Jo Tate. *Critical Companion to F. Scott Fitzgerald: A Literary Reference to His Life and Work* (New York: Facts on File, 2007), 302.
123. The image of the relevant 1850 United States Census page for Baltimore (part of image 173 of 930; NARA microfilm publication M432, Washington, DC: National Archives and Records Administration, n.d.) may be viewed (after free registration) on *FamilySearch.org* at https://familysearch.org/ark:/61903/3:1:S3HY-6X17-DT8?cc=1401638&wc=95RN-ZNL%3A1031350501%2C1031619801%2C1031619802. The Fitzgerald household is detailed in entries 24–6.
124. 'Fitzgerald, Francis Scott Key', in Frederick Adams Virkus (ed.), *The Compendium of American Genealogy: The Standard Genealogical Encyclopedia of the First Families of America*, (Chicago, IL: Virkus, 1930), vol. IV, 183.
125. Janet Thompson Manuel, 'Genealogies', in *Gaithersburg: The Heart of Montgomery County: A History Commemorating Gaithersburg's Charter Centennial Charter Centennial.* Gaithersburg, MD: City of Gaithersburg, 1978, 359.
126. Personal email from Francis P. O'Neill, 23 December 2021.
127. Bureau of the Census, United States. *Heads of Families at the First Census of the United States Taken in the Year 1790: Maryland* (Baltimore: Genealogical Publishing Company, 1965), 89; 91; 88.
128. See Jane C. Sween, *Montgomery County: Centuries of Change* (Woodland Hills, CA: Windsor, 1984),18.
129. Richard K. MacMaster and Ray Eldon Herbert, *A Grateful Remembrance: The Story of Montgomery County, Maryland 1776–1976* (Rockville, MD: Montgomery County Government and the Montgomery County Historical Society, 1976), 11; 13.
130. A glance at the first column (of three) of approximately ninety-five names on the first page of the over seven pages of the Montgomery County 1790 Census returns reveals the surnames 'Corcoran', 'O'Neill', 'Connerlly', 'Lacey', 'Connell', 'Flarharty', and 'Kelpatrick'. *Heads of Families at the First Census of the United States Taken in the Year 1790: Maryland*, 85.
131. MacMaster and Herbert, 18.
132. *Fitz* ('son of') was a patronymic indicator used by the early Normans of Ireland and England that preceded the father's forename. It was eventually incorporated into patronymic surnames.
133. However, although slavery on the north American mainland emerged first in Virginia, Maryland, and a corner of North Carolina, Maryland's number of slaves steadily declined from the beginning of the nineteenth century, and it remained in the Union during the American Civil War. Kolchin, 24; 82

134. Clare Lise Kelly, *Places from the Past: The Tradition of Gardez Bien in Montgomery County, Maryland* (The Maryland-National Capital Park and Planning Commission, 2011), 184.
135. Nancy Milford. *Zelda: A Biography* (New York: Harper & Row, 1970), 140.
136. 'Amory, Son of Beatrice' as the first chapter title of *This Side of Paradise* gives it, barely mentions his father. Stephen Blaine goes on to die 'quietly and inconspicuously', which is more of an appearance than patriarchs make in most Fitzgerald works.
137. Fitzgerald. 'Author's House', *Esquire*, 1 July 1936. https://classic.esquire.com/article/1936/7/1/authors-house.
138. Letter to Edmund Wilson, January 1922, *A Life in Letters*, 331.
139. Fitzgerald to Edmund Wilson, 25 June 1922, in Andrew Turnbull (ed.), *The Letters of F. Scott Fitzgerald* (New York: Scribner, 1963), 337.
140. Fitzgerald, *This Side of Paradise*, ed. Philip McGowan (Oxford: Oxford University Press, 2020), 130.
141. This oral lore remains familiar even in secular contemporary Ireland. See its use in Conor McPherson's drama, *The Seafarer* (2006) and Claire Kilroy's novel, *The Devil I Know* (2012).
142. Princeton in the period in which Fitzgerald enrolled was still an overwhelmingly 'WASP preserve', and continued to attract a disproportionate number of Presbyterian students, remaining in ethos not too distant from the days when Henry James *pater* had been sent there for divinity training by his Ulster-born father. Jerome Karabel, *The Chosen: The Hidden History of Admission and Exclusion at Harvard, Yale, and Princeton* (Boston & New York: Houghton Mifflin, 2005), 71.
143. 'Benediction' is set at a Baltimore Jesuit seminary housing 'some Irish and some tough Irish, and a few French', the distinction between the two Irishnesses suggesting the gulf of race. Regan, '"a good man" in "a fight"' is 'tough Irish', the off-white bruiser of stereotype fit only for 'missionary' work in 'China'. Fitzgerald, 'Benediction' in *Flappers and Philosophers* (London: Collins, 1922), 251; 262.
144. David S. Brown, *Paradise Lost: A Life of F. Scott Fitzgerald* (Cambridge, MA; London: Belknap Press of Harvard University Press, 2017), 17.
145. Harry Saltpeter, 'Fitzgerald, Spenglerian' (1927) in Baughman and Bruccoli (eds), *Conversations with F. Scott Fitzgerald* (Jackson, MS: University Press of Mississippi, 2004), 88.
146. See Pat McQuillan and Mary McQuillan, *The McQuillans of County Fermanagh: Descendants of Mary McQuillan, 1790–1876*, a family document held at the Minnesota Historical Society and posted here: http://freepages.rootsweb.com/~friendsofthehighlandcemetery/genealogy/mcquillan/mcq_tree_web.htm.
147. Bruccoli, *Some Sort of Epic Grandeur*, 11.
148. Walter Benn Michaels, *Our America: Nativism, Modernism, and Pluralism* (Durham, NC; London: Duke University Press, 1995), 25; 27.
149. Fitzgerald, 'Winter Dreams', in *All the Sad Young Men*, 45.
150. Writing of a passport photograph, Fitzgerald remarks: 'It looks rather Teutonic but I can prove myself a Celt.' Fitzgerald to Edmund Wilson, 26 September 1917, in *The Letters of F. Scott Fitzgerald*, 319.
151. Fitzgerald to John O'Hara, 18 July 1933 in *The Letters of F. Scott Fitzgerald*, 503.

152. O'Hara to Fitzgerald, quoted in Charles Fanning, *The Irish Voice in America: 250 Years of Irish-American Fiction* (Lexington, KY: University Press of Kentucky, 1999), 251.
153. Gelb and Gelb, 57–60.
154. Unidentified 1879 critic quoted in Writers' Program of the Work Projects Administration in Northern California, 6; this species of 'Celt' differed from the 'prevailing type in respect of their black eyes and hair, and gypsy-like, tawny complexions'. Erl Rygenhoeg. 'Othello Not a Negro', *American Bibliopolist* 7.78 (December 1875): 260.
155. Bowen, 'The Black Irishman', 204.
156. Terence Dolan, *A Dictionary of Hiberno-English* (Dublin: Gill & Macmillan, 2004), 22.
157. Basso, 'Profiles: The Tragic Sense', 225.
158. Bowen, 'The Black Irishman', 204.
159. Yvonne Shafer, *Performing O'Neill: Conversations with Actors and Directors* (New York: St. Martin's Press, 2000), 9.
160. A. G. Review of *Whence the 'Black Irish' of Jamaica?* By Joseph J. Williams. *Studies: An Irish Quarterly Review* 21(84) (1932): 694.
161. Akenson, 12–57.
162. See Jennifer Nugent Duffy, *Who's Your Paddy? Racial Expectations and the Struggle for Irish American Identity* (New York: NYU Press, 2013), Sinéad Moynihan, *Other People's Diasporas* (Syracuse: NY: Syracuse University Press, 2013), and Diane Negra, 'The Irish in Us: Irishness, Performativity, and Popular Culture', in Diane Negra (ed.), *The Irish in Us: Irishness, Performativity, and Popular Culture* (Durham and London: Duke UP, 2006), 1–19.
163. 'Sheila King', in Julia McNamara (ed.), *The Irish Face in America*. New York & Boston: Bulfinch Press, 2004, 134.
164. Armada survivors who washed up in Ireland were summarily put to death or fled to Scotland. T.P. Kilfeather, *Ireland: Graveyard of the Spanish Armada* (London: Anvil, 1967) 63; Evelyn Hardy, *Survivors of the Armada* (London: Constable, 1966) 5.
165. Amy Blaney, 'Mariah Carey Launches Own Alcoholic Cream Liqueur "Black Irish" in Nod to Her Heritage', *Independent.ie*, 17 August 2021. https://www.independent.ie/irish-news/mariah-carey-launches-own-alcoholic-cream-liqueur-black-irish-in-nod-to-her-heritage-40759695.html.
166. Fitzgerald, *The Beautiful and Damned* (New York: Signet, 2007), 86.
167. Fitzgerald, *Beautiful*, 274.
168. Fitzgerald, *Beautiful*, 290; 244.
169. Fitzgerald, *Beautiful*, 284–5.
170. Fitzgerald, *Beautiful*, 226.
171. Fitzgerald, *Beautiful*, 332.
172. Fitzgerald, *Beautiful*, 339; 347.
173. Fitzgerald, *The Great Gatsby*, ed. James L.W. West III (New York: Scribner, 2018), 130; 131.
174. Michaels, 25; Carlyle Van Thompson, *The Tragic Black Buck: Racial Masquerading in the American Literary Imagination* (New York: Peter Lang, 2004), 109–48.
175. George Bornstein, *The Colors of Zion: Blacks, Jews, and Irish from 1845 to 1945* (Cambridge, MA; London: Harvard University Press, 2011).
176. Fitzgerald, *The Great Gatsby*, 13.

177. After Culloden, Highland landlords relocated the population to the coast in order to create extensive grazing lands for sheep, and the new communities created were swept away in a second cycle of clearance and forced emigration during and after the 1840s food crisis. There were many fewer deaths in the Highlands as a result of the blight, but the subsequent mass emigration mirrored the Irish experience. See T.M. Devine, *The Scottish Clearances: A History of the Dispossessed, 1600–1900* (London: Allen Lane, 2018).
178. Fitzgerald, *The Great Gatsby*, 3.
179. Fitzgerald, *The Great Gatsby*, 180.
180. Fitzgerald, *The Great Gatsby*, 174.
181. Editorial in *The Fiery Cross*, quoted in Dowling, 282.
182. Jean H. Baker, *James Buchanan* (New York: Times Books/Henry Holt, 2004), 9. Buchanan, like Jackson, has been the subject of murals in contemporary loyalist Northern Ireland. See the image on the Northern Irish mural database, Extramural Activity: https://extramuralactivity.com/2004/07/27/buchanan/.
183. Baker, 141.
184. Richard Buller, *A Beautiful Fairy Tale: The Life of Actress Lois Moran* (Pompton Plains, N.J: Limelight, 2005), 173; 5; 3.
185. Fitzgerald, *Tender is the Night* (New York: Scribner, 1982), 267.
186. Suzanne del Gizzo, 'Ethnic Stereotyping' in *F. Scott Fitzgerald in Context*, edited by Bryant Mangum (Cambridge University Press, Cambridge, 2013), 224.
187. Kathy Peiss, *Hope in a Jar: The Making of America's Beauty Culture* (New York: Henry Holt, 1998), 40–2; 113.
188. Mitchell, 25.
189. Peiss, 9.
190. Mitchell, 94.
191. Elias P. Fordham, quoted in Patrick Huber, 'A Short History of "Redneck": The Fashioning of a Southern White Masculine Identity'. *Southern Cultures* 1.2 (1995): 152.
192. Lola Montez, *The Arts of Beauty* (New York: Dick and Fitzgerald, 1858), 43.
193. Caroline Randall Williams, 'You Want a Confederate Monument? My Body Is a Confederate Monument', *New York* Times, 26 June 2020. Online. The 'rape of enslaved African women by slave owners' shaped the genetic make-up of the Americas. Steven J. Micheletti et al., 'Genetic Consequences of the Transatlantic Slave Trade in the Americas', *American Journal of Human Genetics* 107 (2020): 9.
194. Susan L.Keller, 'The Riviera's Golden Boy: Fitzgerald, Cosmopolitan Tanning, and Racial Commodities in "Tender Is the Night"', *The F. Scott Fitzgerald Review* 8 (2010): 133.
195. Fitzgerald, *Tender*, 6; Keller, 132.
196. Nathan Miller, *New World Coming: The 1920s and the Making of Modern America* (New York: Scribner, 2003) 128.
197. Keller, 138; 130.
198. Keller, 134.
199. Thoreau to Emerson, 17 October 1843 in Walter Harding and Carl Bode (eds), *The Correspondence of Henry David Thoreau* (Westport, CT: Greenwood, 1974), 146.
200. Richard Lehan, *The Great Gatsby: The Limits of Wonder* (Boston: Twayne, 1990), 6.

201. Peiss, 149–50.
202. Keller, 135; William A. Shack, *Harlem in Montmartre* (Berkeley, University of California Press, 2001), 36. The dehumanizing use of the descriptor 'chocolate' in reference to Baker by a Fitzgerald Irish-American male protagonist furthers this vocabulary of the performer's consumability. Fitzgerald, 'Babylon Revisited', *Saturday Evening Post*, 21 February 1931, 4.
203. Richard Dyer, *White: Essays on Race and Culture* (New York: Routledge, 1997), 49.
204. Fitzgerald, *Beautiful*, 40.
205. Fitzgerald to Maxwell Perkins, 4 March 1934 in *Life in Letters*, 249.
206. Sarah B. Fryer. *Fitzgerald's New Women: Harbingers of Change* (Ann Arbor, MI: UMI Research Press, 1988), 74.
207. Fitzgerald, *Tender*, 130.
208. Fitzgerald, *Tender*, 199.
209. Fitzgerald, *Tender*, 111.
210. Fitzgerald, *Tender*, 112.
211. Fitzgerald, *Tender*, 161.
212. Fitzgerald, *Tender*, 289.
213. Fitzgerald, *Tender*, 228.
214. Fitzgerald, *Tender*, 233.
215. Fitzgerald, *Tender*, 222.
216. As a consequence of an 1841 mutiny on board the *Creole*, a ship involved in the American coastwise slave trade, 128 enslaved people won their freedom in the Bahamas, then a British possession. When the *Creole* reached Nassau, it was boarded by the harbour pilot and his crew, all Black Bahamians, who assured the mutineers that under British law they were free. See Walter Johnson, 'White Lies: Human Property and Domestic Slavery Aboard the Slave Ship *Creole*', *Atlantic Studies* 5.2 (2008): 237–63.
217. Fitzgerald, *Tender*, 258–9. The Mason-Dixon was an informal boundary between free and slave states.
218. An offensive North American slang term for someone from a Spanish-speaking country in the Americas.
219. Fitzgerald, *Tender*, 260; 261–5.
220. Fitzgerald, *Tender*, 265.
221. Fitzgerald, *Tender*, 265–6.
222. Fitzgerald, *Tender*, 157.
223. Fitzgerald, *Tender*, 19.
224. Nancy Milford, *Zelda: A Biography* (New York: Harper & Row, 1970), 118.
225. 'White skin', notes a contemporary Black African model with albinism, is considered 'a defect or abnormality' when found on what are perceived to be '"non-white" bodies'. Thando Hopa, 'I Am a Black African Woman with Albinism & There's Nothing "Deficient" About Me', *Allure* magazine, 23 August 2021. https://www.allure.com/story/thando-hopa-personal-essay-albinism.
226. Keller, 136; 137; Devon Hansen Atchison, 'Shades of Change' in Cheryl Krasnick-Warsh and DanMalleck (eds), *Consuming Modernity* (Canada, UBC Press, 2013), 169.
227. Fitzgerald, *Tender*, 289.

228. Fitzgerald, *Tender*, 295.
229. Fitzgerald, *Tender*, 295; 298.
230. The final five 'Pat Hobby' stories were published posthumously.
231. Fitzgerald, 'A Man in the Way', in *The Pat Hobby Stories* (New York: Scribner, 2004), 13.
232. Fitzgerald, 'Fun in an Artist's Studio', in *The Pat Hobby Stories*, 128.
233. Fitzgerald. '"Boil Some Water – Lots of It"', in *The Pat Hobby Stories*, 21.
234. Arnold Gingrich, intro, *The Pat Hobby Stories*, x.
235. Maurice Bourgeois, *John Millington Synge and the Irish Theatre* (London: Constable, 1913), 109–10.
236. Gingrich, intro, *The Pat Hobby Stories*, ix.
237. Alan Margolies. 'F. Scott Fitzgerald's Work in the Film Studios', *The Princeton University Library Chronicle* 32.2 (1971): 99–100.
238. Fitzgerald to 'Scottie' Fitzgerald, January 1939, *A Life in Letters*, 383.
239. Fitz-Norman Culpepper hatches a plan to keep the Black men who have accompanied him out of Virginia in perpetual slavery, a state of affairs that continues into the twentieth century, by fabricating a proclamation that the North had lost the Civil War: 'The negroes believed him implicitly. They passed a vote declaring it a good thing and held revival services immediately.' Fitzgerald, 'The Diamond as Big as the Ritz' in *Tales of the Jazz Age*, 157.

Chapter 4

1. Quoted in Malcolm Brown, *The Politics of Irish Literature* (Seattle, WA: University of Washington Press, 1972), 139.
2. Sylviane A. Diouf, *Dreams of Africa in Alabama: The Slave Ship* Clotilda *and the Story of the Last Africans Brought to America* (New York: Oxford University Press, 2009), 7–8. The Act Prohibiting Importation of Slaves of 1807 provided that no new slaves were permitted to be imported into the United States, though the domestic (cross-state) trade persisted. One of the last surviving passengers, Cudjoe Kazoola Lewis (*c.*1841–1935), born Oluale Kossola, lived long enough to be interviewed by Zora Neale Hurston. See her book *Barracoon: The Story of the Last 'Black Cargo'*, edited by Deborah G. Plant and foreword by Alice Walker (New York: Amistad Press, 2018).
3. Unsigned, 'The Golden Corn: He Writes to Please', *Time* 64.22 (29 November 1954): 97.
4. Peter Baniak, 'Alonzo Smythe Yerby, MD'. (Obit.), *JAMA* 272.10 (14 September 1994): 826. Medicare was the Johnson administration's groundbreaking national health insurance corrective to the historical exclusion of poor and minority elderly Americans from adequate care.
5. Although biographers tend to list the name and dates of Yerby's parents alone, Jacques Yerby, Frank's son, and his first wife, Flora Williams, among others, have uploaded further details of the author's maternal side onto a genealogy website. Wilhelmina appears to have been known as 'Willie' and her parents (Frank Yerby's maternal grandparents) were Alonzo Smythe (*c.* 1852–1904) and Ellen Justine Smythe (née Snowden; *c.* 1852–1919). Both were born in Augusta, Georgia and

married in 1874. https://www.geni.com/people/Willie-Yerby/31604060469000l725; https://www.geni.com/people/Alonzo-Smythe/6000000031989812284; https://www.geni.com/people/Ellen-Smythe/6000000031990109881.

6. Veronica T. Watson, Introduction. *The Short Stories of Frank Yerby*, ed. Veronica T. Watson (Jackson, MS: University Press of Mississippi, 2020), xi.
7. The 'one-drop' rule (hypodescent) was a legal principle of racial classification in certain US states that asserted that any person with even one ancestor of African ancestry was legally and socially Black.
8. 'Author Frank Yerby, 76, Dies; Buried in Spain', *Jet* 81.14 (27 January 1992): 13 [runs 12–13].
9. Yerby, quoted in 'Yerby, Frank', in Linda Metzger and Deborah A. Straub (eds), *Contemporary Authors: New Revision Series 1* 6 (Detroit, MI: Gale Research, 1986), 468.
10. Yerby, 'Myra and the Leprechaun', in *The Short Stories of Frank Yerby*, 52.
11. Flannery O'Connor, 'Everything that Rises Must Converge', in *Everything that Rises Must Converge* (New York: Farrar, Strauss, and Giroux, 1993), 7.
12. Lei Lani Nishime, *Undercover Asian: Multiracial Asian Americans in Visual Culture* (Champaign, IL: University of Illinois Press, 2014), 102.
13. Literary texts by Black authors in Yerby's lifetime were considered 'authentic' only when such authors identified themselves or were identified as African American and explicitly treated Black concerns. Gene Andrew Jarrett, *Deans and Truants: Race and Realism in African American Literature* (Philadelphia, PA: University of Pennsylvania Press, 2007), 1.
14. Stephanie Brown, *The Postwar African American Novel: Protest and Discontent, 1945–1950* (Jackson, MS: University Press of Mississippi, 2011), 74.
15. Reconstruction (1865–77) was the post-war process to redress the political, social, and economic legacies of slavery and to reintegrate Southern states from the Confederacy.
16. Darden Asbury Pyron, *Southern Daughter: The Life of Margaret Mitchell* (New York and Oxford: Oxford University Press, 1991, 92–3; 137; 207.
17. Pat Conroy, preface to Mitchell, 15.
18. David O'Connell, *The Irish Roots of Margaret Mitchell's* Gone with the Wind (Decatur, GA: Claves and Petry, 1996), 6.
19. Mitchell, 664.
20. Mitchell, 430. This is a striking contrast to the covert Irish-Native American solidarity within which ersatz 'scalping' occurs in Fitzgerald's 'Bernice Bobs Her Hair'. The part 'Indian' and sympathetic Bernice chops off a tormentor's 'Saxon princess' 'blond braids' and hurls them with a gleeful shout of 'Scalp the selfish thing!' The story derives from a letter that the nineteen-year-old Fitzgerald sent to his sister, suggesting a covert link between her (and, thereby, his) racial otherness and that of Bernice. Fitzgerald, 'Bernice Bobs Her Hair'. *Flappers and Philosophers* (New York: Scribner, 1921), 165; 187; 190; 193; see *Life in Letters* 7–10.
21. Jones, 'Phillip Fitzgerald House', online.
22. Anne Edwards, *Road to Tara: The Life of Margaret Mitchell* (New Haven and New York: Ticknor and Fields, 1983), 16.

23. Tommy H. Jones, 'Phillip Fitzgerald House (ca. 1835, ca. 1870), Clayton County, Georgia.' https://www.tomitronics.com/old_buildings/fitzgerald_house/index.html#_edn1.
24. Pyron, 250–1.
25. Mitchell, quoted in Quinlan, 122.
26. This phrase has been used in Latin, Irish, and English since the late eighteenth century to describe Gaelicized Norman families in Ireland. S. J. Connolly, *Contested Island: Ireland 1460–1630* (Oxford, Oxford UP, 2009), 35.
27. The 'u' was added by the novelist.
28. Joseph Blotner, *Faulkner: A Biography* (Jackson, MS: University Press of Mississippi, 2005), 24.
29. Joel Williamson, *William Faulkner and Southern History* (New York; Oxford: Oxford University Press, 1995), 436. 'Butler' is both an occupational English surname and a prominent Norman surname in Ireland, where it occurs with more than double the frequency in comparison to England. See genealogy portal, Forebears: https://forebears.io/surnames/butler.
30. Williamson, 64–5.
31. Mitchell, 739–40.
32. After the 1931 accusation, the threatened lynching of the boys was replaced by their initial legal lynching by an all-white jury. The trials and retrials of the boys, subsequently seen as a watershed in American racial injustice, dragged into 1937. See Dan T. Carter, *Scottsboro: A Tragedy of the American South* (Baton Rouge, LA: Louisiana State University Press, 2007).
33. W.E.B. Du Bois, *Black Reconstruction in America* (New York: Harcourt & Brace, 1935), 715. Brown suggests that Yerby 'read and relied on' Du Bois. Stephanie Brown, 86.
34. Yerby, *The Foxes of Harrow* (Garden City, NY: Sun Dial, 1947), 157.
35. Mitchell, 628.
36. The impossibility of Irish-African hybridity in *GWTW*'s sealed white supremacist universe is mocked by Alice Randall's 2001 parody *The Wind Done Gone*, in which Scarlett turns out to be mixed-race.
37. See the details in a memoir of enslavement in Georgia and elsewhere of Charles Ball (*c.* 1780–?), a near-contemporary of the fictional Gerald O'Hara (b. 1801). Charles Ball (with Isaac Fisher), *Slavery in the United States: A Narrative of the Life and Adventures of Charles Ball, a Black Man* (New York: John S. Taylor, 1837), 213.
38. However, Pyron makes the important point that Mitchell's narrative reflects the racist representation of Reconstruction in the mainstream 1930s historiography upon which she had to rely. Pyron, 310–11.
39. Stephanie Brown, 75.
40. Mitchell, 60.
41. Mitchell, 65.
42. Mark C. Jerng, 'Reconstructions of Racial Perception: Margaret Mitchell's and Frank Yerby's Plantation Romances' in *New Approaches to Gone with The Wind*, ed. James Crank (LSU Press: Baton Rouge, 2015), 52.
43. Drew Gilpin Faust compares Scarlett and Sutpen, gender/class outsiders to Southern culture who plot their own advancement. Drew Gilpin Faust, 'Clutching the Chains

That Bind: Margaret Mitchell and "Gone with the Wind"', *Southern Cultures* 5.1 (1999): 12–13.

44. Yerby, *Foxes*, 175.
45. Du Bois, Black Reconstruction, 700–1; David R. Roediger, *The Wages of Whiteness: Race and the Making of the American Working Class* (London: Verso, 2007), 13.
46. Yerby, *Foxes*, 375.
47. Jarrett, '"For Endless Generations": Myth, Dynasty, and Frank Yerby's *The Foxes of Harrow*', *The Southern Literary Journal* 39.1 (2006): 54–70.
48. Robert Bone, *The Negro Novel in America* (New Haven, CT: Yale University Press, 1968), 168; 167.
49. A 'morganatic' marriage is one between persons of unequal rank in which the husband's privileges cannot pass to the wife or any children of the marriage.
50. Faulkner, *Absalom, Absalom!*, 17.
51. In the final chapter, beginning in April 1865, we are told that the house is, in part, a 'blackened ruin', while the prologue records that it has been in this state for 'eighty years'. Yerby, *Foxes*, 395; 406; viii.
52. Yerby, *Foxes*, vii–viii.
53. By late in the action of *Gone with the Wind,* the plantation manor at Tara has been reduced—by the depredations of war, fire, occupation, and huge tax bills—to a shell of its former glory.
54. 'there was no continuation of it anywhere [...]. The Plantation system collapsed everywhere, brutally or progressively [...]'. Glissant, *Poétique de la relation / Poetics of Relation*, 63.
55. Mid-century Southern readers were kept in the dark regarding Yerby's racial identity. 'The Golden Corn', 97.
56. Yerby, *Foxes*, viii.
57. See Amy Clukey, 'Plantation Modernism: Irish, Caribbean, and U.S. Fiction, 1890–1950'. Ph.D. dissertation, Pennsylvania State University, 2009, 64.
58. Although Walrond's story is set on an unnamed Caribbean island that may be Trinidad (Mount Tabor is name-checked), 'Great House' is a Jamaican usage for plantation house; see Louise Walsh, '*Dracula* and *Tropic Death*', *Caribbean Quarterly* 64/3–4 (2018): 521–43.
59. 'Waterford' is also the name of an Irish port city associated with the Norman incursion.
60. A 'mulatto' girl approaching the scene next morning feels 'deeply exultant' at 'what had passed there in the night'. Eric Walrond, 'The Vampire Bat', *Tropic Death* (New York: Boni and Liveright, 1926), 234.
61. Clukey, 'Plantation Modernism', 21.
62. Robert Lloyd Praeger, *The Way that I Went* (Dublin: Hodges, Figgis & Co., 1939), 21.
63. Welty, quoted in Dawn Trouard, 'The Promiscuous Joy of Eudora Welty: Missing Bowen in Mississippi', in Richard Gray and Waldemar Zacharasiewicz (eds), *Transatlantic Exchanges: The American South in Europe—Europe in the American South* (Vienna: Austrian Academy of Sciences, 2007), 258.
64. Taking its cue from the sentient house of Poe's 'The Fall of the House of Usher' (1840), Bowen's Big House in the twilight of the colonial presence in Ireland is described from a distance as follows: 'It seemed to huddle its trees close in fright and amazement at the

wide light lovely unloving country, the unwilling bosom whereon it was set.' Elizabeth Bowen, *The Last September* (New York: Random House, 1929), 92.

65. Bowen, *Bowen's Court* (New York: Alfred A. Knopf, 1942), 452; 38; 457.
66. Eudora Welty, 'The Bride of The Innisfallen', in *The Bride of The Innisfallen and Other Stories* (New York: Harcourt, Brace & Co., 1955), 47; 60.
67. Welty, 53.
68. He assumes, for instance, that priests may fine parishioners who miss mass. Welty, 62.
69. His suitcase is suspiciously heavy ('God knew what was inside'); he remarks of a needlepoint image of a rabbit, 'Makes you wish you had your gun'; he refuses the communally shared food, and proclaims that Irish is not a 'real language'. Welty, 73; 57; 58; 57.
70. Welty, 74.
71. Welty, 60.
72. Welty, 62–3.
73. Welty, 63.
74. Welty, 68–9.
75. See Welty, 'Reality in Chekhov's Stories', in *The Eye of the Story: Selected Essays and Reviews* (New York: Vintage1990), 61–84.
76. In a 'Big House' novel set in late colonial Ireland, a family whose '[c]astle and title date from the 1890s' are looked upon coolly by those with deeper histories. Molly Keane, *Good Behaviour* (London: Virago, 2001), 236.
77. Billy Kay, *The Scottish World: A Journey into the Scottish Diaspora* (Edinburgh, UK: Mainstream, 2008), 134.
78. Yerby, *Foxes*, 139.
79. Faulkner, *Absalom, Absalom!*, 17; 8–9.
80. The company's neoclassical and spacious 'Magnolia' was their 'top-of-the-line' offering. Katherine Cole Stevenson and H. Ward Jandl. *Houses by Mail: A Guide to Houses* from *Sears, Roebuck* and *Company* (New York: Wiley, 1996), 13; 19.
81. Glissant, *Poétique,* 64.
82. Faulkner, *AA*, 86.
83. Darwin T. Turner, 'Frank Yerby as Debunker', *Massachusetts Review* 9.3 (Summer 1968): 577.
84. Faulkner, *AA*, 9.
85. Faulkner, *AA*, 16.
86. The moment of time travel referred to in relation to Banville's *Birchwood* is when, in 1910, sometime narrator Quentin Compson and his Harvard roommate appear to briefly travel alongside the enlistees. Faulkner, *AA*, 334–5.
87. Faulkner, *AA*, 227; 242; 225.
88. Faulkner, *AA*, 232.
89. Faulkner, *AA*, 229; 226.
90. Faulkner, *AA*, 227.
91. Faulkner, *AA*, 220; 222; 241. The 'Old Bailey' is the Central Criminal Court of England and Wales.
92. Plymouth Colony was established by English Separatist Puritans in 1620, but the English settlement of Jamestown, Virginia, preceded it by thirteen years. Within

Saxonist rhetoric, to claim descent from those who had landed at Plymouth on the 'Mayflower' was to claim undiluted, originary American whiteness, an association that Jamestown origin did not acquire due to its convict cohort, despite being an older colony.

93. Faulkner, *AA*, 65; 32; 48. This is in pointed contrast to Rosa's father, whose first name ('Goodhue') denotes his unimpeachable credentials.
94. Emily Jones Salmon, 'Convict Labor during the Colonial Period', *Encyclopedia Virginia,* 14 December 2020, online.
95. '[I]n an area with a diverse mix of European backgrounds, which is to say various forms of "Whiteness", the person so dubbed is [...] almost certainly of "Anglo" or, especially, Celtic descent'. Jacqueline Zara Wilson, 'Invisible Racism: The Language and Ontology of "White Trash"', *Critique of Anthropology* 22.4 (2002): 388. Significantly, Quentin's Canadian roommate, from a country with only a short, small history of slavery, does not know the term 'white trash'. Faulkner, *AA*, 181
96. See Glissant, *Faulkner, Mississippi* (Paris: Éditions Stock, 1996), 68; 227.
97. Glissant, *Poétique*, 74.
98. The West Indies enfolds both Barbados and Haiti, the most resonant sites in terms of the earliest history of Irish and African in the Caribbean.
99. Faulkner, *AA*, 244.
100. Faulkner, *AA*, 15–16.
101. Faulkner, *AA*, 60; 22.
102. Faulkner, *AA*, 29–30.
103. Aimé Césaire, *Discourse on Colonialism,* trans. Joan Pinkham, (New York: Monthly Review Press, 1972), 13.
104. Bon, too, embodies a threat to this heteronormative white order in becoming an incestuous object of desire to both Judith and Henry, as does his dainty child, Charles Etienne, who summons up a reference to 'the Irish poet, Wilde'. Faulkner, *AA*, 95–7; 193.
105. The Native American land west of the Appalachian border of the original thirteen British American colonies.
106. Kay, 131.
107. Kay, 143. For a full account of Scots-Irish Presbyterian anti-slavery voices, see Daniel Ritchie, 'Radical Orthodoxy: Irish Covenanters and American Slavery, circa 1830–1865', *Church History* 82.4 (2013): 812–47.
108. Arthur M. Schlesinger, *Robert Kennedy and His Times* (Boston & New York: Houghton Mifflin, 2002), 317–27.
109. James Baldwin, 'Faulkner and Desegregation', *Partisan Review* 23.4 (Fall 1956): 568–73.
110. P.D. East, *The Magnolia Jungle* (excerpt) in Marion Barnwell (ed.), *A Place Called Mississippi: Collected Narratives* (Jackson, MS: University Press of Mississippi, 1997), 186; 190.
111. East, 190; 188; 191.
112. Faulkner, 'The Tall Men', *The Saturday Evening Post* 213 (31 May 1941): 14–15; 95–6; 98–9.

113. Faulkner's beloved Rowan Oak had been built by the Scots-Irish planter, whose roots were County Down Ulster planter. Blotner, *Faulkner,* 651. An image of the house is available at: https://commons.wikimedia.org/wiki/File:Rowan_Oak_2018_2.jpg.
114. Faulkner, *AA*, 241.
115. Quinlan, 224; 25.
116. A Scottish nationalist London designer of Highland ancestry, Alexander McQueen showed tartan wool and torn lace worn by blood-spattered models for a 1995–96 collection called 'Highland Rape' and reprised the looks and the politics in a 2006–07 collection called 'Widows of Culloden'. *Skyfall* depicts the blasted, depopulated landscape of Bond's traumatic Highland beginnings, politically provocative given the context of the debate over the impending (2014) Scottish Independence referendum at time of release. Katherine Gleason, *Alexander McQueen: Evolution* (New York: Race Point Publishing, 2017), 31–4; 147–54.
117. Quoted in Kay, 136.
118. David Yalden-Thomson, quoted in Williamson, 334.
119. Faulkner, 'Appendix: The Compsons', in Malcolm Cowley, ed. *The Portable Faulkner*, revised and expanded edition (New York: Penguin, 1984), 705.
120. Iain Moncreiffe and David Hicks, *Highland Clans* (New York: Clarkson N. Potter, 1967), 87; 91–2.
121. Faulkner, Appendix, 705.
122. Faulkner, Appendix, 707.
123. Likewise, Mitchell's O'Hara justifies his 'ruthless singleness of purpose' in acquiring plantation and human chattel as the hunger 'of an Irishman who has been a tenant on the lands his people once had owned'. Mitchell, 63.
124. Charles W. MacQuarrie, 'Yoknapatawpha County and "Cracker Culture": A Study of the "Celtic" Component in Faulkner's Mythical South', *Faulkner Journal of Japan* 7 (2005). Online.
125. Faulkner, Appendix, 704.
126. Jackson was president between 1829 and 1837.
127. If Faulkner draws from real MacLachlan history, then it seems to have paid him the same compliment: in 1942, the first female chief of Clan Lachlan succeeded her father. Moncreiffe and Hicks, 92.
128. Faulkner, *The Sound and the Fury* (New York: Vintage International, 1990), 320.
129. Blotner, *William Faulkner's Library: A Catalogue* (Charlottesville, VA: University Press of Virginia, 1964), 76–7.
130. James Joyce, 'The Dead', in *Dubliners* (New York: Penguin, 1992), 208–9.
131. Faulkner, *The Sound and the Fury*, 319.
132. Seton Paul Gordon, *The Highlands of Scotland* (London: Robert Hale, 1951), 27.
133. J. V. Ridgely, *Nineteenth-Century Southern Literature* (Lexington: University Press of Kentucky, 1980), 16.
134. George Schuyler, 'Not Gone with the Wind', *Crisis* 44.7 (July 1937): 205.
135. Conroy, Preface, *Gone with the Wind*, 11.
136. Dowd, *The Construction of Irish Identity in American Literature* (New York: Routledge, 2011), 174; Quinlan, 129.
137. Mitchell, 299; 65.

138. Henry T. Crofton, comp. *Crofton Memoirs. An Account of John Crofton of Ballymurry, Co. Roscommon, Queen Elizabeth's Escheator-General of Ireland, and of His Ancestors and Descendants and Others Bearing His Name* (York, UK: Yorkshire Printing Company, 1911), 277–78; Thomas Bartlett, 'The O'Haras of Annaghmore c. 1600—c. 1800: Survival and Revival', *Irish Economic and Social History* 9.1 (1982): 35–6.
139. Bartlett, 36.
140. Maurice Lenihan, *Limerick; its History and Antiquities* (Dublin: Duffy, 1884), 377.
141. The family lore seems to be either inaccurate or erroneous: Although three men from Tipperary named Fitzgerald attended Trinity in this approximate timeframe, none had the first name of 'James'. Alumni Dublinenses: A Register of the Students, Graduates, Professors and Provosts of Trinity College in the University of Dublin (1593–1860); 283; 285; 287. https://digitalcollections.tcd.ie/concern/works/70795b624?locale=en.
142. Mitchell, 61.
143. Aengus O'Daly [Aonghus Ó Dálaigh], *The Tribes of Ireland: A Satire*, trans. James Clarence Mangan (Dublin: O'Daly, 1852), line 15, p. 95.
144. 'Clayton County Georgia: History'. https://www.claytoncountyga.gov/residents/about-clayton-county/history.
145. Mitchell, 58; 401.
146. Mitchell, 62.
147. Frederick Douglass, *The Life and Times of Frederick Douglass* (New York: Dover, 2003), 214.
148. Wilkerson is only fired at the insistence of Gerald's pious wife because of sexual incontinence. Mitchell, 87.
149. Mitchell, 664; 401; 669. The Haitian slave in revolt is, in Grégory Pierrot's telling, an essential trope of Atlantic modernity. See *The Black Avenger in Atlantic Culture* (Athens, GA: University of Georgia Press, 2019).
150. C.L.R. James, *Toussaint Louverture: The Story of the Only Successful Slave Revolt in History; a Play in Three Acts*, ed. Christian Høgsbjerg (Durham, NC and London: Duke University Press, 2013).
151. James, *The Black Jacobins: Toussaint l'Ouverture and the San Domingo Revolution* (New York: Vintage, 1989).
152. Dowd, *The Construction of Irish Identity in American Literature*, 183.
153. Mitchell, 397.
154. Mitchell, 269; 66; 850; 668; 66; 709; 702; 816. Tyler Meredith, Yerby's *Captain Rebel* spin on a Rhett Butler-esque blockade runner in antebellum New Orleans with no illusions about the Confederacy, is of explicit Anglo-Irish Dublin origins. Yerby, *Captain Rebel* (New York: Pocket Books, 1965), 89.
155. Pyron, 250.
156. Anne Edwards, *Road to Tara: The Life of Margaret Mitchell* (New York: Ticknor, 1983), 125.
157. Elizabeth Jane Harrison, *Female Pastoral: Women Writers Re-visioning the American South* (Knoxville: University of Tennessee Press, 1991), 58.
158. Harriet Beecher Stowe's novel drew from Josiah Henson's 1849 dictated memoir of his enslavement. Henson had escaped from the Willow Grove plantation in Montgomery County, Maryland, close to the location of F. Scott Fitzgerald's antecedents. It was

owned by Isaac Riley, who descended from the Gaelic Ó Raghallaigh (O'Reilly) family, hereditary rulers of an Ulster fiefdom broken up in the upheavals of seventeenth-century Ireland. See Josiah Henson, *Uncle Tom's Story of His Life: An Autobiography of the Rev. Josiah Henson*, preface by Harriet Beecher Stowe and introductory note by George Sturge and S. Morley (London: *Christian Age* Office, 1876) and Robert S. Riley, *The Colonial Riley families of the Tidewater Frontier* (Utica, KY: MacDowell, 1999).

159. Pyron, 250.
160. Joseph A. Cox, *The Recluse of Herald Square: The Mystery of Ida E. Wood* (New York: Macmillan, 1964), 69; 160–1.
161. Yerby, *Foxes*, 4; 1.
162. Yerby, *Foxes*, 51; 52–3.
163. Yerby, *Foxes*, 260.
164. Yerby, *Foxes*, 158. See also Jarrett, '"For Endless Generations"', 153.
165. This ambiguity persists in the region. See Virginia R. Domínguez, *White by Definition: Social Classification in Creole Louisiana* (New Brunswick, N.J.: Rutgers University Press, 1986), 151.
166. In the 1920s the term 'Creole' was used in marketing hair and skin preparations to African American women, many of which sought to alter hair texture and skin tone judged to be 'too African'. Peiss, 233.
167. Domínguez, 134.
168. Chopin, 'The Father of Désirée's Baby' [original title], *Vogue* (14 January 1893): 70–4.
169. A slavery-era categorization meaning a person of one-eight Black ancestry.
170. Critics do not agree as to whether Armand was fully aware of his maternal ancestry when he voiced his belief that it was his wife who must be of African descent.
171. 'Colleen' derives from the Irish *cailín*, meaning 'girl'.
172. Yerby, *Foxes*, 81; 155; 170.
173. Yerby, *Foxes*, viii.
174. Yerby, *Foxes*, 90–1; 156–7; 317; 185.
175. Yerby, *Foxes*, 157.
176. Yerby, *Foxes*, 257.
177. Yerby, *Foxes*, 52; 185.
178. Yerby, *Foxes*, 370; 371.
179. Yerby, *Foxes*, 375.
180. *Foxes* does not state this explicitly, but the juxtaposition of an implied *c.* 1798 birth and the name 'Harrow' suggests the traces of the author's research into Irish history in that period.
181. Yerby, *Foxes*, 24.
182. Yerby, *Foxes*, 406.
183. Yerby, *Foxes*, 371.
184. Yerby, *Foxes*, 401.
185. Yerby, *Foxes*, 405.
186. Yerby, *Foxes*, 405.
187. Jerome Mushkat, *Fernando Wood: A Political Biography* (Kent, OH: Kent State University Press, 1990), 160; 87.
188. Yerby, *McKenzie's Hundred*, 224; 267; 263; 266; 268.

189. Yerby, *McKenzie's Hundred*, 266.
190. Amy S. Greenberg, *A Wicked War: Polk, Clay, Lincoln, and the 1846 U.S. Invasion of Mexico* (New York: Alfred A. Knopf, 2012), 24–5; 27.
191. Greenberg, 203–4. Mayne Reid's *c.* 1883 non-fiction account of his experience in the Mexican-American war (posthumously edited by his widow, Elizabeth Hyde), though mostly written in the fast-paced, masculinist 'derring-do' tone of his westerns, has a slippage in which a desecrated American soldier's corpse is admitted to be the just revenge of the local Mexican peasantry for a previous wanton attack on a civilian by another US enlistee. Nonetheless, and as though to counter the San Patricio desertion, Reid's account features a 'brave Irishman' called John Murphy. Reid, 'Captain Mayne Reid and the Mexican Campaign of 1847', *The Illustrated Naval and Military Magazine*, new series, vol. II, 1889, 1152–3; 1157.
192. 'Choctaw and Ireland History', chocotawnation.com. https://www.choctawnation.com/history-culture/history/choctaw-and-ireland-history.
193. 'Yerby, Frank', 471.
194. The first full-length book on the topic was Robert Ryal Miller, *Shamrock and Sword: The Saint Patrick's Battalion in the U.S.-Mexican War* (Norman: U of Oklahoma Press, 1989).
195. 'Yerby, Frank', 471.
196. Yerby to Helen Strauss, 16 April 1964. Frank Yerby Papers, Howard Gotlieb Archival Research Center, Boston University. Box 53, Folder B53 F7.
197. Hoyt W. Fuller, 'Famous Writer Faces a Challenge', *Ebony* magazine, 1 June 1966, 188.
198. Matthew Teutsch, 'Overstuffed and Undercooked: The Film Adaptation of Frank Yerby's *The Foxes of Harrow*', in *Rediscovering Frank Yerby*, ed. Matthew Teutsch (Jackson, MS: University Press of Mississippi, 2020), 90; Yerby, *Foxes*, 353.
199. See Phyllis R. Klotman, 'A Harrowing Experience: Frank Yerby's First Novel to Film', *CLA Journal* 31.2 (1987): 213.
200. On the film set, Harrison asked O'Hara if she disliked him because he was British. Maureen O'Hara (with John Nicoletti), *'Tis Herself: An Autobiography* (New York: Simon & Schuster, 2005), 148.
201. 'Yerby, Frank', 468; 470.
202. Harry Keelan, 'Voice in the Wilderness', *Afro-American*, 18 October 1947, 4.
203. See Diane Negra, *Off-White Hollywood: American Culture and Ethnic Female Stardom* (London and New York: Routledge, 2001).
204. Maureen O'Hara, 18; 24. The actress appeared as 'FitzSimons' in her first two films, but by 1939's *Jamaica Inn* she was listed in the credits as 'O'Hara'.
205. The 1946 change of name from the Irish 'Dougherty' to the Scottish 'Monroe' of O'Hara's 20th Century Fox stablemate, Marilyn Monroe, suggests how Scottishness, by contrast, signalled unethnicized Americanness to film executives of that period. ('Dougherty' was Monroe's first husband's name.) J. Randy Taraborrelli, *The Secret Life of Marilyn Monroe* (New York: Grand Central Publishing, 2010), 115.
206. Maureen O'Hara, 94.
207. O'Hara's oft-cited 'feistiness' was given a '#MeToo' spin in a recent fictionalization, which drew from O'Hara's defiant response to harassment. Anne Enright's *Actress* (2020), mines O'Hara's 2005 memoir, *'Tis Herself*, for source material, which made

headlines because it revealed the mistreatment directed at her by director John Ford on *The Quiet Man* set after she spurned his sexual advances. O'Hara, *'Tis Herself*, 147–52; 163; 167–8.

208. See the portrait of O'Hara in the artwork for the Italian-language film poster at https://www.cinematerial.com/movies/the-foxes-of-harrow-i39394/p/9sicr39i.
209. Mitchell, 815; 816; 245.
210. This association persists somewhat. See Amanda Third, '"Does the Rug Match the Carpet?": Race, Gender, and the Redheaded Woman', in Negra (ed.), *The Irish in Us*, 220–53.
211. Dyer, 132.

Chapter 5

1. Dinah D. Eastop and Bernice Morris. 'Fit for a Princess? Material Culture and the Conservation of Grace Kelly's Wedding Dress', in Frances Lennard and Patricia Ewer (eds), *Textile Conservation: Recent Advances* (Oxford: Butterworth-Heinemann, 2010), 76.
2. Donald Spoto, *High Society: Grace Kelly and Hollywood* (London: Arrow, 2010), xvi.
3. Joseph Lennon has described it as 'one of the Irish literary world's treasures, one not known well enough'. 'Irish Triad: Villanova's Center for Irish Studies Partners with Monaco's Princess Grace Irish Library and Philadelphia's Kelly House' Villanova University press release, 2020. https://www1.villanova.edu/villanova/media/pressreleases/2020/0827.html.
4. That stated, attention to Kelly's beauty in isolation from her whole story obscures the soft power she later wielded as the glamorous, internationally known representative of a tiny principality long overshadowed by its powerful neighbour. Monte Carlo in Monaco, long a gambling mecca was, by the 1950s, under the financial sway of Greek shipping magnate Aristotle Onassis, and had steadily gained a shady reputation for all of Monaco, as an early Fitzgerald effort depicts: As a freshman, Fitzgerald wrote the book and lyrics for a Princeton Triangle Club musical that portrays a tawdry principality peopled by American conmen. The international spotlight brought by the 1956 wedding disarmed French attempts to assert control over Monaco, revitalized its economy and, through Grace's efforts, made it a hub for opera, ballet, concerts, plays, cultural conferences, and readings. Even her unreleased last film, *Rearranged* (1982), a gentle comedy short about mistaken identity in which she plays herself, was a disguised promotion for her beloved Monaco Flower Show. See F. ScottFitzgerald, book and lyrics. *Fie! Fie! Fi-Fi! A Facsimile of the 1914 Acting Script and the Musical Score*, ed. and intro, Bruccoli (University of South Carolina Press for the Thomas Cooper Library, 1996); Spoto, *High Society*, 248–9; 212–13; 266–70. Rearranged remains unreleased as it was unfinished at the time of Princess Grace's death in 1982.
5. Peiss, 64; 66–7; 88–9. Possibly significantly, in light of the ethno-racial 'passing' beauty products potentially provided, an advert for a Kathleen Mary Quinlan face-powder depicts white masks rather than human faces. Image of the 1945 advert at https://hprints.com/en/item/52230/?u=1,3.

6. It might be productive, for instance, to bring the social and ethno-racial meanings of make-up in James's lifetime to bear upon 'The Ghostly Rental', the story in which the daughter, if we recall, plays ghost with the help of face powder.
7. Rachel Carson (1907–1964), the most influential environmentalist of America's twentieth century, was the daughter of Scots-Irish Presbyterian immigrants. Consider also a politico beyond the Tammany Hall nexus such as suffragist and champion of American small farmers, Mary Elizabeth Lease. The Pennsylvania-born daughter of Catholic immigrants from Monaghan, Lease was a firebrand People's Party leader in 1890s Kansas. In addition, greater attention to women complicates received ideas of American Catholic leadership: in 1891, Katharine Drexel, the wealthy collateral ancestor of Jacqueline Bouvier Kennedy, founded the Sisters of the Blessed Sacrament for Indians and Colored People. The steely Drexel had a powerful voice within the Church, and remained unintimidated when threatened with violence for planning a boarding school for African-American children in Philadelphia. Her foot soldiers were Irish-American nuns of working-class Democratic background. The mostly Irish male hierarchy, who had little interest in educating Black children, were 'relieved' to leave this heavy lifting to the sisters. Rebecca Edwards, 'Mary E. Lease and the Populists: A Reconsideration', *Kansas History: A Journal of the Central Plains* 35 (Spring 2012): 28; 29; Suellen Hoy, 'Lives on the Color Line: Catholic Sisters and African Americans in Chicago, 1890s–1960s', *U.S. Catholic Historian* 22.1 (2004): 73; 71; 74.
8. Spoto, *High Society*, 3–4. Strikingly, the term 'main line' is also used to denote the mainstream Protestant churches that dominated Christian America, both socially and numerically, into the period of Grace Kelly's adulthood.
9. David Nelson Wren, *Ardrossan: The Last Great Estate on the Philadelphia Main Line* (New York: Bauer and Dean, 2017), 5. The Social Register or 'Four Hundred' was a directory of a given American city's most prominent WASP families. Into the World War II period, numerous American cities published such directories. See Allison Ijams Sargent, 'The Social Register: Just a Circle of Friends', *New Yorker*, 21 December 1997. Online.
10. Alexis de Tocqueville, *Journey in Ireland, July–August, 1835*, ed. Emmet Larkin (Washington, DC: Catholic University of America Press, 1990), 129.
11. The Irish National Land League was founded in nearby Castlebar in 1879.
12. Bruce Stewart, 'The Princess Grace Irish Library', *World of Hibernia* 6.4 (2001), 66. The library's copy of the Easter Rising-era *Sinn Fein Rebellion Handbook* (Dublin: Irish Times, 1917) has a false spine so that it could be kept on a shelf in disguise. *Annette Ross Anderson*, 'Monaco Direct: Monaco's Grace was Kelly Green', *Grace Influential*, n.d. https://www.graceinfluential.com/post/monaco-direct-monaco-s-grace-was-kelly-green.
13. See Princess Grace of Monaco (transcription of performance at St James's Palace on 22 November 1978 in aid of the World Wildlife Fund), *Birds, Beasts and Flowers* (Exeter, UK: Webb & Bower, 1983), 17; 22–3; 35; 48.
14. Grace further honoured her Mayo grandparents in a foreword to a volume of Irish-themed art four years later in describing them as 'people of remarkable character'. Foreword by Princess Grace of Monaco to Gordon Wetmore, *Ireland: Portrayed by Gordon Wetmore* (Nashville, TN: Nelson 1980), 7. A local Newport-area writer,

Marguerite Gannon, is currently working on a play on John Henry's life in Drimurla. Marguerite Gannon, personal email, 4 January 2022.

15. John O'Hara, *Appointment in Samarra*, Charles McGrath, intro (New York: Penguin, 2013), 11.
16. Bowen, 'Dress', *Collected Impressions* (New York: Knopf, 1950), 112.
17. John O'Hara, *BUtterfield 8*. Lorin Stein, intro (New York: Penguin, 2013), 50–2.
18. Sharon Zukin, *Point of Purchase: How Shopping Changed American Culture* (New York: Routledge, 2003), 200; 198.
19. O'Hara, Introduction, *The Portable F. Scott Fitzgerald*, selected by Dorothy Parker (New York: Viking, 1949), xii.
20. O'Hara, *BUtterfield 8*, 52.
21. Fanning, 250.
22. See, for instance, the use of the quotation in popular magazine *Irish America's* December/January 2008 online potted history of 'Philadelphia's Irish' by Tom Deignan at https://irishamerica.com/2008/01/pennsylvanias-irish/.
23. Spoto, *High Society*, 4.
24. Spoto, *High Society*, 4.
25. The city remained so entwined with Quaker power in American imagination that George Lippard's best-selling lurid urban Gothic novel, which purported to expose the hidden corruption of Philadelphia's ruling class, was titled *The Quaker City* (1845).
26. Adam Douglass ('An Hibernian'), *The Irish Emigrant, An Historical Tale Founded on Fact* (Winchester, VA: Sharrocks, 1817), 184.
27. Gilmore, xx.
28. Judith Ridner, 'Scots Irish (Scotch Irish)'. *The Encyclopedia of Greater Philadelphia*, 2017. Online https://philadelphiaencyclopedia.org/archive/scots-irish/.
29. The Presbytery of Philadelphia was the first organized presbytery in the American colonies. Seven ministers composed the first meeting in Philadelphia in early 1706 with Donegal clergyman Francis Makemie (1658–1708) moderating. Six of the seven clergymen present were Presbyterian ministers who had been ordained in Scotland and Ireland. Alfred Nevin, *History of the Presbytery of Philadelphia, and of the Philadelphia Central* (Philadelphia: Fortescue, 1888), 62–7.
30. Elizabeth M. Geffen, 'Violence in Pennsylvania in the 1840's and 1850's'. *Pennsylvania History* 36.4 (1969): 392. The Loyal Orange Institution (f. 1795), commonly known as the Orange Order, is an Ulster loyalist organization that has traditionally opposed Irish nationalism and Irish republicanism.
31. This was a demarcation line along the southern Pennsylvania border that became the boundary between the free North and the slave-holding South.
32. See John Runcie, '"Hunting the N**s" in Philadelphia: The Race Riot of August 1834'. *Pennsylvania History* 39.2 (1972): 187–218.
33. See the marker at https://commons.wikimedia.org/wiki/File:Lombard_Street_Riot_Historical_Marker_at_6th_and_Lombard_Sts_Philadelphia_PA_(DSC_4614).jpg.
34. E. Digby Baltzell, *The Protestant Establishment: Aristocracy and Caste in America* (New York, Random House, 1964), 73.
35. Zachary M. Schrag, "Nativist Riots of 1844, *The Encyclopedia of Greater Philadelphia*, 2013. Online https://philadelphiaencyclopedia.org/archive/nativist-riots-of–1844/.

36. Tyler Anbinder, *Nativism and Slavery: The Northern Know Nothings and the Politics of the 1850's* (New York: Oxford University Press, 1992), 58. The Know Nothings were a nativist, anti-Catholic and anti-Irish political movement that was briefly powerful in the mid-1850s.
37. Rory Fitzpatrick, *God's Frontiersmen: The Scots-Irish Epic* (London: Weidenfeld and Nicolson, 1989), 261.
38. Smith's celebrated opening runs as follows: 'Serene was a word you could put to Brooklyn, New York. Especially in the summer of 1912'. Betty Smith, 5.
39. O'Neill also represents inter-Irish tensions as a divided family in a one-act play from the same decade (*The Rope*, 1918), in which red-haired Mary Sweeney is a despised 'Papist brat' to her own Protestant maternal grandfather. O'Neill, *The Rope*,in *Early Plays*, 104.
40. John H. Houchin, *Censorship of the American Theatre in the Twentieth Century* (Cambridge: Cambridge UP, 2003), 59
41. 'More than Theatre Riots Greet "The Playboy": Skirmishes and Ejections Follow Hurling of Missiles at Stage in Philadelphia', *New York Times*, 17 January 1912, 2.
42. Dominic Bryan, *Orange Parades: The Politics of Ritual, Tradition and Control* (London: Pluto, 1999), 56.
43. Lucy McDiarmid, 'The Abbey and the Theatrics of Controversy, 1901-1915', in StephenWatt et al. (eds), *A Century of Irish Drama: Widening the Stage* (Bloomington, IN: Indiana University Press, 2001), 68.
44. This was Philadelphia attorney Charles Biddle (1857–1923). Lady Gregory, *Our Irish Theatre: A Chapter of Autobiography* (New York: Putnam, 1914), 293; 'Biddle Family History and Timeline' on the website of their former estate, Andalusia: https://andalusiapa.org/.
45. Clark, *The Irish in Philadelphia: Ten Generations of Urban Experience* (Philadelphia, PA: Temple University Press, 1981), 172.
46. Robert Lacey, *Grace* (New York: Putnam's Sons, 1994), 52.
47. Michael L. Mullan, 'Sport, Culture, and Nation Among the Hibernians of Philadelphia: Irish American Civic Engagement and Cultural Nationalism, 1880–1920'. *Journal of Urban History* 39: 4 (2013), 581.
48. Nathaniel Burt and Wallace E. Davies, 'The Iron Age, 1876–1905', in Russell Weigley (ed.), *Philadelphia; A 300-Year History* (New York: Norton, 1982), 488.
49. Billy J. Harbin, 'George Kelly, American Playwright: Characters in the Hands of an Angry God', in Kim Marra and Robert A. Schanke (eds), *Staging Desire: Queer Readings of American Theater History* (Ann Arbor: University of Michigan Press, 2002), 126.
50. Baltzell, *Puritan Boston and Quaker Philadelphia* (New Brunswick, NJ, Transaction, 2007), 418.
51. Deborah A. Wuest and Charles A. Bucher, *Foundations of Physical Education, Exercise Science, and Sport* (Boston: McGraw-Hill, 2003) 199.
52. John B. Kelly, 'Are We Becoming a Nation of Weaklings?', *American Magazine* 161 (March1956): 28–9; 104–7.
53. Spoto, *High Society*, 5.

54. See https://commons.wikimedia.org/wiki/File:Johnbkellysr.jpg. Similarly, French clothier de TOUJOURS used a photo of a young Kennedy in swim trunks to illustrate their 'Hamptons swimming trunks' spring 2020 offering. https://www.detoujours.com/5-e-shop#/categories-swim_bodysuits. Accessed 22 February 2020.
55. Reginald P. P. Rowe and Peter W. Squire, *Rowing* (London: Longmans & Green, 1903), 151.
56. Spoto, *High Society*, 6.
57. Daniel Boyne, J., *Kelly: A Father, a Son, an American Quest* (Guilford, CT: Lyons, 2012), 81.
58. Mullan, 580.
59. Spoto, *High Society*, 6.
60. Our Rowing Correspondent. 'Mr. John Kelly'. *The Times*, 21 June 1960, 15.
61. 'The Music Halls'. *The Times*, 13 August 1912, 7. The Times Digital Archive.
62. Frank Cullen et al., 'George C. Kelly', in *Vaudeville Old & New: An Encyclopedia of Variety Performances in America* (New York & London: Routledge, 2006), vol. I, 628.
63. Roediger, *The Wages of Whiteness*, 117.
64. Roediger, 'Notes on Working Class Racism', in *Towards the Abolition of Whiteness: Essays on Race, Politics, and Working Class History* (London: Verso, 2000), 65.
65. Arthur H. Lewis, *Those Philadelphia Kellys, with a Touch of Grace* (New York: Morrow, 1977), 23; Foster Hirsch, *George Kelly* (Boston: Twayne, 1975), 21.
66. Spoto, *High Society*, 27.
67. Spoto, *High Society*, 63.
68. While Grace's sartorial choices performed white respectability, Baker's stage costumes produced a politics of 'disrespectability'. See Jennifer Sweeney-Risko, 'Fashionable "Formation": Reclaiming the Sartorial Politics of Josephine Baker', *Australian Feminist Studies*, 33: 98 (2018) 498–514.
69. Spoto, *High Society*, 251–2.
70. Princess Grace of Monaco, Preface, Robert Vavra, *The Love of Tiger Flower* (New York: William Morrow, 1980), n.p.
71. See, for example, Thomas Hauser, 'John F. Kennedy: An Appreciation', *Irish America* magazine (December/January, 2002). https://irishamerica.com/2001/12/john-f-kennedy-an-appreciation/.
72. The reception of Kennedy in Ireland was and generally remains of the uncomplicated 'ethnic pride' variety, and in one Catholic Irish iteration, he is meek and pious. See his image in a mosaic in Galway's Catholic Cathedral (which he visited during his official trip to Ireland in June 1963) in which his hands are clasped in prayer: https://www.project28.co.uk/gallery/galway_ireland/f8ffa586-0d8a-11e7-8a41-02daa0202684.
73. William J. Lynch, 'George Kelly the Man' (biographical essay), *Three Plays by George Kelly*. Foreword by Wendy Wasserstein (New York: Limelight Editions, 1999), 4.
74. See Walter Licht, *Getting Work: Philadelphia, 1840–1950* (Cambridge, MA: Harvard University Press, 1992).
75. Harbin, 126.
76. Spoto, 42–3.
77. Mary McCarthy, 'May–June 1947: The Unimportance of Being Oscar', in *Mary McCarthy's Theatre Chronicles, 1937–1962* (New York: Farrar, Straus and Co., 1963), 107.

78. Lynch, 'George Kelly the Man', 2; 4.
79. Lynch, 'George Kelly the Man', 2.
80. John Cain, quoted in Lewis, 128.
81. Wayne R. Dynes et al. (eds), *Encyclopedia of Homosexuality* (New York: Garland, 1990), 447.
82. Lewis, 129.
83. "Where Are They Now?', *Newsweek*, 75 (2 February 1970): 12.
84. McCarthy, 'March–April 1947: George Kelly' in *Mary McCarthy's Theatre Chronicles, 1937–1962*, 97.
85. George Kelly, *The Flattering Word* in *The Flattering Word and Other One-Act Plays* (Boston: Little & Brown, 1925), 17–18.
86. McCarthy's assessment was made in a mainstream venue during a period in which the term 'queer' was only used in a neutral or positive fashion by members of the gay subculture. See Merrill Perlman, 'How the Word "Queer" was Adopted by the LGBTQ Community', *Columbia Journalism Review*, 22 January 2019.
87. McCarthy, 'March–April 1947: George Kelly', 99.
88. 'Fortune Theatre: Craig's Wife', *The Times*, 1 February 1929, 10.
89. For instance, the Craigs' housekeeper, Mrs. Harold, uses an Irish expression denoting craftiness: 'she would make a nest in your ear'. Kelly, *Craig's Wife in Three Plays by George Kelly*, foreword by Wendy Wasserstein; biographical and critical essays by William J. Lynch (New York: Limelight Editions, 1999), 334.
90. Hirsch, *George Kelly*, 30.
91. The US census taken closest to the year of George Kelly's birth, that of 1890, revealed that 45 per cent of domestic servants in America were immigrants. Of those, 39 per cent were Irish. Faye E. Dudden, 'Experts and Servants: The National Council on Household Employment and the Decline of Domestic Service in the Twentieth Century', *Journal of Social History* 20.2 (1986), 269.
92. Margaret Lynch-Brennan, *The Irish Bridget: Irish Immigrant Women in Domestic Service in America, 1840–1930* (Syracuse, NY: Syracuse UP, 2009), 66.
93. Habegger, 303.
94. Lynch-Brennan, 77.
95. This echoes the dehumanizing strategy of calling all Black Pullman train porters 'George', the racist implication of which was that the company founder, George Pullman, 'owned' the porters.
96. Although their names are early usages of what were to become commonplace forms of derogatory address for Irish and African-American men respectively, Patrick's burgeoning whiteness is the implicit source of his innate sense of his equality with his white employer. Preparing to wed his American sweetheart at the close, Patrick is poised to assimilate. See Dale T. Knobel, *Paddy and the Republic: Ethnicity and Nationality in Antebellum America* (Middletown, CT: Wesleyan University Press, 1986); Joseph Boskin, *Sambo: The Rise & Demise of an American Jester* (New York: Oxford University Press, 1988); John Murdock, *The Triumphs of Love or, Happy Reconciliation* (Philadelphia: Folwell, 1795), 22–3.
97. Lynch-Brennan, 78.
98. Kelly, *The Flattering Word*, 45.

99. Heinz D. Fischer and Erika J. Fischer. *Chronicle of the Pulitzer Prizes for Drama: Discussions, Decisions and Documents* (Munich, Germany: Saur Verlag, 2008), 5.
100. Kelly, *Craig's Wife*, 335.
101. Ester Bloom, 'The Decline of Domestic Help', *Atlantic*, 23 September 2015.
102. Kelly, *Craig's Wife*, 202–3.
103. Kelly, *Craig's Wife*, 366.
104. Patrick Hanks, *Dictionary of American Family Names* (Oxford: Oxford University Press, 2003), 380.
105. William H. Egle, *Pennsylvania Genealogies: Scotch-Irish and German* (Harrisburg: Hart, 1886), 478–92; George Hill, *An Historical Account of the Plantation in Ulster at the Commencement of the Seventeenth Century, 1608–1620* (Belfast: M'Caw, Stevenson & Orr, 1877), 284–85.
106. Hirsch, *George Kelly*, 34.
107. T.A. Daly, 'Kitty's Graduation', *Canzoni* (Philadelphia: *Catholic Standard and Times*, 1906), 71, lines 12–19.
108. Quoted in Howell Conant, *Grace* (New York: Random House, 1992), 12.
109. 'Cinema: The Girl in White Gloves', *Time* magazine, 31 January 1955. 'Debutante' refers to the 'coming out' of young women at the Philadelphia Assembly Ball, an exclusive gathering strictly reserved for members of the city's Social Register. Kelly revealed that it had been a childhood dream to 'come out', but as a biographer observes, she was 'an excluded observer of a world that was held to be the ultimate in terms of class and privilege – which may be one reason why she made such a good job of mimicking the style and customs of that world in her later life'. Baltzell, *Philadelphia Gentlemen: The Making of a National Upper Class* (New Brunswick and London: Transaction, 1989), 163; Lacey, 53.
110. This acronym for White Anglo-Saxon Protestant, used to denote the 'old money' white elite, was popularized by Philadelphia Society insider E. Digby Baltzell in *The Protestant Establishment: Aristocracy and Caste in America* (1964).
111. Spoto, *High Society*, 43; 62; 84–5.
112. Alexis Schwarzenbach, 'Imagined Queens between Heaven and Hell: Representations of Grace Kelly and Romy Schneider', in *The Body of the Queen*, 308.
113. Cintra Wilson, *Fear and Clothing: Unbuckling American Style* (New York: Norton, 2015), 191.
114. Lorraine O'Grady, *Writing in Space, 1973–2019* (Durham, NC and London: Duke University Press, 2020), 8–10.
115. Thomas Harris, 'The Building of Popular Images: Grace Kelly and Marilyn Monroe', in Christine Gledhill (ed.), *Stardom: Industry of Desire* (London and New York: Routledge, 1991), 42.
116. I refer here to James's *The Portrait of a Lady* (1881), in which Isabel Archer is bequeathed a fortune appropriate to her gentility.
117. Peiss, 48.
118. Dyer, 98.
119. Dyer, 122; 132.
120. Dyer, 124; 96.
121. Spoto, *High Society*, 194–5; 95–6.

122. David Nelson Wren, *Ardrossan: The Last Great Estate on the Philadelphia Main Line* (New York: Bauer and Dean, 2017), 5; 7.
123. Nathaniel Burt, *The Perennial Philadelphians: The Anatomy of an American Aristocracy* (Philadelphia: University of Pennsylvania Press, 1999), 281; 450–1.
124. Bosley Crowther, 'Screen: No "Philadelphia Story," This; "High Society" Lacks Hepburn Sparkle Sinatra, Crosby, Grace Kelly Are Starred', *New York Times*, 10 August 1956, 9.
125. Edith Wharton's *The Age of Innocence* (1920) depicts that Newport scene as having passed by the close of World War I.
126. François Truffaut, *Hitchcock* (New York: Simon and Schuster, 1983), 325.
127. Princess Grace of Monaco, 'A Comment' in Spoto, *The Art of Alfred Hitchcock* (New York: Anchor, 1992), xiii.
128. Gene Adair, *Alfred Hitchcock: Filming Our Fears* (Oxford: Oxford University press, 2002), 12; 14–14; British census document images uploaded at https://the.hitchcock.zone/wiki/John_Whelan_(b._%7E1838) provide Whelan's date and place of birth.
129. Lacey, 38–43.
130. Alfred Hitchcock, quoted in Paula Marantz Cohen, *Alfred Hitchcock: The Legacy of Victorianism* (University Press of Kentucky, 1995), 97.
131. Spoto, *High Society*,118.
132. Quoted in Spoto, *High Society*, 48.
133. Spoto, *High Society*, 109.
134. Lacey, 62.
135. Hitchcock received the title in 1979.
136. See the still of this moment at https://offscreen.com/view/hitchcock-kelly.
137. *Dial M for Murder*, teleplay by Frederick Knott, *Sunday Night Theatre* (television series), transmitted on BBC, 23 March 1952; Frederick Knott, *Dial M for Murder* (New York: Dramatists Play Service, 1982), 3.
138. Patrick McGilligan. *Alfred Hitchcock: A Life in Darkness and Light* (New York: Regan Books, 2003), 3.
139. Stephen Whitty, 'Blonde', in *The Hitchcock Encyclopedia* (Lanham, MD: Rowman and Littlefield, 2016), 39.
140. For a survey of this scene, see Mary Burke, 'The Cottage, the Castle, and the Couture Cloak: "Traditional" Irish Fabrics and "Modern" Irish Fashions in America, c. 1952–1969'. *Journal of Design History* 31.4 (2018): 364–82.
141. Tara Stubbs, *American Literature and Irish Culture, 1910–55* (Manchester: Manchester UP, 2013), x.
142. 'Irish Mills Consider American Needs', *Women's Wear Daily*, 25 January 1956, 44.
143. Conant, *Grace*, 130–1; a handmade Irish lace Irene Gilbert gown commissioned by the Princess featured in the 2010 Victoria and Albert Museum exhibition, *Grace Kelly: Style Icon*.
144. For instance, Pittsburgh-born designer Anne Fogarty (née Whitney) traded on the Irish surname she had acquired through marriage to promote a 1954 range as 'Irish-inspired'. Anne Fogarty advert, *Vogue*, 1 February 1954, 96.
145. 'Tweeds, Harps, Currachs Grace Horne's Event'. *Women's Wear Daily,* 21 September 1965, 54.

146. Philip S.P. Conner, *Sir William Penn, Knight, Admiral and General at Sea: Great Captain Commander of the Fleet* (Albany, N.Y: Munsell, 1876), 18.
147. Conant, *Grace*, 86.
148. See H. Kristina Haugland, *Grace Kelly: Icon of Style to Royal Bride* (Philadelphia: Philadelphia Museum of Art, 2006).
149. For my discussion of Kelly's wedding dress alongside the Famine-relief project origins of Irish needlework industries, her family's Famine-era roots, and the colonial contexts of the use of antique Irish lace in British and European royal wedding veils and gowns in recent centuries, see Burke, 'Grace Kelly, Philadelphia, and the Politics of Irish Lace', *American Journal of Irish Studies* 19 (2019): 31–46.
150. William Clark Falkner, *The White Rose of Memphis* (Chicago; New York: Donohue, 1909), 518.
151. Clare Sauro, 'Fashion', *Encyclopedia of Greater Philadelphia, circa*2011. Online. https://philadelphiaencyclopedia.org/archive/fashion/.
152. Kate Haulman, 'Fashion and the Culture Wars of Revolutionary Philadelphia', *The William and Mary Quarterly* 62.4 (2005): 625.
153. The image may be viewed at: https://digital.librarycompany.org/islandora/object/Islandora%3A60201.
154. James Orr, 'The Passengers' (1804) lines 167–70 in Andrew Carpenter, *Verse in English from Eighteenth Century Ireland* (Cork: Cork University Press, 2000), 549; 602; 603.
155. 'Désirée's Baby' was published in *Vogue* 1, 14 January 1893, 70–1; 74 under the title 'The Father of Désirée's Baby'. An insider account of life in 1950s *Vogue* suggests that a pedigreed bloodline was a prerequisite for the editorship. See Grace Mirabella, *In and Out of Vogue* (New York: Doubleday, 1995).
156. Although it is widely cited that this fashion had emerged with Queen Victoria's novel choice of a white gown at her 1840 wedding, under the subheading 'The Bride's Dress!' the Godey's Lady's Book author implies that this hue had always been worn on such occasions. 'Description of Uncolored Fashions', *Godey's Lady's Book*, 1 August 1849: 155.
157. Queen Victoria wore white at her wedding not so much to signal 'purity' as to signal 'privilege'. The wearing of that colour was endowed with the former signifier alone decades after her wedding. Chrys Ingham, *White Weddings: Romancing Heterosexuality in Popular Culture* (New York: Routledge, 2009) 27.
158. Carol Wallace, *All Dressed in White: The Irresistible Rise of the American Wedding* (New York: Penguin, 2004), 39.
159. Dyer, 122; 124–5.
160. See 'Kate and the Dress: A Love Story', *Women's Wear Daily* 201.90 (2011): 4,
161. Caitriona Clear, '"The Minimum Rights of Every Woman"? Women's Changing Appearance in Ireland, 1940–1966'. *Irish Economic and Social History* 35 (2008): 72.
162. Áine Ryan, 'Fairytale Princess Grace Dreamed of Mayo Roots', *Mayo News*, 5 April 2011. Online.
163. Henri Marceau, 'Foreword', *Philadelphia Museum of Art Bulletin* 56.269 (1961): 7.
164. Eastop and Morris, 76.
165. Eastop and Morris, 81.

166. Traditionally, talismanic garments are those decorated with characters to which are attributed occult powers, although theorists of clothing suggest that all garments are talismanic in that they are charged by the interaction with the bodily traces of the wearer. See Joanne Entwistle, 'The Dressed Body', in Mary Evans and Ellie Lee (eds), *Real Bodies* (London: Palgrave, 2002), 133.
167. Viewership figures are from '50 Facts about the Queen's Coronation', an article released by The Press Secretary to The Queen in 2003 to mark the 50th anniversary of Her Majesty The Queen's Coronation in June 1953. https://www.royal.uk/50-facts-about-queens-coronation-0.
168. Eastop and Morris, 76.
169. Tara Harney-Mahajan, 'Refashioning the Wedding Dress as the "Future Anterior" in Plays by Edna O'Brien and Marina Carr', *Women's Studies* 44.7 (2015): 996; 1003.
170. 'She pulled again, but the [bridal veil] resisted almost as though it were being grasped from inside the trunk—she let go, and ... the lace began to be drawn back slowly, in again [...]'. Bowen, 'Hand in Glove', *Collected Stories* (New York: Vintage, 1982), 774. The story is clearly inspired by James's 'The Romance of Certain Old Clothes'.
171. Besides the shared surname, Donleavy's character and the future princess both carry a 'virtue' first name.
172. Kenny, *The American Irish: A History* (London and New York: Routledge, 2000), 221–53.
173. J. P. Donleavy, *The Ginger Man* (New York: Grove Press, 2010), 16.
174. '[W]e behold ELIZABETH, our undoubted Queen'. Bowen, 'An Enormous Channel of Expectation', in *People, Places, Things: Essays by Elizabeth Bowen*, ed. Allan Hepburn (Edinburgh: Edinburgh University Press, 2008), 369.
175. 'The whole country is concerned with the coronation, the whole coronation and nothing but the coronation'. Jacqueline Bouvier, 'Crowds of Americans Fill "Bright and Pretty" London'. *Washington Times*-Herald, 2 June 1953, 4.
176. Pat Kirkham and Shauna Stallworth, '"Three Strikes Against Me": African American Women Designers', in Pat Kirkham (ed.), *Women Designers in the USA, 1900–2000: Diversity and Difference* (New Haven: Yale University Press, 2000), 128–9. The sole exception was the *Washington Post*.

Epilogue

1. William Manchester, *Portrait of a President: John F. Kennedy in Profile* (Boston: Little, Brown and Company, 1962), 72.
2. Beth O'Leary Anish, *Irish American Fiction from World War II to JFK: Anxiety, Assimilation, and Activism* (London: Palgrave Macmillan, 2021), 146.
3. Samuel understands Irish, is referred to by others with vocabulary that evokes the loquacious, mystical Celt, and invokes the nationalist grievance of Gaelic dispossession in naming himself a descendant of kings. John Steinbeck, *East of Eden*, intro. David Wyatt (New York: Penguin, 1992), 143; 8; 10; 11.
4. 'Pat Nixon: First-Generation German-American & Her Lincoln Assassination Link'. Blog of The National First Ladies Library. http://www.firstladies.org/ancestral-nixon.aspx.

5. 'The Day Nixon Came to Timahoe', *Independent.ie*, 20 May 2011. Online.
6. 'The Immigration and Nationality Act of 1952 (The McCarran-Walter Act)', *Office of the Historian* https://history.state.gov/milestones/1945-1952/immigration-act.
7. John F. Kennedy, *A Nation of Immigrants*, rev. ed. (New York: Harper Perennial, 2008), 52.
8. See Ian R. K. Paisley, *America's Debt to Ulster* (Belfast: Martyrs Memorial, 1976). Given Paisley's adamant Unionism and the divisive politics of the period, his use of 'Irish' in this context likely means a constituent British identity within the Union along the lines of 'Welsh' or 'Scottish'.
9. See Michael Harrington, *The Other America: Poverty in the United States* (New York, Macmillan, 1963). The War on Poverty, beginning in 1964, was legislation to administer the local application of federal funds to fight poverty.
10. See Tammy L. Werner, 'The War on Poverty and the Racialization of "Hillbilly" Poverty: Implications for Poverty Research', *Journal of Poverty* 19.3 (2015): 1–19. Although the rural poor whites Harrington investigated tended to come from the areas of historical Scots-Irish settlement, he uses 'ethnic' only in reference to bygone post-Famine Irish, Jewish, Italian, and German immigrant urban enclaves. Martin Luther King Jr's soon-to-follow 'Poor Peoples Campaign' was an attempt to create a more multiracial coalition in response to poverty. Drew Dellinger, 'The Last March of Martin Luther King Jr', *Atlantic,* 4 April 2018. https://www.theatlantic.com/politics/archive/2018/04/mlk-last-march/555953/.
11. Jack E. Weller, *Yesterday's People: Life in Contemporary Appalachia* (Lexington, KY: University of Kentucky Press, 1965).
12. In the period in which he filmed *The Quiet Man,* Wayne remarked to a Hollywood reporter that he was 'just a Scotch-Irish [...] boy'. Randy Roberts and James Stuart Olson, *John Wayne: American* (Lincoln, NE: University of Nebraska Press, 1997), 9.
13. Roberts and Olson, 10; 11; 84.
14. Roger Ebert, *The Searchers*, rogerebert.com, 25 November 2001. https://www.rogerebert.com/reviews/great-movie-the-searchers-1956.
15. The original trailer for *The Quiet Man* may be viewed at https://www.youtube.com/watch?v=WcVd8NXtufM.
16. Descriptions of the Beales' lives and home in 1974 are from the documentary. *Grey Gardens.* Cinematographers Albert and David Maysles. Portrait Films/Maysles Films (USA), 1975. The backstory details are from Sheehy and 'Journey to Grey Gardens: A Tale of Two Edies'. The Bowery Boys New York City History (podcast), 27 May 2021.
17. Grace Cassidy, 'Famed Grey Gardens estate closes for $15.5M'. *Curbed Hamptons.* https://hamptons.curbed.com/2017/12/21/16805042/grey-gardens-sells.
18. The vast and largely deserted Gormenghast Castle of British writer Mervyn Peake's *Gormenghast* trilogy (1946–1959) exists without reference to history of any sort due to the hereditary family's complete isolation from the outside world.
19. Barbara Leaming, *Jacqueline Bouvier Kennedy Onassis: The Untold Story* (New York: Thomas Dunne/St. Martin's, 2014), 43.
20. Sarah Bradford, *America's Queen: The Life of Jacqueline Kennedy Onassis* (New York: Penguin, 2001), 9.

21. A search for 'Jacqueline Kennedy' in the archives of popular magazine *Irish America* (1985–), whose remit is to catalogue the business, political, and entertainment successes of the community concerned, yields eighteen articles on the former First Lady.
22. 'Pat Nixon: First-Generation German-American & Her Lincoln Assassination Link'. Blog of The National First Ladies Library. http://www.firstladies.org/ancestral-nixon.aspx.
23. John H. Davis, *The Bouviers: Portrait of an American Family* (New York: Farrar, Straus and Giroux, 1969), 173–83.
24. Bradford, 3–4; Sheehy, 25.
25. Grace Mirabella, *In and Out of Vogue* (New York, Doubleday, 1995), 124.
26. In the 2009 HBO film remake of *Grey Gardens*, Jackie features as a character.
27. *Lace Curtain* examines the social tensions in a WASP-Catholic marriage just when such distinctions are receding within Irish America. The author's 1926 marriage to Orthodox Jewish songwriter Irving Berlin caused a rift with her family.
28. Schlesinger, 313.
29. Schlesinger, 645.
30. Robert F. Kennedy, 'On the Mindless Menace of Violence', in *RFK: His Words for Our Times*, edited and introduced by Edwin O. Guthman and C. Richard Allen (New York: William Morrow, 2018), 370.
31. The supernatural was central to *The Castle of Otranto*, but by the close of the eighteenth century, Ann Radcliffe's Gothic novels depict the ultimate source of horror as extreme human passion. Thus, Brockden Brown and Faulkner are more in the Radcliffe Gothic vein, but Kennedy Gothic, which encompasses both human-made conspiracy and a relentless family curse, partakes of both lineages.
32. Although persistently believed to be a bootlegger, this may have been a false rumour created to damage JFK's presidential aspirations. David Nasaw, *The Patriarch: The Remarkable Life and Turbulent Times of Joseph P. Kennedy* (New York: Penguin, 2013), 80–8.
33. Details of the JFK assassination and its aftermaths are synopsized from William Manchester, *The Death of a President* (New York: Harper & Row, 1967), Anthony Summers, *Not in Your Lifetime: The Defining Book on the J.F.K. Assassination* (New York: Marlowe, 2013) and Nige Tassell, 'Who Killed JFK? The Case that Can Never Be Closed'. *BBC History Revealed Magazine*, March 2018. https://www.historyextra.com/period/20th-century/who-killed-jfk-president-kennedy-evidence-lee-harvey-oswald-what-conspiracy-theories/.
34. Theodore H. White, 'For President Kennedy: An Epilogue', *Life* magazine, 6 December 1963, 159.
35. See Nellie Bly, *The Kennedy Men: Three Generations of Sex, Scandal and Secrets* (New York: Kensington, 1996).
36. Taraborrelli, 398.
37. Walter Mondale, paraphrased in Neal Gabler, *Catching the Wind: Edward Kennedy and the Liberal Hour, 1932–1975* (New York: Crown, 2020), 515.
38. Leaming, 115–16.

39. Taraborrelli's no-holds-barred account of Monroe's life concedes as much. Taraborrelli, 398–9.
40. Faulkner, *AA*, 21.
41. Edward Klein, *The Kennedy Curse* (St Martin's Griffin, 2004), 11.
42. 'Kennedy Family Tragedies', washingtonpost.com. https://www.washingtonpost.com/wp-srv/national/longterm/jfkjr/timeline.htm.
43. Leaming, 271.
44. Adeel Hassan, 'Grim Aura of a Family Curse'. *New York Times*, 3 August 2019, Section A, 11.
45. Leaming, 288–9; 279.
46. Rosalind Miles, *Who Cooked the Last Supper? The Women's History of the World* (New York: Three Rivers, 2001), 7.
47. McMillan Cottom, online.
48. Leaming, 101–2. The president also seemed attuned to the sartorial: Princess Grace recalled that during a May 1961 lunch at the White House, he correctly guessed that she was wearing the label Givenchy. Princess Grace of Monaco interview with Paul Gallico at the Palace of the Principality in Monaco as part of the Oral History Program conducted on behalf of the John F. Kennedy Library, 19 June 1965. https://blankonblank.org/interviews/grace-kelly-on-jfk/.
49. Leaming, 247. White Russians were the elite ousted by the 1917 Revolution.
50. Edmund Burke, *Reflections on the Revolution in France*, ed. L.G. Mitchell (Oxford: Oxford University Press, 1999), 71.
51. Leaming, 130.
52. Leaming, 132.
53. White, 158.
54. Central Park Conservancy.org. https://www.centralparknyc.org/locations/reservoir; https://www.centralparknyc.org/locations/john-purroy-mitchel.
55. By the time of the Revolutionary War, New York possessed the second-largest number of enslaved people in the nation after Charleston, South Carolina. See 'African Burial Ground: A Sacred Space in Manhattan', National Park Service. https://www.nps.gov/afbg/index.htm. See also Mac K. Griswold, *The Manor: Three Centuries at a Slave Plantation on Long Island* (New York: Farrar, Straus and Giroux, 2013).
56. A somewhat positive narrative of shared African and Irish history and identity that would have gratified Yerby is increasingly visible, as exemplified by the African American Irish Diaspora Network, an organization celebrating African-Irish heritage that was founded in recent years by Dennis J. Brownlee, a prominent New York-based African American with Scots-Irish roots. The manner in which such history is going mainstream is suggested by *A Madea Homecoming*, the 2022 instalment of Tyler Perry's massive Black-centric comedy franchise, *Madea*, which nonchalantly introduced a character called Davi O'Malley, the Black son of a white Irish mother.
57. The Indian-Irish Leo Varadkar was *Taoiseach* from 2017 to 2020.
58. See Andrea Bernstein, *American Oligarchs: The Kushners, the Trumps, and the Marriage of Money and Power* (New York: W. W. Norton, 2020), 62; 76; 153.

59. In 1999, Trump served as Grand Marshal of New York's German equivalent of the St Patrick's Day parade. 'German-American Steuben Parade New York: Grand Marshals', n.d. http://germanparadenyc.org/about-the-parade/grand-marshals/.
60. Nic Robertson and Antonia Mortensen, 'Donald Trump's Scottish Roots: How a Tiny Island Could Shape a President', CNN, 3 November 2016.
61. Josh Dawsey, 'Trump Derides Protections for Immigrants from "Shithole" Countries', *Washington Post*,11 January 2018. Online.
62. Moreover, those who identified as white and Catholic as well as white born-again or evangelical Christians voted for Trump in large numbers. See Siobhán Brett, 'Conway, Flynn, O'Reilly, McMahon and More—Introducing the Alt-Irish Americans', *Irish Independent* 19 March 2017; Jessica Martínez and Gregory A. Smith, 'How the Faithful Voted: A Preliminary 2016 Analysis', Pew Research Center, 9 November 2016. Online.
63. Robert A Orsi suggests that the 'self-righteousness' of many recent prominent Irish-American public figures arises from the anachronistic sense of their cohort as 'citizen-victims' of England and Anglo-America. Robert A. Orsi. 'U.S. Catholics between Memory and Modernity: How Catholics Are American', in R. Scott Appleby and Kathleen Sprows Cummings (eds), *Catholics in the American Century* (Ithica and London: Cornell University Press, 2012), 38.
64. In a study that demonstrated that all else being equal, American employers selected candidates with 'White' names for callbacks 50 per cent more often than candidates with 'Black' names, eight out of nine surnames chosen to represent the former category were of Gaelic or Hiberno-Irish origin. Marianne Bertrand and Sendhil Mullainathan, 'Are Emily and Greg More Employable than Lakisha and Jamal? A Field Experiment on Labor Market Discrimination', (National Bureau of Economic Research Working Paper 9873, July2003), 7, footnote 19. https://www.nber.org/papers/w9873.
65. Liam Kennedy, 'How White Americans Became Irish: Race, Ethnicity and the Politics of Whiteness', *Journal of American Studies* (2021) 1.
66. See the Royal Irish Academy's electronic *Dictionary of the Irish Language*, based on their holdings pertaining to Old and Middle Irish (c.700–c.1700). http://www.dil.ie/search?q=gorm&search_in=headword.
67. See W.A. Hart, 'Africans in Eighteenth-Century Ireland', *Irish Historical Studies* 33.129 (May 2002): 19–32.
68. Máirtín Ó Cadhain's western seaboard rejoinder to *Ulysses* features the mixed-race children of Connemara emigrants returned from London, and Le Fanu's 'The Child that Went with the Fairies' depicts a Black and powerful female fairy in a rural Irish setting.
69. See Audrey Nickel, 'Even Racists Got the Blues', *The Geeky Gaeilgeoir* (blog), 6 September 2017. https://thegeekygaeilgeoir.wordpress.com/2017/09/06/even-racists-got-the-blues/.
70. Rory Carroll, '"Duine de Dhath": New Phrase for "Person of Colour" Added to Irish Lexicon', *Irish Times*, 13 July 2021; see 'recent changes' list at https://www.tearma.ie/. Accessed 14 August 2021.
71. 'Talks about Removal of Mackay Statue', 2 News, 5 October 2021. https://www.ktvn.com/story/43434570/talks-about-removal-of-mackay-statue.

72. Elizabeth Dias, 'Targeting Biden, Catholic Bishops Advance Controversial Communion Plan', *New York Times*, 18 June 2021.
73. Fintan O'Toole, 'The Designated Mourner', *The New York Review of Books*, 16 January 2020. www.nybooks.com/articles/2020/01/16/joe-biden-designated-mourner/.
74. Laura Carroll, 'Vice President Joe Biden's Irish Family History', *Irish Family History Centre*, n.d. https://www.irishfamilyhistorycentre.com/article/vice-president-joe-bidens-irish-family-history–1. Boland's description of an ancestor who also held that position as an 'overseer of other peoples' tragedies' illuminates the conflict such a family background can stir. Boland, *Object Lessons: The Life of the Woman and the Poet in Our Time* (New York: W. W. Norton & Company, 1996), 164.
75. Fulmoth/Falmouth Kearney left County Offaly five years into the Famine, and his destination in America—farm country in Ohio—suggests that he followed the earlier, more Ulster-Irish immigration pattern. Megan Smolenyak, 'The Quest for Obama's Irish Roots,' *Ancestry* magazine 26.6 (November–December 2008): 47; 49.

Selected Bibliography

Archives/Paper Collections

Mitchel and Purroy Family Papers, 1830–1942. Rare Book and Manuscript Library, Columbia University, NY.

Nigble Papers, Race Relations Collections (MUM00377). J. D. Williams Library, University of Mississippi Libraries.

Scotch-Irish Foundation Library and Archives Collection, 1889–2001. Historical Society of Pennsylvania, Philadelphia.

The Warner Bros/Turner Entertainment F. Scott Fitzgerald Screenplay Collection, University of South Carolina.

Frank Yerby Papers. Howard Gotlieb Archival Research Center, Boston University.

Interviews and Emails

Hedlund, Sarah (librarian and archivist, Montgomery History Museum and Archive, Rockville, MD), personal email, 15 June 2021.

McGuckian, Eileen (local historian and author, Montgomery County, MD), personal email, 12 December 2021.

O'Neill, Francis P. (reference librarian, Maryland Center for History and Culture), personal email, 23 December 2021.

Ryan, Annie (theatre director), personal interview (on Webex), 9 July 2021.

Film, Television, Fashion Shows, and Exhibitions

Barbado'ed. Moondance Productions. Transmittted on BBC Two Scotland, 26 April 2009.

Berkeley Square. Perf. Grace Kelly. Based on John Balderston's adaptation of Henry James's *The Sense of the Past. The Prudential Family Playhouse* (television anthology drama series). Transmitted live on CBS, 13 February 1951.

Dial M for Murder. Teleplay by Frederick Knott. *Sunday Night Theatre* (television anthology series). Transmitted on BBC (UK), 23 March 1952.

Dial M for Murder. Dir. Alfred Hitchcock. Perf. Grace Kelly. Warner Bros. (USA), 1954.

Grace Kelly: Style Icon. Victoria and Albert Museum. London, 17 April to 26 September 2010.

Grace Kelly's Wedding Dress. Philadelphia Museum of Art, Philadelphia, ongoing since 2006.

Grey Gardens. Cinematographers Albert and David Maysles. Portrait Films/Maysles Films (USA), 1975.

McQueen, Alexander. 'Highland Rape'. Natural History Museum, London. Autumn/Winter [fashion show], 1995–96.

McQueen, Alexander. 'Widows of Culloden'. Paris. Fall/Winter [fashion show], 2006–07.

The Quiet Man. Dir. John Ford. Perf. John Wayne and Maureen O'Hara. Argosy Pictures (USA), 1952.

Redlegs: Sclábhaithe Siúcra na hÉireann. Moondance Productions. Transmitted on TG4 (Ireland), 28 December 2009.

The Rich Boy. Perf. Grace Kelly. Based on the F. Scott Fitzgerald story. *The Philco Television Playhouse* (television anthology series). Transmitted live on 10 February 1952.

The Searchers. Dir. John Ford. Perf. John Wayne. C.V. Whitney Pictures (USA), 1956.

To the Shores of Tripoli. Perf. Maureen O'Hara. Twentieth Century-Fox (USA), 1942

Skyfall. Dir. Sam Mendes. MGM/Columbia Pictures/Danjaq (USA/UK/Turkey), 2012.

Primary Texts

Alexander, Cecil Frances. 'The Ballad of Stumpie's Brae', in Alexander, *The Legend of the Golden Prayers: And Other Poems.* London: Bell & Daldy, 1859, 48–55.

Berlin, Ellin. *Lace Curtain.* New York: Doubleday, 1948.

Berry, Wendell. 'November 26, 1963', in *The Nation*, 21 December 1963, 437.

Boland, Eavan. 'Quarantine', in Boland, *New Collected Poems.* Manchester: Carcenet, 2005, 282.

Bowen, Elizabeth. *The Last September.* New York: Random House, 1929.

Brown, Charles Brockden. *Edgar Huntly, Or, Memoirs of a Sleep-walker.* Eds Philip Barnard and Stephen Shapiro. Indianapolis, IN: Hackett, 2006.

Burns, Anna. *Milkman.* London: Faber and Faber, 2018.

Chopin, Kate. 'The Father of Désirée's Baby' [republished as 'Désirée's Baby'], *Vogue* magazine (14 January 1893): 70–4.

Chopin, Kate. 'Athénaïse', in *Kate Chopin: Complete Stories and Novels.* New York: Library of America, 2000, 353–85.

Corwin, Jane H. 'A Dialogue between Mr. Native and Mrs. Foreigner, on Literary Subjects', in *The Harp of Home; or The Medley.* Cincinnati, OH: Moore, Wilstach, Keys, and Co., 1858, 15–32.

Crockett, David 'Davy' (with Thomas Chilton). *A Narrative of the Life of David Crockett of the State of Tennessee.* Philadelphia: Carey & Hart; Boston: Allen & Ticknor, 1834.

Daly, T.A. 'Kitty's Graduation', in Daly, *Canzoni.* Philadelphia: *Catholic Standard and Times*, 1906, 71–6.

Donleavy, J.P. *The Ginger Man.* New York: Grove Press, 2010.

Douglass, Adam ('An Hibernian'). *The Irish Emigrant, An Historical Tale Founded on Fact.* Winchester, VA: Sharrocks, 1817.

Doyle, Roddy. 'Home to Harlem', in Doyle, *The Deportees and Other Stories.* New York: Viking, 2008, 179–214.

Ellis, Edward S. *The Fighting Trapper, or Kit Carson to the Rescue.* New York: Frank Starr, 1874.

Enright, Anne. *Actress.* New York: Norton, 2021.

Falkner, William Clark. *The White Rose of Memphis.* Chicago; New York: Donohue, 1909.

Faulkner, William. *Absalom, Absalom*! New York: Modern Library, 1951.

Faulkner, William. 'Appendix: The Compsons', in Malcolm Cowley (ed.), *The Portable Faulkner*, revised and expanded edition. New York: Penguin, 1984, 704–21.

Faulkner, William. *The Sound and the Fury.* New York: Vintage International, 1990.

Faulkner, William. 'The Tall Men.' *Saturday Evening Post* 213 (31 May 1941) 14–15; 95–96; 98–99.

Fitzgerald, F. Scott. 'Babylon Revisited.' *Saturday Evening Post* 21 February 1931, 3–5; 82–84.

Fitzgerald, F. Scott. *The Beautiful and Damned.* New York: Signet Classics, 2007.

Fitzgerald, F. Scott. 'Benediction' in Fitzgerald, *Flappers and Philosophers.* London: Collins, 1922, 247–71.

Fitzgerald, F. Scott. 'Bernice Bobs Her Hair' in Fitzgerald, *Flappers and Philosophers,* 155–193.

Fitzgerald, F. Scott. 'The Camel's Back' in Fitzgerald, *Tales of the Jazz Age.* New York: Charles Scribner's Sons, 1922, 27–60.

Fitzgerald, F. Scott, foreword to Don Swann. *Colonial and Historic Homes of Maryland.* Baltimore: Etchcrafters Art Guild, 1939, n.p.

Fitzgerald, F. Scott. 'The Curious Case of Benjamin Button' in Fitzgerald. *Tales of the Jazz Age.* New York: Charles Scribner's Sons, 1922, 192–224.

Fitzgerald, F. Scott. 'The Diamond as Big as the Ritz' in Fitzgerald, *Tales of the Jazz Age.* New York: Charles Scribner's Sons, 1922, 141–91.

Fitzgerald, F. Scott. *The Great Gatsby,* ed. James L.W. West III. New York: Scribner, 2018.

Fitzgerald, F. Scott. *The Love of the Last Tycoon: A Western,* ed. Matthew J. Bruccoli. Cambridge: Cambridge University Press, 1993.

Fitzgerald, F. Scott. 'May Day' in Fitzgerald, *Tales of the Jazz Age.* New York: Charles Scribner's Sons, 1922, 61–125.

Fitzgerald, F. Scott. *The Pat Hobby Stories.* Arnold Gingrich, intro. New York: Scribner, 2004.

Fitzgerald, F. Scott. 'The Rich Boy' in Fitzgerald, *All the Sad Young Men,* ed. James L. W. West III. Cambridge and New York: Cambridge University Press, 2007, 5–42.

Fitzgerald, F. Scott. *This Side of Paradise,* ed. Philip McGowan. Oxford: Oxford University Press, 2020.

Fitzgerald, F. Scott. *The Vegetable: Or, From President to Postman.* New York: Scribner, 1923.

Fitzgerald, F. Scott. 'Winter Dreams' in Fitzgerald, *All the Sad Young Men,* ed. James L. W. West III. Cambridge and New York: Cambridge University Press, 2007, 43–65.

Furlong, Thomas. *The Doom of Derenzie, A Poem.* London: Joseph Robins, 1829.

Glasgow, Ellen. *Barren Ground.* New York: Doubleday Page, 1925.

Glasgow, Ellen. *The Battle-Ground.* Intro. Susan Goodman. London; Tuscaloosa, AL: University of Alabama Press, 2000.

Green, Paul. *The House of Connelly: A Critical Edition,* ed. Margaret D. Bauer. Jefferson, NC: McFarland, 2014.

Heaney, Seamus. 'The Other Side', in Heaney, *Wintering Out.* London: Faber & Faber, 1972, 34–6.

Irving, Washington. 'The Broken Heart', in Irving, *The Sketch Book of Geoffrey Crayon, Gent.* Chicago & New York: Belford, Clarke & Co., 1884, 73–7.

James, C.L.R. *Toussaint Louverture: The Story of the Only Successful Slave Revolt in History; a Play in Three Acts,* ed. Christian Høgsbjerg. Durham, NC and London: Duke University Press, 2013.

James, Henry. *The American.* Boston: Osgood, 1877.

James, Henry. 'The Chaperon', in James, *'The Real Thing' and Other Tales.* New York: Macmillan, 1922, 179–245.

James, Henry. *Daisy Miller: A Study.* New York: Harper & Bros., 1879.

James, Henry. 'The Ghostly Rental.' *Scribner's Monthly* 12.5 (September 1876): 664–79.

James, Henry. 'The Jolly Corner', in *The Portable Henry James,* ed. John Auchard. New York: Penguin, 2004, 283–318.

James, Henry. 'The Last of the Valerii', in *Henry James: Selected Short Stories*, ed. Michael Swan. Harmondsworth: Penguin, 1975, 13–42.

James, Henry. 'The Modern Warning', in *Henry James: Complete Stories, 1884–1891*. New York: Library of America, 1999, 372–434.

James, Henry. *Notes of a Son and Brother*. London: Macmillan, 1914.

James, Henry. 'Owen Wingrave', in *Henry James: Complete Stories, 1892–1898*. New York: Library of America, 1996, 256–90.

James, Henry. 'The Real Thing', in *The Portable Henry James*, ed. John Auchard. New York: Penguin, 2004, 79–105.

James, Henry. 'The Romance of Certain Old Clothes'. *Atlantic Monthly* 21.124 (February 1868): 209–20.

James, Henry. *The Sense of the Past*. New York: Scribner, 1917.

James, Henry. *A Small Boy and Others*. New York: Scribner, 1913.

James, Henry. 'Some Notes on the Theatre' [review of Dion Boucicault's *The Shaughran*], in Montrose Jonas Moses and John Mason Brown, (eds), *The American Theatre as Seen by its Critics, 1752–1934*. New York: Norton, 1934, 122–26.

James, Henry. *The Turn of the Screw* in The Portable Henry James, ed. John Auchard. New York: Penguin, 2004, 127–235.

James, Henry. *Washington Square*. Oxford; New York: Oxford University Press, 2008.

Jewett, Sarah Orne. 'The Luck of the Bogans', *Scribner's Magazine* 5.1 (January–June 1889): 101–12.

Joyce, James. 'The Dead', in Joyce, *Dubliners*. New York: Penguin, 1992, 175–225.

Kelly, George. *The Flattering Word and Other One-Act Plays*. Boston: Little & Brown, 1925.

Kelly, George. *Craig's Wife*, in *Three Plays by George Kelly*. Foreword by Wendy Wasserstein; biographical and critical essays by William J. Lynch. New York: Limelight Editions, 1999, 281–397.

Knott, Frederick. *Dial M for Murder*. New York: Dramatists Play Service, 1982.

Lavin, Mary. 'Tom'. *New Yorker* 48 (20 January 1973): 34–42.

Le Fanu, J.S. 'The Child that Went with the Fairies', in *Madam Crowl's Ghost and Other Tales of Mystery*, ed. M.R. James. London: G. Bell and Sons, 1923, 74–86.

Le Fanu, J.S. *Carmilla: A Critical Edition*. Intro. Kathleen Costello-Sullivan. Syracuse, NY: Syracuse University Press, 2013.

Maturin, Charles. *Melmoth the Wanderer*. Intro. Victor Sage. London: Penguin, 2000.

McHale, Tom. *Principato*. New York: Bantam Books, 1971.

Mitchell, Margaret. *Gone with the Wind*. Preface by Pat Conroy. New York: Scribner, 2011.

Morrison, Toni. *Beloved*. London: Vintage Classics, 2020.

Murdock, John. *The Triumphs of Love or, Happy Reconciliation*. Philadelphia: Folwell, 1795.

Ó Cadhain, Máirtín. *Cré na Cille* [Graveyard Soil]. Inverin, Ireland: Cló Iar-Chonnacht, 2009.

O'Connor, Flannery. 'Everything that Rises Must Converge', in O'Connor, *Everything that Rises Must Converge*. New York: Farrar, Strauss, and Giroux, 1993, 3–23.

O'Hara, John. Introduction. *The Portable F. Scott Fitzgerald*. Selected by Dorothy Parker. New York: Viking, 1949, vii–xix.

O'Hara, John. *Appointment in Samarra*. Intro. Charles McGrath. New York: Penguin, 2013.

O'Hara, John. *BUtterfield 8*. Intro. Lorin Stein, New York: Penguin, 2013.

O'Neill, Eugene. *All God's Chillun Got Wings and Welded*. New York: Boni and Liveright, 1924.

O'Neill, Eugene. *Desire Under the Elms*, in O'Neill, *Plays: Desire Under the Elms; The Hairy Ape; Welded*. New York: Boni & Liveright, 1925, 15–108.
O'Neill, Eugene. *The Dreamy Kid*, in *The Complete Works of Eugene O'Neill*. 2 volumes. New York: Boni and Liveright, vol. II. 399–421.
O'Neill, Eugene. *Long Day's Journey into Night*. Foreword by Harold Bloom. New Haven, CT: Yale University Press, 2002.
O'Neill, Eugene. *The Long Journey Home*, in O'Neill, *The Moon of the Caribbees and Six Other Plays of the Sea*. Intro. by George Jean Nathan. New York: Boni and Liveright, 1923, 55–81.
O'Neill, Eugene. *The Moon of the Caribbees*, in O'Neill, *The Moon of the Caribbees and Six Other Plays of the Sea*, 1–32.
O'Neill, Eugene. *The Rope*, in O'Neill, *Early Plays*. New York: Penguin, 2001, 101–122.
O'Neill, Eugene. *Thirst*, in *Thirst and Other One Act Plays*. Boston: Gorham Press, 1914, 7–43.
O'Reilly, Jane. *The Girl I Left Behind*. New York: Collier, 1980.
Orr, James. 'The Passengers', in Andrew Carpenter, *Verse in English from Eighteenth-Century Ireland*. Cork: Cork University Press, 2000, 544–49.
Poe, Edgar Allan. 'The Facts in the Case of M. Valdemar', in *The Portable Edgar Allan Poe*, ed. J. Gerald Kennedy. New York: Penguin, 2006, 71–80.
Poe, Edgar Allan. 'The Fall of the House of Usher', in *The Portable Edgar Allan Poe*, ed. J. Gerald Kennedy. New York: Penguin, 2006, 244–67.
Poe, Edgar Allan. 'The Tell-Tale Heart', in *The Portable Edgar Allan Poe*, ed. J. Gerald Kennedy. New York: Penguin, 2006, 187–91.
Poe, Edgar Allan. 'William Wilson', in *The Portable Edgar Allan Poe*, ed. J. Gerald Kennedy. New York: Penguin, 2006, 168–86.
Randall, Alice. *The Wind Done Gone*. Boston: Houghton Mifflin, 2001.
Reid, Mayne. *The Scalp Hunters*. Philadelphia: Lippincott, Grambo, & Co. 1851.
Reid, Mayne. *The Quadroon, Or A Lover's Adventures in Louisiana*. 3 vols. London: W.G. Hyde, 1856.
Reid, Mayne. *The Yellow Chief: A Romance of the Rocky Mountains*. London: Beadle, 1870.
Scott, Dennis. *An Echo in the Bone*, in *Plays for Today: Derek Walcott* Ti-Jean and His Brothers; *Dennis Scott* An Echo in the Bone; *Errol Hill* Man Better Man, ed. Errol Hill. Essex, UK: Longman, 1985, 73–137.
Smith, Betty. *A Tree Grows in Brooklyn*. New York: Harper Perennial, 2018, 187–91.
Solomon, Rivers, with Daveed Diggs, William Hutson, and Jonathan Snipes. *The Deep*. New York: Gallery/Saga Press, 2020.
Steinbeck, John. *East of Eden*. Intro. David Wyatt. New York: Penguin, 1992.
Stowe, Harriet Beecher. *Uncle Tom's Cabin: Or, Life Among the Lowly*. Edited with an introduction by Ann Douglas. New York: Penguin, 1986.
Thomson, Samuel. 'To Captain M'Dougall, Castle Upton', in Thomson, *Simple Poems on a Few Subjects*. Belfast: Smyth & Lyons, 1806, 37–39.
Tóibín, Colm. *Brooklyn*. New York: Scribner, 2009.
Tóibín, Colm. *The Master*. New York: Scribner, 2004.
Twain, Mark and Charles Dudley Warner. *The Gilded Age: A Tale of Today*. Hartford, CT: American Publishing Company, 1874.
Walpole, Horace. *The Castle of Otranto* (Oxford World Classics). Intro. and notes Nick Groom. Oxford: Oxford University Press, 2014.
Walrond, Eric. 'The Vampire Bat', in Walrond, *Tropic Death*. New York: Boni and Liveright, 1926, 210–34.

Warner, Susan. *The Wide, Wide World.* New York: Putnam, 1851.
Welty, Eudora. 'The Bride of The Innisfallen', in Welty, *The Bride of The Innisfallen and Other Stories.* New York: Harcourt, Brace & Co., 1955, 47–83.
Yerby, Frank. *Captain Rebel.* New York: Pocket Books, 1965.
Yerby, Frank. *The Foxes of Harrow.* Garden City, NY: Sun Dial, 1947.
Yerby, Frank. *McKenzie's Hundred.* Garden City, NY: Doubleday, 1985.
Yerby, Frank. 'Myra and the Leprechaun', in *The Short Stories of Frank Yerby.* Veronica T. Watson, ed. and intro. Jackson: MI: University Press of Mississippi, 2020, 51–64.
Yerby, Frank. *Speak Now.* New York: Dell Press, 1969.

Secondary Texts

Akenson, Donald H. *If the Irish Ran the World: Montserrat, 1630-1730.* Montreal: McGill-Queen's University Press, 1997.
Alba, Richard. *Ethnic Identity: The Transformation of White America.* New Haven, CT: Yale University Press, 1990.
Alexander, Doris. *The Tempering of Eugene O'Neill.* New York: Harcourt Brace & World, 1962.
Anish, Beth O'Leary. *Irish American Fiction from World War II to JFK: Anxiety, Assimilation, and Activism.* New York: Palgrave Macmillan, 2021.
Ball, Charles (with Isaac Fisher). *Slavery in the United States: A Narrative of the Life and Adventures of Charles Ball, a Black Man.* New York: John S. Taylor, 1837.
Baldwin, James. 'Faulkner and Desegregation'. *Partisan Review* 23.4 (Fall 1956): 568–73.
Baltzell, E. Digby. *The Protestant Establishment: Aristocracy and Caste in America.* New York, Random House, 1964.
Bankhurst, Benjamin. *Ulster Presbyterians and the Scots Irish Diaspora, 1750–1764.* Basingstoke: Palgrave Macmillan, 2013.
Bartlett, Thomas. 'The O'Haras of Annaghmore c. 1600–c. 1800: Survival and Revival'. *Irish Economic and Social History* 9.1 (1982): 34–52.
Beckles, Hilary. *White Servitude and Black Slavery in Barbados, 1627–1715.* Knoxville TN: University of Tennessee Press, 1989.
Beckles, Hilary and Heather D. Russell, eds. *Rihanna: Barbados World-Gurl in Global Popular Culture.* Kingston, Jamaica: University of the West Indies Press, 2015.
Beiner, Guy. 'Disremembering 1798? An Archaeology of Social Forgetting and Remembrance in Ulster'. *History & Memory* 25.1 (2013): 9–50.
Bernstein, Andrea. *American Oligarchs: The Kushners, the Trumps, and the Marriage of Money and Power.* New York: W. W. Norton, 2020.
Bewley, Edmund Thomas. *The Origin and Early History of the Family of Poë or Poe.* Dublin: Printed for the author by Ponsonby & Gibbs, 1906.
Blair, Sara. *Henry James and the Writing of Race and Nation.* Cambridge: Cambridge University Press, 2009.
Blotner, Joseph. *Faulkner: A Biography.* Jackson, MS: University Press of Mississippi, 2005.
Boland, Eavan. *Object Lessons: The Life of the Woman and the Poet in Our Time.* New York: W. W. Norton & Company, 1996.
Bone, Robert. *The Negro Novel in America.* New Haven, CT: Yale University Press, 1968.
Bornstein, George. *The Colors of Zion: Blacks, Jews, and Irish from 1845 to 1945.* Cambridge, MA; London: Harvard University Press, 2011.
Boskin, Joseph. *Sambo: The Rise & Demise of an American Jester.* New York: Oxford University Press, 1988.

Bouvier, Jacqueline. 'Crowds of Americans Fill "Bright and Pretty" London'. *Washington Times-Herald*, 2 June 1953, 4.

Bowen, Croswell. 'The Black Irishman', in Mark W. Estrin (ed.), *Conversations with Eugene O'Neill*. Jackson, MS and London: University Press of Mississippi, 1990, 203–23.

Bowen, Elizabeth. *Bowen's Court*. New York: Alfred A. Knopf, 1942.

Brown, David S. *Paradise Lost: A Life of F. Scott Fitzgerald*. Cambridge, MA; London: Belknap Press of Harvard University Press, 2017.

Brown, Malcolm. *The Politics of Irish Literature*. Seattle, WA: University of Washington Press, 1972.

Brown, Stephanie. *The Postwar African American Novel: Protest and Discontent, 1945–1950*. Jackson, MS: University Press of Mississippi, 2011.

Brucolli, Matthew J. *Some Sort of Epic Grandeur: The Life of F. Scott Fitzgerald*. New York: Harcourt Brace Jovanovich, 1981.

Brucolli, Matthew J. and Judith S. Baughman, eds. F. Scott *Fitzgerald: A Life in Letters*. New York: Simon and Schuster, 1994.

Brucher, Richard. 'O'Neill, Othello and Robeson'. *The Eugene O'Neill Review* 18.1–2 (1994): 45–58.

Buller, Richard. *A Beautiful Fairy Tale: The Life of Actress Lois Moran*. Pompton Plains, N.J: Limelight, 2005.

Bureau of the Census, United States. *Heads of Families at the First Census of the United States Taken in the Year 1790: Maryland*. Baltimore: Genealogical Publishing Company, 1965.

Burke, Edmund. *Reflections on the Revolution in France*, ed. L.G. Mitchell. Oxford: Oxford University Press, 1999.

Burke, Mary. 'The Cottage, the Castle, and the Couture Cloak: "Traditional" Irish Fabrics and "Modern" Irish Fashions in America, c. 1952–1969'. *Journal of Design History* 31.4 (2018): 364–82.

Burke, Mary. 'Grace Kelly, Philadelphia, and the Politics of Irish Lace'. *American Journal of Irish Studies* 19 (2019): 31–46.

Canny, Nicholas P. 'The Ideology of English Colonization: From Ireland to America'. *The William and Mary Quarterly* 30.4 (1973): 575–98.

Carson, Lorna. *Ulster Scots: Language Movement and Speech Community*. M.Phil in Applied Linguistics Thesis, Trinity College Dublin, 2002.

Césaire, Aimé. *Discourse on Colonialism*. Trans. Joan Pinkham. New York: Monthly Review Press, 1972.

Clark, Dennis. *Hibernia America: The Irish and Regional Cultures*. Westport, CT: Praeger, 1996.

Clark, Dennis. *The Irish in Philadelphia: Ten Generations of Urban Experience*. Philadelphia, PA: Temple University Press, 1981.

Cleary, Joe. 'Irish American Modernisms'. *The Cambridge Companion to Irish Modernism*. Edited by Joe Cleary. Cambridge: Cambridge University Press, 2014, 174–92.

Clukey, Amy. 'Plantation Modernism: Irish, Caribbean, and U.S. Fiction, 1890–1950'. Ph.D.dissertation, Pennsylvania State University, 2009.

Coates, Ta-Nehisi. 'The First White President: The Foundation of Donald Trump's Presidency is the Negation of Barack Obama's Legacy'. *Atlantic*, 15 October 2017. Online.

Conant, Howell. *Grace*. New York: Random House, 1992.

Connolly, Claire. 'Writing the Union', in Dáire Keogh and Kevin Whelan (eds), *Acts of Union: The Causes, Contexts, and Consequences of the Act of Union*. Dublin: Four Courts Press, 2001, 171–86.

Connolly, S. J. *Contested Island: Ireland 1460–1630*. Oxford: Oxford University Press, 2009.

Conrad, Joseph. 'Henry James: An Appreciation'. *The North American Review* 180.1 (January 1905): 102–8.

Corbett, Mary Jean. *Allegories of Union in Irish and English Writing, 1790–1870*. Cambridge: Cambridge University Press, 2000.

Cunningham, Bernadette. *The World of Geoffrey Keating*. Dublin: Four Courts, 2000.

Curtis, L. Perry. *Apes and Angels: The Irishman in Victorian Caricature*. Washington, DC: Smithsonian Institution Press, 1997.

Dabiri, Emma. *Twisted: The Tangled History of Black Hair Culture*. New York: Harper Perennial, 2020.

Daly, Mary. 'Revisionism and Irish History: The Great Famine' in D. George Boyce and Alan O'Day (eds), *The Making of Modern Irish History: Revisionism and the Revisionist Controversy*. London & New York: Routledge, 1997, 71–89.

Davis, John H. *The Bouviers: Portrait of an American Family*. New York: Farrar, Straus and Giroux, 1969.

de Tocqueville, Alexis. *Journey in Ireland, July–August, 1835*, ed. Emmet Larkin. Washington, DC: Catholic University of America Press, 1990.

del Gizzo, Suzanne. 'Ethnic Stereotyping', in Bryant Mangum (ed.), *F. Scott Fitzgerald in Context*. Cambridge: Cambridge University Press, 2013, 224–33.

Devine, T.M. *The Scottish Clearances: A History of the Dispossessed, 1600–1900*. London: Allen Lane, 2018.

Domínguez, Virginia R. *White by Definition: Social Classification in Creole Louisiana*. New Brunswick, NJ: Rutgers University Press, 1986.

Douglass, Frederick. *The Life and Times of Frederick Douglass*. New York: Dover, 2003.

Dowd, Christopher. *The Construction of Irish Identity in American Literature*. New York: Routledge, 2011.

Dowd, Christopher. *The Irish and the Origins of American Popular Culture*. New York: Routledge, 2018.

Dowling, Robert M. *Eugene O'Neill: A Life in Four Acts*. New Haven, CT and London: Yale University Press, 2014.

Doyle, David Noel. 'Scots Irish or Scotch-Irish', in Joseph Lee and Marion R. Casey (eds), *Making the Irish American: History and Heritage of the Irish in the United States*. New York: New York University Press, 2006, 151–70.

Du Bois, W.E.B. *Black Reconstruction in America*. New York: Harcourt & Brace, 1935.

Du Bois, W.E.B. *The Souls of Black Folk*. Oxford: Oxford University Press, 2008.

Duffy, Jennifer Nugent. *Who's Your Paddy? Racial Expectations and the Struggle for Irish American Identity*. New York: NYU Press, 2013.

Dunbar-Ortiz, Roxanne. *Red Dirt: Growing Up Okie*. Norman, OK: University of Oklahoma Press, 2006.

Dunn, Richard. *Sugar and Slaves: The Rise of the Planter Class in the English West Indies, 1624–1713*. University of North Caroline Press, 1972.

Dyer, Richard. *White: Essays on Race and Culture*. New York: Routledge, 1997.

Eagan, Catherine M. 'Still "Black" and "Proud": Irish America and the Racial Politics of Hibernophilia', in Diane Negra (ed.), *The Irish in Us: Irishness, Performativity, and Popular Culture*. Durham and London: Duke UP, 2006, 20–63.

East, P.D. *The Magnolia Jungle* (excerpt) in Marion Barnwell (ed.), *A Place Called Mississippi: Collected Narratives*. Jackson: University Press of Mississippi, 1997, 183–92.

Edel, Leon, and Lyall H. Powers (eds). *The Complete Notebooks of Henry James*. New York: Oxford University Press, 1987.

Estrin, Mark W. (ed.). *Conversations with Eugene O'Neill.* Jackson, MS and London: University Press of Mississippi, 1990.

Emerson, Edward Waldo. *The Early Years of the Saturday Club: 1855–1870.* New York: Houghton Mifflin, 1918.

Emerson, Ralph Waldo. *English Traits.* Boston: Philips and Samson, 1856.

Fanning, Charles. *The Irish Voice in America: 250 Years of Irish-American Fiction.* Lexington, KY: University Press of Kentucky, 1999.

Faust, Drew Gilpin. 'Clutching the Chains that Bind: Margaret Mitchell and "Gone with the Wind"'. *Southern Cultures* 5.1 (1999): 6–20.

Fischer, David H. *Albion's Seed: Four British Folkways in America.* New York: Oxford University Press, 1989.

Fitzgerald Smith, 'Scottie'. 'The Colonial Ancestors of Francis Scott Key Fitzgerald'. Appendix to Brucolli, *Some Sort of Epic Grandeur*, 496–509.

Fitzpatrick, David. *Descendancy: Irish Protestant Histories since 1795.* Cambridge: Cambridge University Press, 2014.

Fitzpatrick, Rory. *God's Frontiersmen: The Scots-Irish Epic.* London: Weidenfeld and Nicolson, 1989.

Fitzpatrick, T. B. 'Soleil et peau' [sun and skin]. *Journal de Médecine Esthétique* 2 (1975): 33–34.

Flannery, Denis. 'Irish Strands and the Imperial Eye: Henry James's "The Modern Warning"'. *Henry James Review* 31.1 (2010): 39–45.

Ford, Henry Jones. *The Scotch-Irish in America.* Princeton, NJ: Princeton University Press, 1915.

Fryer, Sarah B. *Fitzgerald's New Women: Harbingers of Change.* Ann Arbor, MI: UMI Research Press, 1988.

Gabler, Neal. *Catching the Wind: Edward Kennedy and the Liberal Hour, 1932–1975.* New York: Crown, 2020.

Gallup, Donald C. *Eugene O'Neill and His Eleven Play Cycle 'A Tale of Possessors Self-Dispossessed'.* New Haven, CT: Yale University Press, 1998.

Gans, Herbert J. 'Symbolic Ethnicity: The Future of Ethnic Groups and Cultures in America', *Ethnic and Racial Studies* 2.1 (1979): 1–20.

Gardner, Jared. 'Alien Nation: Edgar Huntly's Savage Awakening'. *American Literature* 66.3 (1994): 429–61.

Garibaldi, Korey. 'Irish Heritage in the Literary Remains of Frank Yerby and Henry James'. *Multi-Ethnic Literature of the United States* 44.4 (Winter 2019): 122–46.

Geffen, Elizabeth M. 'Violence in Pennsylvania in the 1840's and 1850's'. *Pennsylvania History* 36.4 (1969): 381–410.

Gelb, Arthur and Barbara Gelb. *O'Neill: Life with Monte Cristo.* New York: Applesauce, 2000.

Giemza, Bryan. *Irish Catholic Writers and the Invention of the American South.* Baton Rouge, LA: Louisiana State University Press, 2013.

Gilmore, Peter. *Irish Presbyterians and the Shaping of Western Pennsylvania, 1770–1830.* Pittsburgh, PA: University of Pittsburgh Press, 2018.

Gleason, Katherine. *Alexander McQueen: Evolution.* New York: Race Point Publishing, 2017.

Glenda Frank, 'Tempest in Black and White: The 1924 Premiere of Eugene O'Neill's *All God's Chillun Got Wings*'. *Resources for American Literary Study* 26.1 (2000): 75–89.

Glissant, Édouard. *Faulkner, Mississippi.* Paris: Éditions Stock, 1996.

Glissant, Édouard. *Poétique de la relation/Poetics of Relation*. Trans. Betsy Wing. Ann Arbor, MI: University of Michigan Press, 1997.

Gordon, Seton Paul. *The Highlands of Scotland*. London: Robert Hale, 1951.

Grande, Sandy. *Red Pedagogy: Native American Social and Political Thought*. Lanham, MD: Rowman & Littlefield, 2004.

Greenberg, Amy S. *A Wicked War: Polk, Clay, Lincoln, and the 1846 U.S. Invasion of Mexico*. New York: Alfred A. Knopf, 2012.

Griffin, Patrick. *The People with No Name: Ireland's Ulster Scots, America's Scots Irish, and the Creation of a British Atlantic World, 1689–1764*. Princeton, NJ: Princeton UP, 2001.

Guglielmo, Jennifer, and Salvatore Salerno. *Are Italians White?: How Race Is Made in America*. New York: Routledge, 2003.

Habegger, Alfred. *The Father: A Life of Henry James, Sr.* New York: Farrar, Strauss, and Giroux, 1994.

Haines, Lindsay. 'Poor, Backward and White'. *New York Times*, 25 February 1973, 5.

Hale, Anthony R. 'Martyrs for Contending Causes: John Mitchel, David Walker, and the Limits of Liberation', in Peter O'Neill and David Lloyd (eds), *The Black and Green Atlantic*. Basingstoke: Palgrave Macmillan, 2009, 197–212.

Hale, Grace Elizabeth. *Making Whiteness: The Culture of Segregation in the South, 1890-1940*. New York: Pantheon, 1998.

Hanna, Charles A. *The Scotch-Irish*. New York & London: Putnam's Sons, 1902.

Harney-Mahajan, Tara. 'Refashioning the Wedding Dress as the "Future Anterior" in Plays by Edna O'Brien and Marina Carr'. *Women's Studies* 44.7 (2015): 996–1021.

Harbin, Billy J. 'George Kelly, American Playwright: Characters in the Hands of an Angry God' in Kim Marra and Robert A. Schanke (eds), *Staging Desire: Queer Readings of American Theater History*. Ann Arbor: University of Michigan Press, 2002, 126–44.

Harrison, Elizabeth Jane. *Female Pastoral: Women Writers Re-visioning the American South*. Knoxville: University of Tennessee Press, 1991.

Hart, W.A. 'Africans in Eighteenth-Century Ireland'. *Irish Historical Studies* 33.129 (May 2002): 19–32.

Haugland, H. Kristina. *Grace Kelly: Icon of Style to Royal Bride*. Philadelphia: Philadelphia Museum of Art, 2006.

Haulman, Kate. 'Fashion and the Culture Wars of Revolutionary Philadelphia'. *The William and Mary Quarterly* 62.4 (2005): 625–62.

Higgins, Geraldine. 'Tara, the O'Haras, and the Irish *Gone with the Wind*'. *Southern Cultures* 17.1 (2011): 30–49.

Hirsch, Foster, *George Kelly*. Boston: Twayne, 1975.

Hogan, Liam. 'The Unfree Irish in the Caribbean Were Indentured Servants, Not Slaves'. *thejournal.ie*,6 October 2015. https://www.thejournal.ie/readme/irish-slaves-myth-2369653-Oct2015/.

Holland, Merlin. *The Real Trial of Oscar Wilde*. New York: Perennial, 2004.

Horne, Philip (ed.). *Henry James: A Life in Letters*. New York: Viking, 1999.

Huber, Patrick. 'A Short History of 'Redneck': The Fashioning of a Southern White Masculine Identity'. *Southern Cultures* 1.2 (1995): 145–66.

Ignatiev, Noel. *How the Irish Became White*. New York: Routledge, 1995.

Jacobs, Harriet. *Incidents in the Life of a Slave Girl, Written by Herself*, ed. L. Maria Child. Boston: Published for the Author, 1861.

James, C.L.R. *The Black Jacobins: Toussaint l'Ouverture and the San Domingo Revolution*. New York: Vintage, 1989.

Jarrett, Gene Andrew. *Deans and Truants: Race and Realism in African American Literature*. Philadelphia, PA: University of Pennsylvania Press, 2007.

Jarrett, Gene Andrew. '"For Endless Generations": Myth, Dynasty, and Frank Yerby's *The Foxes of Harrow*'. *The Southern Literary Journal* 39.1 (2006): 54–70.

Jerng, Mark C. 'Reconstructions of Racial Perception: Margaret Mitchell's and Frank Yerby's Plantation Romances', in James Crank (ed.), *New Approaches to Gone with The Wind*. LSU Press: Baton Rouge, 2015, 38–65.

Johnson, Walter. 'White Lies: Human Property and Domestic Slavery Aboard the Slave Ship *Creole*', *Atlantic Studies* 5.2 (2008): 237–63.

Kaag, John. 'William James's Varieties of Irish Experience'. *New York Times*, 16 March 2020. Online.

Kao, Wei H. 'Troubled Desires and Social Taboos in Eugene O'Neill's and Marina Carr's Dramas of the Land'. *Journal of Irish Studies* 24 (2009): 48–56.

Kaplan, Fred. *Henry James: The Imagination of Genius: A Biography*. New York: Morrow, 1992.

Kay, Billy. *The Scottish World: A Journey into the Scottish Diaspora*. Edinburgh, UK: Mainstream, 2008.

Keller, Susan L. 'The Riviera's Golden Boy: Fitzgerald, Cosmopolitan Tanning, and Racial Commodities in "Tender Is the Night"'. *The F. Scott Fitzgerald Review* 8 (2010): 130–59.

Kelly, John B. 'Are We Becoming a Nation of Weaklings?' *American Magazine* 161 (March 1956): 28–9; 104–7.

Kelly, Mary C. *Ireland's Famine in Irish-American History*. Lanham, MD: Rowman & Littlefield, 2016.

Kennedy, John F. *A Nation of Immigrants*. Rev. ed. New York: Harper Perennial, 2008.

Kennedy, Liam. 'How White Americans Became Irish: Race, Ethnicity and the Politics of Whiteness'. *Journal of American Studies* 56.3 (2021): 1–23.

Kennedy, Robert F. 'On the Mindless Menace of Violence', in Edwin O. Guthman and C. Richard Allen (eds and intro), *RFK: His Words for Our Times*. New York: William Morrow, 2018, 368–72.

Kenny, Kevin. *The American Irish: A History*. London and New York: Routledge, 2000.

Kenny, Kevin. *Peaceable Kingdom Lost: The Paxton Boys and the Destruction of William Penn's Holy Experiment*. Oxford: Oxford University Press, 2011.

Killeen, Jarlath. *The Emergence of Irish Gothic Fiction*. Edinburgh: Edinburgh University Press, 2013.

Kirkham, Pat and Shauna Stallworth. '"Three strikes against me": African American Women Designers', in Pat Kirkham (ed.), *Women Designers in the USA, 1900–2000: Diversity and Difference*. New Haven: Yale University Press, 2000, 123–44.

Klotman, Phyllis R. 'A Harrowing Experience: Frank Yerby's First Novel to Film'. *CLA Journal* 31.2 (1987): 210–22.

Knobel, Dale T. *Paddy and the Republic: Ethnicity and Nationality in Antebellum America*. Middletown, CT: Wesleyan University Press, 1986.

Kolchin, Peter. *American Slavery: 1619–1877*. New York: Hill and Wang, 2003.

Lacey, Robert. *Grace*. New York: Putnam's Sons, 1994.

Leaming, Barbara. *Jacqueline Bouvier Kennedy Onassis: The Untold Story*. New York: Thomas Dunne/St. Martin's, 2014.

Lee, E. Andrew. 'The Image of Irish in the Life and Work of Eugene O'Neill'. *The Eugene O'Neill Review* 35. 2 (2014): 137–60.

Lehan, Richard. *The Great Gatsby: The Limits of Wonder*. Boston: Twayne, 1990.

Lewinson, Edwin R. *John Purroy Mitchel: The Boy Mayor of New York*. New York: Astra, 1965.

Lewis, Arthur H. *Those Philadelphia Kellys, with a Touch of Grace*. New York: Morrow, 1977.

Leyburn, James G. *The Scotch-Irish: A Social History*. Chapel Hill, NC: University of North Carolina Press, 1962.

Linebaugh, Peter, and Marcus Rediker. *The Many-Headed Hydra*. Boston: Beacon, 2000.

Linehan, John C. *The Irish Scots and the 'Scotch-Irish'*. Concord, New Hampshire: American-Irish Historical Society, 1902.

Lynch-Brennan, Margaret. *The Irish Bridget: Irish Immigrant Women in Domestic Service in America, 1840–1930*. Syracuse, NY: Syracuse University Press, 2009.

Mac Domhnaill, Aodh. 'Milleadh na bPrátaí' [The Spoilage of the Potatoes]. *Dánta Aodh Mac Domhnaill* [Poems of Hugh O'Donnell]. Colm Beckett, ed. Dublin: An Clóchomhar, 1987, 45–8.

MacLysaght, Edward. *The Surnames of Ireland*. Dublin: Irish Academic Press, 1991.

MacMaster, Richard K., and Ray Eldon Herbert. *A Grateful Remembrance: The Story of Montgomery County, Maryland 1776–1976*. Rockville, MD: Montgomery County Government and the Montgomery County Historical Society, 1976.

MacQuarrie, Charles W. 'Yoknapatawpha County and "Cracker Culture": A Study of the "Celtic" Component in Faulkner's Mythical South'. *Faulkner Journal of Japan* 7 (2005). https://www.faulknerjapan.com/journal/No7/EJNo7.htm.

Malouf, Michael. *Transatlantic Solidarities: Irish Nationalism and Caribbean Poetics*. University of Virginia Press, 2009.

Manchester, William. *Portrait of a President: John F. Kennedy in Profile*. Boston: Little, Brown and Company, 1962.

Manchester, William. *The Death of a President*. New York: Harper & Row, 1967.

Manuel, Janet Thompson. 'Genealogies', in Manuel, *Gaithersburg: The Heart of Montgomery County: A History Commemorating Gaithersburg's Charter Centennial Charter Centennial*. Gaithersburg, MD: City of Gaithersburg, 1978, 325–410

Margolies, Alan. 'F. Scott Fitzgerald's Work in the Film Studios'. *The Princeton University Library Chronicle* 32.2 (1971): 81–110.

Martin, Maureen M. *The Mighty Scot*. New York: SUNY Press, 2009.

Massue, Melville Henry. *The Jacobite Peerage, Baronetage, Knightage and Grants of Honour*. Edinburgh and London: Jack, T.C. & E.C. Jack, 1904.

McBride, Ian. R. '"When Ulster Joined Ireland": Anti-Popery, Presbyterian Radicalism and Irish Republicanism in the 1790s'. *Past & Present* 157 (1997): 63–93.

McCarthy, Mary. 'March–April 1947: George Kelly', in *Mary McCarthy's Theatre Chronicles, 1937–1962*. New York: Farrar, Straus and Co., 1963, 97–104.

McClymer, John F. 'Of "Mornin' Glories" and "Fine Old Oaks": John Purroy Mitchel, Al Smith, and Reform as an Expression of Irish-American Aspiration', in Ronald H. Bayor and Timothy J. Meagher (eds), *The New York Irish*. Baltimore, MD: Johns Hopkins University Press, 1996, 374–94.

McGilligan, Patrick. *Alfred Hitchcock: A Life in Darkness and Light*. New York: Regan Books, 2003.

McGovern, Dan. 'Eugene O'Neill's Place in Irish Theater Today: Interviews with Irish Theater Scholars'. *Eugene O'Neill Review* 39.1 (2018): 140–62.

McGuckian, Eileen, and Lisa Greenhouse. *F. Scott Fitzgerald's Rockville: A Guide to Rockville MD in the 1920s*. Rockville, MD: Peerless Rockville Historic Preservation, Ltd., 1996.

McNamara, Julia (ed.). *The Irish Face in America*. New York & Boston: Bulfinch Press, 2004.
Michaels, Walter Benn. *Our America: Nativism, Modernism, and Pluralism*. Durham, NC; London: Duke University Press, 1995.
Milford, Nancy. *Zelda: A Biography*. New York: Harper & Row, 1970.
Miller, Kerby. *Emigrants and Exiles: Ireland and the Irish Exodus to North America*. Oxford: Oxford University Press, 1988.
Miller, Nathan. *New World Coming: The 1920s and the Making of Modern America*. New York: Scribner, 2003.
Miller, Robert J. *Native America, Discovered and Conquered: Thomas Jefferson, Lewis & Clark, and Manifest Destiny*. Westport, CT: Praeger, 2006.
Miller, Robert Ryal. *Shamrock and Sword: The Saint Patrick's Battalion in the U.S.–Mexican War*. Norman, OK: U of Oklahoma Press, 1989.
Mitchel, John. *Jail Journal*. New York: Office of *The Citizen*, 1854.
Mitchel, John. *The Last Conquest of Ireland (Perhaps)*. Author's Edition. Glasgow: R. & T. Washbourne, 1876.
Monaco, Princess Grace of. *Birds, Beasts and Flowers*. (Transcription of performance at St. James's Palace on 22 November 1978 in aid of the World Wildlife Fund.) Exeter, UK: Webb & Bower, 1983.
Monaco, Princess Grace of. 'A Comment', in Donald Spoto. *The Art of Alfred Hitchcock*. New York: Anchor, 1992, xiii–xiv.
Monaco, Princess Grace of. Interview with Paul Gallico at the Palace of the Principality in Monaco, Oral History Program for John F. Kennedy Library, 19 June 1965. https://blankonblank.org/interviews/grace-kelly-on-jfk/.
Monaco, Princess Grace of. Forward to Gordon Wetmore. *Ireland: Portrayed by Gordon Wetmore*. Nashville, TN: Nelson, 1980, 7.
Monaco, Princess Grace of. Preface to Robert Vavra. *The Love of Tiger Flower*. New York: William Morrow, 1980, n.p.
Moncreiffe, Iain, and David Hicks. *Highland Clans*. New York: Clarkson N. Potter, 1967.
Monteiro, George. 'Americanism in Henry James' "The Modern Warning"'. *American Literary Realism* 43.2 (2011): 169–74.
Monteiro, George. *Reading Henry James: A Critical Perspective on Selected Works*. Jefferson, NC: McFarland, 2016.
Montez, Lola. *The Arts of Beauty*. New York: Dick and Fitzgerald, 1858.
Moynihan, Julian. 'Hyphenated Americans in Old Philadelphia'. *New York Times*, 9 August 1970, 7; 35.
Moynihan, Sinéad. *Ireland, Migration and Return Migration: The 'Returned Yank' in the Cultural Imagination, 1952 to Present*. Liverpool: Liverpool University Press, 2019.
Moynihan, Sinéad. *Other People's Diasporas*.Syracuse: NY: Syracuse University Press, 2013.
Murphy, Angela F. *American Slavery, Irish Freedom: Abolition, Immigrant Citizenship, and the Transatlantic Movement for Irish Repeal*. Baton Rouge, LA: Louisiana State University Press, Press, 2010.
Murphy, Brenda, David Clare, and Jackson R. Bryer. 'Used Books: Travis Bogard: *Contour in Time: The Plays of Eugene O'Neill*'. *Eugene O'Neill Review* 43.1 (2022): 69–90.
Mushkat, Jerome. *Fernando Wood: A Political Biography*. Kent, OH: Kent State University Press, 1990.
Nasaw, David. *The Patriarch: The Remarkable Life and Turbulent Times of Joseph P. Kennedy*. New York: Penguin, 2013.
Negra, Diane. 'The Irish in Us: Irishness, Performativity, and Popular Culture', in *The Irish in Us*, 1–19.

Negra, Diane. *Off-White Hollywood: American Culture and Ethnic Female Stardom*. London and New York: Routledge, 2001.

Nevin, Alfred. *History of the Presbytery of Philadelphia, and of the Philadelphia Central*. Philadelphia: Fortescue, 1888.

Nishime, LeiLani. *Undercover Asian: Multiracial Asian Americans in Visual Culture*. Champaign, IL: University of Illinois Press, 2014.

O'Brien, Harvey. 'The Final Fortress: The Redlegs and Bajan-Irish Abjection', in Alison Donnell, Maria McGarrity, and Evelyn O'Callaghan (eds), *Caribbean Irish Connections: Interdisciplinary Perspectives*. Kingston, Jamaica: University of the West Indies Press, 2015, 174–86.

O'Daly, Aengus [Aonghus Ó Dálaigh]. *The Tribes of Ireland: A Satire*. Trans. James Clarence Mangan. Dublin: O'Daly, 1852.

O'Hara, Maureen (with John Nicoletti). *'Tis Herself: An Autobiography*. New York: Simon & Schuster, 2005.

Ó Néill, Domhnall. *Remonstrance of the Irish Chiefs to Pope John XXII*. CELT/Corpus of Electronic Texts: A Project of University College, Cork, 2005–2010.

O'Neill, Peter D. *Famine Irish and the American Racial State*. London; New York: Routledge, 2019.

O'Neill, Peter D. 'Memory and John Mitchel's Appropriation of the Slave Narrative'. *Atlantic Studies: Global Currents* 11.3 (Fall 2014): 321–43.

O'Sullivan, John L. 'Annexation'. *The United States Magazine and Democratic Review* 17 (July–August 1845): 5–6; 9–10.

O'Toole, Fintan. 'The Designated Mourner'. *The New York Review of Books*, 16 January 2020. www.nybooks.com/articles/2020/01/16/joe-biden-designated-mourner/.

Painter, Nell Irvin. *The History of White People*. New York: Norton, 2011.

Paisley, Ian R. K. *America's Debt to Ulster*. Belfast: Martyrs Memorial, 1976.

Peatling, G. K. 'Thomas Dixon, Scotch-Irish Identity, and "the Southern People"', *Safundi: The Journal of South African and American Studies* 9.3 (2008): 239–56.

Peiss, Kathy. *Hope in a Jar: The Making of America's Beauty Culture*. New York: Henry Holt, 1998.

Pierrot, Grégory. *The Black Avenger in Atlantic Culture*. Athens, GA: University of Georgia Press, 2019.

Pyron, Darden Asbury. *Southern Daughter: The Life of Margaret Mitchell*. New York and Oxford: Oxford University Press, 1991.

Quinlan, Kieran. *Strange Kin: Ireland and the American South*. Baton Rouge: Louisiana State University Press, 2005.

Reid, Whitelaw. *The Scot in America and the Ulster Scot*. Nelson McCausland, introduction. Down, Northern Ireland: Books Ulster, 2005.

Ridgely, J. V. *Nineteenth-Century Southern Literature*. Lexington, KY: University Press of Kentucky, 1980.

Ridner, Judith. 'Scots Irish (Scotch Irish)'. *The Encyclopedia of Greater Philadelphia*, 2017. Online.

Ritchie, Daniel. 'Radical Orthodoxy: Irish Covenanters and American Slavery, circa 1830–1865'. *Church History* 82.4 (2013): 812–47.

Roberts, Randy, and James Stuart Olson. *John Wayne: American*. Lincoln, NE: University of Nebraska Press, 1997.

Robertson, Nic, and Antonia Mortensen. 'Donald Trump's Scottish Roots: How a Tiny Island Could Shape a President', CNN, 3 November 2016.

Rodgers, Nini. *Ireland, Slavery and Anti-Slavery, 1612–1865*. Basingstoke; New York: Palgrave Macmillan, 2007.

Roediger, David R. *The Wages of Whiteness: Race and the Making of the American Working Class*. London: Verso, 2007.

Roosevelt, Theodore. *The Winning of the West*. New York: Review of Reviews Company, 1889, vol. I.

Rowe, John Carlos. 'Henry James in a New Century', in John C. Rowe and Eric Haralson (eds), *A Historical Guide to Henry James*. New York: Oxford University Press, 2012, 197–217.

Runcie, John. '"Hunting the N**s" in Philadelphia: The Race Riot of August 1834'. *Pennsylvania History* 39.2 (1972): 187–218.

Russell, Anthony G. *Between Two Flags: John Mitchel & Jenny Verner*. Kildare, Ireland: Merrion Press, 2015.

Salmon, Emily Jones. 'Convict Labor during the Colonial Period'. *Encyclopedia Virginia*. Virginia Humanities, 14 December 2020. Online.

Schlesinger, Arthur M. *Robert Kennedy and His Times*. Boston & New York: Houghton Mifflin, 2002.

Schuyler, George. 'Not Gone with the Wind', *Crisis* 44.7 (July1937): 205–6.

Shack, William A. *Harlem in Montmartre*. Berkeley, CA: University of California Press, 2001.

Schwarzenbach, Alexis. 'Imagined Queens Between Heaven and Hell: Representations of Grace Kelly and Romy Schneider' in Regina Schulte (ed.), *The Body of the Queen: Gender and Rule in the Courtly World, 1500–2000*. New York and Oxford: Berghahn, 2006, 306–26.

Shafer, Yvonne. *Performing O'Neill: Conversations with Actors and Directors*. New York: St Martin's Press, 2000.

Sheehy, Gail. 'Inside Grey Gardens'. *New York Magazine*, 10 January 1972, 24–30.

Shoemaker, Nancy. *A Strange Likeness: Becoming Red and White in Eighteenth-Century North* America. New York: Oxford University Press, 2004.

Shome, Raka. *Diana and Beyond: White Femininity, National Identity, and Contemporary Media Culture*. Urbana, Chicago, and Springfield: University of Illinois Press, 2014.

Smith, Abbott Emerson. *Colonists in Bondage: White Servitude and Convict Labor in America, 1607–1776*. Chapel Hill, NC: University of North Carolina Press, 1947.

Smart, Robert. 'The "Vital Blood" of Irish Colonials in America and the Formation of the New Nation', in Christine Kinealy and Gerard Moran (eds), *Irish Famines Before and After the Great Hunger*. Cork: Cork University Press, 2020, 49–60.

Smolenyak, Megan. 'The Quest for Obama's Irish Roots'. *Ancestry* magazine 26.6 (November–December 2008): 46–7; 49.

Spenser, Edmund. *A View of the Present State of Ireland*, ed. W L. Renwick. London: Partridge at the Scholartis Press, 1934.

Spoto, Donald. *High Society: Grace Kelly and Hollywood*. London: Arrow, 2010.

Steen, Shannon. *Racial Geometries of the Black Atlantic, Asian Pacific and American Theatre*. Basingstoke, Hampshire; New York: Palgrave Macmillan, 2010.

Stevens, Hugh. *Henry James and Sexuality*. Cambridge: Cambridge University Press, 2008.

Stewart, Bruce. 'The Princess Grace Irish Library'. *World of Hibernia* magazine 6.4 (2001): 66.

Stubbs, Tara. *American Literature and Irish Culture, 1910–55*. Manchester: Manchester UP, 2013.

Sullivan, Eileen. *The Shamrock and the Cross: Irish American Novelists Shape American Catholicism*. Notre Dame, IN: University of Notre Dame Press, 2016.

Summers, Anthony. *Not in Your Lifetime: The Defining Book on the J.F.K. Assassination*. New York: Marlowe, 2013.

Sweeney-Risko, Jennifer. 'Fashionable "Formation": Reclaiming the Sartorial Politics of Josephine Baker'. *Australian Feminist Studies* 33.98 (2018): 498–514.

Talley, André Leon. *The Chiffon Trenches*. New York, Ballantine, 2020.

Taraborrelli, J. Randy. *The Secret Life of Marilyn Monroe*. New York: Grand Central Publishing, 2010.

Teutsch, Matthew. 'Overstuffed and Undercooked: The Film Adaptation of Frank Yerby's *The Foxes of Harrow*', in Matthew Teutsch (ed.), *Rediscovering Frank Yerby*. Jackson, MS: University Press of Mississippi, 2020, 89–105.

Third, Amanda. '"Does the Rug Match the Carpet?": Race, Gender, and the Redheaded Woman', in Diane Negra (ed.), *The Irish in Us: Irishness, Performativity, and Popular Culture*. Durham and London: Duke UP, 2006, 220–53.

Thomas, Hugh. *The English and the Normans*. Oxford: Oxford University Press, 2003.

Tóibín, Colm. 'Henry James in Ireland', in Susan M. Griffin (ed.), *All a Novelist Needs: Colm Tóibín on Henry James*. Baltimore, MD: Johns Hopkins University Press, 2010, 1–17.

Trouard, Dawn. 'The Promiscuous Joy of Eudora Welty: Missing Bowen in Mississippi', in Richard Gray and Waldemar Zacharasiewicz (eds), *Transatlantic Exchanges: The American South in Europe – Europe in the American South*. Vienna: Austrian Academy of Sciences, 2007, 257–76.

Truffaut, François. *Hitchcock*. New York: Simon and Schuster, 1983.

Turnbull, Andrew (ed.). *The Letters of F. Scott Fitzgerald*. New York: Scribner, 1963.

Van Thompson, Carlyle. *The Tragic Black Buck: Racial Masquerading in the American Literary Imagination*. New York: Peter Lang, 2004.

Vance, J.D. *Hillbilly Elegy*. New York: Harper, 2016.

Walker, Sheila S. 'Everyday Africa in New Jersey: Wonderings and Wanderings in the African Diaspora', in Sheila S. Walker (ed.), *African Roots/American Cultures: Africa in the Creation of the Americas*. Lanham, MD: Rowman & Littlefield, 2001, 45–80.

Westerkamp, Marilyn J. *Triumph of the Laity: Scots-Irish Piety and the Great Awakening, 1625–1760*. New York: Oxford University Press, 1988.

Whalen, Richard J. *The Founding Father: The Story of Joseph P. Kennedy*. New York: New American Library, 1966.

White, Theodore H. 'For President Kennedy: An Epilogue'. *Life* magazine. 6 December 1963, 158–9.

Whitman, Walt. 'Edgar Poe's Significance'. *The Critic*, vol. 2 (1882): 147.

Williams, Caroline Randall. 'You Want a Confederate Monument? My Body Is a Confederate Monument'. *New York Times*, 26 June 2020. Online.

Williams, Eric. *Capitalism and Slavery*. London: Penguin Classics, 2022.

Williams, Joseph J. *Whence the 'Black Irish' of Jamaica?* New York: Lincoln MacVeagh/Dial Press, 1932.

Williamson, Joel. *William Faulkner and Southern History*. New York; Oxford: Oxford University Press, 1995.

Wilson, Jacqueline Zara. 'Invisible Racism: The Language and Ontology of "White Trash"'. *Critique of Anthropology* 22.4 (2002): 387–401.

'Yerby, Frank.' *Contemporary Authors: New Revision Series 16*. Eds Linda Metzger and Deborah A. Straub. Detroit, MI: Gale Research, 1986, 466–71.

Index

A

abolitionism 37, 61, *61*, 117, 124, 125, 126, 130, 140, 193 n. 140
Absalom, Absalom! 8, 27, 103, 106, 107, 109, 110, 111, 113–17, 120, 126, 128, 129, 171
  enslavement in 113, 114, 116–7, 121
  interraciality in 106, 107
  Sutpen, abject whiteness of 114–6
Act of Union (of Ireland with Great Britain, 1800) 21, 36, 44, 51, 53–4
  'marriage-as-political-union' literary trope 53–4, 57, 164, 182 n. 44
Africans, in Irish language and literature 176–7
African Americans 31, 56, 72, 85, 89, 115, 143
  Irish relations with 4–5, 62, 71, 124, 130–1, 140, 143, 157, 168, 175, 179 n. 6
  see also enslavement in the Americas
African American Irish Diaspora Network 175
Afro-Caribbean 5, 66–73, 92–3
Akenson, Donald 68
Alba, Richard 32
Alexander, Cecil Frances: 'The Legend of Stumpie's Brae' 26
Alien and Sedition Acts (1798) 21, 22, 23, 36
American Civil War 16, 96, 107, 111, 112, 123, 130
  Irish and the 62, 95, 105, 108, 110, 129, 194 n. 145
American Gothic 5, 7, 17, 22–4, 103, 106, 109, 126, 175
'ancestor-haunted' *see under* Scots-Irish Gothic
Ancient Order of Hibernians 141
Anglo-Irish 4, 7, 19, 21, 23, 37, 42, 43, 51, 96, 110, 112, 124, 160, 162
Anglo-Irish Gothic 5, 17, 25, 30, 31, 111
Anglo-Saxon *see* Saxonism
Appalachians 21, 81, 114, 149, 164, 180 n. 5

B

Bahamas 99–100, 204 n. 216
Baker, Josephine 97, *98*, 144, 204 n. 202
Baldwin, James 118
Ball, Charles 207 n. 37
Banville, John 110–1, 209 n. 86
Barbados 66, 67, 68, 69, 72, 73
Bartlett, Thomas 123
Beale, Edith Bouvier ('Big Edie') 164–8
Beale, Edith Bouvier ('Little Edie') 6, 164–8, *167*
beauty, women and 6, 96–7, 136–7, 215 n. 5
  Irish 'whitening' and 6–7, 135, 153
  race/racialization and 6, *6*, 7, 45, 96, 99–101, 133–4, 136–7, 206 n. 20
  see also fashion and clothing; Irish complexion; tanning
Beckles, Hilary 68–9
Beiner, Guy 21, 37
Berlin, Ellin: *Lace Curtain* 2, 168
Bermuda 58, 69
Biden, Joe, as 'revenant' 10, 177
Big House (Anglo-Irish) 8, 110–2, 208 n. 64, 209 n. 76
  Big House novel 110, 111, 112
Birth of a Nation, The 63, 130
'black Irish' (white) 4, 5, 7, 8, 63, 91–3, 100
  Spanish Armada fallacy 93, 202 n. 164
Black Irish (mixed-race) 1, 2, 3, 5, 7, 8, 32, 72, 91–3, 104–5, 106, 128–9, 178, 227 n.56
  invisibility of 3, 32, 104
Black Lives Matter 10, 175, 176, 177
blackface 73, 64–5, *65*, 143
Blair, Mary 72, *73*, 197 n. 59
Blair, Sara 55
Bloom, Ester 149
Boland, Eavan 76, 229 n. 74
Booth, Edwin 91
Bowen, Elizabeth 4, 8, 107, 111, 112, 138, 160, 162
Boyne, Battle of the (1690) 21, 107, 122
Brown, Charles Brockden: *Edgar Huntly* 7, 18, 22–5, 36, 116
Brown, John 130
Brown, Stephanie 104, 107
Brucher, Richard 74
Buchanan, James 95, 203 n. 182
Burke, Edmund 20, 172

C

Campbell, Naomi 7
Canny, Nicholas 79, 110
Carey, Mariah 2, 93

Caribbean Irish *see* Redlegs
Caribbean plantations 110, 113
African and Irish differentiation on 4, 66–7, 69, 73, 116
African-Irish joint revolts on 69; 92–3
indentured servants on 8, 21, 64, 66–9, 73, 100, 115–6, 148, 176
Irish planters on 68, 92, 110, 208 n. 59
transported Irish on 8, 67–8, 115–6
see also Barbados; Haiti; Montserrat; Redlegs
Carlyle, Thomas 49
Carson, Edward 51, 140, 141
Carson, Kit 14, *15*
Carson, Lorna 25
Carson, Rachel 136, 216 n. 7
Cather, Willa 34
Catholic Emancipation (1829) 61, 127
Catholic Irish Americans 2, 19, 20, 35, 36
African Americans, relations with 4–5, 62, 71, 124, 130–1, 140, 143, 157, 168, 175, 179 n. 6
conservatism of 3, 10, 144–6, 171, 176
as Gaels 19, 41, 43, 62, 63, 94, 176
grievances of 60, 67–8, 138, 139, 176, 228 n. 63
as 'off-white' 20, 38–9, 46–8, 63, 74, 75, 96, 101, 109, 125, 133–4
pre-Famine cohorts 2, 3, 86–8, 140
prejudice and 35, 56, 63, 126, 140, 148, 166
progressive politics of 10, *10*, 144, 168, 169, 171, 177
Scots-Irish, relations with 35, 36, 44, 125, 139–41, 164
as settler-colonials 3, 64, 74, 105–6, 123
as simian 6, *6*, 45, *45*, 71, 102, 137, 155
stereotypes 20, 31, 50, 88, 90, 91, 101–2, 118, 142, 143, 148, 150–1, 201 n. 143
as undemocratic/corrupt 45, 56, 58, 127
as 'white' 32, 41, 44, 62, 71–2, 93, 135, 159, 163, 176
'whitening' of 4, 5, 10, 134, 159–62, 163–4, 176
see also Catholicism; Famine of 1845; lace curtain Irish; nationalism; shanty Irish
Catholicism 14, 20, 36, 42, 43, 47–8, 68, 78, 85, 87, 88, 105, 131, 145, 154, 156, 169, 177
Celts 2, 4, 43, 64
Césaire, Aimé 117
Chanel, Coco 97, 100
Chopin, Kate 30, 128, 158
Clare, David 66
Clark, Dennis 62, 141
Clay, Edward W. 61, *61*, *92*, 157
Clear, Caitriona 159
Cleary, Joe 5
Clinton, Bill 13
Clukey, Amy 16, 110
Coates, Ta-Nehisi 13
Conant, Howell 153
Confederacy 16, 114, 117, 121, 122, 123, 127, 130
iconography of, in Northern Ireland 16
Irish support of 16, 61, 62, 83, 87, 117, 124, 125, 166
Connolly, Claire 54
Connolly, Sybil 172, *173*
Conroy, Pat 1, 123
Corn Exchange 81, *82*
Corwin, Jane Hudson 14
Cowley, Malcolm 120
Creole case (slave revolt) 204 n. 216
Creoles 14, 127–8, 129, 134
Crèvecoeur, Hector St. John de 20
Crockett, David 'Davy' 14, 19
Cromwell, Oliver 30, 67
Gothic and 30–1, 68
Culloden, Battle of (1746) 3, 18, 44, 94, 120–3
Curran, John Philpot 187 n. 21
Curran, Sarah 187 n. 21
Curtis, L. Perry 155

D
Dabiri, Emma 7
Daly, T.A. 150–1, 159
dime novels 2, 14, *15*
Deevy, Teresa 159
Democratic Party 9, *10*, 10, 12–3, 45, 58, 63, 126, 130, 139, 141, 145, 163, 168–71, 177
Diana, Princess of Wales 51, 159, 172
Donleavy, J.P. 156, 161
doppelganger 7, 26–31, 35, 36, 52, 57, 62, 65, 69, 80, 82, 86, 96, 122, 129, 166
Douglass, Adam 19, 139
Douglass, Frederick 2, 37, 61, 124, 133
Dowd, Christopher 6, 123, 125
Drexel, Katharine 136, 216 n. 7
Du Bois, W.E.B. 70, 72, 107, 108
Duffy, Jennifer Nugent 93
Dunbar-Ortiz, Roxanne 12, 14
Dunn, Richard 67, 68
Dyer, Richard 97, 134, 153, 159

E
Edgar Huntly see Brown, Charles Brockden
Emancipation (1863) 31, 92
Emerson, Ralph Waldo 7, 20, 41, 43, 49–50, 94, 100, 176
Emmet, Robert 3, 4, 21, 36–7, 44
Emmet, Thomas Addis 55, 187 n. 20

enslavement in the Americas 5, 8, 26, 67–70, 93, 95, 99–100, 103, 109, 115–7, 140, 155, 175, 204 n. 216
Catholic Irish and 4, 87, 92, 212 n. 158
indentured servants and 21, 67–9, 115–6, 148
Scots-Irish and 16, 61–2, 95, 119, *119*
transported Irish and 4, 67, 115
see also African Americans; Caribbean plantations; Southern United States

F

Falkner, Emeline Lacy 106
Famine of 1845 3, 70, 75–7, 111, 131, 154
as divider event between Irishnesses 4, 11–2, 18, 19, 35, 36, 47, 50, 58, 63, 88–9, 177
Irish-American memory and 58; 75–7; 89; 192 n. 123
and Scotland 94–5
Fanning, Charles 19, 139
fashion and clothing
Grace Kelly and 156–7, 159–60,
the Irish and 136–7, 148, 151, 156, 157, *158*, 172, *173* 227 n. 48
Jackie Kennedy and 172–3
race and 7, 40, 46, 48, 136–7, 144, 152, *152*, *158*, 157–9
see also beauty; women
Faulkner, William 5, 7, 17, 18, 24, 106–7, 111, 118–20
ancestry and mixed-race family of 3, 106, 120, 157
Compson Appendix 121–2, 123
integration and 118
plantation house of 119, *119*
The Sound and the Fury 120–3
The Southern Reposure 118
'The Tall Men' 118
see also Absalom, Absalom!
Fenty, Betty 67
Fischer, David H. 17
Fitzgerald (Irish dynasty) 42, 82, 106, 199 n. 109
Fitzgerald, Cecilia Ashton Scott 83, 84, 85, 86
Fitzgerald, Edward (father of F. Scott) 83, 84, 87, 88
Fitzgerald, Edward (great-grandfather of F. Scott) 3, 83, 86–7, 88
Fitzgerald, F. Scott 2, 3, 5, 32, 63, 82, 83, *90*
ancestry of 3, 8, 32, 83–9
'Babylon Revisted' 220 n. 202
The Beautiful and Damned 58–9, 89, 93–4, 97
'Bernice Bobs Her Hair' 206 n. 20
'The Camel's Back' 84, 85
'The Curious Case of Benjamin Button' 84, 85–6
'The Diamond as Big as the Ritz' 70, 87, 95, 102, 177
The Great Gatsby 63, 83, 89, 90, 94–5, 151, 175
The Love of the Last Tycoon 16, 95
'Pat Hobby' series 90, 101–2
racio-ethnic anxieties and 7, 8, 63, 85, 88–91, 94, 95–9, 101–2
'The Rich Boy' 151, 187 n. 6
tanning 4, 7, 8, 64, 89, *90*, 91, 96–8, 100
Tender is the Night 6–7, 89, 95–6, 97–101, 164
This Side of Paradise 13, 83, 88, 139
Fitzgerald, Michael 84, 85, 86
Fitzgerald, Phillip 105–6
Fitzgerald, 'Scottie' 84, 86, 88, *90*, 102
Fitzgerald, Zelda Sayre 83, 84, 88, *90*, 97
Fitzpatrick Scale (dermatalogy) 8, 64
Ford, John 134, 155, 164, *165*
Foxes of Harrow, The (book) 8, 30, 103–4, 113, 127–30, *132*, 132–3
Absalom, Absalom!, influence of 109–10, 128, 129
centrality of Black characters in 128–9, 130
Gone with the Wind, contrasted with 103–5, 107–8, 130
Gothic prologue of 109–10, 128
interraciality in 30, 104–5, 107, 127–9
Foxes of Harrow, The (film) 104, *132*, 132–4
downplaying of Black characters in 133, 134
Maureen O'Hara in 133–4
Franklin, Benjamin 4, 21, 142
Fryer, Sarah B. 99

G

Gaelo-American 3, 18, 19, 42, 43, 69, 90, 94, 103, 120, 121, 122, 175
Gaelo-Normans 23, 43, 67, 77
Gaels *see* Catholic Irish Americans
Gardner, Jared 22, 23
Garrison, William Lloyd 61, 193 n. 136
Garvey, Marcus 67, 92
Gelb, Arthur and Barbara 75–6
Gildea, Mary 148
Gilligan, Rich 82, *82*
Gilmore, Peter 19
Gingrich, Arnold 102
Giuliani, Rudy 13
Glasgow, Ellen 2, 3, 14, 25, 125–6
Glissant, Édouard 2, 110, 113, 116
Godey's Lady's Book 158

Gone with the Wind (book) 1, 4, 97, 102, 103, 123
enslavement, as positive in 102, 103, 107, 124, 126
Foxes of Harrow, The, compared with 107–9, 130
Gerald O'Hara (character) 37, 44, 105, 107–8, 123–4
Irish whiteness and 'off-whiteness' in 4, 39, 96, 108–9, 125, 134
Gone with the Wind (film) 97, 102, *108*, 123, 133, 158
Gothic literature 1, 9, 10, 33, 40, 75, 109, 110, 116, 122, 129, 161, 168–9, 171–2, 174
Catholic depravity in 169, 170
cursed families in 26–9, 120–2, 169–71
the threatened beautiful woman in 171, 172
see also American Gothic, Anglo-Irish Gothic; Kennedy Gothic; Scots-Irish Gothic
Grace, Princess of Monaco *see* Grace Kelly
Grey Gardens 10, 164–6, *167*, 167–8
Griffin, Patrick 14, 17, 20, 21, 25

H
Haiti 114, 116, 124–5, 129, 176, 212 n. 149
Hale, Anthony R. 62
Harrington, Michael 164
Harrison, William Greer 78
Haulman, Kate 157
Henson, Josiah 212–3 n. 158
Hepburn, Katherine 153
Herbison, Ivan 25
Hiberno-Irish dialect 71, 72, 149, 151, 197 n. 51
Hiberno-Norman 23, 42–3, 48, 49, 53, 68, 82, 92, 106, 125
as illegible identity 31, 43–4, 46, 50, 57, 133
hillbilly 81, 125, 149
Higgins, Geraldine 1
Hinds, Michael 81
Hitchcock, Alfred 9, 135, 154–6
Famine Irish roots of 9
Hogan, Liam 66
Holmes, Oliver Wendell, Jr 50
hooks, bell 30
Hopa, Thando 204 n. 225
Hughes, Langston 72
Huston, Walter 81
Hyde, Douglas 43

I
Ignatiev, Noel 4, 20, 143
immigration *see* Catholic Irish Americans; Famine of 1845; Irish racio-social...; Scots-Irish
Immigration and Nationality Act (1952) 163
indentured servants 8, 21, 64, 66–9, 73, 100, 115–6, 148, 176
Indian Removal Act (1830) 13, 14, 15, 131
interraciality 1, 30, 61, 72–4, *73*, 78, 104–7, 127–9, 144
Irish, racialization *see* Irish complexion; Irish racio-social...; red hair; whiteness
Irish Americans *see* Catholic Irish Americans; Irish racio-social...; Scots-Irish
Irish complexion (as red / 'too pale') 4, 8, 64, 67–9, 73, 97–8, 100, 118, 134; *see also* Redlegs
Irish Home Rule 50–3, 55, 140
Irish language 2, 18, 77, 125, 176–7
Irish maids 41, 125, 134, 146, 147, 148–9, 157
Irish planters *see* Caribbean plantations; Southern United States
Irish racio-social groupings *see* black Irish; Black Irish; Catholic Irish Americans; Celts; Gaelo-American; Gaels, Hiberno-Norman; hillbilly; indentured servants; Irish planters; Jacobite peers; lace curtain Irish; poor white; Redlegs; Scots-Irish; shanty Irish; transported Irish; WASP; 'white trash'
Irving, Washington 37, 187 n. 21
Italians, as 'off-white' 8, 46–8

J
Jackson, Andrew 2, 5, 7, 12–13, 14–15, 16, *17*, 105, 121, 164, 182 nn. 30-, 1, 185 n. 97
contemporary political uses of 13, 16, *17*, 203 n. 182
as Gothic figure 5, 7, 12–6, *17*, 121, 164
peoples of colour and 13, 14, 15, 16
Scots-Irish 'whitening' and 13
Jacobitism 18, 23, 28, 67, 94, 103, 125
Jacobite peers (or gentry) 3, 44, 45, 103
Jacobs, Harriet 61, 193–4 n. 141
Jacobson, Matthew Frye 46
Jamaica 7, 66, 92, 140, 151, 195 n. 11
James, Alice 148
James, C.L.R. 125
James, Henry 2, 5, 6, 17, 21, 24, 31, *31*, 32, 34–41, 43–57, 135
The American 35
ancestry of 34–5, 43–4
closeted sexuality and Irishness 7, 37, 38, 147
Daisy Miller *39*, 39–41, 46, 48, 50
'The Ghostly Rental' 15–6, 185 n. 97
Home Rule and 51–3
'The Jolly Corner' 35
'The Last of the Valerii' 47–8
'The Modern Warning' 37, 50, 52–3, 54, 55–7

James, Henry (*Continued*)
'Owen Wingrave' 28–9, 30
The Portrait of a Lady 55, 221 n. 116
racio-ethnic anxiety and 8, 34–6, 38–9, 46, 48, 50
'The Real Thing' 47, 48
'The Romance of Certain Old Clothes' 50
Scots-Irishness and 3, 7, 32, 35, 38–9, 43, 51–2, 56
The Sense of the Past 29, 30, 57, 62, 151
A Small Boy and Others 36
The Turn of the Screw 40
Washington Square 36, 151
James, Henry, Sr *31*, 34, 39, 43, 84
James, William 35, 43, 55
Jarrett, Gene Andrew 104, 109
Jerng, Mark C. 108
Jewett, Sarah Orne 2, 13
Jim Crow (laws and era) 7, 74, 104, 130, 143, 180 n. 12
Johnson, Lyndon B. 164, 168, 169
Johnson–Reed (Immigration) Act (1924) 72
Joyce, James 32, 88, 122

K

Kaag, John 35–6
Kao, Wei H. 79
Kaplan, Fred 54–5
Kay, Billy 112, 117
Keating, Geoffrey 43
Keller, Susan L. 97, 100
Kelly, George 6, 9, 32, 142, 143, 144, 145–50, 151, 160
Kelly, Grace (Princess Grace of Monaco) 2, 5, 9, *9*, *98*, 135, *136*, 137, 138, 143–4, *146*, 151–5, 156, 161–2, 227 n. 48
Dial M for Murder 9, 135, 154–5
progressive politics of 143–4
'WASP' persona of 151–6
'whitening' of Irish America and 9, 134, 159–61, 163–4
Kelly, John B. 137, 141–3, 160
Kelly, Mary C. 75
Kelly, Walter 142, 143
Kennedy administration, progressive policies of 10, *10*, 168, 169, 171, 177
'Kennedy curse' 169, 171
Kennedy, Edward ('Ted') 169, 170, 171, 172
'Kennedy Gothic' 5, 10, 163–75
Kennedy, Jackie (Jacqueline Bouvier Kennedy Onassis) 10, 162, 166–7, 169, 170, 172–4, *173*, *174*
Kennedy, John F. 5, *9*, *10*, 13, 56, 145, 163, 168, *174*, 177, 227 n. 48
Kennedy, Joseph, Sr 168, 169
Kennedy, Robert ('Bobby') *10*, 118, 168, 171
Key, Francis Scott 84, 88, 95
Key, Philip 84
Killeen, Jarlath 24, 25
King, Martin Luther, Jr. *10*, 168, 170, 225 n. 10
'King Billy' (William III) 107, 122
Klotman, Phyllis 133
Kolchin, Peter 66, 68, 127
Ku Klux Klan *73*, 95, 107, 125
Scots-Irishness and 63, 95
anti-Catholicism and 63, 72, 78, 126

L

'lace curtain Irish' 64, 125, 149, 168
Le Fanu, J.S. 31, 176, 184 n. 66, 228 n. 68
Lease, Mary Elizabeth 136, 216 n. 7
Lieven, Anatol 14
Linebaugh, Peter 67
Loquasto, Santo 76
L'Ouverture, Toussaint 125
Lowe, Ann 162
Lynch-Brennan, Margaret 148

M

McCarthy, Mary 145, 146, 147
McClure, S.S. 34–5
McCullough, John 65, *65*, 194–5 n. 8
McDiarmid, Lucy 141
McGilligan, Patrick 155
McHale, Tom 188 n. 32
Mackay, John W. 168, 177
McLaughlin, Joseph 141
McMillan Cottom, Tressie 6, 172
McQueen, Alexander 120
Makemie, Francis 217 n. 29
Malouf, Michael 67
'manifest destiny' 2, 44
Margolies, Alan 102
Mason-Dixon line 100, 140, 204 n. 217
Maturin, Charles: *Melmoth the Wanderer* 30, 68
Meagher, Thomas Francis 194 n. 145
Mexican–American War (1846–8) 131, 214 n. 191
Michaels, Walter Benn 89, 94
Middle Passage 60, 70
Miller, Kerby 2, 18
'miscegenation' 1, 40, 56, 72, 158
Mitchel, John 57–8, *59*, 60, 61–2, 103, 125
anti-abolitionism of 8, 60–1, 103
Mitchel, John Purroy 57, 58–60, *60*, 62, 175
Mitchell, Margaret 1, 8, 32, 102, 107
family slave plantation of 105–6
settler-colonial Irish origins of 3, 105–6, 123

mixed-race Irish *see* Black Irish
Monroe, Marilyn 171, 214 n. 205, 221 n. 115, 227 n. 39
Morash, Christopher 66
Monteiro, George 35, 56
Montez, Lola 96
Montserrat 68, 92
Morrison, Toni 107
Moynihan, Julian 39
Moynihan, Sinéad 93
multiraciality *see* Black Irish
Murdock, John: *The Triumphs of Love* 148
Murphy, Gerald and Sara 97
Murphy, Tom 102

N
nationalism (Irish) 37, 43–4, 51–62, 67, 75, 78, 103, 125, 160
Native Americans 12, 14, *15*, 22, 23, 68, 195 n. 26
  Cheyenne 193 n. 140
  Choctaw 131
  Creeks 13, 105, 124
  Delaware 22
  dispossession of *17*, 20, 79, 80, 113, 121, 124
  Navaho 127
  Scots-Irish and 4, 5, 7, 12–15, *17*, 20–4, 79, 131, 193 n. 140
  Seminoles 13, 105
  see also Indian Removal Act; Jackson, Andrew
nativism 1, 14, 141, 143, 148
  as inter-Irish hostilities 140
Negra, Diane 93, 133
'New English' 23–4, 42, 43, 100, 123
New York City, as Catholic Irish sphere 36, 45, 56, 57–60, 62, 71, 130, 141, 175–5
New York City Draft Riots (1863) 130, 131
Nishime, LeiLani 104
Nixon, Richard and Pat 163
Nordic heritage *see* Saxonism
Normans 2, 18, 23, 28, 30, 41–2, 44, 49, 53, 56; *see also* Hiberno-Normans

O
Obama, Barack 175, 177, *178*
  white Irish ancestry of 177, 229 n. 75
O'Brien, Harvey 69
Ó Cadhain, Máirtin: *Cré na Cille* 2, 176, 228 n. 68
O'Connell, Daniel 61, *61*, 124, 193 n. 136
O'Connor, Flannery 104
O'Faoláin, Seán 77–8
'off-whiteness' *see* Catholic Irish Americans; hillbilly; Italians; Scots-Irish; shanty Irish; poor white; white trash
O'Grady, Lorraine 2, 151, *152*
O'Hara, John 2, 91, 92, 138–9
O'Hara, Maureen 8, 104, 107, *132*, 133–4, 144, 154, 156, 164, *165*
'Old English' *see* Hiberno-Norman
O'Neill/Ó Néill (Gaelic dynasty) 19, 42, 77, 78, 82
O'Neill, Eugene 2, 4, 8, 16, 51, 63, 64, 69
  African-Irish Caribbean history in 4, 8, 64–6, 69–73, *71*
  All God's Chillun Got Wings 72–4, *73*
  Black characters and casting of 64, 69-74, *73*, 175
  Desire Under the Elms 66, 74, 78, 79–82, *82*
  The Dreamy Kid 175
  The Emperor Jones 64, 70
  Famine of 1845 in drama of 75–7
  The Hairy Ape 196 n. 42
  interraciality in 72–4, 78
  Long Day's Journey into Night 64, 65–6, 74, 77, 78, 149
  The Moon of the Caribbees 64, 66, 69, 70–1, *71*
  Partition of Ireland in drama of 66, 79
  The Rope 218 n. 39
  A Tale of Possessors Self-Dispossessed 74
  Thirst 66, 69–70
O'Neill, James 64–5, 74, 75–6, 78, 82, 89, 91
O'Neill, Peter D. 1, 60
Orangeism 44, 124, 125, 140, 141; *see also* Unionism
O'Reilly, Jane 30
Orr, James 2, 157
O'Sullivan, John Louis 2, 44
Othello (role) 65, *65*, 74, 91
O'Toole, Fintan 177

P
Paisley, Ian 163
pan-Gaelic; *see* Gaelo-American
Parnell, Charles Stewart 56
Partition of Ireland (1921) 51, 66, 79
Patou, Jean 100
patrilineality *see* surnames
patronyms *see* surnames
Paxton Boys 21, 24
Peg o' My Heart 53, 191 n. 101
Peiss, Kathy 96, 153
Philadelphia, Irishnesses in 23, 91, *92*, 135, 139, 150–4, 159–60
  inter-Irish tensions in 139–41, 150
  see also Kelly, Grace; Kelly, John. B.
Pennsylvania, as Scots-Irish sphere 20, 21, 22–4, 137, 139, 140, 144, 150, 157

plantation house novels 8, 103, 109, 110, 112–3
Poe, Edgar Allan 2, 3, 5, 7, 17, 24, 49
  'The Facts in the Case of M. Valdemar' 27
  'The Tell-Tale Heart' 26
  Ulster ancestry of 25, 28
  'William Wilson' 26, *27*, 28, 29, 31, 33
poor whites 21, 69, 96, 107, 109, 114, 125, 126, 164; *see also* 'white trash'
post-Famine Irish *see* Catholic Irish Americans
pre-Famine Irish *see* Scots-Irish
Presbyterianism 14, 18, 19, 20, 21, 35, 43, 51, 139, 176, 184 n. 76, 186 n. 109, 217 n. 29
Purvis, Robert 140
Pyron, Darden Ashbury 106, 126

Q

queerness *see* sexuality
Quiet Man, The 133, 156, 164, *165*
Quinlan, Kathleen Mary 136, 215 n. 5
Quinlan, Kieran 120

R

racialization *see* Irish, racialization of
Radcliffe, Ann 226 n. 31
Randall, Alice 207 n. 36
Reconstruction 105, 107, 114, 123, 128, 130
'red' skin *see* Irish complexion; Redlegs
red hair 100, 115, 118, 133–4, 218 n. 39
Redike, Marcus 67
Redlegs 4, 67–9, 70, 93, 99, 100, 115, 118
Reid, Mayne 2, 14, 61, 230 n. 193, n. 140, 214 n. 191
Reid, Whitelaw 51
Republican Party 12, 58, 95, 139, 141, 163, 171
  and contemporary Irish America 176–7
  and the Scots-Irish 11, 58, 141, 171
'Rhyming Weavers' 25, 26, 157
Rihanna 2, 67
Robeson, Paul 72, *73*, 125
Roddy, Lalor 81
Roediger, David R. 4, 108, 143
Roosevelt, Franklin 142
Roosevelt, Theodore 13
Rubinstein, Helena 136
Russell, Anthony G. 61
Ryan, Annie 66, 81, *82*

S

Saint Patrick's Battalion 131, 214 n. 191
Sarsfield, Patrick 23
Saxonism 2, 4, 8, 19, 41, 43, 46, 49, 50, 55, 156, 163, 175–6
Schuyler, George 123
Scotch-Irish *see* Scots-Irish/Scotch-Irish
Scotch-Irish Society 139, 179 n. 4
Scots-Irish/Scotch-Irish 2, 4, 7, 19–20, 34
  Catholic Irish, relations with 35, 36, 44, 125, 139–41, 163–4
  contemporary white Protestantism and 11, 13–4, 164, 176
  as distinct from other Irish 2, 4, 8, 18–9, 34, 35, 36
  as frontiersman ideal 13–4, *15*
  fluctuating allegiances of 19–21, 25, 35–7, 50, 55, 117
  Native Americans, relations with 12, 13, 21, 24, 164
  as 'off-white buffer' cohort 4, 7, 13, 20–1, 24, 139–40
  Saxonism and 7, 50, 176
  scapegoating 24, 116, 118
  as settler-colonials 12, 13, *15*, 24–6, 66, 74
  silenced literary voice 5, 24–5
  stereotypes 13–4, 20–1, 31, 51, 117–9
  as 'unethnicized' Americans 11–12, 13–14, 164
  whiteness and 11–12, 13–14, 16, 36, 47, 63, 91, 117–8, 139–40, 148
  see also hillbilly; nativism; Presbyterianism; WASP; Ulster Scots; Unionism
Scots-Irish Gothic 5, 7, 17–8, 24–9, 80, 82, 106
  'ancestor-haunted' motif 26–7, 28, 29, 30, 52, 57, 62
  cursed families in 15, 26–8, 29
  and settler-colonial guilt 5, 25–7, 28–9
Scott, Dred 95
Scott, Dennis 66
Scottish Gaelic identity 3, 20, 94–5, 120
Scottish Gaelic language 3, 115, 120, 175, 176
Scottsboro Boys 107
Searchers, The 164
sectarianism 3, 14, 18, 20, 36, 44, 91, 108, 125, 139, 141, 186 n. 114, 193 n. 140, 196 n. 42
settler-colonialism, Irish origin of 1, 5, 7, 8, 12–3, 25–6, 28–9, 66, 79–81, 105–6, 108–9, 119, 124, 129
1798 Rebellion 3, 21, 22, 23, 36, 37, 55, 157
sexuality 1, 5, 6, 7, 30, 37, 38, 143–7, 171, 188 n. 35
shanty Irish 36, 39, 93, 94, 96, 109, 125, 151, 161
Shoemaker, Nancy 68, 196 n. 26
Sinn Féin 59, 216 n. 12
Smith, Abbott Emerson 67
Smith, Al 63, 126
Smith, Betty: *A Tree Grows in Brooklyn* 58, 140
Solomon, Rivers 70
Southern Gothic *see* American Gothic

Southern plantation system *see under* Southern United States
Southern United States
Irish planters in 1, 8, 13, 16, 103, 105–6, 110, 119, *119*, 124–7, 212 n. 158
'Northern aggression' 61, 124
'one-drop' rule (hypodescent) 104, 206 n. 7
plantation houses 109, 110, 112, 113, *119*
plantation system 8, 68, 69, 107, 110, 115–6, 125–6
pseudo-aristocracy of 110, 112–13
segregation in 47, 104, 107, 133, 136, 180 n. 12
see also enslavement in the Americas
Spenser, Edmund 42, 49
Spoto, Donald 135, 137, 139, 140, 142, 154
Steen, Shannon 74
Steinbeck, John 79, 163
Stowe, Harriet Beecher 126, 212 n. 158
Stubbs, Tara 156
Sullivan, Eileen 20
surnames, Irish 28, 30–2, 40–1, 44, 53, 82, 84, 87, 93, 101, 125, 128
as 'ancestor-haunted' 7, 26–7, 29, 30–2, 52, 57, 62
Black people and 31, 92, 186 n. 10
as 'evidence' of allegiance 7, 23, 31–2, 40–1, 43–4, 52–3, 56, 72, 93, 95, 118, 133, 150
married women and 7, 30, 43, 54, 161, 166
as 'white' 31, 92, 176, 186 n. 110, 228. 64

T

Talley, André Leon 7
Tammany Hall 45, *45*, *46*, 58, 130; *see also* New York City...
tanning, racial meanings of, *see under* Fitzgerald, F. Scott
Teutsch Matthew 104, 133
Thirteenth Amendment (abolishing slavery) 170
Thomson, Samuel 19
Thoreau, Henry David 20, 97
Tocqueville, Alexis de 137
Tóibín, Colm 7, 37–9, 39, 52, 147, 163
transported Irish 3, 4, 31, 58, 62, 64, 67–70, 111, 115, 118; *see also* Caribbean plantations; Mitchel, John; Redlegs
Truffaut, François 154
Trump, Donald 1, 12–3, 14–5, 175–6
as Andrew Jackson's 'return' 12–3
Gaelo-American ancestry of 175–6, 177
Saxonist rhetoric of 176
Tubman, Harriet 13
Twain, Mark 45, *45*, *46*

U

Ulster Plantation 8, 18, 28, 79, 80–2, 150
Gothic representation of 80–2
Ulster Scots 2, 4, 7, 11, 17, 18, 19, 22, 24, 43, 51, 79, 117–8, 139
fluctuating allegiances of 19, 25, 37, 42
as settler-colonists 17, 23, 24–6, 36, 42. 44, 79
1798 Rebellion and 3, 21–2, 23, 36, 37, 57, 157
see also Scots-Irish
Ulster-Scots dialect 2, 25, 26, 157
Underground Railroad 13, 128
Union Army, Irish recruits in 62, 125, 210 n. 145
Unionism 44, 51, 53, 56, 124, 140, 163, 191 n. 86, 191 n. 101
University of Mississippi integration crisis (1962) 118
US Capitol, storming of (2021) 176
US Presidents 5, 12–3, 14–6, *17*, 95, 163, 168–70, 177–8
whiteness and 13, 72, 95, 163, 175, 177–8, 180 n. 12

V

Vance, J.D. 11
Vogue 97, 100, 138, 158, 162, 167, 239 n. 155

W

Walcott, Derek 67
Walker, Madam C.J. 96, 136
Walker, Sheila S. 68
Walpole, Horace 169
Walrond, Eric 2, 110, 208 nn. 58, 60
Warner, Susan: *The Wide, Wide World* 20
WASP 11, 47, 48, 50, 63, 85, 88, 90, 94–5, 133, 144, 146–9, 151, 153, 156, 161, 162, 167
Scots-Irish as 34–5, 39, 49, 138, 139, 150, 221 n. 110
Wayne, John 156, 164, *165*
Wayne, 'Mad' Anthony 100, 164
Welty, Eudora 2, 5, 8, 111–12
Whelan, Kevin 77
whiteness 2, 5, 6–7, 8, 11, 20, 21, 36, 40, 46, 49, 69, 85, 89, 94, 99, 101, 110, 113, 116, 140
clothing and 6, 40, *45*, *46*, 46, 48, 96, 117–8, 144, 151–2, *152*, *158*, 158–60
immigrant hierarchy of 4, 13, 16, 36, 41, 46, 48, 138, 175
photography and 153, 159
whitening cosmetics 96, 97
see also Catholic Irish; poor white; Scots-Irish; WASP; 'white trash'
'white slave' fallacy 62, 66–7

white supremacism 16, 60, 73, 78, 95, 117–8, 130
'white trash' 21, 39, 96, 113, 115, 124, 125, 126; *see also* poor white
Whitman, Sarah Helen 49
Whitman, Walt 28
Wilde, Oscar 4, 37–8, 43, 51, 54, 61, 140, 145, 188 n. 35
Williams, Caroline Randall 96–7, 203 n. 193
Williamson, Joel 106
women (Irish)
  in Hollywood 7, 96, 132–5, 151–6
  invisibility of 14, 135–7, 166, 172
  as simian 6, *6*, *45*, 136–7
  whitening and 5, 9, 96, 215 n. 5
  see also; beauty; fashion and clothing; Irish maids; surnames
Wood, Fernando 127, 130
workhouses 76

Y

Yeats, W.B. 43, 61, 91
Yerby, Frank 3, 5, 32, 72, 103–5, 107–8, 109–10, 113, 126, 127, 129, 131
  Captain Rebel 212 n. 154
  McKenzie's Hundred 127, 130–1
  mixed-race identity of 3, 8, 32, 72, 104, 105, 125, 130–1
  'Myra and the Leprechaun' 104
  racial closeting for Southern readership 110
  Saint Patrick's Battalion, planned book on 131
  Speak Now 197 n. 57
  see also Foxes of Harrow, The (book and film)
Young Ireland Rebellion (1848) 57, 58, *59*, 131